My Name is Sotir

My Name is Sotir

A Memoir *of a* CHILD EVACUEE

As told to

Olga Lexovska Naumoff

Splendid Associates
Dearborn, Michigan

ISBN 0-941983-03-X

Cover and interior design by Sans Serif Inc., Saline, Michigan

Printed in the United States

In memory of all who have carried the faith which has fueled the fire of their hope of freedom and independence, of dignity and equality; to all the unsung, unknown individuals who have yearned, fought, and died in the name of freedom over the centuries; to all Macedonians everywhere; and to the founding fathers of our country who believed "that all men were created equal, and that they were endowed by their Creator to certain inalienable rights; that among these rights are Life, Liberty, and the Pursuit of Happiness," I dedicate this story.

Contents

Acknowledgments

In embarking upon this journey into his past, Sotir has been deeply touched by the support, steadfastness and unflagging love of his wife and best friend, Tina (Noulie), and their children Stefo and Lena; his cousins Risto, Tsila and Sopha; his late brother-in-law, Paul Christou; his very good friend, Alex Gigeroff; and so many other relatives and friends, who supported and encouraged him in this effort. He is most grateful.

I deeply appreciate the trust and respect Sotir has placed in me to bring his story to you. As I jotted down notes, listening to Sotir's recall over the past 4 years, as I urged him to face his past and share his story with others, we laughed and sometimes cried at his devilishness and his bravado. Sotir held nothing back.

None of this could have happened without the copyediting of the manuscript by Sally Lattuca at Turn of Phrase; the cover design, page layout and text design provided by the staff at Sans Serif Inc. Deepest appreciation to Vivian Bradbury for her patient and calming influence during this process and Barbara Gunia's good humor which has helped me through many a night.

As I stumbled into writing this story, two longtime friends were key to my continuing to write: Albert Noyer for inspiration; Norean Martin to whom I owe such an enormous debt of gratitude for her steadfast friendship and for the time spent sending me on-target professional comments and suggestions.

Finally, to my sister, Jo Ann Boyana, who has put up with my euphoria and despair these past 4 years as I tried to tell Sotir's story, there are not enough words that can express my feelings. Thank you, Sis.

I am humbled by and deeply appreciative of the legacy left me by my parents, Anastas (Stanley) and Vasilka. Their lives, experiences, humor, and loving recall of the past has enriched my life far beyond anything that money can buy. They taught me that wherever people have lived there is a story to be told and lessons to be learned that broaden the scope and perspective of history and geography.

Olga Naumoff

Introduction

If ever a description fit the nature and character of the Macedonian people, it is this . . .

Their faith has fueled the fire of their hope for an independent and united Macedonia. In spite of all that the Macedonian people have lived through during the centuries, their passion and their faith have survived. Today, among the Macedonian Diaspora in particular, hope lives on that their faith in the eternal principles of equality, independence and unity for Macedonia will be realized.

There is no written record of the ancient language of the Macedonians. Therefore, how, when, and where did this faith, fire and hope take hold and grow in the hearts and minds of the people? Those two illustrious sons of ancient Macedonia, Philip and Alexander, father and son, evoke exciting and daring images. Emerging from the interior of southeastern Europe, the ancient Macedonians were more familiar with densely forested, rugged mountainous areas and craggy ravines; with valleys, rivers and creeks, than with inaccessible seas that lay beyond their landlocked country. Far to the west and southwest sparkled the Adriatic and Ionian Seas, while to the south the Mediterranean Sea lapped against the shores of southern Europe, northern Africa, and western Asia Minor. It was the East, however, that beckoned Alexander, and history has chronicled his great exploits, which stagger the mind.

But *what if* . . .

. . . Destiny had pulled Alexander to the West or to the North?

. . . Alexander had not died prematurely and the Macedonian Empire did not decline?

. . . Rome had not ascended as a major power?

. . . Slav tribes did not appear in southeastern Europe in the 7th century A.D. and assimilate with the remnants of the ancient Macedonians, Illyrians and Romans?

. . . The venerated Slav brothers, saints Kiril and Metody had not created the Slavic alphabet we know today as the Cyrillic alphabet, establishing a written Slavic language?

. . . Boris, king of the Bulgarians and a descendant of one of the Mongol tribes had not recognized the value of the Slavic written language as a political tool against the Byzantines?

. . . King Boris had decided not to recognize the disciples of St. Kiril and St. Metody—Clement and Naum—as teachers, had not chosen to be baptized as an Orthodox Christian, and had not set up two great centers of Slavic learning in Ohrid, Macedonia and Preslav, Bulgaria?

. . . The Ottoman Turks failed to conquer Byzantium in the early 1400's?

What if, yes, but all of these events *did* take place and the outcome inevitably impacted people, changing the conditions and nature of their survival and the course of their history.

For the Macedonians—as for many other ethnic groups who prevailed for 500 years of Ottoman rule—life was burdened in at least two distinct ways: heavy taxation and the autocratic authority and administration of the Orthodox Church.

The church was controlled by wealthy and powerful Greeks who remained in Constantinople. These Greeks, who lived in the Phanar district, came to be known as the Phanariotes, working hand-in-glove with the Turks. The Phanariotes took particular pleasure in carrying out their Moslem masters' orders of exploitation and harassment of the Slavs. The church exacted enormous fees for the performance of all religious functions, including saying prayers for the dead. They began a ruthless campaign against people speaking in the Bulgarian and Serbian languages and attempted to enforce the use of Greek over the whole of Macedonia, instead of limiting the use of the Greek language to the small southern district of Greece as had long been the custom.

For a number of centuries, the people of Macedonia had been systematically severed from their cultural and language ties in religious establishments, particularly in the villages. Priests had to conduct services in Greek; if they refused, they were replaced by Greek priests.

By the 19th century, as the Ottoman Empire was showing signs of decline and eventual collapse, and as European political power centers were beginning to align themselves to seize control of the various Ottoman lands, ethnic populations in southeastern Europe were awakening to their own opportunities for national recognition and liberation. From America, the concept of self-evident truths such as the equality of man and each man's endowment with certain inalienable rights and, from France, the ideals of *"Liberte! Fraternite! Egalite!"* swept through Europe and reached the obscured pockets of people who had suffered through the long night under the Ottomans. Those concepts gave them hope that the fire of their faith had not died out.

By the end of World War I, most of the Balkan countries, with the help of various European powers, were recognized as sovereign nations—all but Macedonia. Macedonia seemed destined to remain a land subjugated by Greece, but coveted by other foreign governments as they fought for control of the region throughout World War II.

Because of Macedonia's geographical location, none of the major European powers were inclined to let this gateway between the East and the West, this Macedonia with access to the strategic port of Salonika via the Vardar/Axios River, fall into the hands of potential rivals for control of the Mediterranean Sea and the Suez Canal. With the exception of Bulgaria, Macedonia had no powerful neighbors to help her achieve her independence as did the other Balkan nations.

In the eye of the storm, buffeted by competing ideologies, political power brokers, and governmental greed, Macedonians were denied and robbed of their identity, culture, language and in many cases their livelihood. Even though Greece was torn apart by civil war after World War II, Greece, backed by Great Britain and the West, prevailed over its dominance in Macedonia.

What the international community and their leaders failed to comprehend was that the Macedonians would not be content to remain a divided people. They did not comprehend the power of the Macedonian soul. They did not comprehend the depth of the people's patriotism. Throughout the 20th century, the flames of the fire that fed their faith and hope were never extinguished.

What worldly pleasure is untainted by grief?
What earthly glory remains unchanged?

All things are more feeble than shadows,
All things more deluding than dreams.
All human things are vanities.

Where is worldly charm?
Where the passing illusions?
Where the staff of servants and the noise?

Then once more I looked into the graves
And saw the naked bones, and I said,
Now, who is the king and who the soldier?
Who the rich man and who the poor?
All are dust, all ashes, all shadows.

From the *Sticheras* by St. John of Damascus

Prologue

No democracy can long survive which does not accept as fundamental to its very existence the recognition of the rights of minorities.

FRANKLIN DELANO ROOSEVELT, 1938

The end of World War II did not bring peace to Greece. Indeed, that war merely laid the groundwork for the bloody unrest and destruction that followed, particularly in Macedonia.

Although the victorious Allies were determined that Greece establish a representative government within a democratic structure, Greece itself was not prepared.

The seeds of discontent had been sown among the various political factions, by the monarchy in Greece and by the governments of other nations that had vital interests in the country. Among them were the Axis powers, Germany and Italy; the Allies; and the covert interests of their supposed ally, the Soviet Union. Those covert interests of the Soviet Union seemingly remained undetected until it was too late. As a result, the people of Greece, most particularly its largest minority, the Macedonians, were left to reap the bloody, bitter harvest.

The true lure of Greece was not its ancient classical heritage, but primarily its strategic location. Dominance in the Mediterranean Sea and control of the Suez Canal leading to the oil-rich Middle East were the primary goals of each of the interested political factions struggling for power and control of Greece.

The British Lion and the American Eagle had perhaps unwittingly aided corrupt Greek regimes, as they fought the formidable juggernaut of the Axis. The Russian Bear, the erstwhile "ally", of the west while fighting the Axis on the Soviet front, had already staked her voracious interest in the Mediterranean through the various guises of The Peoples' Front thrusts all over the Balkans.

The Communist guerilla bands were active throughout the second World War, sometimes seemingly cooperating with the Allies, but always under the directive of Moscow.

In the ensuing civil war in Greece, they were key actors throughout that horrendously devastating war drama. The impact on the large Macedonian population in Aegean Macedonia was disastrous.

By 1947, the Macedonian Partisan leadership had become increasingly wary and distrustful of the Greek Partisan leadership. As the United States increased its military role in Greece, the Macedonians in the Partisan resistance recognized the extreme peril that would face the population, with particular concern for the children. The Macedonians distrusted the Greek Queen's plans regarding the children, which was to send the children to camps away from the war zone. The parents suspected that it would provide the Greek government a most unique opportunity to Hellenize the Macedonian children.

In cooperation with Tito's Partisans and the Red Cross, the Macedonian Partisan leadership developed a plan to evacuate the children of Aegean Macedonia, which is how the Macedonians refer to that portion of Greece.

That generation of evacuee children is now known as the generation of the ***Detsa Begaltsi.***

The Detsa Begaltsi generation, those who are still alive, are now in their late 50s, 60s and 70s. The memories of that painful time in their lives—separated from family, home and country and taken to foreign lands to reside among strangers—overshadow their daily existence. In their exodus and all that followed, they formed a strong band of brothers and sisters. It has bound them together forever.

Their adjustment to the new—and the difficult readjustment back to the old—make for some poignant stories. Sotir's story is just one, and he shares it with you, unadorned and straightforward with all its visible imperfections.

For those who enjoy pronouncing foreign words as they read, I have written the words with English letters. The meanings are added in English. In the Macedonian language all letters are pronounced.

Here is a short guide to pronunciation of vowels:

A as in the expression *ah.*
E as in the word *get.*
I as in the word *meet.*
O as in the word *loss.*
U as in the expression *oops.*

Before All This —1930's

Dictators ride to and fro upon tigers from which they dare not dismount.

HINDUSTANI PROVERB

During the 1930's, there were ominous signals of the malevolent forces in Europe that were about to unleash their fury over the European continent. The catastrophic potential for dramatic change of the political landscape and the fate of millions of people was inevitable.

From central, eastern and southern Europe, individual men exploited opportunities to mold a totalitarian national mindset among the people with the goal of bringing the world and its resources under their control. To paraphrase President Franklin D. Roosevelt, the names of these men have gone down in infamy: Adolf Hitler, Josip Stalin and Benito Mussolini.

The totalitarian mindset had made its inroad into Greece as well. During the Greek general election in 1936, when a deadlock resulted between the republican liberals and the Popular Front, the balance of power rested with the Communist Party. The Communist Party held only 15 seats out of 285 in the Greek National Assembly, which was a definite threat to the Greek monarchy.

With the support of the Greek King George, Prime Minister General Ioanis Metaxas dissolved the Assembly. Under his rule as a dictator he created a policy of forced assimilation of the Slavs, forbidding them to speak their language in public. This measure revived opposition and resentment against Greece with disastrous results in Macedonia. Another of his decrees was the imposition of the universal military draft, which included the Macedonians. The Greek army was composed of conscripts serving two years, after which they were considered reservists. Life was becoming intolerable for the Macedonians.

The lack of political unity in Greece can be traced back to those who supported the monarchy; those who opposed the monarchy; and the growing strength of the Communist Party.

Mussolini's troops invaded Ethiopia and Albania.

September

- Adolf Hitler's divisions crossed into Poland.
- Britain and France declared war on Germany.
- Italy and Greece made a declaration of friendship.

The wedding of Sotir's parents, Mite and Tsila, T'rsie Macedonia. Sotir's father is to the left of the godfather holding the wedding banner. His mother is wearing a white apron, gold necklace, and flowers in her hair.

A Special Event in the Month of Sechko

The truly passionate are little boys.

MURRAY KEMPTON, 1963

There is no doubt about it. *Lerinchani,* the people who lived in Lerin, remember it well. They remember that the end of January and early February of that year brought more cold wind and heavy snow than any other year in memory, that is, in the memory of many of the villagers of T'rsie. I'm speaking of 1936.

1936, T'rsie, Lerin district of Macedonia. *Sechko*, the month of February, is usually one of the most severe of the winter months back home. Back home is where my heart is and will always be; back home, in T'rsie, in Macedonia.

My *Striko* Done, my uncle, and my father often talked about the bitter cold during

Sotir's father, Mite, circa 1939–40.

Sotir's mother, Tsila, widowed, circa 1950.

Sechko of that year. The entire village had been snowbound. No one could venture out, not even to get water, because of the wind. It blew and howled with such fury, stirring up the snow with such force, that it seemed as if it was going to vent its anger at every house. The strength of the wind bent the strongest trees, and anything daring to stand in its way would have soon found itself sucked up into the very vortex of the wind. The howling sound of the wind echoed through the valleys and hills.

As terrifying as the day was in this month of *Sechko*, Father was struggling to reach his brother, Done, to give him the news. Father pounded on the door and shouted, "Brother, we have another boy in the family. He was born early this morning, during the coldest hours." The door opened and Father, covered with snow, was quickly pulled inside. *Striko* slapped Father on the back, shouting joyfully with congratulations.

The two brothers laughed with joy, hugging each other.

"This boy of yours will be a tough one. He will test everyone to the last. No one can be born on such a day and be weak. May he live long and be strong!"

Sechko, by the way, is derived from the Macedonian word meaning "to cut". Anyway, I guess *Striko* had known instinctively that I would become a hardheaded boy who could stir up a frenzy of emotion; who survived the mischief I frequently created on my own as well as those who visited mischief on me, usually unsuccessfully. It was the more worldly mischief, if it can be called mischief, that enmeshed me and my generation in Macedonia in a struggle for control and power by foreign elements over our native land. They tested the strength and depth of the *Sechko* in all of us.

My name is Sotir, Sotir Nitchov. If you can't pronounce it, that's too bad. But it is *my* name, given to me by my godparents, and blessed in the church.

Don't ever try to change my name, because I have a legacy, a history, and a long memory. I made a promise to my *Dedo,* my grandfather, and myself that I shall never forget my home, my family, my village, my Macedonia.

My memories keep it alive every day of my life. It gives me the incentive, the inspiration, the determination never to bend to anyone or anything, but to live to the fullest, remembering the ones who did not have that choice. You should know that no matter how hard the Greeks tried, no matter how they threatened me or tried to abuse me, I never changed my name.

I think you should also know that I am one of about 30,000 Macedonian children who were not kidnapped, abducted, killed or napalmed. Most of us were able to survive our separation from home and family, in spite of fear and loneliness, because we were evacuated to other countries that opened their doors to us. We are called the *Detsa Begaltsi,* the children who left. It is an appellation that defines our generation forever because of our experiences.

I am one of the Detsa Begaltsi.

T'rsie

In the love of home,
The love of country has its rise.
CHARLES DICKENS, 1840

Lundser. It was my compass, my beacon, my companion. Whenever I sighted Lundser, I knew I was almost home. It was my own personal mountain. Scampering up to its summit, sitting under a tree, a sweet, light breeze caressing my face, was what I imagined a heaven must be.

With eyes closed, my thoughts would drift, without direction, trusting my imagination to alight on something—a thought, a winning moment—anything to unfold its magic in my untried, untested, simple young mind.

From where I sat on my mountain, a panoramic view of my entire world would unfold. Perched like a young *sokol*, a falcon, I would see the valleys, protected by hills and mountains of different shades of green. Here and there the sparkling creeks and rivers winked at me as they made their eternal way from here to there. And there, down there, T'rsie spread out. T'rsie, my village.

The brown and whitewashed stucco houses topped with *keremidi*, red tiles, contrasting against the green of the trees—the variety of colors of the vegetation and the black earth that nurtured us—seemed so beautiful to me, so peaceful, so comforting. Home!

I could see our villagers caught up in the routine and rhythm of daily chores and labors, while the cattle and sheep absorbed themselves in feeding or resting in shade, or just nestled together in their time-honored way. Scenes so beautiful, so tranquil, could only have been created by a master.

The pastoral blend of color, the rhythmic movements of the villagers fulfilling the needs of ordinary country living, greeting each other in friendship and harmony amid the sounds and smells of animals and nature are forever rooted in my soul. They occupy every memory of my childhood, of my short-lived life in my Macedonia.

Oh, fearless ***Sokol****, let me fly with you back to the place of my birth, back to my family that once was, but is no more; back to T'rsie, now in ruins. Each memory encapsulated in its own wet teardrop waits to be released of its pain and sorrow and replaced with the happier times of my childhood. Let me fly with you, Sokol, back to my T'rsie, back to our mountain, to Lundser. With the innocent eyes of my childhood, let me see once again the peace and beauty of my world that once was, but is no more. I will ask no more of you, Sokol. Just let me see everyone and everything as it was. Bring us all back together just one more time!*

Each time I return to T'rsie, I look for sights I knew as a boy. Each time I discover less and less evidence of those who once lived in T'rsie—the large, extended, self-sufficient Macedonian families. As is true of so many Macedonians, *T'rsiani*, those who lived in T'rsie, were energetic, entrepreneurial people whose drive, pride, and their strong sense of independence flourished. Our connection with the land, with nature, held many lessons for us, and we treated both with love and respect, for they nourished us, warmed us, clothed us. Together—land, nature and each other—we were able to survive unspeakable hardships, deprivation, humiliations, and threats of death. Love of land and love of family are intertwined in the minds and hearts of the Macedonians.

My eyes are wide open now, but if I allow my thoughts to drift, they drift back to T'rsie.

Spanning time and distance, T'rsie still exists over there. At first, the outlines of the mountains come into focus. Those luscious greens paint the entire countryside with a beautiful, cool hue, as they seem to curve all around, something like a Turkish moon. I look to the north and smile inwardly as my beloved, familiar landmark, Lundser Mountain, takes shape, beckoning me back. My inward eye moves eastward and rests on Kukul Mountain. Oh, yes. It is still there. Roving over that familiar place, I find myself looking to the northwest searching for *Golenata*. That, too, is still there: the three mountains surrounding the valley where my soul and heart rest, looking down at T'rsie.

Dedo had told us that during the time of the Turks, our village was under the Kostursko jurisdiction. Around 1864, T'rsie was transferred to the Lerinsko jurisdiction.

I feel that I know every inch of land that belongs to T'rsie, from Chaulata Hill, to Plochite, to Palego Hill, south to Bairamovo Hill to Tsiku Livaiche, to Lopushets, Tsusukata and Stogu; through Derveno to Glavieto, toward V'ro, Kukul and Presekata, to the Turianski Ravine and Cheshala. No, I didn't forget Tiza. Tiza was actually a crater in the mountains and became the playground of many of our games. I know the land as well as I know my own name.

When Tome, my unforgettable horse, and I raced with the wind, we touched the boundaries between T'rsie, Nevoleni, Neret, Turie, Statitsa, Psoderi, and Armensko, all Macedonian villages. Tome and I trotted around the many underground springs and galloped along the rivers and creeks. With the plentiful water and fertile land of T'rsie, we were truly blessed.

Tome was like the wind when we raced to Kalugeritsa and down through Tumbata, Dimovski Dol, Gumentsa and Yanina Livada, and then back to T'rsie. It was so great to be young and alive then, to feel so free, so one with my horse.

Why, then, did such horrors, such unspeakable suffering engulf us, tearing our families apart and destroying our way of life?

Where were the humanitarians of the world, the civil libertarians, the cameras and film to record the life and struggle of the Macedonians from the time those lands subjugated by the Ottomans began to break free?

There were those who were granted their freedom, independence, or recognition of their ethnicity in most of the area that is identified as the Balkans. Everyone was granted the dignity of recognition except the Macedonians. Their reward was partition, division of the people among four different countries: Serbia, Greece, Bulgaria and a sliver of land to Albania. The Macedonian was expected to become an instant loyal citizen of the new country by denying his own ethnicity, his language, cultural background, and history.

What outrageous demands had the Macedonians made of the world?

Who gave the Greeks and the Serbs the right to remove every trace of our language, our history, our religion—even our buried dead?

Greeks like to brag that only pure Greeks live in Greece. I don't know about the purity of any Greek. But, contrary to their propaganda, Macedonian villages are very, very old. Much of our written history has been burned, buried or lost in Macedonia, yet T'rsie can be traced back as far back as A.D. 1445 in the Turkish Tax Registry #237 *Tefter,* book, *Kosturski Vilayet.* According to accounts in that *Tefter,* written 50 years after the death of Krali Marko, the last Slavic ruler in Macedonia, there were 30 families listed for T'rsie. The Turks were meticulous about the numbers, because the main revenue came from taxes. Everything was taxed. In this period, T'rsie was producing 230 Turkish kilos of wheat, 120 kilos of *yakmen*, barley, and 10 kilos of beans. Taxes were also levied on beehives, honey, melons, flour mills, pigs, as well as on all fruit and vegetable produce, vineyards, sheep cattle, and whatever farming equipment and building structures existed on the property.

Later, in 1841, *Tefter* #16, Lerinska Nahia, T'rsie was listed as having 72 families. T'rsie was under the jurisdiction of Halil, son of Hadji Hassan, which passed after time to Jusuf and Mustafa, sons of Ibraim, became the authorities over T'rsie.

In 1861, a monk by the name of Gerasim Popanastasov had returned from the

A view of the village, T'rsie. Photo taken by Sotir many years later.

St. Gora Monastery to T'rsie, his birthplace. Father Gerasim's baptismal name had been Traiko. On his return, Father Gerasim was determined to erect a beautiful church in T'rsie. With the help and skill of the villagers and others, by 1866 a school building was added, attracting students from surrounding villages as well.

I can't describe the pride I feel in my heart that my Dedo's grandfather, my great-great grandfather, was one of the villagers who helped to erect the church. Father Gerasim has become a legendary figure, having trained over 20 priests in the old Slavonic liturgy. He trained students to become *psaltars,* chanters, who sing the responses during the church services. Students were taught to read prayers and the books of the apostles. The holy Father survived the determined efforts of the Greek Bishop of Kostur to eliminate him. By 1900, T'rsie's population had increased to 960 Macedonians.

On May 20, 1901, almost two years prior to the St. Elia Uprising, *Illinden,* the legendary Macedonian revolutionary, Marko Lerinski, sounded the battle cry for independence from the Turkish yoke of tyranny in the village of T'rsie!

Why do I remember these things? Why must I remember these things? Perhaps the answer lies in a quote from Cicero, who lived in the first century, B.C.:

To be ignorant of what had occurred before you were born, is to remain a child. For what is the worth of a human life, unless it is woven into the life of our ancestors by the records of history?

From the Beginning

Everywhere, we learn only from those we love.

GOETHE, 1825

I am also known as *Sote* by family and close friends. Dedo liked to call me *Sotiraki*, but Sotir is my name. Here in America, I am also called Nick. Figure that one out! Maybe they thought it was too hard to pronounce, or perhaps it was too STRANGE? Don't ask.

Since the King of the Greeks, George, appointed Metaxas Prime Minister in 1936, allowing him to become the dictator of Greece, I had to be born. I was destined to be his nemesis and to those like him, for the rest of my life.

The first 8 years of my life were among the happiest. I was part of a large family, a simple, frugal, hardworking, proud people, tending to the business of life and survival and life all over again. I knew I was loved. I also knew that I tested that love often as I grew. I was really a little gangster, fearless, independent, mischievous, often quite uncivilized. My parents, Mitre and Tsila, short for Dimitar and Vasilka; my grandparents, Dedo Vasil and Baba Tsila; my older brother, Stefo; my sister Tsotsa, the affectionate nickname for Sofa; and eventually another little sister, Mara, made up my immediate family.

There were aunts, and uncles and cousins, all of whom took their turn trying to keep me civilized. God knows they tried! But, I knew they loved me; even when they threatened me with the direst of consequences, I knew. I loved them just as fiercely, but we didn't talk about it. We didn't have to. As passionate a people as we have always been, we have learned to control our expressions of love and affection for the appropriate time and the appropriate circumstances. That's the Macedonian way. You don't often, if ever, hear a husband or wife address each other as "honey" or "sweetheart" or "dear". That's private stuff, for Pete's sake. Maybe that's why Macedonians are described as *stoic*. I am hardly a stoic person, but I don't go around calling anyone "honey" and that other stuff.

Whenever I could, I roamed the valleys and hills, and later the forests, freely and happily. Child molestation was unheard of and the safety of children was everyone's responsibility. As soon as I could walk, barefoot and free, pantless sometime as a little kid, I embraced my freedom of movement. I led the mischief among my cousins and friends. Mischief was really my middle name, a force to be reckoned with among my enemies, an undisciplined devil among my neighbors.

As an absolutely fearless soul, I loved to observe people. I learned early on in my life how to read people. I listened to their voices as they spoke. I watched their body language, their give-away mannerisms. I learned. Yes, I learned that a change of tone in voice, a twitch of an eye, a change of posture, a furtive glance, or a slight tremor of the hand spoke volumes, and I more clearly understood what they were really saying. Relationships told me a lot, of course: who related to whom, who could keep a secret, who liked to take risks, who the jackasses were, who was respected, and who was not. Man, I was good—very, very GOOD!

But, I knew the **law**. I mean I knew who was the **L A W**, at least for our family, and that was **Dedo**. You can be sure that I always worked, or played, or did the devil's work so that I would remain in Dedo's good graces. Even when I exasperated him, driving him to the breaking point, I knew he loved me, and even approved of my effrontery in some instances. One look into his eyes told me volumes. So I tried to be as circumspect as I possibly could be around him. I really think I was his favorite. Yah, me! I *like* to think that. I really do, even though he was a tough judge and jury regarding me and my escapades.

I loved my Dedo Vasil. I still do. He is always in my thoughts.

So there we were, a little more than a half century ago, living large, well, large for *us*. We had a large family altogether; grandparents, their three sons and their wives and eventually fourteen children. In time, each of the sons acquired his own property, but we belonged to each other. And that was just fine. You could even say we adopted the motto of the Musketeers of France: **ONE FOR ALL, AND ALL FOR ONE.** Of course, at the time, who knew about Musketeers?

From my earliest years, I was totally aware of the various places and villages around us. I already had a favorite town, Lerin. There are those today who call it *Florina,* but the Macedonian heart keeps beating Lerin, Lerin, Lerin!

Lerin was only about 3½ hours from T'rsie; that is 3½ hours as the donkey trots. T'rsie sits in the lap of our beautiful mountains, which I love to recite: Kukul, Lundser, Chereshata. Lerin, situated on the Lerinsko *polie,* field. The Nevolski Hills and the Klepala/T'rsianski *ridovi*, hills, on one side, while on the other side of Lerin the Brezoitsa/Vlashki *livadia*, meadows, and the Bufski/Moteshnitsa Mountains looked down on the town. Lerin was our center for commerce, transportation, administration, postal service and the *police station.*

I remember going to neighboring villages like Armensko, Statitsa, Neret, Psoderi, Nevoleni, Bouf and Oschima. Much later, I discovered that a world existed even beyond, beyond Lerin and beyond Kostur, and that "beyond" world thought of us, if they thought of us at all, as non-existent, or as poor, ignorant, uneducated, boorish peasants.

Before Macedonia was discarded by the "Powers That Were"; before they separated Macedonians from each other, most of the villages had their own schools. Some of the larger towns like Solun, Lerin, Kostur had gymnasia, which the more gifted attended. The more intellectually endowed, and those families who could afford it, sent their sons on to the various universities in Sofia, Vienna, Constantinople, Athens, Belgrad, Rome, Paris, Moscow. They formed the intelligentsia in Macedonia, strongly influenced by the ideas of the West, and by the literature regarding the French and American revolutions. These became our teachers, physicians, merchants, engineers, lawyers, merchants, and—our own revolutionaries.

We may not have been worldly, but we weren't stupid. In our own environment, in our own way, we knew the way of our world. Each family owned some land, some property and some animals. Some, of course, owned more than others. Entire families worked their own *nivias,* farms and fields. We used old-fashioned, simple, hand-made plows and tools, the methodology used by generations in Macedonia.

We did not starve. We may have gone hungry at times, but starvation? I don't think so. Nature taught us how to conserve and protect the land. We have a deep and profound respect for Mother Earth. We were provided with the forests for our building needs and warmth; with the sparkling streams, creeks and rivers and lakes for the clear, refreshing water, and fish. Mother Earth gave us the rich, productive soil for our vegetables, delicious fruit; plants for the dyes that gave color to the yarns used for homespun clothing, blankets, and *kilimi,* carpets.

Our animals, the sheep, goats, cows, bulls, oxen, pigs, hens, roosters, horses, mules, and donkeys, provided us with the hides for our outer clothing, shoes, and packs. They gave us milk, cheese, and eggs. They provided transportation. They taught us lessons in life and death.

As you can imagine, life was a pretty busy proposition for every member of the family, including little children and the elderly. Everyone was a productive member of the family and each could work at something to contribute.

Most of the men had the skills of craftsmen, some quite creative, which made it possible for them to earn a little more *pari*, money. During the winter months, the men often went to other towns and cities to hire out. This practice still is called *na pechalba.* Many men went to other countries, including Turkey, and some even as far away as America, Canada and Australia.

Like most of the village kids in Macedonia, I was a shepherd, moving with the sheep as they grazed up and down the mountains. From my perch on Lundser, listening to the chatter of birds and gazing at the graceful swoops of *sokols* from time to time, I could see patches of rye, corn, potatoes, oats and beans. It looked as if Mother Earth had designed a quilt to cover the land. There was such a graceful curtsying of the stalks in the wheat fields when the wind rippled over them. Those fields looked as if golden waves were moving with the wind.

When I think about it, we were really self-sufficient back then, quite self-supporting, except for lack of cooking oil, sugar and salt. That had to be bought or bartered in exchange for something.

Before the terror that befell us all, we were a tight, close-knit village. Everyone knew everyone else. We knew what the relationships were, not only in our family, but just about everybody else's, as well. This knowledge was very important, because Macedonians were vigilant about even a hint of incestuous relationships. The health and welfare of the entire village was everyone's priority.

Whenever Nature wanted to test our resolve and our strengths, whether it was fire, flood, drought, or storms, all the villagers would come together to help in some way. Each family contributed whatever it could.

Grandparents, and all the elderly, were given the greatest respect. They held the greatest influence over the family, particularly over the sons. The elderly were the first to be seated, the first to be served food, the first to be sought for the mark of approval.

We kids, even my band of gangsters and I, learned the necessity for a strong work ethic. We learned and respected the role of each family member, and the methods of survival in difficult situations. We learned by watching, listening, following directions and doing. We put our trust in our family, our land, our forests, our animals and our traditions. When we deviated and began to place our trust in foreign ideas and men, we learned what the terrible consequences of distrust can be.

I must have been about 3 years old when Benito Mussolini's armies invaded Albania. Maybe just 4 when Il Duce demanded that he be allowed passage through Greek territory, which meant marching through Macedonia. While it was an important event that was going to touch and begin to change our lives, at the time. it made no difference in my life. My world was family, village and Lerin. Even the words *Italiantsi,* Italians, and *Germantsi*, Germans, had absolutely no meaning for me. But, I definitely understood what *Grtsi* meant. We all knew what *Grtsi* meant, and it wasn't good. *Grtsi* meant Greek!!!

Yet, young as I was, I felt something was spooking the grown-ups. Thinking about it now, I guess I was sensing the appearance of some kind of change making itself known in subtle ways. It felt like the clouds were ever so slowly forming into darkening shapes. You couldn't make out what the shapes resembled. They weren't coming from any one particular direction.

I can't exactly place the day or time when I began to feel spooked, but I remember that something was happening. You know how it is when the sun seems to be shining brightly, but the wind has died down? The birds begin to gather and fly around in greater numbers, looking for some place to go and there is less chirping, just the overhead flutter of a multitude of wings? Like when our animals, sensing something, begin to be more restless, more agitated, bellowing and grunting, and it doesn't have anything to do with the weather, as if Mother Nature is sending her own alarm signals to her creatures, large and small? That's what I felt, spooked.

In time I began to overhear bits of conversations here and there, and I became more and more aware of these new words: *Italiantsi,* Italians; *Albantsi,* Albanians.

From time to time, Father was called to work as a medic for the Greeks, but that didn't change anything. Father often went to Lerin on family business for a couple of days, or even weeks. Our lives still went on in the routine way.

At that time I didn't even know the word "*Partizan*", what it was, or what it meant. It could have been a country for all I cared.

As my cousins and I grew, we began to take on more tasks. During the growing and harvesting season, Baba and Mother prepared the lunches, which always contained delicious homemade bread, cheeses and olives, some wine. The young brides, the newly married, all called *nevesti,* would take the food to the men and women working in the fields. I was assigned to bring food as well. It was a pretty, pleasant time, then, for you could hear the singing from the fields. In fact, you heard singing coming from four or five different fields, sometimes responding to each other. The work was hard and the days were long, but the singing seemed to release the fatigue.

We had wonderful holidays, especially, *Velikden,* Easter. It was a 3-day celebration. I always associate *Velikden* with that delicious smell of bread baking and lambs roasting outdoors.

Baba would gather the plants: *chimerika,* from which the red dye was made, and Mother would boil the plants along with *korupki,* bark from trees, and onion peels to release the color. Eggs were always dyed red for Easter because that symbolized the crucifixion and the resurrection of Christ. Eggs have always been the symbol of life to us.

There was a tradition called *chakanie* at Easter and we all looked forward to it. We could challenge anyone, young or old, to see how many cracked boiled eggs we could collect, to proving that you had the strongest egg. That's what *chakanie* was. Even the adults enjoyed the challenges. The way to crack the other person's egg was to cup your own egg with your hand so that only the pointy part of the egg was visible, and then strike the other egg as hard as you could. Each of us hoped that we would have the strongest shell on the egg, because we could collect the cracked eggs and after a while have a little egg feast!

The *chakanie* took place after Easter service, when everybody headed towards *sred selo,* the center of the village for socializing. Then, it would be home for the entire family and guests to feast on the tastiest roast lamb in the whole wide world.

The best way to create the hardest egg, which no one can crack, is to follow this procedure:

1. Take a raw egg.
2. Drill a hold in the shell carefully with a needle.
3. Suck the egg out.
4. Fill the shell with wax.
5. Seal the egg with more wax.
6. Boil and color the egg!

Take my word for it. You will have collected the most cracked red eggs at Easter. I guarantee it!

Spring was filled with special holidays and colorful traditions. May, when we celebrated *Guirguivden*, or *Gergiden*, which is St. George's feast day, the gypsies would take off during this time, returning somewhere around *Dimitrovden*, on the feast day of St. Dimitri.

On St. George's feast day, after church, young girls would make their way to the fields, bringing their Easter eggs, flowering branches of walnut trees or weeping willows, and a container of wine. They sang as they went, dropping parts of the flowering branches and bits of eggs on the fields, sprinkling the fields with wine. Talk about pretty! This tradition was supposed to guarantee lots of *bereket*, meaning a very rich harvest!

Every year we celebrated the Macedonian Insurrection of August 2, 1903, the feast-day of St. *Elia*, commemorating a day of defiant heroism and sacrifice, when Macedo-

A view of Lerin. Photo by Sotir.

nians tried to get the world's attention to correct the abuses of the Ottoman Empire in Macedonia. We were fighting only for basic civil rights. It was from these annual celebrations, that I began to understand our passion for justice, equal rights, freedom from tyranny, motivating generations of Macedonians to sacrifice their lives. Our celebration took place at the Monastery, just over the hill overlooking T'rsie. The church, St. Elia, by the Monastery is surrounded by chestnut trees.

Our most religiously observed *praznik,* holiday, is the feast day of Sveta Bogoroditsa, St. Mary, the Holy Birthgiver of God. People would come from many villages and the town of Lerin as well, to participate in the *panagir*, festival. To me it seemed like thousands came to the church in Yanina Livada, near Lerin, which encompassed a part of T'rsie, Kalugeritsa and Moteshnitsa.

We never thought of birthdays. Because we usually were named after a saint, we celebrated our namedays instead. We observed namedays without losing time to complete our chores. *Vrshanie zhito,* the sifting of wheat by tossing the wheat in the air with pitchforks or shovels, had to be done in season. It was something to see how the wind picked up the *shlupki*, the shell, which allowed the grain to fall to the ground, creating a huge pile of grain. I was always tempted to jump into the pile. Had I done so, I would have gotten my butt poked!

1940–41

Men must have corrupted nature a little, for they were not born wolves, and they have become wolves.

VOLTAIRE, 1759

External developments were rapidly moving Greece into a precarious situation. Prime Minister Winston Churchill urged the establishment of the SOE, the British Special Operations Executive, which was stationed in Cairo, Egypt. Its key role was to set Europe ablaze by fostering a spirit of resistance to the Germans through resistance movements. These movements could also act a a fifth column when the time came for the Allies to invade. As Italy and Germany accelerated their drive to achieve power and control throughout Europe and beyond, the SOE made plans to send a military mission into Greece. The purpose of these missions was to coordinate acts of sabotage to be carried out by *andartes,* right-wing Greek guerillas. The Greek monarchy and influential personages had not been altogether opposed to the Germans. Resistance to the Axis occupations was imposed primarily from the outside—by the British.

In Yugoslavia Communists appeared to gain in strength due to the severe measures against pro-Bulgarian sentiment among the Macedonians in the Vardar Banovina, *Vardarska Makedonia.* These Macedonians seemed inclined toward alignment with the Axis.

Intermittent welcoming overtures from the Communists in the Pirin region of Bulgaria to Ivan Mihailov's IMRO were made in an attempt to unite Macedonia into a communist state.

Toward the end of the year, in an effort to prevent Yugoslavia's objections to German intervention in Greece via Yugoslavia, the Germans offered the port of Salonika to the Yugoslavs. Simultaneously the Germans also were offering the Bulgarians a door to the Agean Sea by way of Greek Macedonia and Thrace.

April 1940

- Greece formally recognized the Italian Empire, which included Abyssinia.
- The major powers in the Greek kingdom allied themselves with England.

May/June

- Belgium and France fell to the Nazis.

July

- Greek political resentments erupted in Crete. Metaxas moved quickly and ended the revolt.
- An Italian submarine sank a Greek cruiser at anchor at Tenos.

October

- Mussolini sent an ultimatum to Greece, demanding free passage across Greek territory. Metaxas refused.
- The Italians met stiff Greek resistance that pushed them back across the Albanian border. Macedonians refer to this as the Albanski Boi, the Albanian War.
- Greece reluctantly agreed to have the RAF operate in conjunction with the Greek air force, and the Metaxas government remained reluctant to involve British troops.

January 194l

- Metaxas died.
- Greece pushed Italian troops back into Albania.
- The Third Reich parachuted regiments into Crete. Crete fell.
- The Greek king, his government and British troops evacuated Greece.
- The RAF (British Royal Air Force) virtually became the Greek Air Force.

February

- Germany and Bulgaria signed a secret protocl.
- Bulgarian troops began occupying large sections of Macedonia for joint administrative purposes with Germany.
- The Yugoslav government signed the Axis Tripartite Pact, surrendering any plan to acquire the major Greek port city of Salonica.

April

- Divisions of the Third Reich invaded Yugoslavia en route to Greece.
- The Third Reich troops reached Athens, and the Germans set up their own collaborationist government.

And Speaking of Chores

Work spares us from three great evils: boredom vice, and need.

VOLTAIRE, 1759

Did I have chores? Did I do any work? Oh, you betcha! All of us had chores to do, and believe me, we all did them, though some better than others, I'm sure.

One of my Baba's chores was to gather *koprivici*, nettles, and *tservenka,* a red wheat, and mixed them with other foodstuffs to feed the *bishki,* the pigs. As I mentioned earlier, during the growing season, my cousins and I had the responsibility of taking lunches to the workers in the fields. Baba would make a delicious *mandzha,* a stew, and fill the *grne,* one of our ceramic or wooden pots, for us to carry to the fields. Other times we were charged with the gathering of vegetables from the garden, which we would do with great delight, but not necessarily from our own garden!

I always tested the time-honored ways of doing things. I remember the day when Baba, as usual, told us exactly what she needed from the garden, and we did what she asked. We brought back all the vegetables from the garden. But it was a neighbor's garden that we raided. I guess we weren't all that clever, because we were spotted. In the past our neighbors had been mighty vocal in their complaints to my Baba. You see I had led my gangsters into neighboring gardens before. Whenever we thought we had been spotted, we would hide out, and return later in the evening for supper. This time we thought we had gotten away with our little garden caper. We hadn't, of course, because our entrepreneurial venture ended quite noisily.

Supper that day was, as always, delicious; Baba could make anything taste great. Baba was ready for us. Upon seeing us coming in innocently, as usual, she called to us, "Oh, yes, my boys. Come and fill your bellies with this wonderful food from our neighbor's garden!" She was not pleased.

Dedo nailed us with his look. "Why couldn't you get the vegetables from our own garden?"

Armed with my smug impudence, which stemmed from my sense of immunity from Dedo, I answered, "Well, their garden was closer. And anyway, this way we will have more food for the next time." Wasn't I a smart ass?

Dedo ignored me and my impudence. He tilted his head toward Father.

"See how much damage was done and pay them."

That ended our garden capers . . . for a while.

I loved shepherding, out in the open, free and uninhibited. Many of the older shepherds carried a flute-like instrument, a *kaval* or a *shupelka*. As the sheep grazed around them, the shepherds liked to play their *kavals*. I tell you, when some of the shepherds played their flutes, as they rested on the slopes of the hills and mountains, the wind would often pick up their sounds, carrying the melodies into the valleys and hills and fields. You could just imagine the branches and leaves swaying and dancing in the breezes, as the huge, open-aired amphitheatre filled with melodious sounds. The valleys echoed with the music. No megaphones or microphones or other sound-enhancing gizmos were needed. The mountains and the valleys were the directors and technicians, as the shepherds produced the symphonies for these impromptu concerts.

Sometimes, the shepherds, the *ovchari,* competed with each other. One or two would be playing *kavals* on one side of the mountain, and another two or three on the other. All one had to do was just sit on any slope, with the breeze fanning your face, lean back and enjoy the heavenly musical competition. Heaven on earth? Oh, yes.

I loved working with Father. By watching him work, whether in the fields or caring for our animals, I learned valuable life lessons. He cared about all living things. You could tell that by watching him care for both people and animals. He was very fair in his dealings, and he expected fairness in return.

Father was magical with sheep. He looked after them as if they were his children. After we moved the large, adult flock of sheep out to graze, father would allow the little lambs loose in the wheat field. We used to sow half of the wheat field in the fall. By the time *Baba Marta*, the month of March, and *Treven*, which is April, came around, that wheat field would be about six inches high and to me it resembled a blue-green sea, small waves rolling in the wind. I wish you could see with my eyes that joyful sight of the little lambs, running all over the field, jumping and falling as they skittered about. They did try to graze, but it was obvious to me that they didn't know how. Or maybe they didn't like grazing, because they would shake their heads, making funny sounds. They used to make me laugh, watching them, and the memory still makes me smile.

When it was time to bring the flock back, as soon as the sheep approached the fields, the little lambs would scamper toward them, following the direction of the bleating sounds. Only the river separated the flock from the lambs, preventing the little ones from reaching their mothers. Like little soldiers, the lambs would line up as close to the river as they dared, but they wouldn't cross over. Those lambs wouldn't even get their feet wet. They were just good, obedient, but anxious little soldiers waiting in formation.

Just before the *bulog*, or flock, would reach the river, it was the job of us kids to steer the lambs into the *ambor*, the barn. Now the bleating was stronger and louder in the *ambor*. The mothers in the flock, hearing the lambs' cries, would bleat back at them as if to say, "I'm coming! I'm coming!"

My cousin Risto and I had the task of steering the *bulog* along the river toward the bridge to get them across. Once we maneuvered them into the *ambor*, you should have heard the bleating. Such a cacophony! Young and old, bleating until they heard a familiar sound that identified mother to lamb. What a tremendous noise!

Talk about reunions! Even if the mothers could wait to find and feed their babies, those babies couldn't wait. When we opened the doors of the *ambor*, absolute chaos reigned.

It was beautiful, funny and crazy. The mothers who couldn't find their lamb immediately, went sniffing at first one lamb and then another, until she found her baby. Sometimes, the lambs, in their impatience, would try sniffing and smelling to find their mothers, but their efforts weren't very efficient. Risto and I often helped them, and once they were reunited, mother and lamb, and suckling started, all other sounds ceased. Suckling was now the name of the game!

After the feeding frenzy had ended and all were safely within the *ambor,* lambs lodged between their mother's legs, we all felt it was a job well done. Dedo loved those moments. He was so proud of his healthy flock, but above all, he loved them. As the lambs grew, Dedo liked to sit outside on the ground and admire them. Dedo sported such a unique smile whenever he felt proud of something or someone or something he really admired. That smile creased his face from ear to ear, and lit up his eyes!

The lambs and the flock always brought that smile to his face. I used to love to tease him about that. I remember him saying to me, "Wait until you grow up. You'll find out!"

I never did find out what he meant. Destiny had other plans for me and other Macedonian kids like me.

Usually, around the end of *Treven,* April, and the beginning of *Urezh*ar, the month of May, we had to return with the *bulog* to the village. By the early part of *Urezhar*, Dedo would have selected about 200 lambs to take to Lerin to sell to the *khasapi*, the butchers. He marked the lambs that were to be selected, with either red or yellow paint. The *khasap*i always came into the *kaliva* earlier than the time planned for the sale, to make their own selections before the others. That didn't please Dedo. He wouldn't allow them to make their own selections without his presence.

"I'll tell you which ones I am selling. I will make that decision, not you!" he would say in no uncertain tones.

If a *khasapin,* a butcher, protested, Dedo did not hesitate to cut him off.

"You will buy from the ones I decide to sell, or not at all. If you persist, I will raise the price. So let's not waste any more of my time!"

Whichever of us kids happened to be around when the *khasapi* arrived, whether it was Stefo, Risto, Ilo or me, Dedo always asked us if we had any favorite little lamb or baby goat. If any of us pointed to one that happened to have been marked for sale, Dedo would indicate to the khasapin, "No, not that one."

"But we have already agreed to the deal."

"Well, we agreed, but now we will have to disagree. My grandson bought that one," he would reply with a straight face.

Oh, he was one of a kind, that Dedo of mine. He could not be intimidated. He showed no fear of anyone or anything. He was, without doubt, the most stubborn of the stubborn individuals in the entire world. If he felt he was right, nothing could move him from his position. And always, his family came first. I guess that's why I admired him so much, and he knew it.

Dedo loved to test me. Sometimes he would deliberately make me angry to the point of no return, then he would come at me and say, "I got you, didn't I?' He would chortle with delight when that happened.

Because he got such a kick out of testing me, I learned to hide my anger so that I couldn't be "gotten" when I didn't want to be "gotten". These were excellent lessons that I learned, and they served me well in confrontations with others, even as I grew older. I should amend that. It served me well most of the time, not always.

It was always good to have my cousin Ilo with me in Lerin because he was a good companion. While there were other kids from T'rsianska Mala that I knew, I always felt much better with Ilo there. T'rsianska Mala was a district in Lerin that had been populated by families from our village for generations. Folklore has it that Lerin itself was founded by T'rsiani.

For about two summers, Ilo and I spent most of the time coming and going between T'rsie and Lerin, fulfilling various errands and chores.

I don't remember the year, but one winter, Ilo's brother Risto, and I spent our winter in Lerin as shepherds, grazing our flock in a large area outside the town. We led the sheep to Brezoitsa, above the Dzade Road, leading to Bigla Mountain and the town of Prespa. Dedo had leased the entire area to have our sheep and goats graze there. In the winter, the sun heated this open area from morning to sundown, making it ideal for grazing. Snow never lasted long here.

That winter was such a memorable one. Nature had so much to teach me, more than I could ever learn from books. It was the time for the birthing. I felt such awe. Sometimes there were as many as 15 or 20 lambs born in half a day.

When the birthing was over, either Risto or I would holler for our parents to come and help count the number of newborn lambs. We tried to keep the mothers and newborn together, isolated from the rest of the flock for that day, to avoid any accidents.

There I was, barely 6 years old, watching the miracle of birth. I felt so many emotions, but I always felt a little sad, seeing the efforts of the little lambs, struggling to get upright on their legs. Hearing their weak bleating, calling for help, as their mothers stood on guard, unable to do more for them, I found it hard to hold back and not try to help them. Sometimes Mother Nature is a tough teacher for both animals and humans.

The new mothers cleaned their lambs by licking them all over. There were a couple of the new mothers, maybe about three or four of them, who seemed a little ornery, as if they didn't want or even like their new-born. They made no attempt to clean their babies. In fact, they stomped and kicked at their poor little lambs, so we had to watch them very carefully in case any of the sheep rejected their lambs.

What I am about to tell you now might disgust you, but I had to do it. There was one mother sheep kicking and stomping her helpless little lamb so badly that I couldn't stand it. I tried to kick the sheep to stop what she was doing, but she was determined to kill her own baby. I was so upset that I reached out and grabbed a heavy piece of wood nearby and hit that sheep as hard as I could.

I did it. I killed her and saved that little lamb. Now I had created an orphan, which was the farthest thing from my mind to do. There were other mother sheep whose babies did not survive their birth. So I did what people have done for years, what I had seen my father and Dedo do. I skinned one of the little dead lambs, with all the mucous on the skin and draped it over the new orphan. It didn't take long for the new mother to sniff it and adopt it. Maybe I did a good deed for a change to balance out the other.

When evening settled in, we brought the new mothers and little lambs to the barn. I don't recall the month during which the birthing began, but within 30 days it was all over. Then, more work had to be done to ensure their survival. Father impressed me so, the way he had the routine all down pat. He made sure that all of the lambs were fed and given appropriate medication. He recorded the number of males and females, and then branded their ears. I am still filled with admiration for him and the way he gave such care to every detail.

Each day, the lambs had to be separated from their mothers, so we children had to move the mothers and the rest of the flock out to graze. Before we started out, the mothers would bleat at their lambs, as if to reassure them they would be back, and the little ones would respond with their own bleats. This also saddened me, the thought of their brief separation from each other. I felt as if it were happening to me. I wondered if the little ones felt abandoned by the ones who fed them when they were hungry. Did they feel insecure?

A few years later, I was going to revisit those feelings, when I had to be separated from my own mother.

But that was later . . .

. . . I only know that I remember feeling happy and secure in my own world, being with my family and living in T'rsie and Lerin. I liked the smiling, friendly faces of our people, as they greeted each other, trusted and respected friends and neighbors. I loved the beautiful colors in the clothes Mother, my aunts and the other women in the village wore, those bright cheerful colors of green, blue, red and yellow, colors that Nature supplied in her plants and grasses. The women also wore lots of white. All of the young girls and new brides wore white scarves, or *shami,* on their heads, to keep their hair neat while outdoors. Except for women who were in mourning, very few wore black.

In the evenings, when the weather permitted, on holidays and special occasions, villagers gathered in the middle of the village, or *sred selo*. After chores, and tables had been cleared, men clustered in groups to talk and exchange ideas, or play cards, or *tavla*, backgammon. Children were usually running around, teasing each other, or inventing games of their own. Later the women would show up on the other side of the square, catching up on the news of the village.

Some of our villagers formed an instrumental music group that played together frequently. Eventually, someone would start singing and others would join in. The songs led to *oros,* the circle dances, and everyone enjoyed their evening together, relaxing in friendship, relaxing from the daily routine of life. The older folks were a part of this communal life as well. They watched with love and pride etched on their faces as they saw their families, the children, relatives and neighbors enjoying themselves.

The instrumental musical society of T'rsie and their friends. Sotir's father is standing, second from the right. Their western style hats were important, as was posing for pictures.

Good, happy, times.
What happened to us?
Why did it have to happen to us?

Finders are not Keepers

Age imprints more wrinkles in the mind
Than it does on the face.

MONTAIGNE, 1850

You know, you could have compared us kids to beavers. We created swimming pools in several different places. Wherever there was a river, stream or creek, we would build ourselves a swimming area. We were coming home one afternoon and parted into different groups heading for our houses. The villagers' *bashtchi,* vegetable gardens, were located a little below the village, downhill. Many of the *bashtchi* were reinforced by stonewalls to hold the earth because of the hilly contour of the land. We reached Done Georgiev's house, situated below ours. From the window of our house I could look over the roof of his. Ilo caught up with me, and we began our usual tussling, pushing and running. Not paying much attention to where we were goofing around, we suddenly found ourselves by a much taller wall, at least thirty feet tall. On top of the wall was Done's *gumno*, the area of his property used for threshing, and to the right of his *gumno* was his *plemna*, the barn. Now is this an opportunity for some action, or what? I looked at Ilo with supreme confidence and challenged him, "I'll bet you I can climb this wall."

"Yah, you could, but you won't because you know you'll fall and end up like a rabbit on a skewer. Can't you see those bean and tomato stakes? They look pretty sharp and heavy."

I shot back, "I'm going to try it."

Nobody, not even Pincheto, had climbed this wall and he was the best climber among us. I started to scoot up to about the middle of the wall and found a flat rock, which gave me some leverage to pull myself up. But the rock wasn't strong enough and gave way, making me lose my balance. I found myself landing with a thud on the ground below. I wasn't hurt. Ilo pragmatically had removed the stakes because he was pretty certain that I wasn't going to make it to the top. I hit the ground hard. While still on the ground I looked up to where that darned rock had been lodged. There was quite a gap, a very deep gap there. Ilo also had been looking at the gap and pointed upwards. He kept looking with increasing curiosity.

"You've got to climb back up and see what's in there."

As we both kept examining it from where we were standing, it seemed that the hole or the space had been made in a curious way. It was possible to place something in there. The wall itself was constructed with what we call *plochi*, flat bricks of a reddish-brown mud mixed with straw. It was a very sturdy wall. Definitely this was a challenge, or maybe even an opportunity of some sort for someone. Nothing ventured, nothing gained, right?

I picked up a short stick to put in my pocket and began my ascent up the wall. The stick was to be my probe for snakes because they like to curl up in these kinds of places. I have found bird nests in the gaps of walls like these. As I neared the space in the wall, I probed with my stick and touched something. I couldn't dislodge it, but being a determined, stubborn little cuss, I persisted. I poked and poked, first upwards then down and around and finally pulled something out. It was a little pouch made of animal hide, which fell to the ground where Ilo was waiting.

"*Pari*! *Ima Pari*!" Ilo shouted. "There's money in it!'

That was all I needed to hear. I shoved my entire hand in, all caution aside, while with the other hand I held on to the wall, rather precariously. I worked my toes into the small cracks in the wall, and reached farther into the space and pulled whatever I had my hands on with all my strength. All that effort found three more pouches. Certain there was nothing more there, I scrambled down the wall quickly.

We each took two pouches and went by my aunt's outdoor *furna*, the oven, where the bread was baking. Her *furna* was only a few feet from the church, where the roads to Lerin, Turie and Statitsa meet, leading to *sred selo*, the center of the village. While there, Ilo and I divided the coins and started what must be a universal boys' game, I'm sure. You know, where one guy throws a coin on the ground and the next guy tries to hit or touch it with his own. Whoever hits or touches the other's coin, takes it. We played with the coins as if they were stones for quite a while, without a clue that these were *napolioni, gold coins.* As we were playing, one of our villagers, a man called Daiko, saw us. He was going to pass us, but something caught his eye, so he stopped, turned and came back. When he realized what was in our hands, he looked at us in amazement.

"Where did you get this *pari*?"

Daiko shook his head and began to mumble to himself. We heard him say, greatly impressed, "*Breh,* wow! *Abre vidi, vnutsite na Vasil Nitchov igre so napoliani!* He looked at us in amazement. "Vasil Nitchov's grandchildren are playing with gold pieces, *breh, breh, breh*!"

Hearing that, Ilo and I scooped up the coins from the ground and ran over to our Aunt Kolitsa.

Both of us shouting at once, "Strino, Strino, look what we found!"

Curiously, she asked, "What is it?" and then her look changed to one of consternation. "Where did you find them?"

"In Done Georgiev's wall."

She took some in her hand and turned them over and over.

"Did anybody see you? Did you tell anybody?"

"No, no. Just Daiko saw us playing with them."

"Well, if Daiko knows, the whole village will know. Too bad."

We all sat down to count them. There were fifty gold pieces in each pouch; a total of two hundred coins. My aunt cautioned us to keep our mouths shut, not to say anything until my father came home. She kept the coins for the rest of the day.

When Father came home, Strina came over with the coins and told him what had happened. He called to us and asked us to confirm what Strina had told him. He wanted every piece of information from us, every detail from the very beginning. We held nothing back, because we knew that this was something very big. After he was satisfied that he had the entire story, there was only one course of action. The coins had to be returned.

"We are going to go to Done's house and give him back his coins."

Strina objected. Her position was that this was a finder's keeper's situation.

"No way," Father replied. "If these coins are Done's, he gets them back, all of them."

It was then that he explained how and why Done and his neighbor, Risto Tricov, hadn't spoken in years. Done had accused Risto of stealing his gold coins. Apparently, Done had forgotten where he had hidden his gold coins, and in desperation he accused his neighbor and his own son, Tane, of the theft. As Ilo and I listened to Father, our eyes opened wider and wider and our mouths formed perfect o's. What a story.

My aunt still kept on insisting that we should keep the *napolioni*, but she could not budge my father. It was the right thing to do and the only thing to do, and he would not budge from that.

"We will go over to Done's house and ask him a few questions." That was that.

The three of us, Father, Ilo and I walked over to Done's house and found him sitting on his porch. My father greeted him.

"Good evening, Uncle Done."

To me Done always appeared to be a mean and angry man. This evening was no different. He eyed me, feeling it was not going to be a good evening if I was on his property, and he responded gruffly, "Good evening."

"Uncle Done, the boys were playing in your yard and by the *gumno*, and they found something. . . . "

Done didn't even let him finish. He jumped to his feet. "What kind of damage did they do this time? I didn't have time to go there today. What is the matter with you? Can't you control your boys? Why can't you keep them at your place? They always cause trouble, especially your imp. He almost busted my head with a rock the other day!"

Father, getting to the point of the visit, said, "Listen, *Striko*, Uncle. I want to ask you something very important, so just give me a few minutes."

Still, very inhospitably, he asked, "What is it you want?"

"Have you lost any money?"

Warily, unwilling to admit to anything, "What if I did?"

"It is important that you tell me how much, where and when and how you lost it."

"Go away. What I did or did not lose is my business."

"*Striko*, please. Tell me, so that I can tell you how you can get them back."

This made Done look up at my father very carefully, deliberately, assessing him. With a changed tone, somewhat softened from his earlier gruffness he spoke.

"Mite, sit down. You and everyone else knows that they stole my *pari* and my own son helped them." He was pointing in the direction of his neighbor Traicov's house. "Isn't that the greatest shame?"

"Listen, *Striko*. I have a feeling that nobody stole your money. Do you remember how much there was? Give me an amount, and see if I can help you remember where you had hidden it."

"Why are you so concerned, so interested?"

"Because the boys found something. Unless you tell me where you hid your money and how much you had, I will turn it over to the church."

Done searched my father's face, and then, finally, he spoke. "I . . . I put the money in my wall. Lots of *napolioni.* Maybe one hundred fifty or more. Now, I don't remember exactly."

Father felt reassured enough to show him two empty pouches.

"Do you recognize these?"

Done eyed the pouches and there was instant recognition in his eyes. He looked at my father.

"Yes, they look like my *kesinia*, my little purses, but they are empty. Who took the *napolioni*?"

"Nobody took your *pari*. Here are your *napolioni*. The boys found them while they were climbing your wall."

With a joyful cry, he clutched them in his hands and started to walk toward the door of his house without even so much as a thank-you to my father.

Seeing Done's son coming towards the house, and his daughter-in-law standing in the door, my father called out to Done, "Wait a minute."

"What do you want now?"

In spite of Done's obvious annoyance and displeasure at this moment, my father insisted that Done count his money in front of us, including his son, Tane, and his daughter-in-law. Done obviously did not want to do this, but Father insisted that it was only fair to everybody that he do so. Father particularly wanted Done to verify the amount. After much reluctance and persuasion, Done found himself counting his precious *napolioni* slowly and very carefully. His count—two hundred *napolioni*! Satisfied that there were enough witnesses to confirm the return of the money, Father, Ilo and I left for home.

When we arrived, one of the family asked what our reward was for finding the money and returning it. With supreme impudence, I answered, "*Shibak*!" meaning zilch, zero, making a gesture with my thumb and forefinger.

My aunt was still furious that we returned the money to this unreasonable old miser. She kept mumbling, getting angrier by the minute. Father tried to mollify all of us, saying that perhaps tomorrow he might give the boys something. Everyone snorted. We all knew Done very well. As for the reward, I 'm still waiting.

It was my father who had compassion for the old man. He was convinced and tried to convince all of us that we did the right thing. "The man has worked hard to save those *napolioni*. So why is everybody upset? Forget it! It is done."

End of story.

Portents of Change

In a brief space, the generations of living beings are changed And like runners,
Pass on the torches of life.

LUCRETIUS, FIRST CENTURY, B. C.

But for the occasional drone of an Italian warplane, or the sound of strafing in one field or another, the pattern and rhythm of my life had not changed much. For the grown-ups it had. Change had come, and though it hadn't personally touched me yet, it was coming.

In fact, my life seemed to be getting better and better, filled with even more mischief and adventures. Every now and then I could feel some kind of change outside my own little world. Words like *sloboda*, freedom; *nese turpi*, can't bear it; *nash ezik*, our language; *Makedonia i Rusia*, Macedonia and Russia, peppered the conversations among the grown-ups. They held no great import to me then. I didn't have to deal with the philosophies of freedom, or having to be patient, or having to "bear" anything.

I was Sotir, and I was free and I avoided "bearing" everything I could. As for language, wasn't Macedonian our language? That's what everyone spoke, and that was what I spoke. That's what our whole village spoke! I just carried on, living and experiencing life, and so far, it was good!

From time to time I noticed strangers would appear in our village. They seemed to come and go, and nobody made much of that, as far as I could tell. Yet, there was an aura of secrecy about them. It was then that I became conscious of the phrase *Albanski Boi,* Albanian War. I heard that phrase at home and in the village among the villagers.

And it wasn't too long after that, that some of the men began to leave the village. A lot of the younger men left. Even Father had to leave. That's when I realized that there was something or someplace called Albania. That's where he was heading, I think, but at the time I really didn't know. I didn't know that the men had been drafted into the Greek army and ordered to report to Lerin. I didn't know then that they were to be deployed somewhere on the Albanian front.

It didn't take long for bad news to float back to all the surrounding villages. In our village, the news came that Krsto Balkov, Goge's father, and Kole Yankov, Pincheto's brother were the first casualties from T'rsie. Goge was one of the kids in my gang. He took the news very badly, and was never quite the same again. The terrible news changed him totally.

We saw and felt more of the changes of the twin whirlwinds of death and destruction. The bright colors women wore began to be replaced with black, the symbol of mourning. I didn't see the expressions of the joy of living on the faces of the villagers.

Joy seemed to evaporate, and was replaced with sadness and uncertainty. Black was worn not only by the family members who had lost a son, a brother or a husband, but by so many of the other villagers as well. They were expressing their common sorrow for the families. In Macedonia, one's loss was everyone's loss. Life was so hard to support under the conditions that had been imposed on Macedonians, so that one loss touched all.

Everyone needed time, the passage of time to recoup and to carry on. Not that I comprehended then. After all, what is time to a kid of 5, 6 or 7 years of age? Time went on forever. It was unending. Had 2 years passed since Father left? As the men began returning home, it crossed my mind that the *Albanski Boi* had ended. Father also finally returned, physically unharmed. He had served much of his time as a soldier medic in the army hospital in Lerin. Our house was filled with tears of joy, on his return. I was so proud of him!

After our family reunion, after he had eaten and rested, he then told us the story of his survival in the bunker. Was he ever my hero then! Let me tell you, I couldn't hear the story often enough. I had always felt Father was somebody very special, so I think you can imagine how I felt as he talked about his near-death experience.

The Greek army had built bunkers and a military post up in the mountains Kula, Lopushence and Kalugeritsa, between Lerin and Nevoleni, the village northeast of T'rsie and south of Lerin. Greek soldiers, which meant the Macedonians, were posted as sentries. Father was one of the sentries. As Italian planes swooped over the area and dropped their bombs, Father's bunker was a direct hit. Father and the others were buried under the wreckage and debris.

For several hours, the other soldiers tried to dig them out, even though they thought they had been killed. They kept on digging, and luckily, the men were still alive! Alive to die another day?

Some of the soldiers had hidden on one of the mountains in the peaks of Kulata. They survived, too. Father was such a hero in my eyes, but it was hard to ignore the tears of despair and worry that flowed down my mother's face. I couldn't look into the faces of my grandparents. They feared for our future. But did I fear anything? Not me. Absolutely not! After all, Father was home. He had a great story to tell, and I was going to have some great adventures myself!

However, there was such bitterness among the villagers. The Greeks had been getting their asses kicked. Dedo and the elders had learned that the Italians had managed to reach Kostur, and then advanced into Yanina, Larissa, the Greek territory. Angry that the Macedonians had been drafted under the command of Greek officers who did not know the territory and were unable to stop the advance of the Italians, the elders feared that more and more Macedonian men would be sent to the front lines and that more Macedonian blood would be spilled to save Greece. Someone always had to save Greece! Their thoughts could be read by looking into their eyes:

How much more blood do we give for Greece?

Every village draftee had been sent to the front lines immediately, with little training, few real weapons, and no preparation. They were simply exhorted to fight. They fought furiously and managed to push the Italians back, deep into Albania, almost to the Adriatic Sea. More and more of the returning soldiers spoke of their horrible experiences fighting on the Albanian front.

Many lifetimes later, I met a friend, Pavle Vasilovski from the village of Bouf, who shared his bitter, painful memories of that terrible time.

Pavle: "Thousands of Macedonian men and boys were recruited one way or the other by the Greeks to fight on the Albanian front. The Greek soldiers were running away, abandoning their positions. Some were found frozen during the winter of 1939, without guns or shoes."

"Eventually, the Macedonian and Greek brigades started pushing the Italians back into Albania, not too far from the capital, Tirana. The Italians were in full retreat. The bitterness among the Macedonian fighting men was great because the Greek command not only exploited us, they still discriminated against us. The Greek generals sent the *Makedones,* as they called us, to fight where the Italians had strong strategic positions. Food was taken from the *Makedones* to feed the southern and islander Greeks. Wounded Macedonians were left to die, without treatment. That was under Greek orders.

"That will never be forgiven or forgotten. We were treated worse than dogs. That was our reward, our recognition for saving their Greek asses in their war."

Pavle's bitter recall of that time was echoed by many of the veterans of the Albanian War. These same veterans in Greece were also survivors of the Resistance during World War II and the civil war in Greece that followed. Pavle joined the Partizans and worked as a commissar-organizer for them. He survived that ordeal. He eventually came to America and lived with his son and his wife, my sister Mara, for a long time before he died.

But for the occasional drone of an Italian warplane, or the sound of strafing in one field or another, the pattern and rhythm of my life had not changed much. For the grown-ups it had. Change had come, and though it hadn't personally touched me yet, it was coming.

Ciao/Arrividerci

Civilization is the lamb's skin in which barbarism masquerades.

THOMAS BAILEY ALDRICH, 1903

I remember only one horrible incident with the Italians, and that is when they came into our village. I don't ever remember the Germans coming to T'rsie. The Italians did come, and for one reason only, and that was to arrest my Aunt Kolitsa.

I guess there have always been *shpioni,* traitors, spies, and collaborators, but you would never think that there would be any among our villagers. I always felt we were like one large family, looking out for one another, sharing joys and sorrows with each other.

As I mentioned earlier my *Strina,* Aunt Kolitsa, was targeted by these *shpioni,* because her niece was married to Petre Novachkovski, one of the commissar-organizers in the Partizan resistance movement in *Vardarska Makedonja.* Later he was assigned to Aegean Macedonia. Because of his role in the Partizan movement, which was sweeping all across Macedonia, Petre became a man wanted by the Italians, the Germans, and the Bulgarians.

I guess there is a Judas in any community, because one of the village informers reported to the Italian authorities that Petre was in the village, which at the time of the report was true.

Whenever Petre and his two companions came into the village, their visits were brief. At my father's specific request, they never went to my *Strina's* house. They were told never to make contact with her or with any member of our family. Father wanted to protect her and the children, my cousins Kotse, Lena, and Naso.

Petre was a good friend of my father. Many times he came to the fields where we were working. They talked briefly and privately, and then Petre would just disappear.

It is still one of the most disturbing memories of my young life, the day *Strina* Kolitsa and my cousins were arrested, except Kotse because he was not home. The Italians dragged her to the center of the village, *sred selo*. There, where everyone could see, they beat her with their rifles and their fists. I don't know how many soldiers were doing the beating. All I know is that no one could come to her defense. No one dared. When the Italians tired of beating her, my aunt and cousins were hauled like sacks of potatoes and placed on mules to be taken to jail in the village of Zhelevo. Kotse turned himself in a week later.

At the moment of their arrest, Father and Uncle Tsande left immediately for Lerin. There he sought out Dobrev and Kalchev, the two Bulgarians working with the Germans, to do whatever they could do, including offering some sheep in a deal for their release. Apparently Father and Uncle Tsande achieved something, because when Father returned he at least had Kotse with him. However, after he brought Kotse into the house to be cleaned, fed and rested, Father again left for Lerin to meet Dobrev, and then went to Zhelevo one more time.

It took a week for *Strina* Kolitsa to be released. No official charges were made against her or Kotse. The Italians were hoping that by humiliating her and the children before the entire village, *Strina* Kolitsa would be forced to reveal where Petre was. She never knew where he would be, but the authorities were not convinced. They did not arrest her two other children; we kept them with us.

I don't know what price my Father paid, other than the few sheep, or what our family paid to get their release from the Italians, but I remember Father saying, "Nothing is more important or more valuable than getting Kolitsa and Kotse released."

Strina Kolitsa was never the same after the beating.

We were never able to identify the informer.

Kotse joined the Partizan movement. How could he not?

1942

They are Macedonians. Their Macedonianism is not artificial. It is natural, a spontaneous and deep-seated feeling which begins in childhood, like everyone's patriotism.

CAPTAIN P.H. EVANS
Report on the Free Macedonia Movement Area Florina, 1944,
to the British Foreign Office

There was a disparity between the Greek official view of what they termed the *minority* population in Macedonia and the Macedonian view of themselves. The British were unaware of the disparity when the SOE, Cairo, dispatched British paratroops into the mountains of Macedonia.

As the paratroops were dropped from the British planes, attempts to make contact with leaders of resistance movements inside Greece led to confusion. In the Italian-administered zone in Macedonia, Bulgarian and pro-Bulgarian Macedonian sympathizers formed security units known as the *Ohrana Battalions,* as the Communist Greek and Bulgarian Partisans began to appear. The Communists exploited the Macedonians at every turn. The Bulgarians remained dominant until 1943.

In Yugoslavia Tito began to play his pivotal role in Macedonia. He appointed the head of the resistance movement in Yugoslavia, code name, TEMPO, as his representative to meet with Andreas Tzimas of the KKE Political Bureau and the central Committee of EAM. TEMPO's plan was to set up a Balkan Resistance Headquarters, coordinated jointly by Yugoslav and Greek Partisans, liberate the town of Kostur, *Kastoria*, and install a unified command. By the end of the year, 10 million German garrison troops were stationed in the Balkans.

By the time the Germans were preparing to withdraw from the Balkans later in the war, Ivan Mihailov, chief of the IMRO, who had maintained friendly relations with the Germans, unsuccessfully attempted to establish an autonomous Macedonia.

April:

- The Communists attempted an uprising in the Bitola/Prilep districts.
- The Bulgarian Army and Gendarmerie put down the rebellion and executed 12 local Communists.
- The people reacted with strong protest demonstrations during which the Bulgarian Gendarmerie commander and 15 gendarmes died.
- An outbreak of resistance movements spread throughout Greece. A breakdown of law and order was prevalent. Starvation faced the nation.

June:

- The Bulgarian government conferred Bulgarian citizenship on Macedonians of Bulgarian descent.
- Bulgarian sympathizers in Macedonia displayed Bulgarian flags and formed bands midst rumors that the Bulgarian army would occupy western Mcedonia.
- The Greek Gendarmerie and local administrative officials followed the retreating Greek army south.
- Supported by the Germans in Solun, *Salonica,* Bulgarians organized a Bulgarian Association. Identity cards were issued entitling the bearer to special privileges and rich food rations.
- Bulgarians organized and secretly armed their followers in western Macedonian districts through liaison officers with German military headquarters.
- TEMPO and Andreas Tzimas met at Grammos.
- Rommel's army in North Africa retreated after the Battle of Alemain.

October:

- The Germans reached Stalingrad.
- British officers were flown into Greece to join with KKE, ELAS and EDES leaders to coordinate the *andartes* and begin sabotage against the Germans and Italians.

Kotse's Wedding

Happiness is brief.
It will not stay.
God batters its sails.

EURIPIDES, 408 B.C.

I've met a lot of people who have the impression that every marriage in Macedonia is an arranged affair. Most often that wasn't the case at all. Sometimes parents, grandparents or close relatives would plan, hopefully, that one of their children might marry according to the family's preference. It didn't always work out that way. Maybe one marriage in 200 might have been arranged, and maybe more frequently in past generations. The approval of family was always important, however. Young Macedonians paired off because of mutual attraction subject to the approval of the family, and true love prevailed.

I remember overhearing conversations among the women talking about the virtues of this girl or that one, and about the kind of dowry a particular girl would have. At the *pazar*, the marketplace, sometimes real negotiations were carried out in terms of the size and quantity of a particular girl's dowry, making that girl highly desirable. A dowry was a real marketing tool for those who had material instincts.

Father was the first person I had ever heard who spoke out against this custom. He and some of his friends were discussing this as they sat around talking together. Dedo was also present. Someone asked, "What if the parents of the girl can't afford a dowry? So the girl cannot be married?"

"Dowry?" Father turned to my cousin, Kotse. "Kotse, when you decide to marry, marry the girl you love, not her dowry!" Wow, I thought, no *prike,* dowry!

Kotse's wedding is locked firmly in my happy memories. Since Kotse was one of Dedo's grandsons, my parents' nephew, and my cousin, we were naturally the groom's immediate family. If I remember correctly, this is how the wedding unfolded.

In a Macedonian family, a wedding is an event in which just about everybody plays a key role, except us gangsters. Heck, the entire extended family on both sides, and in many cases, almost the entire village has a part to play.

One week before the Sunday of the wedding, it was our responsibility to take the wheat to the flour mill where it was to be ground into flour for the wedding breads. After the flour was blessed, the grinding began. There was an awful lot of teasing and joking going on among the grown-ups, which I didn't get at all. But it sounded like fun, so we kids tagged along. We laughed when the adults laughed, just happy to be feeling good about *their* good feeling.

We took the flour to the house of the bride. Singing and teasing was going on there, too. Friday was the day designated for the baking the *kolak,* the wedding bread, and the smaller round breads, the *kolochinia*. What a ritual that was!

I should mention that we have a lot of symbolism in our customs and ceremonies. For example, an attractive, young, unmarried girl is selected to start the baking process, mixing the yeast and water, adding the flour and eggs and the other ingredients at the appropriate time. Her beauty, youth and virginity symbolize the qualities the young bride-to-be will bring to her marriage, and the preparation of the bread is to ensure that the newlyweds' lives will be bountiful and graced with children.

The women around her began to sing a kind of serenade, I guess. That's what it sounded like to me. And again, what was with the funny comments? I was all eyes and ears, but I understood *nishtcho*, nothing. The *kolak*, the wedding bread, is usually a work of art, to my eyes at least. It is decorated with sugar, almonds, raisins, and braids made from the dough.

This *kolak* is prepared for the godparents, because it also serves as a formal invitation to them and their family. A beautiful *kolak* is also an acknowledgement of the important status the godparents will hold in the newlyweds' lives.

A large round bread or *kolak* is made for the best man, while the smaller *kolachinia* are prepared to be distributed to the grooms' men called the *kulupchi* and to the bridesmaids who are the *kulupchitsi*.

These breads are pulled apart into pieces and offered to the relatives and villagers, as a kind of announcement and invitation. The yeast is placed in a bowl decorated with *bosiluk*, basil.

"The yeast is being started,
started by close relatives,
and first cousins."

That's how the serenade of the yeast ritual began, but I don't remember the rest of the words. The work, the ritual, and the laughter went on for some time.

Now the *kum* and *kuma,* or, as we say, the *nunko* and *nunka,* the godparents, are much honored guests and are very respectfully treated. Dedo and Baba and my parents, who were standing in for Kotse's father, and the entire Nitchov *soi,* clan, were treated with great respect by the bride's family. All the adults in our family received a large *kolak*, a bottle of wine, and homemade cheese from the bride. This custom was called *na kolache.*

Saturday! Everybody was busy doing something. The houses of both the bride and groom were filled with friends and relatives. Our house was jammed. Baba and Mother kept shooing us gangsters away from the kitchen. They were kept very busy preparing food and drink for the men who sat around talking, singing, and sounding happier and sillier with each drink. They got so happy that they started to dance as they were singing. Kotse was teased by the men, but I didn't pay much attention. I was more interested in sneaking some of the food the women kept serving to the men.

We kids kept running back and forth between the bride's house and ours. Their house was just as noisy. There was just as much teasing of the bride, and a lot of joking and storytelling. I decided to listen in. Just then, one of the women began another teasing serenade, with the others joining in, like a back-up group.

Ah, why doesn't God say, my dear young one,
Let it rain; let it pour and let it flood.
Let her mother be carried away
Because she didn't allow her daughter
To have who she wanted
Who wanted her, as well.
Oh, what a true love we had!

I didn't need to hear any more of that! So back to our house. They were still baking more bread there, too, and serenading as well. This is what I remember hearing:

Oh, you colorful room,
So decorated with three bands of wood;
Each wall plastered in white
And painted blue.
Where is your young bride
To hustle and bustle in your room?

I went to look at Kotse . . .

Was he sweating? Was he happy? Did he really want to get married? Why? On this evening the groom is supposed to invite his future in-laws to his house.

Then I heard it again, the serenading and the droning by the women:

Ah, you new moon,
How beautifully you shine tonight!
Tonight I will gather the in-laws
Each with quick horses . . .

And on and on. I really wondered what Kotse was thinking. Was he really enjoying this?

I was hungry again.

With the bride's wedding dress in his possession, Kotse invited the *nunko* and his groomsmen into the house. As he did so, another serenade began:

Come in, Nunko, come in.
The coffee is ready.
The beds are made.
Tables are spread
With white cloths
With white breads
With roasted lamb
And red wine.
Come in, Nunko, come in.

The day before the wedding arrived, and Kotse had to be shaved on this day. So there he was, my cousin Kotse, sitting on the chair, taking in all the jokes and teasing, and making his own comments as well. I was not sure what all of that was about then, but I tell you Kotse looked very happy.

While the men seemed to be enjoying themselves at Kotse's expense, we heard:

The groom is being shaved.
Who is shaving him?
Why, his closest family and relatives;
His Nunko and his groomsmen!

My cousins and I watched and communicated with each other using only facial expressions, when we weren't eating or fooling around.

There were shouts of "*Da se kerdose!* May they be blessed." "*Do godina so mushko dete*, within a year a little boy!" These words were heard throughout the day and throughout the village. I kept thinking, we guys are pretty important. It's great to be a man!!

By this time, the *kulupchitsi* were dressed in their better clothes and they were handed white aprons. They had the honor of formally inviting the godparents, as well as the *probratim*, the best man, to the wedding. We gangsters followed them, uninvited as usual; as the groom's wedding guests went to the bride's house, to toast the bride-to-be with drinks from the decorated *pagurche*, a flask containing homemade *rakia,* prune brandy.

We kids didn't get any *rakia*, but we could see that the *rakia* worked its special magic and really loosened everybody up, because the joking and teasing increased. Singing and dancing began again. The women of the household joined in the first toast to the bride, but then went about setting food on the table. And all of this *befor*e the ceremony!

When I heard the rooster's first *kikoriko,* cock-a-doodle-do, Sunday morning of the wedding, I thought I had just gone to bed. Those roosters showed no mercy. We had to get up and get going. The band that had been hired to play for the weekend had been playing since Friday, almost continuously. And here they were, ready to lead the way to the bride's house.

I already knew the line-up. The band would lead, then the godparents. The *nunko* had the honor of holding the wedding *bairak,* banner, high with an apple on the top of it.

He was followed by the nunka, then Kotse and his *pobratim*, his best man, then the family, and the rest of the wedding party. You should have seen us! Everybody looked so special, so clean and neat! Really special, even me. *I* wore shoes, that's how special!

As we walked toward the bride's home, the villagers lined up along the road, shouting out congratulations and well wishes. In front of the bride's home, an egg had been placed in a tree, hanging from a high branch. Now this called for a member of the groom's party to shoot at the egg and break it before we could claim the bride. I can't remember who it was, but a shot was fired, the egg was broken and a great shout came from the wedding party. I guess that was a good thing? I think I'm going to let you figure out the symbolism this time.

The *nunko* was still holding the banner with the apple on top. What did the apple mean? I don't know. Maybe a sign of good health? Our side began the serenade:

Oh, you young bride,
Come out and greet us,
So that we can see your face,
Your pink and white face.

As if we didn't know what she looked like! The bride-to-be came out, her head down, smiling, but not too much, just modestly. And then, one more serenade from us for her, her parents, and their guests:

Who dressed you so beautifully?
Was it Tsila, the moon?
Or Kicha, the black gypsy?
Was it Kilja, that barrel of meat?
Or Lina, that black ash?
Your sisters tend pigs.
Your brothers are blockheads.
We found and killed a flea behind your ear!

Everybody laughed! But it was time now for the whole affair to be legalized. The *nunko* and *nunka,* the groom and bride-to-be, and the rest of the bridal party started the walk to the church. The godfather placed the *bairak or forubitsa*, two words for the wedding banner, outside the church.

The wedding service began as the priest met the bridal party at the entrance of the church and led them toward the altar. Everyone else followed except us gangsters. We knew how long our Orthodox ceremony was, so we spent our time in the churchyard, peeking into the church occasionally, to gauge how things were progressing. It was interesting to watch some of it, but heck, it was a long process. Let me tell you, when you marry in the Orthodox Church you really know you are going to be married—forever!!! It seems to take that long.

Finally we heard a commotion coming from the church. The ceremony was finally over. The bride and groom appeared at the door and paused as rice, candy, and money were tossed at them. We kids scrambled to collect the candy and money as everyone else headed *sred selo*, to the center of the village to celebrate with toasts, drinks, food, and some serious dancing.

The *tapan* player, the drummer, began the beat, signaling that the first *oro,* the wedding dance was about to begin. There was an important order to the *oro*. It had to be led by the godfather, holding the *kolak*, then the godmother next to the bride and groom. Next to the groom were the best man, and then the parents. The groomsmen, the bridesmaids, the families and relatives lined up also, as the *oro* began joyfully, seriously in that slow, dignified movement. As the *tappan* controlled the pace of the dance, the clarinet pierced the air with the first notes, and the other musicians joined in.

Around and around the *oro* wound, as the godfather, symbolically held the *kolak*

Kotse's wedding. He is wearing a cap. His wife is to his right in white apron.

over everyone's head, and as the *oro* goes on, making special comments to the dancers and they to him. It seemed as if the whole world had joined us on this joyous day.

The dancing went on all evening and the *kaleznitsi* kept the rest of the celebration going all night at our house. I have no idea how late it continued.

Kotse's wedding was for us a time of music, laughter, good humor, with everyone dressed in their colorful best. It was a moment of wellbeing. We were secure, the center of a total family event in which the entire village happily participated and shared. We were together as God intended us to be, continuing the cycle of life, enveloped in the comfort of our ages-old traditions. It was a time celebrating our way of life. That's what I remember so well, celebrating life, our way of life.

I think Kotse's wedding was the first—and the last—time I saw our entire family, all the Nitchovs, all of our relatives, all of the villagers, young and old alike, relaxed, enjoying, sharing, laughing, singing and dancing, happily anticipating the future.

Destiny, however, was forging ahead with something else in mind.

Dedo Vasil

To forget one's ancestors is to a brook without a source;a tree without root

CHINESE PROVERB

I went with Dedo frequently when he was planning to plow the fields. He enjoyed waking me early in the morning, sometimes as early as four or five o'clock.

"Come on, get up, Sotiraki. We have to plow the fields today."

I would jump up and be ready in no time. All I had to do was put on my *pintsi*, the kind of shoes we wore back then, usually handmade of leather, with pointed, slightly curved toes. We had a secret; we slept with our clothes on most of the time. After I splashed a little water on my face, I was ready to go.

You would have loved our *pintsi*. I even made some out of rubber tires that had been left by the Italians. We Macedonians don't like waste!

In the fields Dedo would get the oxen and start plowing a few *brazdi,* a few rows, at a time. Then he would call out, "Sotiraki, come over and take the plow for a couple of minutes, while I enjoy a few winks."

Sometimes those few winks went from a few minutes to a few hours. Dedo's sleep was always instant and deep. Not even once would he open his eyes to see how I was doing. He had that much confidence in my ability. From time to time I would hear him murmur, "Just plow a little bit longer, a few more *brazdi.* I'll take over shortly."

At times I felt that he would never wake up. Only as the sun blazed directly overhead, high in the sky, would he awaken, shielding his forehead with his hand as he peered toward the fields. Pride always swelled up in me when he would exclaim, "*Mashala*, Sotiraki. You have plowed the entire field! Why not release the oxen and come over here by me for a little lunch." *Mashala* is the Turkish word for bravo.

I would do that, feeling quite puffed at the compliment he paid me. Dedo was always concerned about all his animals. He did not want them over-worked; he made certain that they were fed as well.

There was a certain ritual that Dedo followed as he prepared to plow. Standing in the field, he would make the sign of the cross slowly, reverently, touching his forehead with the thumb of his right hand pressed against the first two fingers. This signified that God the Father, Christ the Son, and the Holy Spirit were one and the same. His hand moved down to his mid-section, to his right shoulder, then to the left.

He prayed aloud in his direct manner. "Now on this day we need your help, *Gospo.* Give my animals the strength they need to get their job done. Thank you, *Gospo.*" Then the sign of the cross, again.

That was Dedo. Just a straight request from him to *Gospo.* It was important to start the day's work by telling *Gospo* what was needed, including His help. He always counted on *Gospo's* help. *Gospo*, by the way, is our word for God.

It's funny. As religious and as practical as he was, Dedo was also superstitious. When we headed for the fields, if a cat or any other animal crossed his path, he would walk around the path the animal took, even if it took 20 minutes to do so. That always made me impatient. At such times, I would inform Dedo in no uncertain terms that I would not stop. I would just keep on going, and I did. Crossing an animal's path was no big deal as far as I was concerned. Let the animal go around *me*! On days like that, I would be in the field with the oxen harnessed, plowing a few *brazdi* before Dedo showed up.

Typically Macedonian, the only time he made superstitious comments was when something unforeseen or unfortunate happened. For instance, when the plow broke or if one of the harnesses snapped, or even if one of us happened to trip and fall, he would say, "So and so *te pochudi,* put a hex on you!" That's when I would really get down and dirty with my comments. I just didn't believe in superstition.

In my most refined way, I would make a crude sound, then point to my crotch and say, "This . . . this has a hex on it. Maybe someone, somewhere, put a hex on it. Who knows?"

I'm not sure what my point was, except that superstition was bunk as far as I was concerned. But Dedo, instead of being outraged, always laughed. He would tap me on the head while shaking his head, saying, "Sotiraki, Sotiraki, what a *chudno,* wonderful boy you are!" Yep, I was *chudno* in Dedo's eyes. Ha!

Dedo and I became so close. I loved to tease him and bring him to the point of anger, but never beyond the point. That's when he would look at me, puzzled, "Who are you like, boy? You are as mean as your Dedo Ilo. He wasn't afraid of anything or anybody either. That has to be where you get your meanness from."

After an episode of teasing he would add, "But your work ethic and work habits, those you get from Dedo Nitcho." This was always said with great satisfaction. He was always able to justify my actions and character.

My Dedo knew our family history so well and he never tired of talking about it. When he spoke of them, it was as if they had lived here until yesterday, they were so alive in his mind. Let me tell you about them.

Dedo Ilo was my Dedo's youngest brother. Dedo Vasil was the oldest, then Dedo Pasko, followed by Dedo Lazo and Dedo Ilo.

Dedo Nitcho was my Dedo's grandfather. My great grandfather, named Tanas, took his grandfather's first name, Nitcho, as our family name. Dedo Tanas became Tanas Nitchov.

Now *Nitcho* is not a common name. It was probably a kind of nickname. For example, you might hear someone called *Ditcho,* which is a nickname for Andrea. *Andriko* is the familiar form of Andrea as is *Andriche.*

Andriche or *Ditche* could be used to address a kid and the name would stick as he grew up. As a grown-up his friends might continue to use the name. I always swelled with a little pride when I would hear about Dedo Nitcho.

According to my Dedo Vasil, Dedo Nitcho was one of the original T'rsiani who founded *Staro* T'rsie, the old village of T'rsie. Many of the older villagers knew that Dedo Nitcho was one of the original founders.

I can hear Dedo even now tell how the villagers had to move to a different location and so established themselves in Kalugeritsa. But in a short time they decided to leave Kalugeritsa because it was situated in an open area, leaving them vulnerable to Turkish attacks and roving bandits.

So many other Macedonian villages found themselves in the same situation and sooner or later moved their villages to different locations to avoid danger and harassment. Dedo trekked over the hills and mountains and established the present location of T'rsie. It was so remote that the feared and hated Turks dreaded going over the mountains to hunt them down. This was how Macedonians avoided paying *rushvet* or *faide,* the taxes to the Turkish Aga or Beg. The entire village moved to a safer location.

Resettling T'rsie in the high mountainous area had many advantages. The mountains and forests of Macedonia served as fortresses and sentinels in times of danger. There were several ideal places for v*ardishtcha* or lookouts on any side of the mountain. You could detect early when friends or foes were on their way to the village. Each villager learned how to travel through the mountains under cover of darkness.

From the time we were children we learned the secrets of our forests and caves. We knew every animal path and the dangers therein. Water, which is critical to both man and beast is plentiful around T'rsie. Our forests were our source for building homes and farm equipment. Our mountains were our refuge and our homes.

It was easy to see why Dedo Nitcho and the others decided on this new location for T'rsie. As I began to recall my past, it just occurred to me that T'rsie means *to seek, to look for*. Was that the origin of the name of our village?

Good old Dedo Nitcho! He lived to be 119 years of age. His son, Dedo Tanas, my great grandfather, lived to be a 108. My Dedo used to chortle, "I'm going to bypass Dedo Nitcho and my father, Tanas, Sotiraki. Just you wait and see!"

During our lunch breaks, when we paused from the plowing, Dedo often talked about the old times and about our family history. He reminisced often about the family's hard times and their struggles for survival during the Turkish occupation, and the hardships following Illinden, the two Balkan Wars, and the First World War.

Preceding each event, each conflict, there was such hope that Macedonia would gain her independence and her freedom. He even spoke about how he and his brothers had to split and establish their own homesteads. Any move meant making a new beginning with practically nothing. So it was with true pride that he would point things out to me and say, "See over there? I bought that from so and so."

He could remember who sold him each of his fields. I knew, without his telling me, how hard he had to work to earn everything that he now owned. He was proud of his achievements; he wanted me to share in that pride. And I did.

By our modest village standards, by our little Macedonian T'rsianski standards, Dedo was a rich man. If a villager had many fields—which we call *nivia* or *livadi*—if he owned livestock such as cows for milk and butter, 600 to 800 sheep, plus goats, horses, oxen, bulls, mules, and donkeys, he was considered a rich man.

Dedo used to say, "There is enough wheat in the *ambari*, the silos, to feed the entire village!" By the time his sons, my father and my uncles, grew to manhood and worked with him, Dedo would remind all of us grandkids how hard our fathers worked. He tried to motivate us to love our work. We really tried, but we were still kids.

Dedo loved all his sons, my uncles, Kole, Done, Vane, and my father, Mite. I loved them all, too, but Dedo will always have a special place in my heart.

Very few pictures of those closest and dearest to me have survived the devastation and destruction of our lives, land, property, and hopes. Each memory has become like a precious snapshot nestled in my memory album. Bright, laughing snapshots of weddings, christenings, name days, religious observances, faces of close relatives, and best friends pass before me in moments of contemplation.

There was so much happiness, so much singing and dancing back then. We had few disappointments or losses within the family then. We were such a close-knit family of kinfolk. My father and his brothers, my uncles, got along very well. I just don't remember conflicts or arguments between them. We kids, my cousins, my brother and sisters, and I—felt more like brothers and sisters than like cousins.

My mother, Tsila—her full name was Vasilka—took care of all of us. After my uncle's second marriage, my cousins grew up thinking of Mother as their mother! She cared for us all equally. Among us, our birthdays seemed to fall almost 2 years apart. Risto was maybe 3 or 4 weeks older then my brother, Stefo. Ilo was 6 weeks older than I. Risto and my sister, Tsotsa, were a couple of weeks apart. My baby sister, Mara, and the baby, Tanas, born to my uncle's second wife, were of the same age.

Perhaps I have talked too much about my Dedo. But to me he was so unique in character that memories pop up, one after the other, in quick succession, often unbidden. I loved him, even when he would deliberately anger me so that he could enjoy seeing my reaction. He loved to watch my seething emotions boil over. I can still hear him, "Aha, I got you that time, didn't I?"

So I learned not to let him see my frustration. That's when he would try even harder to get me to explode. Eventually, he would give up with the comment, "He is not from the Dimovski *soi,* his mother's clan. I know that. He is pure Nitchov. Ha! He is Dedo Nitcho incarnate. From that kind of . . . ."

I would interrupt him. "Ha, yourself. I am a carbon copy of you," I loved to say to him. "Just like you, a stubborn, bossy tsar, a pasha, an aga!!"

"All of those things, am I? " was Dedo's response. "Yep, and a lot more," I would taunt back. "Sotiraki, Sotiraki," he'd shake his head. "You were born one mean little kid."

"I can't help that, Dedo, but why do you say I am such a terrible boy? Don't I do everything you ask of me? Have I ever said 'No." to you?" Then, petulantly, I would go on, "Dedo, you sound like the rest of the villagers, accusing only me when something bad happens. 'Who did it? Why, blame Sote, of course'!"

"Wait a minute here, son. Think! What do you call a boy who cuts off the buttons from the shirt of every kid who passes by our house as they go to meet their parents coming back from the pazar?"

"I only cut off two buttons, Dedo, for the fun of it."

A formal photo taken in the 1950s of Baba Tsila and Dedo Vasil, seated, with Mareto standing next to Baba, Mother, and Tsotsa behind Dedo.

Planting a cherry tree on the property in Lerin, with a very aged Dedo and Baba seated on the ground. Tsotsa, Mareto and mother, Tsila standing.

"Oh, is that so? Didn't you plug Todor Georgiev's *oja*, the chimney? Didn't you bust Tsile's head, and Gospo only knows how many more? Didn't you break Linka's windows? Or burn Pando's gates? And who overturned Dedo Petre's *ulishcha,* beehives? You broke Mite's nose and closed his eyes. He couldn't see for a whole week! I could go on and on. I had to pay for some of those things. You know that, don't you?"

Of course I did.

I loved that man, my Dedo. He was small in stature, but he was tall in his humanity. He felt things deeply. Yes, he was proud, stubborn, but also very fair. He loved to barter for whatever was needed, whether it was to acquire a better, more strategic field, or a more productive area, or a super animal. He never cheated or lied to anyone. In his eyes the lowest form of human being was anyone who lied or tried to cheat him. If anyone ever did, it would only happen once, never twice.

There's a kind of legend about Dedo's sense of obligation and honesty the family likes to tell. It seems that Dedo once borrowed a gold coin from a man in Poleto, a little village near the town of Lerin. He and this man often traveled together on buying and selling trips. After some time, they lost contact with each other, and it bothered my

Dedo that he hadn't repaid this man the gold coin he owed him. He tried to contact the man's relatives as to his whereabouts, but was never able to locate him.

Years passed. Dedo always carried the gold coin on him in the event that their paths would cross again. After some passage of years, Dedo finally heard from the man's relatives that he had died somewhere *na pechalba*. Upon hearing the sad news, Dedo went to the man's village church, bought and lit some candles in the man's memory, and donated the gold coin to the church in the man's name.

He often talked about his friend, feeling terrible that he didn't actually repay his debt by placing the gold coin back into the man's hand. He used to say to all of us, "Whoever gives you something in your hand, you are obliged to repay it, placing your repayment in his hand!"

Dedo cautioned us from time to time that things will not always go the way they should, but that doesn't give us the right to give up. We were to keep trying to reverse things for the better. Even if it hurt to make changes, it would be far better for only one to suffer instead of two or more!

Dedo, the most decent, honest, generous, and scrupulously fair person who has ever influenced my life. That was my Dedo Vasil.

Tome—Joyous Soul Mate & Vesko—Shining Warrior

It is as natural to die as to be born.

FRANCIS BACON, 1625 A. D.

What year was it when one of our mares died giving birth to a foal—a colt? It caused a lot of discussion in the family about issues of life and death. I was mesmerized. How would the little colt survive? If it were to live, who would take care of it? Is it right to kill an innocent? It would have to be destroyed. Dedo did not want to hear any more of the discussion. He decided for all. It would have to be destroyed. That was final.

Now, as it happened, Baba, who had not ventured to give her opinion because, as usual, she was busy, by the *ambor,* the barn, which was under the balcony. She had heard the discussion. Loudly, indignantly, still outdoors, she voiced her outrage, "Aren't you ashamed? How can you think of destroying a helpless, living thing? Have you no feelings? Get out of there, now."

All this outrage was directed at Dedo. She stalked into the stall.

"Give the colt to me," and she proceeded to take charge. To us, "Bring me some blankets!"

We dashed off and brought her the blankets. She looked at us in exasperation after seeing what we brought her.

"Not the *new* ones!"

But she wrapped the blankets around the little newborn, anyway. She informed Dedo that we kids would help her care for the colt. Father carried the colt in his arms into the room with the stove. Gently, Baba started to clean it with warm water. After that she warmed some milk and poured it into a bottle. Father gave Baba one of the rubber gloves from his medicine bag. He had pierced one of the fingers of the glove which Baba fit over the bottle, making a nipple. She held it to the colt's mouth and he began sucking away. It seemed to be healthy enough because it gulped about two or three *kanatchki,* pitchers, of milk. We kids thought of it as Baba's baby, at first.

Over the next few weeks and months, Baba increased his food intake to include *kasha*, which is bread soaked with milk. As soon as Baba felt he was ready for more food, she began to chew the food she had for him, and then stuff it into his mouth. The colt ate everything she gave him! I watched with astonishment, then said aloud, "I hope you didn't do this to me. Yech!"

"Oh, ho! If you only knew how many times,"

"Euuu! Yech, yech, and double yech!" I loved Baba, but . . . !

At the time, I thought it was pitiful how she spoiled the colt. Was this the way to treat a horse? For a while, only Baba was consumed with thoughts of how to feed him and take care of him. Eventually, we all began to take responsibility for him. When he first slept with me, I really liked it. As he grew older, we all became more and more attached to him, especially me. I felt a special connection to him. I kept urging him to come upstairs with me for company. He didn't have a name.

He became a member of the family now, with full citizenship. Whatever the family ate, the colt ate. I talked to him all the time. I loved to pull his ears hard and then run. He would come right after me. He liked to sleep at my feet.

As the little colt began grow, both Dedo and my father told us to bed him in the *ambor* with the other horses and animals.

Father said, "Be sure to bed him a little away from the other horses and animals, until they get used to him."

He was a happy, playful little pony. Every time he saw Baba outside, he ran up to her and played with her by pushing her with his head, ever so softly. It was as if he knew that she was old and that he had to be careful not to hurt her. It was such a tender sight to see, a real love connection.

I could see that Dedo was beginning to look at our little pony with interest and a little pride. He really was a clever little pony and a very quick learner. We kids had a pole with ropes attached to it in our front yard. We always enjoyed grabbing a rope and spinning ourselves around. Our pony thought it looked like fun, so he joined the fun and ran around the pole as we were spinning. That was great fun.

Then, I began to wonder, would the colt race with me? I decided to challenge him. He liked racing. The way he liked to play the game was to let me have the lead. Then he would try to outrun me, which he usually did.

We were competing with each other once, when we ran into Father.

"What's *Tome* doing here?" he asked.

I smiled and shrugged my shoulders. Tome. Tome? Tome! The name stuck to our little pony. He was our Tome. No, he was *my* Tome!! We didn't mount him for a year, and I never used a saddle on him.

In time, Tome grew into a large, strong horse. He was beautiful. His gray and white coat with black spots on his graceful long neck . . . the white patch in the middle of his forehead, extending all the way down just short of his nose, made him seem so beautiful to me. Tome was tall with very skinny shins. What a beautiful, healthy horse he was. It seemed that he could be trained to do anything. He was definitely smarter than I could ever hope to be.

We often played the game of "Dead." This is the way we played . . . I would fall down and lay absolutely still. Tome would come over and nudge me with his front leg, and roll me over and over until I got up, alive, and ready for action again.

Sometimes, when he was overly excited about something, he would raise himself on his hind legs and whinny for all he was worth. He was absolutely magnificent when he did that. Whenever he was excited, I could calm him instantly, just by blowing into his nostrils.

My favorite way of riding Tome was to wind my legs around his beautiful, strong head, my head dangling under his, and race with the wind. I never fell, and he never tired. He never threw me off. You couldn't tell where the horse ended and I began—we were one body, one spirit, one mind—my Tome and I.

Whenever we rode on level land, I would give him his lead to see if he would race with me. It was hilarious because I could never outrace Tome. Nevertheless, he always played along with me and let me have a head start.

Dedo decided that Tome would never be used for plowing, and he would never feel the weight of a *samar*, a pack saddle. Instead, Dedo declared to all of us, "If you are good boys, Tome will be yours to play with!"

When we were younger, Dedo had given us a little white donkey called, believe it or not, *Belo Magarche*, white donkey. It was ours to play with. *Belo Magarche* never felt the weight of a *samar*, either.

You can see why I loved my Dedo. He understood kids. He understood me. Eventually, everyone knew Tome was mine. I wish you could have seen us together. He followed every direction I gave him. If I told him to take the oxen to their grazing field, he would do that. If we needed water and were some distance away, all we had to do was put a *zobnik* around Tome's neck. A *zobnik* was a waterproof *torba* or food bag. Tome would trot over to wherever there was water, go into the water, kneel down to fill the bags, and bring the water to us.

If we were caught in a deluge of rain, he would take the lead and bring us home.

If there was a problem in crossing a river, he would stop and turn around to warn us kids and the other animals as well. He would stand on his rear legs, the front legs pawing the air, and whinny.

We all got to know him very well, but he knew us even better.

There was a 3-mile stretch of road up the mountain from Derveno-Machoets and V'ro Preseka. If you go through Kukul, it's a 5-mile stretch. This is where I loved to race with Tome. At Machoets there are grazing fields and water, so this place became our headquarters. I loved to hop on him, *sans* saddle, and ride him up to Derveno, our starting line. At that point I would jump off and we would align ourselves next to each other.

On the count of three we would both sprint. Tome would let me keep up with him for about 5 yards. As I dropped behind, he would look back, then slow down until I caught up with him. Then we would run "even" for a few more minutes before he put on speed for another 100 yards. Again, he would slow down. As soon as I got close to him, he would turn around, bare his teeth and laughingly, pityingly, whinny at me, as if to say, "Okay sucker, haven't you caught on yet? You can't seem to catch me, eh? Come on, boy, can't you do better?"

I would pretend to threaten him. "One of these days, I'll beat you. You'll see!"

I talked to Tome all the time. From time to time he would nod his head. Then, again, he would let me get ahead of him by about 50 more yards and, with a couple of sprints, he would catch up. From behind, he would nudge me with his head, as if he knew that I was getting too tired to go on with the game.

We often had an audience of *volovars*, cattle herders. They enjoyed our races, always rooting for Tome. Tome's reward from the *volovars* was bread, which he enjoyed.

I was always the underdog in these races with Tome. How I loved those days! It seemed that our animals were such unique breeds. My cousins and I had fun herding the oxen. Sometimes we grazed them close to the Turianski *sinor*, border, steering them toward the villages of Statitsa, Armensko, Neret, Psoderi or Oschima. Herding made us all familiar with the different personalities and strengths of these animals.

One of the sports we indulged in was ox-butting oxen from the other villages. We would bet our lunches on our ox, and it was winner-take-all. For a few years, we kids from T'rsie were considered the champs, thanks to our "Vesko" and "Ilo's Badzheto"—our favorite oxen. These two, Vesko and Badzheto, were the best from our village, and we won most of the competitions.

Vesko was not very big, nor very small either. But he was a very good combatant. He was raised from a small *telentse*, a calf, somewhat like the way we raised Tome. All of our animals were very well fed. There was plenty of *zhito, seno, chemka, echmen* and *trifil* (wheat, hay, corn, oats and clover).

One of the secrets of Vesko's success in competitions was his *ostri rogovi*, sharp horns, which were filed to a very sharp point, capable of cutting anything. Vesko was the best—he was just one of a kind. I never met another like him.

Now you have met Tome, my soul mate, my joyful steed; and Vesko, my fierce, shining warrior.

The Lottery

It is a wise father that knows his own child.

SHAKESPEARE, THE MERCHANT OF VENICE

The one serious rift in our family occurred when Uncle Done remarried. Our new aunt was a total misfit, which was so obvious to everyone, especially us kids. She couldn't agree with anyone in the family on any given thing. Until she entered our lives, the brothers, my father, my uncles, and their families, lived under one roof harmoniously.

With this new daughter-in-law, Dedo and Baba tolerated much, trying to overlook the many squabbles she generated. This was very difficult for my grandparents.

Everything came to a head just before the christening of my little sister Mara, and Tane, my uncle's son. Since both were born within the same week, it was decided that they would be christened together by the same *nunko*. The nunko, the godfather, was from the village of Statitsa. His family had been godparents to our family for many generations of Nitchovs. That's usually the way it is in Macedonia. Godparents were held in the highest respect by the families.

In preparation for this sacred ceremony, the baptism of children, Baba and Dedo, Father and the uncles trekked to Statitsa to extend the formal invitation to the godparents for the christening on the following Sunday. Having done that particularly pleasant duty, Mother, Baba, and the other aunts began the preparations for the feasting that follows the ceremony. A specially selected lamb was killed and prepared for the roast. Exceptionally fine bread was baked for the blessing by the priest.

Some time during the night when all of us were asleep, my new, unpopular aunt scooped up baby Tane, stole some of the lamb and as much of the baked goods as she could carry, and left for Lerin. She apparently had been hatching this plan for some time, because she already had a different godfather for the baptism of Tane in Lerin!

This was not only a gross embarrassment to our entire family—it was a sacrilegious act, an act of enormous disrespect to my grandparents. To steal off in the middle of the night with a grandson, to have acquired a new godfather, to keep her plans secret from her own husband, and to steal the bread made for the priest's blessing was unheard of. It was a violation of the gravest order; a violation of human decency.

Unfortunately the deed could not be undone. Nevertheless, my little sister Mara's christening took place as planned, without the bread and with a little less of everything else.

After the christening, we were all worried about Dedo. How is he going to handle this very personal blow to the entire family? His face and mouth were set. There was no question that a major decision was about to be made that would affect us all.

Monday morning, he left for Lerin to contract builders. We call them *maistori*, men who are masters in their trade. Dedo had decided to build a new house with very thick walls. Dedo bought my mother's former home from her father, Dedo Dimo, and hired the *maistori* to build a large home on it.

A very early picture of the Vasil Nitchov family. Seated is Dedo Vasil, holding his grandchild, Dina, and a very young Kotse standing next to him. In the back row are, left to right, Striko Kole, Strina Kolitsa, Mite, (Sotir's father, about 16 years old) Baba Tsila next to him. Next to Baba is Strina Doneitsa and Striko Done.

Dedo was in full charge. He told the *maistori* that he wanted a full *izba*, a basement, with a *keral* for storing wine, cheese and meat. The keral served as a cooler, as well. The house was to have four large bedrooms. There was to be an outdoor oven right next to the house, and a large barn connecting with the house. The *gumno* in front of the house was to be a few yards out, and everything was to be surrounded by a wall. All this was to be built with black rocks and painted with whitewash. The floors were to be made of wood, except the kitchen area, which was to be the only room with a dirt floor. Father worked with the *maistori*, selecting, hauling and cutting the wood to size. Believe me, Dedo was designing a very modern house for its place and time. It was a truly great house.

The rooms were heated by the *kiunzi* or stovepipes and ducts. Dedo made sure that there was another heating stove between the rooms for additional heat. Dedo focused the strength of his anger and humiliation on building the house. He had also come to another major decision. For Dedo, the time had come to split up his property among his sons and himself, because they could no longer remain together as one large compatible family.

The one uncle, my Uncle Vane or John, had emigrated to America, and up to this point was unmarried. Therefore, Dedo made it clear that if Uncle Vane ever returned to T'rsie, he was to be given a share of the property. Dedo's oldest son, Uncle Kole was not going to get his full share, because they had a falling out before he left for Australia. The property was to be split between my father and Uncle Done. He emphasized, however, that if either of the two other sons returned, there would be a re-draw for equal shares.

Before the division of the property, however, Dedo gave the old house to Uncle Done. The new home would house my grandparents, my parents and us four kids, Stefo, Sofa, Mara and me, Sotir. He selected some property for himself and Baba, with the understanding that after he and Baba had passed away, the property would go to the son who was living with Dedo at the time of his death. He chose to live with my father. Tome was not included in the drawing. Dedo kept him out. He was not going to have a *samar* put on Tome. Dedo ruled and no questions were asked.

Dedo decided on a lottery. Because there was no draw for me, I was chosen to be in charge of the drawing. He placed red, white and spotted beans in a can. Each of the beans identified a specific field or farm and its location. My father held a red bean. Uncle Done had the white one. The spotted bean was Uncle Kole's. Dedo used the same procedure to divide the animals, cows, horses, oxen, and sheep.

The first draw was for the mare. It went to Uncle Done. For some reason, which to this day I don't know, Uncle Kole was not in the draw for the horses. I drew until everything was split down the middle, evenly. The *bulog*, flock of sheep, about 800, was divided in half, which meant that the sheep would have to be marked all over again. Uncle Kole was left with less than a third of the sheep, but when we herded them they were as one flock.

Father also got Vesko, which was my very personal favorite ox. The village property was equally divided among the three brothers. Dedo kept a few fields just for himself and Baba. However, the property in Lerin was divided into two parcels between the two uncles. After everything had been divided, each son began to work and maintain his own fields. It was understood, however, that as long as Dedo was alive, he would control everything if any conflict or quarrel erupted between them. That kind of problem never occurred.

Following the split, we moved into the new house as soon as it was completed. We moved from *Gorna Mala*, the upper district of T'rsie, to *Dolna Mala*, the lower district. Of course, I had to form an almost new gang of *surtutsi*. I still kept the original gang in tact. It was only during snowball fights that I played with the *Dolna Mala* gang against the *Gorna Mala*. So, of course, you know which gang was winning most of the fights. *Dolna Mala*, naturally. The villagers used to say, "That *Turcheto*, young Turk, makes the difference!"

I loved our new house. There seemed to be so much room, lots of space indoors and out. It was a house that filled me with such pride. Dedo impressed me with his determination to do everything to improve our lives while he was still able.

I loved my Dedo. I loved my life. Who wouldn't have?

The Piglet Caper

You pay a great deal too dear for what's given freely.

SHAKESPEARE

Dedo had given a piglet to one of our neighbors who had mentioned that she wished she had one. She was surprised by Dedo's gift, but very appreciative. She constructed a little pen for this piglet and intended to raise it. Of her four children, one of her sons, who was very timid, hung around with me and my gangsters.

As luck would have it, her son Done, my little band of Turks—as some of the villagers described us—and I were passing by the little pen. At that moment, spontaneously, a wonderful, brilliant and rather delicious thought struck me.

I stopped and turned to the gang. "How would you like a little roasted piglet?" They gave me a look, and each promptly informed me that I was nuts. Where was I going to find a piglet? I pointed and said, "Right there."

Done protested. "That piglet is ours. Your grandfather gave it to my mother last week!" And I replied to him, quite cavalierly, and not without some arrogance and smug assurance, "So what? He'll just have to give her another one."

My young Turks looked at me skeptically, but I could see that they were greatly tempted. I turned to each of them, Ilo, Mite, Gavre, Done, Pincheto, looking at them, daring any one of them to grab the piglet. I could see that nobody had the guts. So, I gave an exaggerated sigh. It was up to the leader, of course, to show them what courage and leadership was all about.

Rising to the occasion, I reached into the pen and grabbed the struggling, squealing piglet. But I had a good grip on it, and we all ran like hell to a place called Chemer, where our family owned a field. We used it many times as a *batchila*, a combined sheepfold and dairy, where we made our cheese and butter from sheep's milk. No one was around at the time.

I am going to spare you the details, but we killed the little piglet and cleaned it very carefully and thoroughly in the nearby river. Being the connoisseurs that we were, a couple of kids went back to their houses to get salt and *merugie*, our word for herbs and spices and whatever other ingredients they could find.

The rest of us built a fire by digging a little hole in the ground, building up the heat with branches and sticks. This was a familiar procedure for us because we used to cook pumpkins and squash over the fire in the same way. We scooped up mud from the river and molded the mud around the piglet. Now the charcoal in the pit began to glow nicely. Man, we were busy little chefs, working out everything to perfection. We saw ourselves as Class A gangster piglet chefs, the best in all of T'rsie and Lerin. No, the best in all of Macedonia!

We placed this little piglet in the heated pit and put some hot charcoal on top of it. There was one problem we faced, however. None of us really knew how long the piglet should roast. A little problem, but not for long. We just had to rely on our sense of smell. And that's what we did. We spent the couple of hours gabbing away, boasting about our exploit and how we got away with it, and finally, our noses began to tell us the piglet was done.

Were we lucky! It turned out terrifically delicious. Really the best, the tastiest pork we had ever eaten. We sat down around the pit and ate that little sucker, the entire thing, even sucking out the bones. What a feast! What an accomplishment! My legend was going to be enhanced even more.

I had learned from Father and uncle how to roast fish and meat in this way, so I became the king-fisher, the smart-ass, the culprit, and the guru in the technique of roasting piglets. One of the lessons I had learned was that when the mud had hardened after a time, whatever you were roasting is removed from the pit and the mud casing is broken. The skin sticks to the inside of the mud cover.

Believe me, never has roast pork tasted as delicious as this one did. I can still savor the taste to this day!

Evening was coming on, so we knew it was time to go home. As we came to Done's house, he went around the back to avoid seeing his mother right away. His mother saw the others of us and came out fuming. She followed me home because she was going to see that justice was done to me.

She knew what had happened. I thought, how could she have seen me? Apparently she had, and had already informed Dedo about the theft of her precious little piglet. As I came to the house, Dedo came out of the door.

Pointing at me, Done's mother, Kita, in a quivering voice, shouted at Dedo, "That little Turk stole my piglet. Nobody else. He did it."

I walked into the yard, nonchalantly, innocently, followed by Ilo. I had an unconcerned smile on my face, happy as a lark, hopping from one spot to the other, without a worry in the world, and greeted Dedo. "Hello, Dedo, how are you?"

Dedo, eyeing me carefully, replied, "Oh, I'm just fine. And you two *surtutsi*, rascals, would you be hungry by any chance?"

"Oh, no, Dedo. We ate earlier."

Done's mother could take no more. "See, they took my piglet!"

Dedo, in a controlled voice and manner said, "Kito, just give me a minute. I'll be with you in a moment."

He came back to us. "I want to know what you boys did today." Ilo and I looked at each other, and Ilo spoke out, "You tell him."

"Why not you? Are you a mute?" I retorted.

Dedo, with great patience, spoke directly and slowly, "I am waiting and I want to know now."

"Should I start from the beginning or . . . ?" I asked, politely.

"From the beginning," said he in reply, "and come closer. I can't hear very well."

I came as close to him as I could. I fingered the corner of his jacket, cast my eyes downward and in my most seductive, gentle voice began my little story softly and somewhat sweetly.

"Dedo, about noontime we were by Strina, Aunt Kita's house. Then we saw the piglet. Then we grabbed it."

In a soft voice, Dedo asked, "Who saw it first, and did all of you grab it?"

"No, I grabbed it. It was my idea. In fact, the others didn't want me to do it, but I did it."

Still softly, Dedo said, "Now, you get another piglet and give it to Kita, and you will assure her that this will never happen again."

I did what he told me. Strina Kita thanked Dedo, but she would not look at me. Dedo turned to me, "I suppose you are not hungry any more."

I didn't answer because Baba was calling everyone to the table for supper. There was a general hum of conversation, full of talk and laughter, everything as usual.

Dedo turned to me. "I cannot understand where you get such ideas, doing the things that you do. I can't wait to see you grow up and see what you will become." He shook his head from side to side.

One of my cousins piped up, "He is going to be a big vagabond, a hoodlum. That's what he is going to be!"

Dedo didn't comment further, but I was watching him carefully, and then he glanced at me with a covert smile!

That is what I remember most about the day of our piglet caper, that interesting smile on Dedo's face as he looked in my direction. What was he really thinking?

Life was good, then, and there were all kinds of fun. I felt as if the entire village was ours, our playground, our inspiration, to do whatever our impulses dictated. There were several little groups of kids that hung together, but I have to admit, with no modesty whatsoever, that my gang of Turks, *surtutsi*, rascals, was the tops. Everybody used to say so, though I do not include the adults in this assessment of my gang.

The Burning Curiosity Caper

Enquire not what boils in another's pot.

THOMAS FULLER, M.D.

I knew what bullets looked like from the time I was barely able to walk. Both Dedo and Father always had a rifle, which we never touched. It never occurred to me to do so. I also knew what bullets sounded like.

By the time I was 6 or 7, my cousins and I were able to find plenty of time to get into mischief. We all had chores to do, but there is just so much kids our age were able to do. So we had time for adventures and capers.

We could always find time to explore and test things in our own way. I had a lot of curiosity about things. It was not unusual for me to find things that I had no business finding, which brings me to the evening my cousin Ilo and I found a case of bullets. That discovery developed into a fiery little caper that had an interesting consequence.

As I said, we knew what the bullets were capable of doing, and we knew what kind of sound they could make. What an opportunity to find out how much noise a case of bullets could make! I was not one to pass up an opportunity of this kind, no matter what.

I could talk Ilo into any kind of adventure, so I said to him, "Let's empty the *barut,* gunpowder, in the bullets, and throw the *barut* into the fireplace and see what happens, okay?"

You should have been there! I never saw anything like it! It lit like a bomb! What a show!

We burned down the fireplace, chimney and some stuff around the fireplace. Then the *plemna,* the barn, where the wheat was stored caught fire.

I certainly picked the opportune time to start a fire, even involuntarily! It was wheat-threshing time and the adults were in the *gumno,* the yard, threshing the wheat and bundling the *slama,* the hay. Everyone was working there threshing the wheat when they saw the barn on fire. They worked quickly to put the fire out and save the wheat and hay. They saved us all from an even greater catastrophe.

Miracle of miracles, neither Ilo nor I were even singed by the huge flames that burst out. Talk about fireworks!

There were more fireworks to come. Dedo came running into the house, madder than the proverbial hornet. He was fit to be tied, fuming hotter than the flames that burned everything to the ground. Ilo managed to run away, but I got stuck in the kitchen, trying to put the fire out. Who even thought it would cause this much damage? I impressed myself with my stupidity at this point, not only because of the damage to the property, but facing Dedo's outrage? That really was stupid!

Baba came running as well. More than anything, she wanted to know what had happened, because all she could hear was Dedo cursing and shouting, getting closer and closer to where I was. I had no place to hide, then, quickly a thought came to me. I'll stand behind the door, and when he walks in, I'll run out and he won't be able to catch me! What a brain!

"Where are those *Turtsi,* those Turks?" he demanded angrily of Baba.

"I don't know."

"I know Sotiraki had something to do with this. Nobody else would even think of doing such a thing, burning everything down, that *turchin*, that Turk!"

Baba kept protesting she didn't know where I was, all the while shielding me behind the door, holding her apron wide open. She kept protesting, "No one is here. No one is hiding here. Go away, Vasil, go look around."

She had given me away. I could tell by the way she spoke. I knew I was caught. So I decided to face the music. I put a smile on my face as Dedo grabbed my arm, slammed the door shut behind me, and pulled me toward the window, pointing toward the yard where the rest of the family and neighbors were. They weren't standing still. They were busy putting out the fire and cleaning up the mess that was left. I could only see part of the threshing floor. Dedo was shaking me with the intensity of the fury he felt.

"Aren't you ashamed? You could have burned down the whole neighborhood, with so much hay and wheat that was stored. It doesn't take much to start a fire! What were you thinking? But I forgot. Sotiraki doesn't think!!"

He was shaking my arm harder and harder with each word. For a minute I even thought he might pull it right out!

"You're not a baby any more. When are you going to grow up? When are you going to start thinking first?"

Now Baba was getting more than a little frightened at his display of almost uncontrollable fury. She kept warning him not to hit me. Then she began to curse Dedo, threatening him.

"If you hit him, may your arm wither and fall off!"

Now those were very strong words for Baba to use. I knew I had to speak up.

"Baba, I'll deal with Dedo. Don't worry."

Dedo Vasil suddenly stopped. All of a sudden it occurred to him that maybe I was hurt.

"Are you hurt?"

Whew!! It was at that moment that I knew I was safe. No matter how angry I could make him, I knew he would not do anything to hurt me physically. Outside, I am sure everyone thought that I would finally get the beating of my life, which I had earned and deserved! By the time Dedo and I walked downstairs and into the front yard, the *dvor,* we were actually talking and laughing about the whole caper.

Were the others shocked? Were they surprised? Were they expecting me to be crying my eyes out? You betcha.

Father was so upset that he stalked over from where he was working and began scolding me so severely that Dedo jumped all over Father. Dedo was defending ME! You can't convince me that adults aren't a strange species.

"Don't bother Sotirki. What happened was your fault," Dedo said, pointing to the bullet cases. "You left those cases in the *yavur* and you know better than to bring such things here. We have children . . . ."

I interrupted Dedo, not realizing that I was about to add fuel to the fire of his outrage. "Dedo, there are *pushki,* guns, in there, too."

Suddenly, Father realized that a far greater danger was lurking, which could involve more than child-like pranks and carelessness.

"Don't go near there again! DO YOU UNDERSTAND? DON'T TOUCH ANYTHING. STAY AWAY FROM THERE!"

To Father Dedo said sternly, "You better get rid of everything. Get those things out of here before someone gets hurt or blows us all up." There was another message they were sending to each other, but it was a silent one, communicated only with the eyes.

In fairness to Father, all of those cases and guns were very well hidden and out of our reach. I don't even recall how we stumbled onto them. Was it Ilo who might have seen Father and Uncle Risto hauling the cases and hiding them. All I can recall was that I was climbing the roof looking for I don't know what, when I spotted the cases. Anything that I saw that was new, different or strange, I had to explore and examine and test. So I opened a case. It was filled with guns! No one ever explained how they got there.

In a week's time, everything was gone. I didn't know how, when or who cleared them out, and I never asked.

Oh, about Ilo. He finally found the courage to return home. He asked me quietly if Dedo had spanked me. Negative, I told him, but I added that Dedo was going to spank him.

"Why me? You were the one who did it."

"It's not about that, " I told him quite seriously.

"What do you mean? What was it about then?"

"It's because you ran away. You know he doesn't like that," I said a little accusingly, but "put on," of course.

Dedo just happened to come by at that moment and saw us. He strongly scolded the red-faced Ilo, shaking his finger at him.

"The next time you do something, you must face it. Don't run away. If you are wrong, admit it. And if you are right, then stand up and own up to it. By running away you are considered guilty whether you are or not. Understand?"

Boy, did we ever. From that point on, we really had Dedo under control. If we found ourselves doing something that was forbidden or wrong, afterwards we would inform him first, by ourselves. He would then ask us if it was the right thing to do and support our position.

However, if one of us, well truthfully, it was usually me, but if one of us got into a fight, he would demand, "Did you beat him up or did he beat you up?"

I always claimed I was the winner, and his response to me was always an approving, "Good for you!"

Somehow I always felt Dedo enjoyed our confessions of mischief and fights.

The Alpha and Omega of My Greek Education

Education makes a people easy to lead,
But difficult to drive;
Easy to govern,
But impossible to enslave.

LORD BROUGHAM, 1828

I have only negative memories of my brief education in my village school. Here's the thing. The people of our village, T'rsie, built one of the first Slavic schools in the region in 1865. It was a beautiful three-story structure. Our legendary priest, Father Gerasim, had built the church and then the school with the enthusiastic support of the people. Although today it is politically incorrect to say it was a Bulgarian school, that is what it was.

We referred to it as a Macedonian school, and it operated fully until the beginning of the Balkan Wars, in 1912–13, and resumed only after World War I had ended. Children from neighboring villages, such as Nestrum, Pozdivishcha, Kumanovo, Chetirok, Zhelevo, attended our school.

Father had told me that the school, after reopening, continued until the 1930s when the Greek regime replaced teachers with Greek teachers to teach nothing but Greek. They remained until the late 1930s.

During World War II there was no school at all. Anything written in Slavic was either destroyed or defaced during the thirties.

I remember very well how everyone tried to avoid going to the Greek school. Nobody, but nobody, wanted to be taught Greek. It was a foreign language to all of us.

Father's generation had gone to the Bulgarian school in T'rsie, and most of his generation knew how to read and write in Bulgarian. Father had served as a chanter in the Old Slavonic language of the Church during church services. As a child in T'rsie, I had never heard a church service in Greek.

As the Greek authorities began to realize that the Macedonian children were not attending their Greek schools, a law was passed making attendance compulsory or the parents would be penalized with fines and other punishments.

Macedonians could not afford to be fined, so they tried to force their children to attend the Greek schools. Father tried to tell me in so many different ways the importance of a real education. He wanted all of us to become something besides farmers or shepherds struggling to make a livelihood. He often spoke of the day when—and that it would come very soon—he assured us, we would have our own schools. He meant Macedonian schools. But, he impressed upon us that we had no choice but to go to the Greek school for a while.

"Anything you learn, no matter in which tongue, will be in your best interest. The more you know, the better. If you can learn German or even Albanian, learn it. But right now you have to go to Greek school, and so you will have to learn Greek. We have no choice right now. I wish, oh, how I wish we could have our own schools, but we can't yet."

I can hear the disappointment in his voice even today. I tried to digest Father's words, but I honestly could not follow his logic at the time. What was he really saying to me?

Anyway, the day came when I had to go to that foreign Greek school. As luck and the devil would have it, my gang—Ilo, Gavre, Mite, Pincheto, Kole and I—being approximately the same age—ended up in the same classroom. Ha! For that auspicious entrance to the school on the first day, I had awakened early, washed my face, put on some decent, clean clothes, and brushed my hair with the same brush I used on Tome, my horse.

Ilo and I started out. As we walked toward school, the other children joined us. When we got there, the bigger and older boys and girls went into the building first, and then we followed. Up this point, going to school hadn't seemed to be too awful. In fact, it was kind of fun, because everyone we knew was there, too, talking, joking, looking pretty good, in fact.

I was ushered into a classroom, and then the teacher shut the door. In that instant everything changed for me. I felt that something ominous had happened to me. I felt trapped. I began to feel isolated and claustrophobic at once. I had to get out of there and fast!

I looked at the person who was to be our teacher and took an instant dislike to him. This *ovchar*, this sheepherder, had been saying something, when suddenly, I saw him strike some of the kids' palms with this special switch made from a willow branch, a thick willow branch. I could almost feel that pain.

I saw the tears running down the faces of those kids, and that was the end of school for me. I was definitely going to get out of there. No way was I going to let him hit me like that. No way in hell! That bastard was punishing the kids because they were talking to each other in Macedonian!

They didn't understand what he was saying. I must have been the second kid to protest then and there. How could we learn Greek if we didn't know what the words meant in the first place and couldn't ask each other if they knew?

"*Skase eki*!" the oaf thundered at me.

"I don't know what that means," I said to him, defiantly. He swaggered over to my desk, striking his left palm with that switch in his right hand, with a look in his eyes that could kill. He made a motion with his finger on his ugly lips, and held it there for a few seconds. He then turned around and went to the blackboard. I looked at Pincheto and Ilo and pointed in the direction of the door. They nodded in agreement, but how?

I whispered, "Water—to drink water."

The *ovchar* heard us and came back swiftly to where I was sitting. "No talking in that *glossa,* language. Only *Eleniki*, Greek!"

Again, I spoke to him in Macedonian, grabbing my crotch, making a swishing sound. All I wanted to tell him was that I needed to go to the toilet. They were located on the corner of the school. I figured if I could make it to the lavatories, I would be free, never to return. At least, that was my strategy. It backfired.

The idiot thought my gesture meant, "Piss on you." He came toward me to teach me a standard Greek lesson. With this switch in his hand and a calculating look on his face, I knew that he was going to make this effort an Olympic one. I knew what was coming and just as quickly stood up by my desk, ready to run. The laughter that swept over the entire class infuriated him even more.

As I grabbed my crotch again saying, "Shishy. Shishy," he leaned over me and with disgust in his voice uttered, "Anixe to herry." It meant, "Open your hand."

As he tried to force my hand open, preparing for his Olympic-level strike, I was more than prepared for him. Watching him closely as he raised his arm, just as he was about to hit my hand with all the force he could muster, I pulled it away and he missed.

Without the slightest hesitation, I ran through the doorway, made a right turn, and shortly found myself in the *leika*, the playground. I spent the rest of the day there, by myself, fooling around, thinking.

When school was over, I joined Ilo and the rest of the gang as they headed home. After we had snacked, we went outside again. The gang was a little miffed with me because they had to stay in all day. I reminded them that they could have escaped when that bastard was chasing after me.

That evening, during supper, Dedo asked me about school. Ilo looked at me and spoke, "Eh, no good. We don't understand the teacher, and he hits the kids with this switch."

This didn't surprise Dedo at all. He said to all of us, "Then our Sotiraki is going to have a hard time, eh, won't he." It was more a statement than a question. Ilo slipped up and made the remark that I was already in trouble. Up to this time I had been quite silent.

Dedo immediately asked, "What trouble? What did he do?" That's when I decided that I had better speak up.

"Ilo," I began, feeling noble and righteous, "I will talk about me. I'll tell Dedo." I made my declaration loud and clear. I was not going to that school again. No one was going to beat me with his sticks.

We skipped the next three days of school. You don't need to know where we spent our time. The family didn't know until the village official came over to warn the family that if the children did not attend school, the family would be heavily fined.

When we finally returned home that day, Dedo confronted us. He told us of the heavy fine he would have to pay because of our actions. We stood our ground for a while and then gave in only when Dedo became convinced that someone had to tell that teacher to stop hitting us. He had to relax the rules until we learned to speak Greek.

On that condition we did go back, and that jerk seemed to be more "cooperative" with us. But no matter what, I couldn't stand the monotony and the boredom. Ilo, Mite and Pincheto had been separated from me. Gavre was the closest one to me. I told Gavre that I had had enough and that I was going to leave. But how? It was the same old problem. Recess was 2 hours away.

I was getting desperate, and desperate men have to do desperate things. So in desperation, I deliberately banged my head as hard as I could, face down, to smash my nose and cause it to bleed. I did it! It was bleeding beautifully, so that I could now holler, "*Miti, Miti.* My nose is bleeding." The teacher came over to my desk and told someone to take me over to the *chezma*, the drinking fountain next to the church a few meters from the school. Once there, I splashed some water on my face. The front of my shirt and pants were messed up with blood. It was wonderful.

The students who were with me said that we had to go back. Dramatically, I protested that my nose was still bleeding. I told the kids to go ahead. I was not going back, so they returned. I took off for a place called Solische and Skrkata, outside the village. Ilo arrived home from school first and asked Mother and Baba where I was. They told him that I was in school with him.

"No," Ilo told them. "He broke his nose before noon and never came back." I was arriving home just then and had met Uncle Done on the way. He took one look at me, shook his head and asked, "Who hit you? Who did you fight with?"

"No. There was no fight, *Striko*, Uncle, this happened in school in that idiot's . . . " Before I could finish, Striko became so angry, he started cussing at the teacher, thinking that he had given me the nosebleed. "I'll kill that Greek jackass. He will never hit another kid again."

"No, no." I told him how I did it to myself, to get out of there. He looked at me, his look slowly changing from anger to amazement to approval. He laughed. "*Na Striko mush!* My man!" With that, we both walked toward the yard leading into the house.

However, the rest of the family did not quite appreciate my little trick. I told the family once and for all that today was the last day of school for me. I was not going to go back. I was going to herd the sheep, and I reeled off several different chores that I was going to take on. Even Uncle took up my cause. "I don't think the boys should go to that school. They are not learning anything. Let's wait for Mite to get home and we'll discuss this again. Every kid in the village is complaining about the school." Mite was my father's name.

Dedo spoke up. "And when they come to collect the fines, what do we tell them?"

"Don't pay them. The officials in the towns who are responsible for the schools don't know who is collecting the fines and who is not going to school here. Somebody else is pocketing those fines."

I don't know how long the school functioned. I know it didn't last long because the Partizans were increasing their presence among the villages. I do know that the schoolteacher packed up and left for Lerin. This was about the time I began to see more Germans, more soldiers around us.

So much for my Greek school education. I think that was the last of the Greek school in T'rsie. I remember that around 1946 and 1947, we had a Macedonian teacher, Petre Temelkov, from our village. But only a few of the older boys and girls attended for a short time.

Much later, after the so-called civil war, the Greeks destroyed our big, beautiful school building and built a small single story one, around 1952. The "wonderful" Greeks removed the Cyrillic letters of the name of our church. The only thing remaining on the stone on which the name of the patron saint of the church, St. Nicholas, was carved in stone, is the dove, and the year the church was built.

By 1975, the Greeks had removed everyone from their homes, closed the school and everything else they could find. The Cyrillic letters of the names of the dead in our cemetery were defaced. Today, the village is empty, almost everything in ruins, where a vibrant, passionate people, the Macedonians of T'rsie, had lived and thrived and died over several centuries.

A picture of one of the last classes of students in the Macedonian school in T'rsie, circa, 1928.

The Devil Made Me Do It!

It is one of the blessings of old friends that you can be stupid with them.

EMERSON, JOURNAL, 1836

Even though some memories bring tears to my eyes, there are others that sometimes make me laugh out loud. I did so many outrageous things in my young life—when I was free to roam and test the world around me—that were frequently embarrassing to my family and to my gang of Turks, as well.

This escapade did not have any repercussions, which is another way of saying that Dedo and the family did not hear about it. Here's what happened.

Reading alarming signs that the Devil was luring us into mischief of all kinds, our grandparents and parents tried to mold us into decent little Orthodox Christians. A distinct feature of the Orthodox Church is the beautiful *Iconostas*, the partition of icons facing the worshippers. It is usually a beautifully carved wooden structure, separating the temporal from the spiritual world.

The center of the *Iconostas* features the gates through which only the priest and the bishop may enter. The gates are beautifully carved by local craftsmen. These gates symbolize the heavenly gates. Nobody, but nobody, can simply walk up and go through them. The priest's assistants, the altar boys, and sometimes during the baptism of a boy, the godfather, the father, and other male family members are invited by the priest to join in the special blessings the baby receives inside the gates. No female is ever allowed into the altar area at any time. Never!

During church service, I would see only two people going through the gates into the altar. It became such a curiosity to me, a puzzle, and eventually, of course, a challenge, because not even the altar boys could go through the heavenly gates of the *Iconostas*. They had to use the doors on either side of the Iconostas. Why? I kept wondering. No explanation was ever given that I had ever heard.

Maybe no one dared to ask. It bothered me a lot that only the priest and his assistant could enter the heavenly gates. My father, who as I have mentioned was a *psaltar,* a chanter, who assists the priest during services, had warned me in no uncertain terms that I was not to try to go into the inner sanctum, ever. *Period!*

My, my! I could sense a challenge building within me. Well, as luck would have it AGAIN, as it did so frequently for me, we were playing under the church's *trem*, which is an area that extends from the walls of the church outward. The *trem* was covered and was long and wide, providing some protection from the sun. It also protected us from getting wet when sudden rainstorms occurred.

As we had no plan for the day, my gangsters and I had no focus for activity. We meandered around until we found ourselves under the *trem*. The church door was open, and then, Bingo!, suddenly I had a plan and decided to try it out on the guys.

"Hey, the church door is open. Why don't we go inside and take a look at the altar. Let's see what the priest is hiding there."

My cousin, Ilo, looked at me as if I had suddenly gone nuts. Shaking his head, "You're a *budala*, stupid one. Don't you know that nobody can enter the altar except the priest? We can't just walk in!"

"Well, the priest . . . He's not here, is he? We're here!" The thought of going into the altar had stunned everybody. No one budged. I started toward the door. "I'm going to go in and look."

As I headed for the door, I peered in every direction, but there was no one around, so I went in. Still, no one inside, either. Good!

Our church was built in such a way that it captured the sunlight, reducing the need for artificial light. During the day, light poured in from the dome and the upper side window. All the windows had colored glass, red, blue, yellow, gold and other colors. The church was large and really quite beautiful.

From the balcony, where we kids stayed, prayed and played during our long church services, you could see everything and everybody. In the middle of the church and on the sides near the walls there were chairs and benches. A beautifully carved Bishop's chair was placed on the steps leading to the altar. If you were downstairs, when you stood up, you could not see all the people.

As a young boy, I thought it was one of the most beautiful churches I had ever seen—and that memory still holds today. It was the one Father Gerasim built, *Sveti Nikola*, Saint Nicholas.

As I paused in the middle of the church, drinking in its awesome beauty, Kole, Ilo and Gavre came in silently, cautiously, and joined me. The gang really hadn't thought that even I would be so bold as to enter the altar. But, on the off chance that I did decide to do it, they wanted to be witnesses. The rest of them crept in. That was all I needed. Their presence made it necessary to go forth! I went up to the *Iconostas* and entered the heavenly gates; I heard their collective gasp.

It was so beautiful in there; I thought I had entered heaven. There was this big table, covered with the most beautiful cloth I had ever seen or even imagined existed. It was unbelievably, stunningly embroidered on the top and covered with gold crosses. This thing of beauty hung down to the floor on all sides. There were many books, candleholders, cups and *candila* or candles. Everything looked as if it were made of gold. There were more beautiful icons, which the worshippers rarely saw during a service, except for special holy day services. There were chairs, hangers, and bottles of wine. On one side hung the priest's robes. Some were black and others were in gold and silver, richly brocaded and embroidered.

I had never seen such splendor. I was overcome with amazement and awe. The boys had been whispering at me, and eventually I did hear them. "What are you doing? You should come out of there." They were getting a little more than uncomfortable. They felt they were committing some great sin.

But I couldn't leave just yet because I had spied a white robe, one of several, and a weird scenario was formulating in my head. I was going to become a *samovil*, a ghost. I put the white robe on over my head, and found a way to be able to see through the robe. I sneaked out of the side door of the altar, unobserved, moving very quietly until I was directly behind the boys. Standing quietly behind them for a second, I then let out an unearthly scream.

You should have seen their faces as they jumped sky-high. I had scared the living daylights out of them, and they ran off as fast as they could—like scared rabbits—out of the church. They couldn't move fast enough!

Once they were gone, I took off the robe and hung it on the rack. I fluffed it out, so that from a distance it would look like someone standing there, which gave me an idea for still another scenario. I decided to complete my ghostly charade and went back into the altar. I turned everything upside down, *candila*, chalices, trays, everything, and arranged them in front of the altar. I arranged one of the priest's robes on the floor, and faked the shoes with some clothing. Then I placed one of the platters at the top of the robe, covering it with one of the black robes. I arranged it so that it looked like the stovetop type hat that our priests wear. Finally I placed a wine bottle close to the head.

Had anyone walked into the church at that moment and looked toward the altar, the gates open, you would have thought the priest was sprawled behind the heavenly gates. The rest of the robes were strewn around the floor. Well, my task was completed, so I took off, leaving the gates open, and walked out of the church with no one the wiser because no one was around.

The gang was waiting for me by the *trem*, and they were really pissed at me, although they managed to laugh at themselves a little. They were embarrassed, definitely uncomfortable, and they showed it. So what?

I decided to go to the school building and see if there might be some action around there. Some time passed, maybe an hour or two. One of the gang saw Ziso, the

A view of the interior of the church, St. Nikola, T'rsie, Macedonia, built in the late 1800s by Father Gerasim and the villagers of the period. Sotir is to the right, holding a camera. Photo taken in 1988.

Pitroup, the churchwarden, running out of the church. Ziso looked panicky. He was talking to himself as he headed toward the *chezma,* one of the drinking fountains. He thought he was alone.

We dropped whatever it was we were going to do, and went up the stairs to see what was going on. We had already forgotten about our little church escapade. Heck, wasn't that a couple of hours ago? In gangster time, our escapade was an ages-old affair. But, I had to remember. The guys hadn't seen what I did inside the altar. Ilo whispered to me, "I'll bet that Ziso saw a devil in the church."

At that moment Ilo turned to me, with growing suspicion. "What did you do in there?" I, innocently, with an injured expression of unbelievable depth on my face, "Wha . . . ? Nothing!"

Kole came running. "Hey, I heard Ziso saying "*Popo padna. Pian e.* The priest has fallen. He is drunk!" I reminded Kole that the priest wasn't in the village. He had gone to Statitsa.

Suddenly Ziso stopped his mumbling as he saw Baba Nesha Rukova coming toward the *chezma*. She had overheard us, and she reassured Ziso, "*A bre nemame Pop. Kakov Pop? Da ne si bolen*? There is no priest here. What kind of priest? Are you ill?"

Poor Ziso couldn't answer, and he wasn't about to go back to the church alone. He waited until someone else showed up before he moved from the spot. The way Ziso was carrying on, you would have thought he saw the devil himself!

An old gravestone Sotir unearthed in the desecrated T'rsie cemetery enscribed in Slavic letters, dated 1750.

A view of the upper part of a church, showing only the sculptures of the dove and the cross. Every trace of Macedonian lettering, sculpture, and pictures have been eradicated.

The gravestone of Father Gerasim, which reads: Here rests Father Garasim, 1870–1891. He was buried behind the altar in back of the church.

Word got around in time. Everyone in the village heard what had happened, and they had a pretty good idea about the identity of the culprit behind Ziso's devilish experience.

No one told on me. I certainly had nothing to say.

It probably was the devil himself, up to his fiendish tricks. And in the church!

Little did I know that my days of foolish pranks in the village were coming to a quick end.

1943

It was not the easy-going peasants who started the resistance to the Germans in the mountains. That was the last thing they wanted; they had hardly seen a German, or noticed the slightest difference in their way of life, until the talkers from the towns arrived with exhortations to take arms against the invader. For the peasants the resistance movement meant the loss of their livelihood, the burning of their homes, the looting of their property, all of which they endured as long as they believed the cause to be a good one but none of which they would have inflicted upon themselves without prompting . . . The ordinary man in the street, in the field, on the hillside . . . was not even free to stay still, for even the decision to stay at home and do nothing was a positive decision involving concrete consequences. He was obliged to choose between alternative leaderships offered to him to become either a collaborator or a Communist, or whatever it might be . . . .

COMMANDER C.M. WOODHOUSE, Allied Commission to the Greek Guerillas

The leadership and strategy of the guerilla bands in the mountains were provided directly or indirectly from Athens and Moscow, but the guerillas came from the indigenous peasantry of the region. The BMM appeared in Northern Ep;irus and encountered SHTAB.

German divisions were active from Korce, Albania to Lerin, *Florina,* Greece. The BMM's strategies were to link up with the Albanian, Serbian and Greek resistance movements, and make direct contact between various political leaders. The plan was to divide the region into four regions, each region to be under the command of a British lieutenant colonel. The BMM sent Nick Hammond as liaison to Macedonia, but Greece was cold to Myer's idea of an independent Macedonian resistance movement.

The BMM gave undivided support to ELAS, while also supplying EDES with arms and increasing amounts of gold. Gold sovereigns in English, French and Italian gold called *napolioni* by the guerillas were brought in bags. The Greek forces of Colonels Poulos and Krsokhou, and the armed villagers of Mikhalagas in west Macedonia did the Allies a service by accepting arms to fight EAM/ELAS.

Brigadier General E.C. Meyers, Commandant of the BMM, 1942–43, convinced that the Greek colonels were not up to the task of sabotage, decided to use *andartes*, the right-wing active guerilla bands in Thessaly and Macedonia.

EAM/ELAS viewed the *andartes* as a challenge to their own pursuit of leadership, and General Zervas, the leader in the mountains of EDES, as a collaborator with the Greek king. EAM/ELAS issued death threats to the *andartes* unless they joined EAM/ELAS. EDES came to be regarded as the asylum for everyone who hated and feared the KKE.

A prisoner-of-war camp in the Pindus Mountains was formed to hold German and fascist prisoners. No prisoners were taken on either side as a captured guerilla did not live very long.

January:

- Germany accorded approval to Mihailovich in Yugoslavia.
- Tripoli fell to the British 8th army.

January–December:

- By February, the German army reached Stalingrad.
- The covert policy of the USSR to capture the political leadership in the Balkans focused on the resistance movements.
- Yugoslavia was eventually dominated by Tito; Albania by Enver Hoxha; Bulgaria by Georgi Dimitrov.
- The USSR declined to assist the Allies in bringing together rival guerillas, deeming it interference in the internal affairs of another country.

Spring/Summer:

- The British war Cabinet approved support to Greek guerillas willing to support the Greek monarchy.
- North Africa was cleared of Axis troops.
- EAM/ELAS attacked the PAO in Macedonia.
- Mussolin fell. Italy was invaded by the Allies.
- King Boris of Bulgaria died mysteriously.
- Mihailovich attacked German shipping on the Danube.
- KKE accused Colonel Zervas of being a fascist conspirator. The KKE and ELAS were convinced the British were going to impose an unwanted monarchy.
- Rival resistance groups collaborated with the Germans, and armed collaborators expanded the forces of Mikhalagas in western Macedonia.
- BMM suggested Colonel Bakiridz take command of all guerilla forces.
- Germans captured five Greek generals and sent them to Germany.
- Destruction of Asopos railway viaduct and the Gorgopotamos convinced the German High Command that the Greek resistance movements controlled two-thirds of Greece.

- German troop reinforcements rushed into Greece to aid the remaining Italian forces.
- The Pan-Slav Committee in Moscow acclaimed Tito and denounced Draja Mihailovich of Yugoslavia.
- From Cairo, the Greek king cabled reassurances to Prime Minister Churchill and President Roosevelt that the Greek people would have free elections to form a government of their choice after Greece was liberated.
- Greek exiles blamed the British for the creation of EAM/ELAS.
- Representatives of Yugoslavian, Bulgarian, and Albanian Partisans attended the EAM/ELAS congress in the Greek mountains.
- EAM strongly criticized Macedonian leaders for seditious propaganda, and proceeded to organize Macedonian leadership as an integral part of ELAS with equal rights.
- Allied troops landed in Sicily.
- The National Bands Agreement was signed by EAM/ELAS; EDES; EKKA; PAO; and BMM. All guerilla bands were to accept and receive military direction from BMM headquarters, although each band could retain its name.

August:

- ELAS allowed Macedonian schools and newspapers to function, and increasing numbers of Macedonians joined EAM/ELAS.
- KKE allowed Macedonians to form independent units. SNOF was formed and their organized guerillas took to the fields.
- EAM and SNOF clashed constantly.
- A delegation from the mountains met with the Balkan Section of the SOE in Cairo to discuss the unrepresentative nature of the Greek king's government and to delay his return to Greece before a plebiscite was held.
- The value of the guerilla campaigns began to diminish.

August–September:

- ELAS integrated relations with the LNC of Albania; with Tito's lieutenant, TEMPO, in Yugoslavia; with SNOF leaders; and with the Bulgarian Partisans.
- The Italians capitulated. ELAS confiscated and kept Italian weapons.
- The Germans proceed to divide the remaining Italians against themselves.
- The Aegean islands were captured by the Germans.
- BMM was transformed into AMM. German troops moved northward.
- EAM/ELAS, convinced the occupation was ending, requested the BMM to advance the entire allocation of gold sovereigns for 1943.

October:

- KKE, ELAS attempted to seize power and attacked all rivals except EKKA.
- Italy declared war on Germany. Rival resistance groups collaborated with the Germans. Armed collaborators expanded the forces of Mikhalagas in western Macedonia.
- The Greek king again appealed for unity.

November:

- The Jajce Conference of the Anti-Fascist Council of the National Liberation of Yugoslavia established a Macedonian nation equal to the federeated republics of Yugoslavia. The Conference completely disavowed Bulgarian pretensions over the people of Macedonia for their pro-Bulgarian sentiments.

December:

- The Bulgarian Fatherland Front rejected the Jajce Resolution because the Bulgarians considered Macedonia the cradle of Bulgarian Renaissance. The Fatherland Front declared itself in favor of Macedonia for the Macedonians.

Yamata!

Do not eat your stew from the same bowl as the Greeks.

Dedo Vasil Nitchov

One of the Italian Army supply depots was located in Lerin. As the Italian War was winding down, and before the Third Reich made its way into our lives, the Italians began their retreat. They left huge amounts of food, ammunition, medical supplies, and uniforms. In short, they left everything needed to feed, clothe and provide for an army. Word spread quickly through Lerin, and looting began on an unbelievable scale. Everybody ran to loot whatever they could before the Germans came on the scene. Uncle Done said to me, "Everybody is grabbing whatever they can in town. Come on, Sote, let's go and see what is left. Maybe we can find something. Just grab whatever you see."

So I tagged along with Uncle Done, and I can tell you, I had never seen such bedlam. Everyone was grabbing something, shouting, running as if they had all gone mad. I guess war makes scavengers and madmen of all of us. Hey, it was great fun! I grabbed what I could, which wasn't all that much; maybe some salt, or was it sugar?

and a few cans of biscuits. It was about all I could carry. It was then that I first heard the expression: *yamata*. It means a stroke of good fortune.

Hurrying back to the house, we ran into Father, Uncle Traian, Krsto Stoikov and a bunch of other men I didn't recognize. Uncle Done was astonished at what the others had looted. He turned to me, speaking loudly enough so that Father and the others could hear him clearly, and said, "Look at my brother and those other idiots, hauling guns, bombs and ammunition. Everyone with any sense would have grabbed food and clothing!"

When we passed our *kaliva*, our barn, my eyes bugged out. The whole place was stacked with boxes of rifles, machine guns, ammunition and bags with the Red Cross emblem on them. There were blankets, rain slickers, army uniforms and also other things that were not visible. At my uncle's urging, I joined him and took some blankets, shoes and slickers. Our logic was that what we were taking wouldn't be missed by anybody!

However, Dedo was thoroughly upset. White with anger, he approached his sons and Father's friends and asked them to sit down. Out of respect for Dedo, they did. Then in his sternest voice and most deliberate manner, trying to control his anger, he began, "Boys, I don't know what has gotten into you. Here we all are worried about food and clothing in these very upsetting and difficult times, but," he turned to face his sons directly, "what have you and your shitty friends here brought to our home?" He paused for a second or two, not expecting an answer, but wanting the question to sink in their heads. "By morning you are to get rid of everything. I don't care where, but I do not want any of that garbage on my property. Do we understand each other?"

Silence.

By daybreak of the next day, the loot had been loaded on horses, mules, and an army truck that someone had brought to the property by the river. The men had been busy all night. Where it was to be delivered, only Father, Uncle Traian, and their friends knew. Dedo was so furious with my father that he railed at him for several days.

"You and your cohorts are accomplishing nothing except loss. When will you learn that you do not eat your stew from the same bowl as the Greeks? They will deceive you. Remember my words. They will deceive all of you. You act as if you have no brain or the ability to reason. Sit down on your asses and take care of your families. Don't go creating problems for the people. Don't listen to those bums!'

As the Germans began to arrive, they brought with them their prisoners of war and set up the camps in the Kondopulskite and Moteshnitsite *livadia*, meadows. For the first time we Macedonian kids began to see men of different nationalities in these prisoners of war. There were many Russians and Ukranians, and much later came the Italian prisoners. It was at this time that I became aware that farther up in the more mountainous villages, the Partizani were forming fighting units. From time to time we began to hear of skirmishes with the Germans.

When and where did these other Partizani come from? If anyone knew, not a word about them was heard, not out loud at least.

The prisoner camps stretched out all the way to Moteshnitsa following the path of the river. We began to see more Italian prisoners. Having developed an entrepreneurial frame of mind by now, we kids saw some real opportunities for gain. We started a trade with the prisoners, offering food in exchange for raincoats, handguns, boots, belts, saddles. Sometimes we gave them chickens, turtles, snakes or rabbits. Whenever the German guards saw us, they chased us away. As you can guess, they never caught us because we were smaller, faster. Besides, this was our territory. Kids always know the good escape routes. We liked to go through some wires down by the river and on to the other side where the road leads to Armensko Moteshnitsa. Then, too, there was another escape through Kalugeritsa and Yanina Livada. Oh, we knew our territory, alright!

From time to time we would hear of prisoners escaping. Circulating among the villagers was the big story that a large number of mostly Russian and Ukrainian prisoners of war had escaped. Father gave us strict orders not to go near the camps for a few days. Now *that* aroused our curiosity, but we obeyed his orders. Father and Uncle Traian looked as if they were preparing to go somewhere. I asked where they were heading. Uncle pointed towards Lundser and then toward Bigla. Well, that was the direction they were supposed to take.

A little later, when Father thought I wasn't around, I heard him say to Uncle, "I'm not sure if there were enough food and guns for the escaped prisoners, but our responsibility ended with the successful delivery of more than 3,000 guns and ensuring their escape."

I couldn't hear what Uncle Traian replied.

Oh, wow! I kept eavesdropping on their conversation as they discussed who was going to take the leadership in the mountains. Once again I heard the names Kole, Petre, and Naso, and for the first time I heard a new name, TEMPO.

Who was he?

After some time had passed since the big escape, the temptation became too great, even though we were warned not to go near the camps again. We couldn't stand it. We had to try to restart our trade with the prisoners. Not a good idea! This time the guards began to shoot over our heads, although never at us. It became a little hairy. Finally, the guards succeeded in scaring us away for good.

Our *yamata* had come to an end!

Achtung!

Laws are silent in time of war.

CICERO, 52 B.C.

I remember very clearly when the German troops entered Lerin. They marched right through the city, passing St. Nicholas Church, the cemetery and the *Kondopoulo*, which was located across the river facing our property in Lerin. Kondopoulo was owned by a family who had been relocated to this area from Asia Minor during the Greek/Turkish population exchanges.

Oh it was something to see those Germans march! We all watched wide-eyed. I remember running across the river many times just to see them. This was the real thing! These were how real soldiers *should* look. With their strange-looking helmets, spic-and-span uniforms and coats, their shiny boots. Yep. They looked the way soldiers ought to look. I remember thinking to myself—I didn't know the word then, but I do now—they were *disciplined!* Without knowing anything else about them, I looked at them with such admiration. Wow! Real soldiers! I was so impressed.

They didn't bother anyone at first. They never stole from us. They never made passes at the women. Everyone agreed that they weren't like the *Italian* soldiers. Those Germans were something else!

Like everyone else, I became aware of another kind of "German soldier". At least that's what we thought they were. But they weren't German. An incident occurred some time after they first appeared that clarified who the "other Germans" were. This is what happened.

We heard shooting one day and we kids began to see a large number of men gathering near the edge of our property. Naturally, curiosity being what it was, my cousins and I wanted to see what was going on. There was no fear in us; just a lot of curiosity. So we ran through the fields toward the sound of the guns. We dashed toward a pear tree, which was close to the crowd, and scrambled on up to the branches. This is what we saw.

A lot of men were gathered there, and we saw that one man asked each individual to repeat something he said to them. We could hear him speak and, surprisingly, we could understand him. He was asking them to repeat this phrase, "*Sheise i shes kozhi ot kozi,* 66 hides from goats."

After each man repeated the phrase, the one in charge gestured each individual to one side or the other. This was beginning to interest me, because it was obvious that there were going to be two teams. I thought that maybe there was going to be a new game. Maybe these men were going to make up farm teams, lining up for a game. Good. I loved competitions.

How wrong I was. What we saw was not a game. It definitely was not a sight for young eyes, or even for old ones. We made no sound as we watched, transfixed. About twenty or so men were selected from one side and lined up on the other. Those spiffy, disciplined soldiers that I had so admired at first, now aimed their rifles at one side of the men lined up and, on command, fired. We looked at something unbelievable. The men fell to the ground, almost at one time. What we were watching were executions. Executions!

For the length of time we stayed in the tree, maybe 25 or more men lay on the ground, all over, on all sides of the field. We kids waited, glued to the tree. No on paid us any attention. Every eye was fixed on the horror happening in front of us. When the shooting ended, the soldiers left without taking the bodies with them. They just left them there, as if they were animal carcasses, as if they had never been living, breathing men only minutes ago.

Suddenly a truck covered with a greenish-brown tarpaulin drove up to the church. A second crew of soldiers loaded the bodies into the truck and left. The truck turned right, and from that point we couldn't see any further. We knew that the road they were on would take them to the center of town. What we had just witnessed was the efficiency and ruthlessness of the *Gestapo*, aided by other strangers.

Father came looking for us. When he saw us still up in the pear tree, he called, and we scampered down. Simultaneously, words spilled out of our mouths as we told him what we had seen. As we hurried toward our house, he listened intently, lips closed tightly.

Later, Father learned that those "others" were Bulgarians. These Bulgarians had been identifying which men were Greeks and which were the Macedonians by asking them to repeat the phrase, 66 hides from goats. In Macedonian it was *sheise i shes kozhi ot kozi.* If the man was identified as a Bulgarian, his life was not at risk. The Greeks gave themselves away because they could not pronounce the phrase properly. To Greeks the '*sh*' and '*zh*' sounds are difficult to pronounce.. Father told us that the two Bulgarians were working very closely with the Germans. I couldn't tell what Father thought of the Bulgarians, but they were certainly a new element in our lives.

In spite of the new *visitors*, I was enjoying the times I spent in Lerin on our property there. Going back and forth from our village to the city was always full of adventures. Many times I was placed in charge of the property, including the house, while the grown-ups tended to other things.

I was made the guardian of the vegetable garden. We had, tomatoes, peppers, cucumbers, leeks, onions, melons, cherries, pears, apples and the seven or eight fields of corn.

During the summer periods, the German soldiers would come to buy our fruits and vegetables, whatever we had available. We communicated using hand signals and facial expressions.

In the beginning, when we couldn't quite understand each other, one of the Germans attempted to go into the garden to point out what he wanted. Seeing him take that liberty, I began to holler at him at the top of my Macedonian voice. And I could holler pretty good. I gestured to him furiously, trying to make him understand he was not allowed in the garden. I even swung a stick at him in my fury. I didn't care if he was a German soldier or not. *I* was in charge and *he* did not have *my* permission to go into the garden. He seemed to enjoy our encounter and laughed at me, but he did stop. He never went into the garden again without permission.

The next day he brought a man who spoke both German and Macedonian. However, his dialect was different, which I eventually learned was Bulgarian. The Bulgarian proved to be very useful. His name was Mladenov and he seemed to be a very big wheel. He set things straight between my German and me. It was understood that no one would come into the garden if there was no adult from the family also present.

The Germans were to pay for everything on the spot, which they always did. From that point on, I felt reassured there weren't going to be any further problems. They would point at what they wanted and pay me, then I fetched it for them. It got so that I would allow them to pick out what they had paid for, because I watched them like a hawk, ready to pounce and peck if I had to.

Many times they would tap me affectionately on my head or my back, saying something in German, laughing at my expression. I always charged them more than I usually charged our own people. The German money wasn't all that good anyway. It was mostly paper money, kind of reddish, long, wide, with holes punched in it. I would collect a basketful of this paper money, which brought smiles to Father and uncle.

"Seems like you made some friends, Sote. Too back you can't speak their language."

Everyone commented on the German soldiers. As I said before, they never bothered any of our women. If they saw a woman working in the fields, they would avert their eyes. Only if a male showed up would they initiate any conversation.

The Germans trained on the outskirts of Lerin. They held maneuvers all the time with their tanks and firing machine guns at their targets. One of our neighbors had an orchard next to ours. He also was originally from Kafkasos in Asia Minor. His name was Petros and his son was Ari. Petros and Father became good friends, and so did Ari and I. Father coached Petros in his pronunciation of our words like *chardak*, balcony; *chorapi*, stockings; *chekan,* hammer; *kozha,* fur or hide; *zhena*, woman; *zhelka,* turtle; *shishe,* bottle; *shipka,* fork; *shareni,* colorful; *bohchka*, barrel.

I was curious. Petros knew our language. Why was Father doing this? Soberly, Father explained, "Yes, he knows our language, but because of the way he pronounces our words, the Germans can tell he is different, not a Macedonian like us. Remember the other day when the Germans were separating the men and then began shooting some of them?" I nodded, solemnly.

"Well, they could tell who was Greek and who wasn't. Kalchev and Dobrev told me that they identified the Greeks by their accents and pronunciation."

Ohhhh! I understood now. Of course! The Greeks have a hard time pronouncing the sounds of "ch" and "sh". When they try to pronounce our words with the those letter combinations, they say "tz" for the "ch" sound and "s" for the "sh".

On a few occasions these same two Bulgarians would come to us to buy sheep or cattle for the Germans. I watched and listened to them very carefully as they spoke, because I could easily understand them. Although the Germans seemed to be careful and respectful of our way of life, I had seen another side of them in that ugly, frightening spectacle. The memory of those executions and the horrible disregard for human life remains a vivid memory of a terrible time.

Still, I went over to the area where the Germans held their maneuvers, firing their rifles and guns. I saw that empty shells were left where they dropped. I had heard that there was a place in Lerin where empty shells were bought. Needless to say, I, Sotir, the entrepreneur, magically appeared.

Since I liked to collect empty shells, why not collect them and sell them in town. And I did!

Just call me Sotir—or Sote—the Entrepreneur. Either way, it has a nice ring to it, don't you think?

The Chicken/Rooster Caper

He who deals with a blockhead will need much brain.

SPANISH PROVERB

I was coming home from Skrkata, our play area, where just a few barns stood. My gangsters and I often used the barns to hide any ill-gotten goods. These "goods" were usually stolen from army trucks. They were useful little toys, such as dynamite sticks, hand grenades, bullets, fuses, and whatever else we could lay our curiosity-laden hands on. Some of the boxes that we helped ourselves to hadn't even been opened.

I had stopped to check out our loot. The box of dynamite sticks was particularly appealing to me, so I picked up three or four sticks. I put all but one in my pocket; that one stick I kept in my hand.

One of the intriguing things about a dynamite stick is that you can pinch, pick, and roll the stick into marble-sized balls. Isn't that useful? It was useful for me, because it helped me invent a new game, requiring very little strategy—while making a wonderful noise. I particularly liked to flick my incredibly useful dynamite marble, just as any kid would flick an ordinary marble, in any direction, and just let nature take its course. Great stuff!

As I headed toward our house on this particular day—within a yard or so from our house—I flicked my "marble" toward the chicken coop, which also housed the roosters. I watched, fascinated, as a lordly rooster strutted over to the "marble", picked it up, and ate it!

Faster than I can recall the incident, that silly, strutting rooster flipped over on his back, feet pointed to the sky, as if accusing God for allowing this indignity to happen to the lord of the hen house. I stared. There was no movement whatsoever. Terrific!

I decided to throw a few more "marbles". As I kept throwing, a couple of my gangsters came around. They became intrigued by my new game, and they started to make their own "marbles" and toss them. What a sport! You should have been there to see the remarkable scene we were creating. There were chickens and roosters all over the village, falling flat on their back, their feet pointing straight up.

As the villagers became aware of what was happening outside and saw chickens and roosters on their backs, a number of them started coming after us. But we had the head start. Like buckshot, each of the gangsters ran in a different direction. It was every man for himself.

I, however, found the optimum place to hide, a *furna,* an outdoor oven. The oven had already been prepared for baking, so it was loaded with branches and wood. Having the advantage of being short, I moved some of the firewood so that I could hide more comfortably.

But my luck was finally going to run out because Panduitsa, the woman who lived there, was about to start the fire in the *furna* to bake her bread! By the time she went back into the house, the oven had started to smoke and the fire was gaining momentum. I was determined to stick this out, one way or the other, but my eyes started to smart from the smoke and my throat filled right up with it.

I felt the urge to cough. I knew I had to be quiet, but I couldn't suppress the cough, so I muffled the sound as it escaped my lips.

Panduitsa did not hear me, probably because the fire was making its own crackling sounds. I kept willing her to get away and go back into her house—just move away, *nooooowwwww!*

But my mental telepathy was not working. The fire was heating up. I had no choice. My situation was impossible. I had to get out. I didn't know where she was at the moment, but I had to move and move *nooooooow!*

So I pushed aside the branches and burning wood, and took off at a speed that can only be described as lightning quick. I ran toward one of the creeks and stuck my head in the water, drinking as much as I could. Finally cooled off—which must have taken an hour or more—I headed for home.

Poor Panduitsa! She had prepared about 20 loaves of bread for baking. Thinking that her *furna* was hot enough, she had started to clean out the ashes and place her dough inside. She was stunned; then, outraged to find her oven cold! Having 20 loaves of bread ruined was no small matter.

When things of this nature went wrong in the village, there was only one place to go to find the answer. Panduitsa went directly to our house to vent her anger, outrage, loss, and frustration.

When I finally came home, Mother greeted me with, "What did **you** do today?"

The family was looking at me, waiting. There was no way out, so I told the truth, knowing that we would have to pay for my "creativity" again. This time, though, so did the families of some of the other gang members.

A little item had slipped my mind, though. I had forgotten that I had left a stick of dynamite on the windowsill.

The day after my little caper, my sister, Tsotsa, found what she thought was a piece of *alva,* a sweet made of sesame seed and other stuff. Believe it or not, that's what she thought. She didn't know whose it was or why it was left there, but she took a large bite or two this "delicacy".

We almost lost Tsotsa. She was in a coma for a couple of days. Had it not been for Father's skill, she would have died. Even though I took absolute blame for it and expected the most severe punishment—which I rightfully deserved for my disregard for everyone's safety, including my own—I was not punished!

Instead, Father sat me down. He was determined to reach me somehow to help me develop a sense of responsibility toward others as well as for myself. We were alone together for a long, long time. I deserved a severe punishment. But I didn't receive it.

Somehow, some way, Father drove into my head that I had to change. I had to grow up.

Neither Father nor Dedo ever struck me.

Horseknapped

Opportunity makes the thief.

ENGLISH PROVERB

In spite of the war around us, we tried to go on with our lives as normally as possible. We still went back and forth from our village to Lerin many times. Sometimes we kids would be sent alone, leading our horses or mules, loaded with farm products. It was on one of these trips that I experienced, for the first time, how close the war was. I was about 7 years old.

Dedo had instructed me to take the *pravda,* the mules, horses and mares, to Lerin. This was the way we transported products to and from the village. Villagers loaded my horses with sacks of fresh bread and gave me specific instructions. I was to take the path leading to the church, St. Bogoroditsa, where someone would meet me, and from there I was to continue on to Lerin. St. Bogoroditsa was located under the peak of Clepala—a secluded, quiet place, like many of our Orthodox churches and monasteries. I reached Yanina Livada—which resembles a small crater, a *ramnina*, as Dedo used to say. It was 10 or 11:00 in the morning, which I knew by the position of the sun.

As I approached the church, people were waiting for me, all right! Maybe 2,000 were assembled, from V'ro Derveno to the church, all *Partizani* as far as I could see. What a sight that was! As I arrived at Plochite, I could hear guns rat-a-tatting and shells piercing the air. They were fighting nearby, towards Kalugeritsa and Lerin. So what? It didn't scare me, and I didn't really concern myself with the noise. I just assumed it was a training exercise. The Germans used to do this from time to time, so it seemed to be business as usual. After a year of fighting, I was used to it. I didn't see any problem.

The people knew who to expect and were waiting for me. They were the *Partizani.* They unloaded my horses quickly, and told me to go home. That confused me. Did they know something I didn't? Should I go home to Lerin or back to T'rsie? I decided that I should return to T'rsie.

As I turned the *Pravda* to go, Ilo Dimovski gave me a sealed letter, instructing me to deliver it to father—no one else. I immediately stuffed it inside my shirt. I had seen Ilo before, talking to my father privately in Lerin. He was also known as *Goce*, the Commander, the head honcho, the general of the *Lerinski* and *Kosturski Odred,* the *Makedonska Brigada,* Macedonian Brigade. The *Brigada* consisted of 3,300 to 4,000 men and women. Much later I learned that the *Brigada* was 98% Macedonian.

With the sealed letter inside my shirt for my father, I started for Lerin instead with my little group of animals. Down the road, I stopped to water the animals and refresh myself. I could hear shells exploding all around, but I had heard shelling and shooting before. It was a part of our lives now, so I gave it no more thought. After all, I had instructions from Dedo and a special letter for Father. Since my horses and I were ready, I continued on my way to Lerin.

On the road to Kalugeritsa, I reached an area that bordered Yanina Livada. A few of our T'rsiani still had homes and fields there. From this point I could easily see and hear from a great distance. I could even hear people calling to one another. As I was passing through I heard a terribly loud explosion, followed by several others, just above me, very close. So close, in fact, that some branches from the trees above fell at my feet.

Shells began to hit the houses. I was still on my mare when I saw the houses explode. One of the shells exploded right in the middle of *Striko Petre's giumno,* Uncle Peter's yard. I heard screams and shouting. There was a lot of confusion down there. It didn't sound good, and it didn't look good. People were gesturing and shouting about something terrible—but my mare trotted on, carrying me farther and farther away.

I reached Kalugeritsa, passing my mother's family home and saw Ilo Maleganev and Itso Mangov. Further along, I spotted my Cousin Goce. Some had machine guns. Occasionally they fired a few rounds. No one stopped me, even though I could hear and see explosions all around. I had never been afraid of that noise. It was too familiar a sound. Besides, I had a mission, and it was a mission I was going to complete.

The terrain was hilly and the roads curved around the hills. I had reached Tumbata. There were lots of streams and creeks. Some of the crossings were out in the open, while a few horse-steps downstream you were hidden from view. From Tumbata I was heading for Shupurka. The path there would bring me to Chaulata, the hill which obscures Lerin from view.

I was familiar and comfortable in this area, but then I began to feel bullets whizzing by. The animals were getting nervous. In spite of that, I continued on to Shupurka, where there is an *izvor,* a natural well. The water came from the mountains. Our T'rsiani had built a beautiful water basin, a *chesma* with a *kopanka* (water trough) for the animals to drink from. From this point the road twisted again, and then flattened, almost straight, following the outline of the hills. I could see Lerin as well as Moteshnitsa and another little T'rsiansko settlement. I was moving as fast as I could to reach Chaulata, the barren hill where the road bends, almost forming the letter *C.* A green road sign informed travelers of the distance to Lerin, and to other destinations. As I rounded the bend in the road, exposed, I heard Doneitsa Mangova shouting at me, "Turn around and go back. Go back now!"

Go back now? No way. I ignored her. I had a mission to complete, even though Tome was trying to warn me, as he usually did when he sensed something dangerous. He was whinnying and balking. He stamped his feet and reared onto his hind legs. He did not want to proceed. But my mission! The letter for father had to be delivered!

Although I had never felt the heat of bullets before in my life, as they tore through the air next to me, I knew where the heat was coming from. They made a funny sound. I could see that some of the bullets had cut off branches of the short, bushy spruce trees. We call these trees *kopachki* and *smreki.* I could hear the thud of bullets as they hit the sandy earth. The road sign, too, was being riddled by bullets.

As I followed the road I felt a bullet hit my mare, knocking off the handle of the *samar,* harness. I grabbed the *chakulets,* in the back of the *samar,* dismounted, and saw that she had been grazed. I put some dirt on the wound, placed a small blanket over top and, using the *polopashnitsa,* the belt, held her cut together. I realized I would not be able to get to Lerin. I had no choice but to turn around.

I headed back toward the *chesma,* under which there is a *mrasarnitsa,* a very cold area, which makes and preserves ice in Nature's way. The *mrasarnitsa* is very deep and almost completely underground. The roof is just a few feet above the ground. I tied my horses with a long rope. They would have enough movement for grazing. I jumped off my mare, tied her loosely, and sat down by the tree. Leaning against it, believe it or not, I dozed off. From the time I had left St. Bogoroditsa, there had been so much noise that, in this little *livada,* meadow where a soft breeze blew, it seemed as though I was in another place, another world.

I don't know how long I had been dozing, but something awakened me. I peered around, and I could see the *Partizani* fleeing. Then I saw the Germans running after them. Seeing that, I jumped into the *mrasarnitsa*, and hid in a corner, I covered myself with *snopie,* sheaves of straw. The *Partizani* scattered quickly. This was their land, They knew every inch and they managed to disappear.

The Germans, having lost sight of the *Partizani*, paused. Then I heard footsteps approaching the *mrazarnitsa.* When the noises stopped, I could see someone looking around, cautiously, then turning back. As I watched him leave, I thought there must be hundreds of soldiers out there, maybe thousands, but no one saw me. I was safe.

Then I heard voices.

Raising myself to the little window, I watched as the Germans placed their wounded soldiers on the backs of my animals. They put a bandaged man on my mule. After loading their wounded, the German followed the creek to Moteshnitsa, across the river toward Lerin. They headed toward Tumbata. I knew they were going to have a serious problem. They had to cross the river, and my mule would never cross a river. I know of only two people who could make him—my father and my brother, Stefo. No one else.

That darned mule wouldn't budge no matter what the Germans did. The poor bandaged soldier on her back could not get loose. His hands had been tied to the rope that ran from the mule's head. Finally, the mule went berserk; he spooked and started running toward our property in Lerin, following the river, dragging that poor soldier along. I knew he would be dead by the time the mule reached home.

I knew I had to get out, but I heard those voices again. I couldn't understand a word! I hid under the *snopie* again. There were footsteps coming toward me. I could see a few Germans passing and glancing inside, but no one saw me. They continued on their way.

So, I waited. As the last two Germans were moving past, one of them turned around and came into the entrance of the *mrazarnitsa*. He had seen something. Pointing his gun in my direction, he shouted. I didn't know what he was saying or if he was shouting at me. I tried to be still under the straw. He fired his gun and the bullet just missed me. Some of the straw from above fell on top of my head. He kept firing. Two other Germans came inside. One of them started talking in my direction in a demanding voice, raising his hands up. I realized that they had seen me and were telling me to come out with my hands up!

I pushed the straw forward, and as it fell toward the floor, I was exposed, holding in my hands my black rubber shoes, the *pintsi* I had made from tires. They motioned to me to walk out of the *mrazarnitsa* ahead of them. I stood on the road with my hands up. I was still only about 7 then, and didn't know if I would make it to 8 years old. The soldiers started to laugh as they talked to each other, looking at me. One of them came close, smiling, raising his hand towards my head. I ducked sideways, quickly. He stepped back and motioned me to step forward. I did. Another soldier offered me something, but I shook my head, no! The German who had originally spotted me, and fired at me, put his hand on top of my head and messed up my hair. It was as if he was my uncle, patting me on the head. He was smiling at me now. The earlier look on his face, which was quite ugly and mean, had disappeared.

We stood like that for a few minutes, then two more people showed up, one in civilian clothes, the other in an officer's uniform. They both looked impressive. Behind them, a few yards back, stood a group of about 15 soldiers. The civilian came to me, looked me over carefully and then spoke in German to the officer. They paused and then looked at me again.

The civilian started talking to me in Greek, which I could not understand, but I knew it was Greek. I think he was trying to learn where the Partizans were, how many. When I didn't respond, he started slapping my face. That was all I needed. I could feel my blood rushing to my head and I started shouting at him in Macedonian, challenging him!

"Go ahead, hit me. Hit me, you bastard. Hit me harder! You don't have any strength. Go ____ your mother!"

Two soldiers stepped forward to stop him, but the officer said something, and they backed off. One of them winked at me and made a fist. The civilian hit me a few more times. He backed me up toward the little road. Right beyond the edge, a little lower, was a steeply banked creek. If you were to fall into it, you would go straight down, through vines and roots, and into the water.

I thought quickly. One more slap from this creep, then I'll jump into the dark creek. The hell with everything! With my precious rubber shoes in my hand, I was ready for him, as defiant as ever. He slapped; I fell. I jumped and went through those vines very easily, and made my way down into the water. After rolling a bit, I took off like a rabbit. There was gunfire, but the bullets were hitting the other side of the creek. I don't know what happened next with the Germans, but I found myself running beside the main river. I could see that some of the river-bank was caked in blood, but I did not stop to look. It wasn't *my* blood!

I finally came to Klodencheto. The water ran out of the rocks that we use for drinking water. I spotted Father hiding our mule in a secluded area in Marvor's orchard. I ran toward him. He saw me and stopped. He splashed some water on my face and made me sit on the ground next to him.

"What happened? Why didn't you return to T'rsie? Didn't you see the fighting?"

I told him the whole story. Nobody had said anything to me about turning around to go home when I was at Sveta Bogoroditsa. Only when I got to Chaulata did I realize that a real battle was happening. I told him what had happened to the horses.

"I know. I saw them being led into the schoolyard, but the mule went directly to Lerin. The soldier that was loaded on the mule is dead, down by the Urba. I don't want you to go anywhere near there. Do you understand?"

I understood.

"Later," Father went on, "the Germans came and picked him up. A few of them came by the *kaliva* and talked to me for a few minutes, and then left."

Father never told me what they talked about. I never asked.

Father kept looking at me, not at all sure that I was alright. He shook his head over and over.

That evening, Father went to find the horses. How he managed, I don't know, but he came back with all of them. All of them except Tome.

The letter that was entrusted to me to deliver to Father was still inside my shirt, but I had forgotten all about it.

Dedo was so upset, so angry, that the fire in his eyes could have burned down the house. I said nothing, but smiled at him occasionally. He said nothing to me.

Tome Comes Home

What a man has honestly acquired is absolutely his own,
Which he may give freely,
But cannot be taken from him without consent.

SAMUEL ADAMS, 1768

The German officer who took Tome told my father that the horse was his and not to bother to come back again. When Father told me that, I decided to go by the school building where they were keeping Tome. Boy, I was pissed. That German was going to keep Tome? I didn't think so, and not for long.

As I was changing my shirt, back home, the sealed letter that was given to me by Ilia for Father, fell out of my shirt. I had forgotten it! I scooped it up and went into the garden where father was. I gave him the messy, sweaty letter. He tore it open and went inside to read it.

After a few minutes he came out. "Tell Dedo that I will be back later," and he headed out toward Lerin. Until Dedo arrived an hour or so later, I was alone, snacking on some fruit and going over what had happened. I had no idea where Dedo had been, but I found out in a hurry. The woman who had tried to warn me when I was near Maleshnitsa, Goge Mangov's mother, and others came to tell Dedo what they saw.

Now Dedo looked at me very hard.

"Where is your father?" Oops, I had forgotten to give him Father's message. So I told him. "Did he get Tome?"

"He didn't say. I don't think so." Then I told Dedo about the letter.

He became so upset, so very upset, he started cursing. "Oh, those shits. What am I going to do with your father? He has gotten himself involved with those crazies . . . !" Dedo turned around, still cursing to himself and headed for the *livada.* I followed him, just in case. "He doesn't mind his own business, "but he flits here and there involved in crazy things. He has gotten himself involved with crazy people!" There was nothing I could say to him.

We went to get the mule and brought her into the *kaliva*. Dedo prepared something to eat and we ate silently. Later, Father showed up as I was sleeping. I had left Dedo sitting there. When he saw Father coming in the door, he began to ream him out. That's what woke me. As I listened they were going at it hot and heavy, but eventually, still arguing, the voices seemed a little calmer.

I listened more carefully. "Petre's son was killed today in the yard."

I remembered, then, that earlier in the day, I knew something terrible had happened as I was on my mission to Lerin. The cries and shouts coming from the little T'rsianska hamlet as I was passing by must have been just at the time when Tsile, Petre's son was killed. It was the shells. Tsile was their target. Why?

Dedo was telling Father that Doneitsa Mangova came to the house earlier to check on how I, Sotir, was doing. She was afraid that I might have been killed or wounded too. She knew that I had been caught in the shooting between the Partizani and the Germans. Had I survived? Of course! When she saw that I indeed survived, Dedo told Father that Doneitsa furiously scolded him. "How could you, with your brain, send a little boy in these times . . . poor Petre!"

After Dedo had said what he had to say to Father, Father tried to explain to Dedo what happened. Dedo was in no frame of mind to listen to anything he had to say. "Quiet! No more of this. Why have you become so involved in these things? It isn't as if you don't have enough to do here. You are all going to gain zero. Nothing! Don't waste your time . . . " Father cut him off.

"Enough, Father. Stop. I take care of my responsibilities and you know it. Don't worry," Father tried to reassure Dedo, "I will continue to do everything that needs to be done, and on time. You know that very well. You don't have to worry about anything." With that exchange, Father walked out the door.

Dedo came over to where I was sleeping to cover me up and found that I was awake. "You *surtuk,* rascal! Aren't you asleep?"

"How can I sleep with you two making all that noise? Why were you arguing?"

"We were not arguing. But we don't understand each other, either. Now go on, sleep. You're still very young. These matters are not for you."

He lay down beside me, and in a few minutes he was snoring away. I don't know where Father went, but with Dedo next to me, I felt better and soon I fell asleep.

In the morning, I saw that they were both working in the fields. I joined them with a "*Dobro utro*, Good morning." They had been talking about Tome. They had promised three heads of sheep to someone, but had not heard from him yet, whoever "him" was.

Dedo said, "You know, I'll take Sotiraki with me. We'll go down to see what the situation is and how soon we can get our horse back." Great! Father nodded in agreement. Dedo and I walked toward the school grounds where they kept Tome. The school itself had a large yard fronted by stone walls about 4 to 5 feet high. Black iron gates leading into the school were closed.

I ran up the road toward the gates calling, "Tome. Tome." Nothing. No whinny of recognition. A guard came up to me and said something, which of course, I didn't understand. Then he gestured, indicating he wanted me to get going, to get out of there. Eventually, and very reluctantly, I did.

Turning around to walk down the road, I heard a horse coming from the main road. It was Tome! There he was with a saddle on his back, his tail cut short, and his *griba*, the hair on top of his neck, trimmed short. A man in uniform sat on top of my Tome.

Just as I was running to catch up with Tome, another rider joined the men. "That's my Tome. Give me my horse," I demanded with all the strength I could muster in my voice. They looked at me, saying something to each other, which I could not understand, and urged their horses forward. One of the two took out a whistle and blew it several times. Immediately I was surrounded by soldiers, they were all around me. They chased me away without hitting or dragging me. They just steered me away from the officers.

Meanwhile, I could see Tome was acting very unsettled. He was spooking and snorting. The officer decided to get off Tome, so I returned to the school to find Dedo. I found Dedo talking to Dr. Agitase. Later on I learned that Dedo was recruiting him to help us get Tome back. It was then that I heard the name Kalchev for the second time.

Rumor had it that this Kalchev, the Bulgarian, was well respected by the Germans. Whatever the details of the negotiations were for Tome, it went on for several weeks.

During those weeks I went to see Tome every chance I could and talked to him, reassuring him that he was going to come back home.

Ilo had finally arrived from T'rsie, which made me very glad because he could join me in visiting with Tome. We went to the gates almost immediately and called to Tome. He would come trotting. Not even the guard could stop him, but they did keep the gates closed. All we could do was stroke his head as we spoke to him until we were chased away.

Now there were two of us feeling really bad. It hurt to see Tome locked up. He was so used to roaming around, free, playing, having fun. Now he was in prison and I couldn't stand it. To be locked up? Unthinkable! I just had to do something to free him, but what?

We visited Dedo Ilo, my Dedo's youngest brother. He always had some kind of treat on hand for us kids, and he always asked about Tome. I really liked Dedo Ilo because he always had a story to tell about his youth or how wild he was, his experiences as a *komita*, guerilla, or how he lost one of his legs up to the knee. He also had a son named Sotir.

On this particular day, as he was telling us one of his stories, the word *grabi* popped out at me. *Grabi* means to take. I blinked several times. That was it! Dedo Ilo gave me the idea. I was going to take back my own horse. How? Well, I would find a way, because there had to be one. I talked to myself, "Think, stupid. Think!"

Now, my gang and I had developed some skills in "grabbing" things, like apples or tomatoes from a neighbor's garden. You know what I mean? But grabbing gates? That would be a problem. Dedo Ilo was still story-telling, but my mind was elsewhere. I had even stopped munching on my *felka,* the slice of bread that Baba had given me.

Dedo Ilo whistled at me a couple of times, and I snapped out of my thoughts. I looked at him, and with a knowing look, and said, "I know how, Dedo."

"Let me hear what you are thinking."

"You know, we see these big *kamioni*, these trucks, going in and out of the gates. I can get under one of them somehow, go in with the truck, hop on Tome and ride out of there while the other *kamioni* are moving through." Brilliant of me, I thought and I looked for approval.

"That's not a good idea. You're going to be smashed by one of them because there are a lot of holes and ruts in the road. No. No."

I refused to let Dedo Ilo discourage me. "You know what? When the *kamioni* are entering and leaving, I will signal Tome to come to the gates. We just have to time it. They don't have Tome tied down, you know."

I didn't need anyone's approval. Ilo and I thanked Baba and Dedo, and we left. We spied on the movements of the *kamioni* for a couple of days. Here we were, Ilo and I, about 7 or 8 years old, planning, scheming, strategizing the rescue of Tome as if it were a real war campaign.

Tome's routine involved being washed and scrubbed down with a *chetka*, a brush, before he was put through exercises by walking around the yard. They fed him over on the far side of the gate. The plan was perfect. We went home to tell the family of my plan. Father had just left for T'rsie and Dedo was there by himself. Looking for his whole- hearted support, we revealed our well-thought-out plan.

When we finished, we looked at him expectantly. But, he strongly objected and ordered us not to go to see Tome anymore. He reassured us that he was going to get Tome back, but we just had to be a little more patient. He also revealed that he had paid off some people to get him out.

I exploded, "*Iaitsa*! Those people just take your money and don't do a thing. They don't care about Tome." I was awfully disappointed in Dedo, and I used an inappropriate manner toward him. *Iatisa* can mean eggs, but in the manner in which I used the word, it really had a nasty meaning, probably something like "balls."

"Watch your mouth or I'll stuff you with hot pepper."

I shut up and ran out toward the river. To pass the time, I started throwing stones into the water. Shortly, Ilo joined me. He suggested we go across the river and into the Kondopoulo orchard and just hang out. We didn't give any thought to the security guard there. So off we went, through the orchard, to Ilo's Aunt Gina's house and stayed there awhile. After that, with time still pretty heavy on our hands, we walked over to the main road, passing under the Nikokiriko School by St. Nicholas Church, turned left and headed home across the river.

We were halfway toward the river when we heard the whinnying of a horse, coming from the main road. Without turning around I said to Ilo, "That's Tome. I know it's Tome!" It was. We looked to see two German officers going through the orchard on horseback. A couple of miles in length, the orchard had a small path down its middle. The two officers were cantering slowly, with about 50 horsemen behind them. I guessed that they were all guards.

I said to Ilo in whispers, "Let's wait by the crossroad. They'll go through there." Ilo looked a little skeptical, but he didn't really object, so we waited there. When they came abreast of us, one of the horsemen pulled up and stopped to speak to the riders behind him. They came close to where we were sitting on top of the cement canal wall. Tome couldn't contain himself. He was as happy to see us, as we were to see him. He started to act up restlessly.

The officer gave the reins to another soldier to hold Tome down and try to quiet him. They just couldn't. I ran up to Tome, grabbed his head and put it alongside my face. He calmed down. There were no more problems as we nuzzled each other. The soldiers started talking among themselves as they watched us, pointing. We couldn't understand what they were saying to each other. Finally, the officer took another horse to ride, and Tome was to be led back to the yard by one of the soldiers.

It wasn't easy to lead Tome, but somehow the soldier managed and we watched them disappear into the orchard. My mind was made up. Nobody was going to stop me. I was going to take Tome back and I wouldn't think of the consequences. He was my Tome. I told Ilo and he agreed with me. We SHOULD take Tome.

So we headed back to our *kaliva*, which really is half house, half barn, where Dedo was. "I needed you two. Where were you? Where did you disappear to?"

"Oh, here, there, everywhere." Then I told him how we stopped to visit Dedo Ilo and Aunt Gina and the rest of it.

Dedo said nothing, but he gave me a look.

The next morning Dedo took us into Lerin and told us to meet him by Vasil Kirev's Bakery. He didn't mention any particular time, but just that we were to meet him there. Well, Ilo and I knew what we were going to do, and headed for the school, arriving in perfect time. There was a big convoy coming down the *dzade*, the paved highway leading to Bigla, Prespa and Kostur. I looked at Ilo. He looked at me.

We were off like a shot. Sometimes life can be absolutely perfect. This was one of those times. Trucks were driving in and out. It was a moment out of my dreams. There was a lapse between arrivals and departures because trucks were being unloaded. We had to spot Tome to be certain he was not being guarded, so Ilo sneaked in and found him. I was crouched on the top of the wall by the gate.

Ilo came around the back of the side wall. He whispered to me, "Call Tome. He is free, but there are a lot of trucks around there." I called Tome's name several times. He heard me instantly, found his way around the trucks and came trotting to me. The soldiers were very busy working, hauling stuff, walking and crossing all over the place. They had no time to observe a horse. While Tome stood at the gate no one seemed to notice. Caring about a horse was the last thing on those soldiers' minds.

Reassured, when Tome was close enough, I jumped on top of him. He just sprinted off, down the main street. We rode about two blocks toward our *kaliva*. That's when we heard the whistles.

The air was filled with the sound of whistles. The guards were being alerted. An officer's horse was galloping away. Stolen? No way! Ilo ran towards the bakery where he was supposed to meet Dedo. Urgently, Ilo said to me, "Don't stop anywhere. Go straight home."

Tome and I practically flew like the wind together. Tome, my joyous companion and I, together again. We were like the *T'rsianska* wind, the winds of T'rsie, and we were flying home!"

We galloped through the Turkish section, hoping no one saw us. We passed Pelopida's Café up the road and took the T'rsianska Mala road, past the Dulio, across the creek and past our *kaliva*. Then we galloped along the river toward Moteshnitsa and Armensko, left to Yanina Livada to Sveta Bogoroditsa Church. There we stopped to refresh ourselves with water and trotted upwards through Garishche.

We were in heaven, Tome and I, seventh heaven. We were free at last to take to the wind, to frolic at will, to trot contentedly. We were home at last. We played our game of running and stopping. I would pretend to be tired, which was his signal to get behind me and just nudge me with his head. With that he went ahead and huffed and puffed. Shaking his head from side to side, he bared his teeth and whinnied.

After a while, I lay down on the ground knowing he would come back and make as if he were going to bite my ear. He never had bitten me before and he didn't this time either, but he did pull. He knew I would get up. I looked about to see if anyone was around. No one! We were too far from Lerin. We had passed Plochite, Derveno, and then Machoets, very familiar land. This was where we grazed our cattle almost every other day, every year. This was the road Tome and I had raced all the time.

Once again, I swung around under Tome's neck and wound my legs around that beautiful neck. I put my face against his, and rode upside down. Did I say heaven? You betcha! We're going home! We're going home, Tome! Tome! Tome! Oh yeah! I pressed my face against his neck harder. We reached V'ro, where you can see T'rsie. From this point a traveler. One can go down towards Kofkamen and Fashite, then Lenishche, Trite, Buki, Stranata, Leika, Skurkata and, ta-da! You are home, if T'rsie was your home.

We were home. I wish you could have seen Tome when we reached V'ro. He reared up on his hind legs, front legs pawing the sky, and just pranced. He ran up and down, whinnying with joy. To me, he was singing and dancing, singing from the heart and dancing with happiness.

Baba was the only one there when Tome and I trotted in. She had come out for something, unaware that we were there. When Tome saw her, he trotted over to her, to play, grabbing at her hair covered by her *shamija*. He played at biting at her hands and she laughed. She, too, was happy to see him.

"Oh, Baba's little Tomche. What you have gone through! Now that you're home, everything will be all right." She kept saying these words to Tome, just to be talking to him, and he kept nodding, going around her. I couldn't take it anymore.

"Baba, I'm here too!"

"Oh, you're Baba's little boy. You rescued our little pony. Oh, how wonderful," she said, hugging me happily. Nothing can compare to loving hugs from a beloved Baba.

I walked toward the house and went directly to the *noshvi,* she shelves where she kept fresh baked bread. I was so hungry that I couldn't wait for anybody or anything. I grabbed half a loaf and went outdoors. Baba and Tome were still there, talking and nuzzling each other. Tome finally came over to me and took a huge bite of the bread in my hands.

"There's cheese in the *grne*, the pot, Sote." I didn't need any cheese. I had everything I wanted in the whole world. Tome and I finished that loaf in no time at all.

Evening was beginning to close in, and everyone was coming in from the fields or from wherever they had worked that day. Father and Mother came in from Staro T'rsie, at the most beautiful time of day, early evening. As they reached the house, Tome ran out of the *avlia,* stall, to greet them. You should have seen the pleased looks on my parents' faces. It made me doubly happy. I had done a good thing for once, I thought.

"See, you kids were worrying over nothing," Father said. I couldn't believe it. He thought that the money he had paid someone and the three sheep's heads that Dedo offered had brought Tome back to us.

When I heard what he said, I boasted loudly, "Yeah, they took your money and sheep for nothing. It was Ilo and me that brought him home today."

Astonished, Father asked, "How did you do that and where was Dedo? Didn't the Germans come after you?"

"I left Ilo and Dedo in Lerin. I don't know anything more, because Tome and I didn't look back or stop to ask!" I felt so smug, so pleased with myself.

Father looked at Mother and Baba and told them that he was going to go to Lerin the next day to look into the matter. Before the evening was over, all the Nitchovs had come over, even some of the neighbors to hear about Tome and me.

Two days later, Ilo and Dedo came home. Dedo started looking for me as soon as he arrived, but I was with my gangsters going over my exploits. By late afternoon I showed up at the house.

As soon as he saw me, the first words out of Dedo's mouth were, "*Bre Surtuk*!!" Whenever Dedo began anything with those words, I knew that he was upset. No he was furious, and that I would be in for it. I knew his moods and habits so well, that I was always prepared for him, especially when the words, *bre surtuk,* you rascal, were uttered!

"Bre *surtuk*! Come here and sit," he thundered at me. We were both very close to the manure pile. At the same moment Uncle Done arrived, finally finished with his chores. He came over to me smiling and started to congratulate me for bringing Tome home.

By this time Dedo could barely contain himself; he was ready to lay into me. When I sensed that, I grabbed a wooden chair to bring to him so that he could sit more comfortably.

With nothing but love and concern for his well- being, and comfort oozing out of me, I said to him, "Here, Dedo, make yourself comfortable and sit down. Since we're going to be here for awhile, maybe I should bring you a glass of wine?" I knew he liked to drink a little wine before meals.

"Sit down and shut up. Don't give me this baloney," he snapped at me.

"Okay, okay. I just want you to be relaxed. I'm expressing my respect. Isn't that what you always preach to us?"

Still trying to jolly him up, I spoke, "Oh, Dedo, how fearful you are. Here, you can see I brought Tome home and nothing..."

"You have a wooden head. Don't you understand anything that I am saying to you?"

"Yes, I do understand. But there's nothing to worry about."

Uncle Done piped in. "Father, leave the boy alone. He did good. He was able to do what neither you or I could. Someone played us for chumps, that's all."

"Oh, fine! And what if they had killed the boys, what would you have said to that?"

"Father, haven't you . . . " The sentence went unfinished as Dedo exploded higher than a kite.

He shouted at Uncle Done. "You should be ashamed of yourself for talking like that. It is a shame that a grown man talks like a kid. You don't understand anything either. Shame on you."

But Uncle had left the house without even hearing what was coming out of Dedo's mouth. I had to speak. "Dedo, forgive me. I won't do that again. I just couldn't help it. Don't get mad."

"Sotiraki, you were there the other day when your Uncle Petre's son was killed." Tears were filling his eyes. Just then it dawned on me that Dedo had a deep fear that we would all be killed. He was terribly worried. He knew what wars were all about. I certainly had no idea, but I felt I was beginning to learn. To this point, war seemed to me a kind of game, uniforms, guns, marches, bombs blowing up, because my life went on almost as usual. I had no clue of the dangers lurking all around us in this most dangerous of times and places.

Dedo calmed himself a little, and he motioned to go toward the house where Baba had set the *sofra*, the table. We were having Baba's delicious *manja*, a stew. As we ate, Dedo still couldn't take his mind off the Tome rescue.

"Sotiraki, weren't you afraid?"

"In a way, yes, but . . . "

Ilo or Stefo, or maybe Risto interrupted me to assure Dedo that no way was I afraid of anything. They made cracks like: "Dedo, even the devil runs from Sotir." Or, "He doesn't know the meaning of fear, of shame." Or, "He's a dope. He understands nothing." Or, the best one, "Sote and the devil are brothers."

As they wisecracked, they laughed at their own wit. I just listened, commenting only once, "One of these days, you will get yours. Just wait and see; I'll get even." On that note, Dedo immediately stopped the exchanges with a sharp voice. "Enough. No more."

And that was it. Everybody shut up. There was no more conversation on that subject or any other subject that evening. I was content to keep on smiling. For you see, Tome, my joyous companion, and I were together again. I think only Tome could understand my feeling of enormous triumph and satisfaction.

Death Does Not Blow a Trumpet

Death does not blow a trumpet

DANISH PROVERB

Tome died of a poisonous snake bite.

It was a very hot summer day. We were grazing our herd at Machoets, between Derveno and V'ro, above the village of Neret. When we were together, Tome was always very playful. On this afternoon, however, Tome did not seem to be himself. He just stood where I had left him, even though he usually liked to be around me. This was strange behavior for him. What was wrong?

I walked over to him and started talking to him, to my buddy, to my heart's companion. As I talked to him, he looked at me, and then rolled his eyes.

Why hadn't I noticed this before?

Why hadn't I checked him out right away? If I had, maybe I would have spotted what the problem was.

Why didn't I do that?

What was the matter with me?

I thought maybe he just needed a run, just the two of us, flying into the wind, as we loved to do, my legs entwined around his neck and my face under his where I could breathe into his nose if I wanted. I mounted him, and positioned myself. He wouldn't move. I tried patting him again as I talked.

This painting by his late brother-in-law, Paul Christou, shows Sotir's joyous companion, Tome, racing against the wind.

I nuzzled against him, my face against his . . . and there it was. I discovered the problem—a swelling on the right side of his head. As I looked closely, I could see that his skin had been punctured. Immediately I pulled out the little knife that I always carried and made a cut in the puncture. I tried to suck out the poison. I sucked as hard as I could, thinking this would help him. But Tome started to sweat. I knew I had to get him home. With a little prodding, we reached the front of our *plemna.* Quietly, Tome collapsed and stretched out on the ground.

I yelled out for Father. Whatever he had been doing, he stopped and came over to us. He saw the problem right away and sent a couple of the kids to get some help from some of the villagers who had experience treating snake bites. They tried everything to help Tome, but nothing seemed to work.

I went numb. All I could see was my beautiful Tome, stretched out on the ground. My Tome, who was normally so full of life and joy and energy, now on the ground, unmoving. I stretched out next to him and wrapped my arms around him for the rest of the evening. Just as the sun had finally set, Tome raised his head, turned to look at me, as I lay there clinging to him. He had not made a single sound, not a whimper or a whinny. He just looked at me and died. Just like that.

Tears still fill my eyes whenever I think of that moment, that last . . . final look Tome gave me as if to say, "I have to go now, buddy. I have to leave you."

I couldn't let him go.

How could I let him go?

Tome!

Tome!

1944

Revolt and terror pay a price. Order and law have a cost.

CARL SANDBURG, 1936

Chaos reigned in Greece despite radio appeals for unity by the Greek king from Cairo, Egypt, and from Moscow. Infighting within and among the various guerilla bands was brutal as each vied for power and control over regions.

By early spring, the threat to ELAS by rival guerilla bands such as PEEA, EDES, EKKA, and SNOF, grew. Serious dissension erupted with the KKE. Several factions with the KKE were at odds: those favoring violence; those favoring infiltration; and those favoring strict adherence to the Moscow party line. Fear also arose within the KKE that British authorities would declare war on EAM/ELAS.

British recognition of the status and leadership power of a guerilla band would ensure the band arms, ammunition, gold and eventual control over all of Greece.

Assuming that the USSR was an ally, the British prodded them to send a mission to Greece. ELAS expected to receive gold, arms and ammunition from the Soviet mission. The Soviets expected to find an army equal to Tito's Partisans. Both were disappointed.

Next door to Greece and Macedonia the civil war in Albania had fully erupted. The covert policy of the USSR was reflected in its support of the Albanian Communist guerillas; in the repudiation of the exiled Serbian king, and in the appearance of Bulgarian Communist guerillas in eastern Macedonia and Thrace as the Fatherland Front took over the Bulgarian government.

From August through October, Colonel Zervas' guerilla fighters were considered resistance fighters against the Germans.

The AMM assumed the role of the BMM during this period. By October, the AMM handed over a relatively intact Greece to the Greek people with the caveat that Greece was to settle its own future under a unanimously recognized government, and that the help of the Allies was to be unanimously welcomed.

Instead, the Greek government policy again deteriorated into revolutionary violence between EAM/ELAS and the Anglo-Greek authorities without any trace of intervention.

By the end of October, most of the Balkans had been liberated from the Germans.

January:

- King George of Greece and Moscow Radio appealed for unity in Greece.
- The Soviets informed the Greek ambassador in Moscow of their support for united Greek guerillas.
- A Greek royal decree deprived collaborating Greek guerillas of Greek membership.

February:

- A truce among EAM/ELAS and EKKA was reached at Plaka Bridge.
- KKE and EAM were recognized as one organization.

March:

- PEEA, with Bakaridis and Ivolos, set itself up in the mountains to raise the quality of the resistance movement.
- The Soviet press acclaimed PEEA. PEEA and the Greek government agreed to the formation of a new government, representative of all opinions.

April:

- Bulgarian Communist guerillas appeared in Eastern Macedonia and Thrace.
- Bulgarian troops occupied Lerin (*Florina*), Kostur, (*Kastoria*), and Voden (*Edessa*).
- The Red Army reached the borders of Romania.
- The Greek king declared the next Greek regime to be determined by free elections after the liberation of Crete.
- EAM and EDES confronted each other.
- ELAS attacked EKKA, murdered its leaders and scattered EKKA, practically annihilating the band. The Koutsania Conference clarified the extent of the KKE menace.

May–July:

- Britain sought discussion with the Soviet Union on the danger of their divergence of policy toward Greece. The Soviets rejected, on the basis that whatever was happening in Greece was entirely a Greek matter.
- EAM/ELAS was denounced before the representatives of PEEA, EAM, ELAS, and the KKE at the Conference of Lebanon. Delegates agreed to a coalition within a government under Papandreou.
- The KKE repudiated the Lebanon Charter and the coalition within the Papandreou government. Internal dissension erupted in the KKE.

- PEEA and EAM demanded the resignation of Papandreou.
- Belgrad was liberated with the arrival of the Red Army and Tito.
- The Casserta Agreement signed by Generals Zervas and Saraphis placed their forces under the Greek government.
- Albania was liberated as Hoxha arrived in Tirana.

August:

- Yugoslav Macedonia became an officially federated state: The Peoples Republic of Macedonia.

September:

- SNOF pressed for pure Slav Macedonian Partisan bands independent of ELAS.
- KKE officially proclaimed Macedonia an inseparable part of Greece.
- Papandreou supported appointment of British General Scobie as Chief of Allied Forces in Greece.
- Communists agreed to the formation of the Gotsev Macedonia Battalion under ELAS leadership.
- SNOF negotiated to incorporate OHRANA.
- Greek Supreme Commander Serafis ordered the 9th ELAS Division to attack the Gotsev Battalion. The KKE committee of Lerin (*Florina*) vetoed the attack. Markos helped Gotsev cross the Greek/Yugoslav border.
- Germans left Bulgaria. The USSR declared war on Bulgaria. Bulgaria then declared war on Germany.

October:

- ELAS instructed Markos, Kikitsas and Bakirjis not to enter Salonica *(Solun)*. The instructions were ignored.
- EAM informed a small British Commando band of parachuters in Chalcidice that their help was not needed and that Salonica was in the hands of the Partisans.
- SNOF leaders met with KKE regional bureau for Macedonia to discuss terms for joining the liberation struggle of EAM; the inclusion of pure Macedonian units; the establishment of the Macedonian Liberation Front; the placement of Macedonians in administrative posts in Macedonian towns and villages; and an end to the persecution of the Macedonians.
- EAM turned down SNOF demands.
- SNOF reverted to TEMPO's command.
- British and guerilla troops entered Patras in October; Athens a week later; Salonica by the end of the month.

November:

- German troops began their retreat, and most of Greece was left in the hands of EAM/ELAS.

December:

- British authorities demanded all *andartes* and guerilla bands to disband and hand over their weapons.

A Message from Leon

Whatever God has brought about is to be borne with courage.

SOPHOCLES, 401 B.C.

By this time, up to about 20 of the younger men from our village had left to join the *Partizani.* My 15-year old cousin, Goge, went with them. The first girl to become a *Partizanka* was 15-year old Sofa Palachova. It was about this time, I think, that for the first time I heard the words *Vardarska Makedonia.* I wondered if *Vardarska Makedonia* was just beyond Kalugeritsa.

It had to be summer that day. I remember it so well, but I can't remember the month. Father was working on a farm beyond our village. I was doodling around the house when I heard my aunt, the one we called *Nevestata,* the bride,who was Kotse's wife. I ran to her and could see that she was crying.

"Sote, Sote, go tell your father. The Partizani were here!" she was sobbing so terribly.

I took off in a flash and ran all the way to a place called Chestakot, about a half hour from our home to find Father. He saw me running over the hill and immediately let go of the oxen. He ran to meet me by the river. He knew. He knew something serious had happened.

"*Shto ima?* What's up? Anything wrong?"

Breathless from running so fast, I blurted, "Kotse. It's about Kotse and the *Partizani*. Strina told me to tell you."

"Which way did they go?"

"Toward Turie. I heard someone say something about Vicho."

In just seconds, Father set his priorities in order.

"Listen, Sote. Let the oxen and the horse graze for a while and then bring them in later. Tell them at home that I might be late getting back. Very late", and with that he took off on foot in the direction of Turie.

When I came back home, everyone was upset, Baba, Mama, all the aunts, crying and wailing as if everything was lost. Neighbors and friends gathered at the house. Everyone tried their best to put a positive spin on the situation, but the concern and sadness enveloped everybody. That's when I learned that some of the men had joined the Partizans voluntarily, but others had been tricked into joining.

It was at that moment that I recalled a man named Petre, originally from the village of Oschima, who had married my Strina Kolitsa's niece. Petre became one of the chief recruiters for the Partizans. He had come to our house many times, of course, as a relative, but he also came with his two friends, Naso and Kole, to discuss with Father the *Partizanstvoto*, the Macedonian Partizan movement. Kole, Petre's friend had given many speeches in the village, prior to all tricks they played to get the young men to join the Movement.

On one occasion the three of them revealed their true mission. They happened to be present at a wedding celebration. As they were dancing the *oro*, our line dance, *sred selo* the villagers saw the guns that they had under their coats. *Shpioni,* spies or informers, and we had some in our village, passed on the information to the authorities. By the next day soldiers came into the village looking for them. Everyone was suspect, but the soldiers couldn't find the three they were looking for. That was bad news.

Although some of the men would be able to return, many more of them returned home wounded in body and spirit. Many would not return at all.

For the first time I began to see deep, tragic lines etched in my Father's face. Dedo and the other uncles, all strong men, were grief-stricken, sobbing the way our grown men do. I didn't quite understand what was happening yet.

It was Father who had to be the one to break the news to my aunt and the family. He had learned what had happened after he left me with the oxen. It was about Kotse.

Father and Kotse had been almost inseparable. Although there was a 7-year difference in age, and they were uncle and nephew, they were actually closer than brothers. Kotse's father, Kole, my father's brother, had left for Australia in the l930s, leaving my Aunt Kolitsa with three children. Married Macedonian women are known by their husband's name for the rest of their lives. Kole, which is short for Nikola, was Striko's, uncle's, name. Therefore Strina is addressed as Kolitsa. Dedo and Striko Kole had a serious falling out over Dedo's perceived harsh treatment of Baba. After Striko Kole left, Father and Striko Done assumed responsibility for his family.

Eventually Dedo's attitude toward Kole softened. He decided to send Kotse to the village of Neret, a couple of donkey hours from our village, to learn the tailoring trade, so that he could become a terzia, a tailor.

On the very day that we heard about Kotse, my cousin Dina's husband had returned. Both cousin Ilo and I ran to greet him. We hugged him and clung to him for a few moments, and then we ran to my aunt's house to join them in the happy reunion. We did not know what else to do, so happy were we to see him, alive.

But Kotse. Oh, Kotse. He had only been with the Partizans for such a short time!

Kotse's son was born after he had left. Cousins Ilo, Risto and I used to take the baby, nestled in its homemade cradle, outdoors. We played different games with him and kept him occupied much of the time.

Kotse had a dog he had named Leon. Baba never like Leon, but it was Leon who

Strina Kolitsa (Aunt Velika) Nitchov, her children Lena, Nase, Kotse, and Kotse's beloved, faithful dog, Leon, circa 1938–39.

tried to communicate an ominous message. Leon had begun to whine for a period of a month and a half, always facing northwest. He kept it up to the point that Baba had started to mutter that something bad was going to happen. She said that she could feel something was not right. I guess all animals have a way of communicating with us, if we only take the time to try to understand. Baba was right on track.

When Father got details about Kotse's death, we understood that Leon was the first to know that Kotse had died, for it was at that time that Leon, facing the northwest, had begun to whine. Kotse was killed northwest of our village.

He never lived to see his son grow into manhood. Kotse's death left a stone on each of our hearts, which we all carry to this day.

Sowing and Reaping Among the Innocent

Ignorance of the world leaves one at the mercy of malice.

WM. HAZLITT, 1821-22

Surely there can be no doubt that the seeds for continued war were sown by the occupation of Macedonia. There were so many, so deviously tantalizing and conflicting ideas, hopes and promises dangled before our eyes that they were bound to enfold us in the most bloody, unimaginable, unforeseen consequences for all of Macedonia.

But first, let me tell you about the end of the German presence. I remember vividly the sights and sounds of planes buzzing, diving at, and strafing the German convoys heading in a westerly direction from Lerin toward Prespa, Mala Bigla, Bela Voda and Bigla itself. That day my cousins and I were grazing oxen in Badoma and Ramni V'r, when we first heard the planes and then saw them.

We left the oxen to their task and ran to the top of Ramni V'r to see what was happening. The planes came up from the vicinity of Statisa, soared up and over Ramni V'r, and then dived over the village of Armensko.

These were not Greek planes. The planes fired at the convoy and then disappeared only to return and sweep over the area again. We could even hear the rat-a-tat-tat-tat of the guns. The grown-ups called the planes *Tito's Shtukas*. It was absolutely exciting to watch all the action. From where we were on the hill, as the planes began their swoop,

I swear I could see the masked faces of the men in the planes. At least they looked like they were wearing masks.

They flew over our high mountains, and then they would come down through the low, deep valleys, which were flanked by *preseki*, hills on either side of the valleys. There were lowlands throughout. We couldn't believe how much damage those planes could do.

We saw trucks burning and the Germans running. Some of the Germans were able to hit the ground, while others fell on the spot, dead or wounded. Can you imagine that we were eyewitnesses to the routing of the mighty Germans?

After a series of actions like that one, I remember that the Partizans became more visible in greater numbers in the villages as well as the mountains. They were moving about more freely. We did see a few Greeks among the Partizans. These Greeks were from the families who were part of the population exchanges between the Greeks and the Turks. We all knew there were some Vlachs in the movement. Vlachs were Macedonians of Romanian descent.

All kinds of rumors were making the rounds. One of those was that the Greeks in the leadership of the Partizan movement worked for British and Greek intelligence. Regardless of rumors, in spite of the shooting and killing, our life as we knew it had to go on.

The days and months were still filled with the necessary chores that the seasons demanded be done. Fields still had to be plowed, seeds sown, harvests collected. Animals were still being born as some were dying, and their needs had to be met.

There seemed to be a more hopeful attitude and confidence re-emerging among the grown-ups. Confidence sprung from the greater presence of the Partizani. The Partizani were at last going to accomplish great things for the Macedonians. Boys and men and young women, too, were eager to join them.

"We're going to be free! We are going to have a free, united Macedonia," "We're going to have our own schools. We will be able to speak our language!" The young adults openly expressed their views and confidence that a free and united Macedonia was at hand.

The elders were hopeful, too, but they had lived a lifetime of hopes, hopes that remained unfulfilled. They urged caution. It was such an impossible dream.

There were those Macedonians in quasi-leadership positions as well as in the ranks of the Partizani who knew better than we did how real the Greek threat was to us. In spite of the warnings against trusting Greek leadership, the determination and the will to achieve freedom, unity, independence, vibrated in our voices and shone like a light from our eyes. If the energy of the young and the belief in the righteousness of our cause could be the decisive factor, we would achieve our goals for a free, united, independent Macedonia.

And then all hell broke loose again. The Greek Royal Air Force had come to life and began to bomb villages, civilians, and livestock—anything that moved. Again we saw people arrested and jailed without trials. We heard of executions and hangings and beheadings.

Today, I am a middle-aged man, but I can still see fields strewn with maimed and dead horses and livestock. These wounded animals, sheep, goats, oxen, bulls, cows, horses, donkeys or mules had to be put out of their misery by the very people who owned them. No human could bear that sound—of animals moaning or crying out in pain. They were so helpless.

Most people cared for their own animals and treated them as family. The possibility of disease spreading and polluting the earth and the streams was a genuine concern. But at the time—I was a boy of about 10, then—I still could not understand why anyone had to kill the animals. How could anyone be so cruel? We lost 300 sheep at Dreno, near the boundary of *Gorna Statitsa*, upper Statitsa. We had to move our remaining livestock to Prespa for safety.

Many times civilians and children alike would get trapped in the fighting between the Partizani and the Greek Royalists. No one knew when or where the fierce battles would break out. No more outdoor cook-outs, because the Greeks took it as a signal that the Partizani were around. All cooking had to be done indoors. Well, now, war or no war, that took away some of joy of the outdoors as far as we mindless gangsters were concerned.

Don't worry. We quickly worked out a strategy to outfox the Greeks. This is what we did. My gangsters and I built three or four fires in different places, about a half-mile apart. Using more instinct than smarts, we would select the one place where we felt it was safe to do our cooking or roasting.

The strategy worked occasionally, and as you can imagine, we didn't heed the constant warnings from our families. They kept telling us that we were only encouraging the Greeks to shoot us more. When we were scolded, we listened with the most serious, solemn, and attentive expressions on our faces. It was hard to stop us, because we saw ourselves as merely playing a game, not too different from playing hide-and-seek, don't you see?

Whenever the Partizani evacuated our villages and our surrounding mountains, the Greek *andartes* or *burandari*, would seize the opportunity to sneak in and surround the village. On one awful yet vivid day, the burandari summoned all of the old remaining men, some of the women and children into the middle of the village. They decided they were going to make an example of these hapless people, so that the rest of the villagers could see what happens to if you harbor Partizani and don't inform on them.

Using rifle butts, black whips, and wooden sticks as their weapons, these brave, heroic, bastard "*special forces*" beat the living daylights out of old frail bodies. These *kesagee*, vengeful animals, these cut-throat bullies particularly enjoyed the sport of hitting their victims with all the strength they possessed, until the screaming and howls of pain deafened everyone.

These sadistic Greek military police from Konomladi and Neret, and the burandari who did their dirty, cowardly work got a special thrill when they kicked their victims sprawled on the ground. No one dared to move or help those poor souls because if they did, they were as good as dead.

As the beating was taking place in the village, a few of us kids were caught outside the village by the river Leika. I knew I was in for it. One of those bastards began to ask me questions about my father. How could they know I was Mite's son? I thought. There was no way I was going to give them any information. Besides, I didn't know the Greek language. Dedo himself couldn't speak Greek except for the few words he needed to get by.

I did know that *ne* in Greek means *yes*. In our language, *ne* means no. Because of this confusion in the meaning of the word and my attitude, I was whipped. I didn't cry. No matter how much I was beaten I wouldn't give them the satisfaction of crying. The asshole with the whip became angrier and whipped me harder. I wouldn't give in.

As it happened, Dedo Traiche happened to come along on his way back from Kalugeritsa and he stopped. He walked over to the one who held the whip, and explained to him that I didn't understand the difference in the meanings of certain words. He also told them that I never cry. I told those guys that even if they cut my balls off, I wouldn't cry. That was a big mistake. I still have some of the scars because I couldn't keep my mouth shut.

We told Dedo Traiche, not to go beyond the *plemni*, the barns, because he would be seen and beaten. He could hear the terrible cries coming from Stranata, across the village. He had no idea what was going on.

Having finished teaching their object lesson to the villagers, the "pride of Greece"—to me they were one more example of the "shame of Greece"—left the village laughing, arrogant, and proud, as if they had just won a great moral Greek victory by mercilessly beating the helpless old and the defenseless young Macedonians. They were teaching us stupid, miserable Macedonians, young and old, how great their military power was, how glorious their cause in support of their magnificent *Elada*.

Tell me, could you forget such a scene? Could you forgive such a people or a country? This scene and hundreds like it will never be forgotten. Each generation will hear, and shed their tears of frustration over such oppression and brutality. It will not be forgotten! After the "pride of Greece" left our wretched wounded lying helplessly in the middle of the village, the women who had managed to remain hidden, came out to carry the victims to their homes, where they remained bedridden for weeks and months, trying to heal.

No doctors, no nurses or medicine were available for them. Nothing except the love and care of the people, using whatever home remedies they had. I watched as the old Babas salted sheepskins and wrapped the bodies of the wounded to help them heal.

Some recovered eventually. Some were maimed and crippled for the rest of their short lives. Some died from the pain and shame of the humiliation of the vicious public beating they endured. What hope could have been left for them? To live and be beaten again another day?

You have to understand that those *burandari* never left a village without plundering and looting, taking whatever meager food, clothing and other items they could loot. Sometimes the final gesture on their part was to torch a village.

If you think about it for a moment, it was as if their criminal activities were perfectly timed. They seemed to know how much time they had to accomplish their filthy deeds. By the time the Partizani returned, the "pride of Greece" managed to slither away, like the snakes they were.

Andartes, burandari, pushkari, the three faces of Greek evil, the handmaidens of Greek injustice, occupy a special designation, listed among the most despicable species of human beings. *Pushkari* are the turn-coat Macedonians, the *Grkomani*, the *Grecophiles*. They were among those who did the greatest evil through their espionage work for the Greeks. And the Greeks used them well in their criminal activities against the people.

Many years since that horrific time, I have sometimes come across these loathsome creatures, these Judas, living comfortably in the United States and Canada. They probably were able to get to these great countries before anyone else. They should have been left to rot in Greece with the other bad seed in that land.

The Turning Point

A man may die,
Nations may rise and fall,
But an idea lives on.
Ideas have an endurance without death.

JOHN F. KENNEDY, 1963

The ugly character of war was beginning to leave its imprint on us. Yet, the world knew little and cared less about us. Our lives and deaths were of no consequence to others, particularly the Greeks under whose regime we had suffered for decades. To those powerful world leaders in whose hands our destiny lay, our land, our people were mere pawns to be used to their advantage in their war games.

Where were the journalists, the photographers, the reporters from the outside world? All sides used us to achieve their own ends, while men like my father gave his life's blood fighting for every Macedonian's ideal.

Is it unreasonable; is it treasonable to want to live with dignity, a free man?

Is it unreasonable for him to speak the language he had heard from the cradle, listening to the lullabies his mother and grandmother sang to him in their precious language?

Is it sacrilegious for him to listen to the Old Macedonian Slavonic liturgy, which is still heard throughout the world, and to worship in the language of his father, and his father's father, and their ancestors, spoken beyond the reaches of time?

Can it be illegal to read our history, to celebrate our creativity, to sing our songs, to have pride in our heroes and heroines, to know of our cultural background?

Where were you, oh world, when we needed you so that you could see how we lived, to understand our pain, to lead us out of the days of darkness and oppression we thought were behind us when the Ottomans were defeated? Empty promises of a free, independent, united Macedonia were dangled before us by the Germans, Bulgarians, Yugoslavs, Greeks, aided and abetted by Great Britain, and/or the Soviet Union. You let Macedonia became the setting for one of the bloodiest massacres in recent history.

Turning their pent-up fury against us, the Greeks not only killed and tortured our people; they burned our homes, destroyed our farmlands and indiscriminately and dispassionately slaughtered our defenseless animals.

No one in the free world paid much attention. Who had ever heard of Macedonians, so why should anyone care? Macedonians simply didn't exist! The fruits of the ambition of these countries were left in Macedonia to rot. Propped up by the British, the Greeks, rising from the ashes, could not help but rejoice in their hearts that the Macedonians were being cleansed out of their own land.

How wrong they were. They simply didn't understand the depths of our passion for our land, our communal history, our dignity and our self-respect. The Greeks, though, were beginning to see that the Soviets and British were going to solve the problem of their decades-long effort to cleanse themselves of every trace of the Macedonians and their hated language from Macedonia.

I remember one particular day in Lerin. The authorities had forced a large crowd to gather by the cemetery. There was something different about this crowd. Being the nosy, curious kids that we were, we crept closer to the action to see what was going on.

What we saw was a horrible, senseless, inhumane thing for anyone to see. The Greeks were about to teach us stupid Macedonians a Greek lesson on man's inhumanity to man.

The Greek authorities were ordering three men to dig holes in the ground. I recognized two of the three men, and it was all I could do to keep my mouth shut. Something really creepy was happening.

One of the men was from the village of Bouf. The other, whose name was Gilo, was from our village, T'rsie. I knew him so well because his son, Pandel, was a friend of mine. We often played together. I wanted to shout out to him, to say something, anything, but I held back.

What was happening here? My mouth was open, ready, to yell. As I looked over, suddenly, I spotted the old man, Gilo's father, who then was about 75 years old. The old man was hanging on to a tree limb, shaking with grief, trying to keep from falling. He cried out to Gilo, saying his name over and over and over, weeping, begging, barely able to stand. "Gilo! Gilo!"

His voice, his voice was so weak! That cry of a father's agony! I will never forget that sound. The Greeks were about to tear his heart out for the old man knew what was about to happen. They were rather enjoying the scene and its effect on the people.

Nobody moved to help the old man. No one dared to comfort him. Fear was everywhere in the cemetery that day. No one dared to move because of the presence of the evil that surrounded everyone.

I couldn't say a word. I just stared, my heart thudding in my chest, taking in this whole terrible scene. I remember seeing Gilo's mouth. His lower lip had cracked open, bleeding. The Greeks were now really into it, enjoying the whole event, shouting at the three men, calling them and the onlookers *puli vulgari,* meaning Bulgarian scum. Every filthy epithet, every curse they could think of, they hurled at their poor victims and those of us who were witnessing this cruelty. To my young ears, the Greeks sounded like men gone mad.

And then the shots! I will never forget the sounds of the shots.

Although gun and rifle shots were familiar sounds to me by now, this, this was a horror beyond anything I could have imagined. Gilo and the other two men collapsed into the holes they had dug. They fell into their graves, and I will never forget the look on the faces of those hateful Greeks, or the filth that spewed from their mouths.

I will remember everything that happened on that day in Lerin, to the end of my days. I can never forgive the Greeks, never, ever.

There had been no trial for these three men. The accusations, which were made against them, were never verified. What was their crime? Well, they were Macedonians, and every Macedonian was suspected of helping the *Partizani.*

British gold found its way into the hands of those who were willing to spy for the Greeks. There was no evidence against the three. But, hey, to the Greeks it didn't matter if there was no verification. This strategy of accusation without proof worked well for the Greeks in their effort to frighten and intimidate the Macedonians, to keep them from supporting the Partisan resistance movement.

As it turned out, in Gilo's case, one of the neighborhood kids was coerced into accusing Gilo of having a radio concealed to transmit information to the *Partizani.* Nothing could have been further from the truth. In fact, Gilo, intending to remain neutral, was one of those men who resisted recruitment into the Partizan movement.

Years later, after the conflict ended, the Partizans confirmed that Gilo had never been recruited.

Each day, tension grew more intense as the horrors increased. The Greek strategy of intimidation became more and more severe and occurred more frequently. The Greeks and their agents recruited spies among the greedy to inform on their neighbors; to openly accuse them. More often the accusations were anonymously made. Even the children were objects of intimidation and manipulation to inform on their parents if they or anyone else spoke Macedonian in their homes or in the fields, or anywhere else!

My own Uncle Tase was hanged on Clepala Mountain near St. Bogoroditsa, but not before the Greeks had tortured him for weeks. They pulled out his teeth and then his fingernails. They beat him so severely that his agony could be heard throughout Kalugeritsa and Yanina Livada!

As informers and spies were courted, the informers targeted specific homes. By the summer of 1947, in late July and early August, our village began to be systematically torched. The arsonists and gunmen Macedonians called *pushcari* had the honor of torching the houses in sequence to create the maximum terror in the village.

The very first houses torched were our new house, which had been built 2 years prior, and Vane Pandov's house. It happened during *vrshanie,* the harvest season when entire families were involved in harvesting the wheat and other grains. The hay was being bundled into bales and hauled from the fields.

When the *pushcari* burst into the house, they looted everything they could lay their hands on, and then applied the torches. My brother, Stefo, escaped within minutes before the *pushcari* burst in. When I saw what was happening, I could only think of the horses.

I cut the ropes that tethered the horses and chased them toward the *dire,* creek. Stefo led the horses into the *dire* and managed to hide them. I recognized the torchers from the village of Rokovitsi and I knew who they were. I will never forget them.

One of them had tried on my brother's *guna,* a cloak-like homemade garment made of goat hair. It takes a lot of work to make and becomes a strong garment, an excellent protection against rain and cold.

Those "brave, heroic Greek soldiers," the "pride of Greece," watched their lackey *pushcari* as they looted, pillaged and torched. When the "pride of Greece" left, only the charred remains of the smoldering houses were left for the villagers to see.

Ironically, two of the torchers visited us here in America. One of them had come from Australia and they both came to our home, because one of them was a relative of one of my sisters-in-law. We invited him to stay for dinner and of course the conversation revolved around Macedonia. As we talked he said, "I know T'rsie. I have been there."

This was my moment, and I responded, "I know you were. You were the one that stole my brother's guna. Do you remember pushing that old Baba as she tried to take back her grandson's guna?"

He turned a brilliant red in the face and mumbled something that sounded like, "I don't think it was T'rsie." He couldn't wait to leave and they did so, very quickly. No coffee for them. They were in a real hurry!

Already with the Partizan movement, Father and so many others had joined because they believed that it was the only option they had to preserve, liberate and unite Macedonia. Father believed that the Partizans would put an end to the discrimination, humiliation, and murder that the Greek regimes had instituted to remove any trace of Macedonian past. Father believed, as so many others did, that they were forging a brighter future for our generation, so that we could live free from the constant specter of the hated Greek tyranny and corruption, even though they were partners in the Greek Partizan movement.

I can still hear the songs, the passionate songs of freedom, of independence, of the dawn of a glorious new day for the Macedonian people. However, that wonderful pattern and rhythm of our village life had been bloodily interrupted and changed forever.

The sounds of shelling in the middle of the night became the norm, which sent us running to our safe places for cover. The bloodletting began to take on a life of its own. In spite of the obvious danger around us, my gangsters and I were always on the lookout for anything that looked dangerous or forbidden. Bullets, grenades, anything different became our new toys. And then, we discovered LAND MINES! And, a new game was invented.

The mines had been placed on the paths and roads normally traveled by the villagers, adults and children alike. Some of the mines were placed in the ground, but others were hanging from the branches of trees, wired for tripping by a horse or donkey. We heard that some kids had been killed when unaware, they had stepped on one.

So my gangsters and I looked for the mines. We found it great fun to defuse them as we cleaned them out. This was not a task for little fools. Nevertheless, sometimes we would pick up a mine and throw it as far as we could to watch it explode. Wow, what a sound that mine could make! It was dangerous, yet thrilling at the same time. I know that the danger was discounted for the thrill we got by throwing a mine with all our might just to see and hear the explosion.

Mother was less than thrilled with me. She kept warning me and threatening me with serious consequences. I listened, but I didn't hear, because I ask you, what more serious consequence of Fate could happen to me when Fate had made me a Macedonian?

I pretended to get the message every time my Mother harangued me, but we were living in a world with danger all around us: explosions, injuries, beatings of innocent people, shootings, torching, the terror and hopelessness, the smell of death and dying.

Nothing could shock us any more, could it? We were getting used to this new normalcy. Anyway, I felt that an invisible shield was keeping me safe. Somehow I was immune to injury and death. That had nothing to do with me. The war was over, supposedly; there were no more Germans or Italians. Maybe some Brits were still left among the guerillas. The Allies were victorious and the war, supposedly, had ended for Greece.

By 1944, I was 8 years old. There were all kinds of rumors floating around. Something seemed to be in the wind, a change of some kind was beginning to engulf us. A lull in the kind of action we had lived through settled in for a while. There was a lot of traffic in and out of the village and lots of *maubet*, conversations about the *Partizani*.

I didn't know what Partizan meant, but I knew that it meant good, and that they were on the side of the Macedonians. Everything I heard about them confirmed the thought in my mind that they were the good guys. After all, Father had joined the *Partizani*, and he was not only one of the good guys, he was the best.

I might have been overhearing important bits and pieces of information in the talk swirling about me, but heck, that was the business of the grownups. I had my own life to live. Everything around me was still comfortably familiar. I had Vesko, my bull. I had my chores—that had not changed. I had my gang of Turks, but most importantly of all, my family was all around me. Dedo was in charge and all was right with my world. Life was still good. I was still my fearless self. After all, I was born free, and I intended to remain free and unafraid of either man or beast.

I was free to watch the birds, especially the *sokols* sweeping over the fields and plains on their way to their perches, or maybe they were scouting around for food. I still took our animals out to graze, looking out for mines, of course. I could still lie down on our good, fertile soil and gaze at the sky. I still could let my imagination take flight as freely as I felt, flying on the wings of a *sokol*.

I never had to worry about a change in the weather, because the animals would give me the signal early enough to take action. If a storm headed our way, before I could see the storm signals, the flock would start tracking back down the mountain by themselves, heading for the barn. The goats would come down to the lower areas. And the lower the area they sought, the heavier the storm was going to be.

The sounds they made always brought me back to reality. They huddled together to protect themselves and me if we were caught in a deluge. They never let me down, whether they were sheep or horses, oxen or cows. They knew how to communicate with each other and Nature.

Nature never let us down. Mankind did, time and again. Neither they nor we T'rsiani had any inkling of the severity of a storm in the making that would strike us shortly.

Within a few months after the Second World War was said to have ended, some of the T'rsianski Partizani began to return to the village. There were so many mixed emotions among us as they returned. When there was joy in a household at a safe return, every one rejoiced. But this time, because of the experiences of the Macedonian people of the last several years, joy was in short order.

Those who did come back were emotionally wounded. They came back disillusioned, bitter, and depressed. So very many men never returned. The families often did not know where the men were killed, and for them there was no closure.

1945

The disease of Greece was the imposition of a modern political system on a partially primitive society . . . the chief impediment to Greek political stability is the Greek politician . . . A Greek politician can have as acute a brain as an English or French politician; often he has a more acute one and an astonishing insight. He can talk as well as any western politician, if not better; and that is all he can do.

COMMANDER CHRISTOPHER M. WOODHOUSE,
Allied Mission to the Greek Guerillas.

Although the atomic bomb ended World War II for most of the world, the war did not end for Greece. The sharply divided political factions continued to vie for the hearts, minds and loyalty of the population. Several Greek Regents had been named to head the government and had been replaced. Despite pleas for unity from the King, political tensions, threats and indiscriminate accusations of collaboration with the Nazi were rampant. The Communists in Greece sought to destabilize the country and create a vacuum of power from which they could gain control. Commitments were made to the Macedonians by the KKE, ELAS, EAM, regarding their reunification, their autonomy and equal rights. Zahariadis on his return to Greece declared his support for Macedonian self-determination, only to reverse himself a few months later.

Tantalizing prospects emanated from Yugoslavia to annex Aegean Macedonia, at first also supported by the Bulgarians. However, the Macedonian Partisans appealed to EAM for recognition of an all-Slav Macedonian organization of its own to be known as SNOF.

Britian and the United States continued to pour money and personnel into the country with the goal of stabilizing Greece and implementing democratic procedures. The Allies pressed Greece to hold a plebiscite, write a constitution and then hold free, democratic elections.

The British were committed to the return of the monarchy to Greece; strongly supported by the right wing political faction. The Liberal party favored a kingless democracy, while the Left, mentored by Moscow, were determined to establish a socialist people's republic.

Terrorism and brutality from the Right bloodied Greece, to the outrage of foreign journalists.

The Greek cauldron, boiling with political intrigue, uncontrolled passions, broken promises, and a disillusioned Macedonian population who had always harbored a deep distrust of all things Greek, was about to spill over.

The cynical role of the USSR, through its emissaries in the Greek communist organizations, ensured the imminent next round of war in Greece, hitting Macedonia hard.

January:

- Plastiras replaced Papandreou as head of the Greek government.
- EAM sent General Scobie new terms for armistice.
- General Scobie withdrew offer of armistice because of Greek treatment of prisoners and seizures of hostages.
- British troops enter Salonica (*Solun*).

February:

- The Varkiza Agreement was signed between the Greek government delegation and delegations from the Left, calling for the disarmament of all EAM resistance fighters and the punishment of all Nazi collaborators.
- As some ELAS units began to disarm, other entire ELAS units crossed into Yugoslavia and Bulgaria.
- Greece began to increase terrorism and persecution of minorities.
- The Yalta Conference coincided with the opening sessions at Varkiza.
- Greece asked for British support against Yugoslav pretensions in Macedonia, expressing worries about Hoxha's Albanians, Tito's Yugoslav Partisans, and the Bulgarian Fatherland Front.
- The Red Army crossed the Oder Line.
- General Eisenhower's armies crossed the Rhine.
- The Greek Ambassador was informed that the USSR would not send an ambassador to Athens.

April–May:

- The Greek National Guard and Gendarmerie entered western Mcedonia.
- The Greek king again broadcast a plea for unity.
- EAM outlined violations of the Varkiza Agreement via memo to Harold MacMillan.
- Yugoslavia embarked on a campaign to discredit Greece.
- The Allies finished off war in Europe.
- Tito formally recognized the Albanian government under Enver Hoxha.
- The Right in Greece organized nationalist demonstrations on King George's nameday.

- Bulgarian Communists supported Yugoslav initiative for annexation of Greek Macedonia.
- The X party under General Grivas became the direct action instrument for the Royalist Right Wing faction in Greece.

June:

- Zahariadis returned to Athens in a British plane; officially recognized NOF and supported the principle of self-determination and respect of the rights of the Macedonians.
- NOF was admitted into EAM.
- The KKE exploited the suffering people, brought down successive Greek governments, formented rebellion, and continued to spur the resistance movements, disintegrating public order.

July:

- Kossovo was adjusted to the Yugoslav frontier. Bulgaria designated a small western corner to Macedonia.
- The Bulgarian and Albanian press launched violent reactions against the Greek government.
- The Red Army increased its strength in Bulgaria.

August:

- The atomic bomb ended World War II.
- Zachariadis reversed his position, and declared Macedonia would remain Greek.
- Terrorism from the Right began to affect every corner of Greece.
- Foreign journalists expressed their outrage at the sheer brutality of publicly presenting severed heads for payment in Greece.

September:

- Britain continued to pour money and missions into Greece to implement democratic procedures.
- The Greek delegation was ignored at the Foreign Ministers Conference in London. Greece was excluded from the negotiations on terms of the Italian peace treaty. Molotov refused to meet with the Greek Regent.
- The Greek Regent returned to Greece with a detailed order for the plebiscite, the constitutions and elections.
- Administration in Greece became practially non-existent as politicians began to lobby the voters.

October.

- In the British House of Commons, it was announced that British troops would opposed attempts by either the Right or the Left to seize power in Greece.

November:

- The United States announced a 25 million dollar loan to Greece through the Import/Export Band, and another l0 million dollars in 2 months for the purchase of US Army supplies which had been left in England.

December:

- EAM toured the Greek provinces to organize political pressure for their candidates.

Life in the Greek Cradle of Democracy

He who is as faithful to his principles as he is to himself is the true partisan.

William Hazlitt, 1839

After the German retreat, Greek chaos and repression intensified. We began to see different activities in Lerin. With the Germans gone, political winds began blowing from every political direction and gaining momentum in Macedonia.

Political demonstrations became more frequent and noisy. Every political party held a demonstration it seemed to me.

I must have been 9 or 10 years old when I saw and heard my first real political demonstrations. I remember it very clearly. We happened to be in Lerin, tending to our property, when EAM/ELAS demonstrations were held. These were the Communist parties. The KKE graffiti was everywhere. The party members waved the red flag with the sickle and hammer. I'd never seen anything like that.

The Communist leaders gave speeches and the people cheered loudly, especially when they made nasty comments about the other political parties. Promises of a better life and of equality were made to the spectators, and the crowds again loudly cheered the speakers. Not everyone supported EAM/ELAS, of course.

Two of the political parties, ELAS and the Royalists, seemed to be the largest and most-important ones. ELAS and the others always spoke of the Royalist Party as the "fascist" party. As far as I was concerned the only difference between ELAS and the "fascist" Royalists was that the "fascists" weren't with ELAS. That's all I knew about them, and I didn't care to know anything more.

I don't know how the elections were carried out, but we learned that the Royalists won and ELAS came in second. The King's Greeks were in power again, and promises to the people were forgotten. As soon as the results of the elections were posted, all opposing political parties were outlawed. The thousands belonging to the other parties were arrested. The Greek "democratic" procedures were such that many of those arrested on one pretext or another were exiled and jailed in the Greek islands. Many of them did not survive their imprisonment. For us it was another lesson in how Greek "democracy" works in the land of "the cradle of democracy."

From this point on, the Macedonians' situation got nastier. Again, everyone of Macedonian origin was suspected of something or other. Discrimination became worse. Again our language was prohibited, especially in public. Churches were closed. Cyrillic letters etched on the grave monuments in the cemeteries were defaced. The Greek authorities did everything they could to erase the Slav presence in Macedonia.

Beatings and fines became more frequent. Humiliation reached new levels for those persisting in declaring themselves Macedonian. Word spread among the people of the executions of Macedonians who refused to give up their birthright.

At one point I remember many of our people were forced to sign some kind of paper or affidavit. It had a special name, but I don't remember what it signified.

Much later I learned that over 100 T'rsianie were sent away "eskoria", jailed in the islands. Some spent 10 years or more in jail.

During this time the Greek authorities felt they were finally beginning to get somewhere. Getting rid of those *Makedones* in Greece seemed to be a real possibility now. Cleansing Greece of those pesky Slavs was going to be achieved one way or another.

There was little left for the Macedonian people in that kind of oppressive atmosphere. After 50 years of Greek harassment, humiliation, and civil and human rights violations, anger could no longer be suppressed. Emotions were in turmoil, and the political pressure on all sides was felt by everyone. Eruption into civil war was the inevitable climax, with great loss on both sides, particularly among the Macedonians.

Were there alternative choices for any of us at that time in that place? You see, that really is the crux of the situation. Even not making a choice, was considered a choice by one faction or another, and came with its considerable consequences.

And so, life in the village, although much changed by loss of life, damage to property, and humiliation, still had to go on. For about a year, things seemed to settle down into the routine of carrying on. Each family had to pick up the slack where there was a missing father, a husband, a son. Everyone worked twice as hard and twice as long. Almost no time was left for grieving or to wonder what tomorrow would bring.

We just had to get through today in the "cradle of democracy."

Countdown

When the world has once begun to use us ill,
It afterwards continues the same treatment
With less scruple or ceremony . . .

JONATHAN SWIFT, 1711

Frustration, resentment and anger against the Greeks' injustices began to build in me daily. I missed not being free, free to find adventure in the mountains; free to sit with my back against a tree and watch a falcon wing by, swooping down toward the valley and then up and around again. How wonderful it would be to be a falcon, I thought. I missed being able to play and do the nutty things that all village boys have done for generations. I missed the competitions we used to have with the boys from the other villages to see who could throw a stone the farthest, or who could pee the highest.

But most of all, I missed my father. I missed those evenings spent together when the sun was beginning to dip over the mountains, and you could see the last of the *sokols* making their way home. We used to sit around the supper table and listen to his stories about old Macedonian heroes and the times of the *chetas,* armed bands. Life under the Turks was not easy, which gave rise to the *chetas* and the *voyvodas,* the chieftains.

Conversations about the Insurrection of 1903, *Illinden*, always made the old-timers wonder was it worth it to lose so many lives and still not be free. Those wars seemed so far away. We were at war again, with an enemy we knew well. This was our real war, I thought. Will it be the final one?

All of us kids liked to hear ghost stories or funny stories, but we heard them no more. We used to hear about America, Canada and Australia, where relatives and friends had gone, but the letters had stopped coming.

Our days, though, were busier. The elders kept count of the wounded, missing or dead from our village. Their heads would shake from side to side in disbelief. Prayers were mumbled, but eyes looked toward heaven, "*Gospodi, Gospodi, Gospodi*!" God, God, God, what have we done?

All of the able-bodied men were gone. Had a stranger wandered into our village, he would have thought that the village consisted only of old men, women wearing black and children. Faces were etched with sorrow, fear, resignation and despair. Once shining eyes were dulled from grief and tears. The women covered their heads with black scarves, and wore only black clothes. The children were still children, but not quite carefree.

Gone were the smiles, the jokes, the teasing, the joy found in song and dance. Death and doom enveloped us all. But even during those unstable times, we had hope that things would get better. That sense of hope provided a small measure of security and charged our fighting spirit.

Women, young women—girls—were being recruited to join the *Partizani.* Teenage boys were rapidly becoming men. The *Partizani* needed their youthful passion and strength. Those of us who were younger began to take on the chores of men, work that we would never have done if our father and uncles were home.

We never knew when the *Partizani* would emerge from the mountains, silent, unseen. They materialized when their supplies of food were depleted and they disappeared just as quickly. Family life was disrupted, and the impact on us kids was brutal. We didn't care about things the way we used to.

The sound of heavy gunfire coming from the mountains became more frequent, closer. Whenever I heard the guns, I wondered, is that Father shooting? How far away is he tonight? When will it be over? Yes, we were scared, and the fear made us mean, angry and resentful, but most of all, that fear led to thoughts of vengeance.

When the memories of that time surface, I ask myself the same questions over and over again.

Was it worth it?
What choice did we Macedonians have?

What choice would I have made if I had been in Father's shoes?

Could I have lived under the Greek authorities if I had been a man?

Could I have lived with their arrogance, their harassment had I been an adult?

Would I have lived with the constant humiliation and intimidation that the Greek authorities imposed, unable to keep my name, not allowed to speak my language or go to my church?

Could I have been denied my own ethnicity, allowed the schools to close, books to be burned, cemeteries and graves plundered, my birthright destroyed?

Would I have been able to call myself a ***man****?*

As the clashes between the Royalists and the *Partizani*, spearheaded by the forces of the Greek National Liberation Front and Liberation Army, ELAS/EAM**,** became uglier, and casualties mounted on both sides, Macedonia became the flashpoint of action. Every civilian was in greater danger each day. Every man, woman, child, and animal was a target. The safety of the children, the protection of the children: *how could the children be protected?*

These discussions became more open, not only within families, but in the village as well. It was becoming clearer that the *Partizani* were planning something. The more active *Partizani* were talking about strategic movements, personnel, safe havens. Within our family, the talk was subdued. Dedo, Baba, Mother, the older uncles we address as Dedo, expressed their fear of the uncertain future, and tears flowed when there was talk of the children. I overheard that some of us might have to be sent to Yugoslavia. Yugoslavia? What was a Yugoslavia? Or a Tito, a Stalin, or a Lenin? Were they mountains? People? Places?

In spite of all that we were hearing, my cousins and my other gangsters, as well as my enemies, tried to be as normal as we could. We still did chores. When we could get away, we still played with each other. We still swam, and we rode our donkeys or horses. Throwing stones at each other was still a part of our lives. With our mothers and our grandparents, we continued to go to the *pazar,* the marketplace. Mischief and children may be inseparable, but our lives, our options were getting narrower, and we felt it.

1946

What counts is not necessarily the size of the dog in the fight—it's the size of the fight in the dog.

DWIGHT D. EISENHOWER, 1958

While the British and American governments developed an Anglo-American Balkan policy which could be integrated into an Anglo American Greek policy, the Soviet government policy was on its own covert track in Macedonia and in Greece.

Armed units of NOF, which was working to win national rights within the framework of democratic Greece were under the guerilla commander, Markos Vafiades. NOF's willing volunteers and recruits spread their network in the Voden (*Edessa*), Lerin (*Florina*), and Kostur (*Kastoria*) regions.

With no secure government in firm control, chaos, rumors, conflict, extreme violence was ongoing in Greece.

January:

- Rumors circulated that Left wing guerilla bands were re-forming in Macedonia.
- The Soviet government complained at the UN Security Council that the presence of British troops in Greece endangered the peace of the world.
- Britain promised the withdrawl of troops after the Greek elections.
- The Security Council debate clarified the issues Greece faced: the choice between the USSR and the Western countries; the choice between the Left and the monarchy.
- EAM demanded representation in any Greek government.

February:

- EAM requested postponement of elections for 6 months to prepare a list of candidates.

March:

- The Greek Prime Minister offered guaranteed freedom of movement of all party candidates.
- The KKE refused to mobilize all the Party's forces for armed struggle, signaling the end of the Democratic Army.
- Zachariadis boasted his army would be in power by 1948.

April:

- Within a year of the elections, Greece had already had three Prime Ministers and five governments.

May:

- As British troops were being withdrawn, renewed fanatical guerilla wars began as SNOF bands were dispatched to join the ranks of Greek guerillas. Gotsev was appointed a colonel in the Yugoslav army.

June:

- Roaming Communist guerilla bands created a desparate situation in Macedonia.

September–October:

- Martial law was imposed on northern Greece to combat guerilla movements.
- Zahariadis was prosecuted for making a speech deemed an incitement to disorder.
- Army officers previously associated with ELAS were sent into exile without trial.
- The King returned to Greece and made attempts to form a broader government and was deadlocked each time.
- Britain refused to supply the Greek government with arms for the protection of civilians in northern Greece, i.e., Macedonia.

Sulio

Children are a poor man's riches.

English Proverb

We saw Father from time to time, and when we did our world was whole again. There was no question about it now. He was a Partizan. What else could he be?

I often I looked at my mother's face when Father was home; I could see her emotions reflected in her eyes. There was happiness seeing him safe and well. There was fear, exasperation and worry also, but she knew he had no choice because of his character.

As a Macedonian woman, a wife and a daughter-in-law respectful of her position in the family, she knew there was no way she could let her feelings be known to the rest of the world. But she carried a heavy burden in her heart.

I recall a very special evening when Father returned with four or five men. Of course, Baba and mother bustled around them, preparing and serving drink and food. I hung around trying to be a little invisible (ha!) and useful at the same time.

I listened to the plans they discussed. They were preparing for their next mission. The leader of this group of men was actually the commander, a man called Kosta Suleymanov, nicknamed Sulio. He was so impressive to my eyes. He was from the village of Chereshnitsa, Kostursko. I took an immediate liking to him and grew to admire him. He had a tremendous reputation and commanded respect from friends and enemies alike. The Greeks feared him. Whenever word spread that Sulio's *Partizani* were in the vicinity, the Greeks never initiated any action if they could avoid it.

I was so honored to be allowed to pour a pitcher of water for him when he wanted to wash his face. I remember he looked at me with approval and smiled. He nodded his head and said to me, "You're all right, boy. Too bad you are not old enough to come with me and join the Partizani. You would be a force to contend with. I think you could show those dirty Greeks a thing or two."

I was lifted to the clouds, my face burning with pride. Both pride and admiration for him skyrocketed. I'll never forget that moment or him, either. Sulio became a legend among us.

There was a particular incident, which became a favorite story to tell and retell about him. It seems that *burandari* had captured some of the *Partizani* from the *Kuidy Partizanski* Battalion. They had been given the responsibility of controlling and protecting the T'rsianski Mountains. The Kuidy Battalion had been tripped up on several occasions, so the *Partizanski* headquarters decided that they had to dispatch Sulio's battalion quickly to regain T'rsianski regional control.

While most of Sulio's men were from the Macedonian villages, there were some *arnauti*, of Albanian extraction, and the *prosvigi*, who were born in Macedonia. The *prosvigi* were the offspring of the Greeks who were part of the population exchanges with the Turks decades earlier. However, Sulio never accepted any Greek Partizans from the south. He warned us, "I cannot trust those Greeks. If any of us are killed, it will be by one of those Greek Partizans. Watch your back always. Have your eyes on your back!"

On another evening when Father and Sulio returned—it was either in the spring of 1946 or 1947—they were so jubilant. They had just returned from *Vitsi (Vicho)* Mountain, where 70 *Partizani* scored a major victory over the lousy Greeks. One of the five-star Greek generals and his unit had the unenviable mission to attack and destroy the *Partizanski* Battalion there. It didn't happen.

The *Partizani* fought hard and defeated the Greeks. *Tetin*, Uncle Trian, one of many of our people who fought on Vicho, told the story of how they shot the Greek general riding a white horse. He commanded 1,500 men.

The return of the *Partizani* was a joyous moment. Everyone was smiling. "Today we caught and fried the biggest fish of those *burandari*. They couldn't find us, much less catch us. We are too swift for them. We know every inch of that area, and they don't know where their asses are!"

The Partizani defeated a five-star general! Our *Partizani*, mostly young men in their twenties and younger, beat down the general! OORAH!

As the story was told over and over, the younger guys began to sing and dance in celebration of their victory. We were invincible. We could never lose!

Sulio was a realist, however. Once again he cautioned everyone.

"Don't trust the Greeks. Tell me, why do you think that *SHTAB*, Partizan headquarters, is preparing to appoint a Greek to be the next commander if I am killed? They have it all planned to take over completely and run the show after we win this fight. They want to get rid of all us Macedonians. They never liked us and they never will. Our leader was tricked into agreeing to the plan of putting a Greek second in command in every unit, and, one-by-one, the Macedonian leaders are being eliminated, killed or exiled. Don't you think that those Macedonians knew what was going on? Yet they could do nothing but keep on fighting and dying."

He said this as if it were inevitable. Sulio always made you think, then think, and think again.

It made me ask myself what Father had committed himself to. Was it going to be worth it?

After that night, word came to Sulio that the *burandari* were planning a surprise attack again on the *Kuidys* Battalion. Wily Sulio had a plan for them. He was anticipating a counter-attack. His strategy was not very complicated. He was going to set a trap for the *burandari*. The plan was to allow the *burandari* to approach deep into Sulio territory. Unaware that it was a trap until it was too late, the *burandari* would advance, giving the Partizani the opening to fire from the rear, right and left. Sulio would then open with a fierce attack from the front and then purposely pull his Partizani back.

The *burandari* were surrounded on all sides. The entire skirmish lasted about half an hour. There wasn't much fighting, but there were many *burandari* captives.

The captives were made to strip down to their underwear. They had to take off their shoes, also. So, almost naked, and barefooted, Sulio released them to return to Lerin or to their camps. And believe it or not, some stayed and joined Sulio's brigade! How do I know this is what actually happened? Let me tell you.

About six of my gangsters and I were caught right in the middle of the whole skirmish. If the fight had lasted a few more minutes, we might have been captured by the *burandari* and maybe held for ransom! Some of the soldiers who had been allowed to escape ran toward Lerin, crying out, "Sulio ate us up. They killed us all."

Dedo Traiche was coming into our village with his horses and donkeys at about the same time. He had heard and seen the *burandari*. As Dedo Traiche came into the village, he asked everyone he saw, "Who is this Sulio? Show him to me so that I can kiss him. Those poor, dumb Greek soldiers running naked and scared, was a beautiful sight to my old eyes."

This episode marked the last time I saw Father alive.

Father must have been with Sulio from the very beginning. How they met, I probably will never know, but I see them now enshrined in a golden memory radiating hope and defying hopelessness. They were two men bound together in life as in their death, living and dying for justice for the Macedonians. I don't have a photograph of the two of them. Photographs sometimes do fade. But their golden memory will never fade. They will remain, Sulio, the Commander, the warrior, with his faithful comrade, my father, Mite, the medic, in charge of the medical care for the *Partizani* throughout their brief, doomed, gallant fight.

There is a very old saying among us: "You can not drive straight on a twisting road!"

In the late spring of 1972, my wife and I returned to T'rsie for the first time since I had left, 20 years before. We had a difficult time there, but managed to overcome obstacles.

During that time I met one of the Greek secret police who had been working in our area since 1946. His name was Giorgios. He knew everybody in our family, especially my father. We talked about many things past and present, but mostly of the past. Interestingly enough he confirmed the account of the defeat of the Greek general and his unit. There is a commemorative plaque of the defeat at the foot of Vicho Mountain.

Although Giorgios was a Greek and was a member of the secret police, he was of enormous help to us while we were there, especially in Solun, Salonica. He was different from the Greeks I had met in my lifetime. He was a real human being, with the emphasis on ***human***. *We spent over 12 hours together, just talking, and 4 more hours on the train.*

For his assistance, understanding and humanity, for the first time in my life, I expressed my thanks to a Greek, to Giorgios.

1947

$3,600 for every ragged, ill-fed Partisan holding the mountains; 250 American officers involved in day-to-day decision-making; a regular army of 136,000 men equipped with artillery and armor, supported by 50,000 National guards, had been letting 25,000 Partisans of the Democratic Army slip through their fingers.

AMERICAN SENATOR GLEN. H. TAYLOR
Estimate of American Spending on President Truman's Report.

1947 was defined by the Truman Doctrine, which addressed American spheres of interest which included Eastern Europe in general. The United Nations Security council earmarked 100 million pounds for Greece, which the USSR opposed.

The United Nations General Assembly found Albania, Bulgaria, and Yugoslavia had given support to the guerillas fighting against the Greek government and called on these countries to cease offering their assistance.

In retaliation to the guerilla bands' strong rebellion against the Greek government, the Government launched a series of drives to exterminate guerilla action.

February:

- The United States inherited the British role in the Mediterranean.
- Guerilla rebellion expanded to violent new levels and kept planning for a free government in the Macedonian mountains.

March:

- Britain withdrew economic commitments and military support from Greece.
- Guerilla war intensified in the Greek mountains to coincide with the British withdrawal.
- A British brigade was left in Bulgaria to counter Soviet troop presence there.
- Prince Paul assumed the Greek throne after his brother, King George, died.

May:

- The Truman Doctrine in combination with the Marshall Plan clarified the issues in Eastern Europe as a contest between a Western system, headed by the United States, and that of the Soviet Union.

September:

- A Liberal/Populist coalition replaced the Greek government in September and, by October the Greek Communist press was suppressed

November:

- A joint Greco-American staff was formed to fight the guerillas.
- Another 35 Communists were executed in various Greek prisons, which brought the total number of people killed under the joint American-Greek staff to more than 4,500.
- By the end of the year, the KKE Party was banned by law.

December:

- The Democratic Army's Macedonian headquarters lauched a major attack on Konitsa. The Greek government forces countered with air support, giving them the experience of an unexpected victory.
- The Democratic Army lost 650 men, dead or wounded.
- The Greek rebel radio announced the formation of a provisional Greek Government in the mountains, with Markos as Prime Minister.

The Plan

Who takes the child by the hand takes the mother by the heart.

Danish Proverb

My gangsters and I heard about "The Plan." There was a "Plan" in the works that had to do with all of us kids, but we didn't know anything about it.

I was 11 years old going on 12. We knew the grown-ups were talking about The Plan but they didn't have the details either. Partizan spokesmen came into the village to lay the groundwork with Macedonian leaders in the village for acceptance of The Plan. The leaders knew that it was not an easy plan to propose, so they tried to approach the villagers with a rationale that they could accept. This was the rationale based on the intelligence the Partizans were getting from their most trusted people:

"The Americans are running the war now. There is an American named General van Fleet in charge. We are all in greater danger than ever. They have brought in heavy guns and a new weapon, and we will be their guinea pigs. Their bombs are going to shoot out flames that will kill every living thing in its path. These bombs have something called napalm. It burns the earth, rocks, people, and animals!"

The spokesman paused and looked into the face of each man present. He knew that the next piece of information would be something no one would ever have expected. There was an attentive silence. Every eye was on him.

"Every child from the ages of 2 to 14 years of age is to be evacuated. Children under 2 and all infants are to remain with their mothers, because many women nurse their children up to the age of 2.

"There will be several young women selected to accompany the children and be their surrogate mothers for the duration of this war. They will be called *maiki*, mothers. Each *maika* will be assigned 10 to 12 children for their care and protection.

"Our count is that about 87 children are to be evacuated from T'rsie. The children will be in safe hands."

Safe hands? In times of trouble we always fled into the mountains with our own families. We knew every inch of our mountains. Hadn't our forests always protected us? Wasn't it the most logical, practical way, to hide in the mountains? They were our guardians! As families we remained together as safe as was possible, but we were together!

Now it was going to be different! There was stunned silence. What they had been told hit each man very hard. Each was either a father or a grandfather and the thought of sending their children somewhere without an adult relative of their own with them was beyond anything they expected to hear.

There is nothing more sacred to a Macedonian family than a child. To send a child away—even for his or her own safety and welfare—not knowing where they were to be sent, nor for how long, having no one with them except other children from the village, how were they to do this?

Were there no other options?

To this day, I cannot believe there were no other options.

I don't know how much discussion there was, but there was no doubt about the danger the Macedonian people were facing. Able-bodied men were continuously being recruited by the Partizans and by other guerilla bands. This meant that, with the children gone, there would be only women, babies, and old people left in the village.

How would they survive? That thought was on every man's mind. Nevertheless, each family had to be told of The Plan and the date for the planned evacuation.

The children were to be evacuated by the first week of March, the month of *Baba Marta*. So while we kids tried to guess what was in the works for us, I knew nothing concrete until Dedo decided to tell us.

I remember once when one of the guys in the village had kicked me in the stomach. I had not seen that sucker punch coming, and it really hurt. I have never forgotten the pain, nor did I ever forget the kid who did it.

That was the same pain I felt when Dedo talked to us about The Plan and what each of us, grown-ups and children alike, had to do. We kids were going to be sent away. What did that mean?

All I knew, all any of us kids knew of the world was T'rsie, maybe Lerin, or some of the villages we visited with parents. Our world was our mountains and hills and valleys and every goat path in them.

We knew the rocks and caves and every forest and what kinds of trees were good for firewood.

We knew the creeks and rivers.

We knew where the monastery was where we held our religious celebrations.

We knew each other.

We knew how to speak Macedonian.

We couldn't read or write yet, because our schools had been closed since the fighting began. But we knew nothing of any other *dunia*, any other *svet*, any other world.

Who was going to meet us? What would we be doing? I wasn't scared—not much. I simply didn't want to leave everything I knew, everything I cared about, and everybody I loved.

Leave Mother?

Dedo or Baba?

Stefo?

Uncles and aunts?

No!

I wouldn't admit to anyone that I might be scared. Dedo assured me and my cousins that everything was going to be for the best for all of us, and that there was nothing to be afraid of.

I knew I could trust my Dedo. He would never let me be hurt by anyone. He trusted me to be strong. I would have to go when the time came. He depended on me not to let him down. In his own way he was trying to stir up my courage, by having me see him looking and talking with confidence about the future.

He didn't talk about it again. Our departure was a given. His eyes, though, had a different look. I don't know how to describe it, except that when he looked at us, it was as if he were seeing someone else, and, perhaps, hearing something spoken a long time ago: *Taka bilo pisano.* That is how it is written.

In the summer of 200l, while traveling through Macedonia, my wife and I talked with many of the people who lived through the war years and had excellent recall of the period. Over and over we shared our experiences, our emotions with each other, and our understanding of the reasons why the Macedonian children had to be evacuated.

Our friends thought the Greek guerilla leader, Zachariadis, had plans to free young mothers and recruit them into the Partizans. With the children separated from their mothers, they could be more easily brainwashed and turned against their Macedonian parents and anything Macedonian.

The other sinister character in the scenario at the time, it was felt, was the Greek Queen, Frederika. It was also said that she initiated the recruitment of the Macedonian children to convert them into Greeks, and to any nationality except Greek. Everyone seemingly held the children in the highest *priority!*

1948

All is riddle, and the key to a riddle is another riddle.

EMERSON, 1860

The bitter struggle by the various factions vying for power and control of the hearts, minds and loyalty of the Macedonian people could only lead to dire consequences. The years 1948–49 proved to be grim, grizzly times for the population.

Competing ideologies, charismatic leaders, demagoguery of every hue bombarded the Macedonians. The KKE and ELAS attempted to induce the Macedonians to join their army, DAG, the Democratic Army of Greece. NOF had issued a declaration urging Macedonians not to join the Greek Army, claiming the Macedonians were already building a new life in the free regions. Of the DAG, 30 percent were Macedonians who favored secessionist or autonomist solutions for Macedonia.

IMRO, the Internal Macedonian Revolutionary Organization, was also making strong efforts to influence the Macedonians through the distribution of leaflets and public announcements. NOF painted the IMRO as a terrorist organization, and worked uncompromisingly to smother the IMRO influence.

IMRO strategy at this point was to support a plan for an independent and united Macedonian state under the protection of the United States, Great Britain and the Soviet Union. The plan had unanimous support of the non-communist Bulgarian-Macedonian organizations in the United States and Canada, and the Bulgarian opposition parties. There was also support for an IMRO proposal for an independent Macedonian state outside the framework of Yugoslavia.

None of the proposals came to fruition.

Tito's treachery was revealed soon after Yugoslavia was expelled from the Comminform, which served to end Yugoslav support for the Cominform oriented Greek guierillas. This took the Greek Communists by surprise. Tito's treachery played a decisive role in the outcome of the fierce battles at Vitsi (*Vicho),* and Grammos in 1949.

March:

- Radio Athens announced that 3,000 bandits were surrounded in Peria and would be exterminated the next day.

May:

- Martial law was declared throughout the country after the Greek Justice Minister, Christos Ladas, was murdered. Hundreds of resistance officers were shot and the victims were scattered all over Greece. The mass execution of those who were condemned to death for offences committed before 1944 was ordered by the Greek government. The Ministry of Justice issued orders to speed up court proceedings before the middle of the month to shoot 2,961 people who had been condemned.
- A storm of international protests was aroused, including the AMM. Among the protests:
- *The Manchester Guardian* . . . "The Greek Government's decision to execute Communist prisoners by way of reprisals fills one with shame and dismay . . . "
- *The Daily Herald* . . . "What can be the effect except to intensify passions which already divide the Greek nation, and to provide the communist enemies of Greece with invaluable propaganda?"

The Macedonian Trail of Tears

Remember your name, Sote.
Remember who you are!

Dedo Vasil Nitchov, 1948

It was a beautiful March day in 1948, cold but sunny. Slowly, quietly, the families began to bring their children *sred selo*, to the village square. The day and time for our departure had arrived.

We were leaving all we had ever known, taking only the clothes we were wearing. The girls had scarves to cover their heads and protect their ears, their hair swept back from their young faces. They were dressed in homemade coats and sweaters to warm them, their feet in woolen socks and homemade *pintsi,* shoes.

We boys, our hair grown longer since summertime, when our heads were shaved almost to the scalp, were dressed in modest clothes, long pants, our stocking feet also covered by our homemade *pintsi.* We carried homespun *torbas,* bags stuffed with homemade bread and cheese. It was not much. We had no idea how long our trip would be or where we were going. We carried as much food as we could.

The younger children clung to their mothers and grandparents for all they were

"Starting the Macedonian Trail of Tears" by Alex Gigeroff.

worth. They buried their faces in the adults' hands so that you could only see half of their little faces, eyes looking fearfully around. They were terrified. There was subdued murmuring among us, an occasional sniffle.

I made an effort to put on my "Sotir" face and attitude. We kids from T'rsie were going to be together—we weren't going to be alone—I was sure they wouldn't even separate the "bad" kids from the "good" kids.

As I looked around, I could see that we were all beloved children, and at that moment it hit me. We were leaving. My eyes stung. I couldn't swallow. I lost my cool. I wiped my face quickly because I didn't want them to see tough guy, Sotir, the free *sokol*, crying. I pulled myself together and put on my "cool" look again.

Finally, all of the children, 87 of us, from the village had been accounted for. It seemed like we had been standing in the square forever, and yet not long enough. Were we waiting for a Pied Piper to lead us away? There were no Pied Pipers for us Macedonian children, only stark reality. The square was quiet, except for muffled words and the sound of sobbing, primarily from the mothers and grandparents. Agony etched its path in parents' faces, confusion spilled out with the tears of the children. Where were we going?

Children clutched family members who held them even more tightly, as if they would never part. Cries and laments from the mothers and the grandmothers began to rise. Most of the young men and fathers were absent from this sorrowful gathering. They had been recruited—or had fled to escape recruitment.

As we huddled around our families, we kids began to cast furtive glances at one another, for courage, mostly. I remember thinking, "What's he looking at? Is she scared?"

I wasn't going to let anyone read *me*. I struck an air of cool disinterest, as if this were just another day. I told myself we're going on a journey, a new adventure lies ahead. We are going to a safe place. That's what Dedo told me. I started to think about what I was going to do and how I would act.

As I thought about my new role and shifted my gaze, going from one family to another, I was kind of surprised to see that babies, carried in their mother's arms, had been brought to the square. My eyes widened. Are they going to send small babies with us too? My simple brain began to understand a little more clearly that this was serious.

Suddenly, our time was up. No more gazing, no more speculation or posturing. I heard cursing. The old men! They cursed their fate. They had lived long enough to see their children taken from them! These old men no longer had the strength or power to stop the unbearable sorrow and pain everyone was feeling. They cursed from the deepest part of their souls, spitting out their hatred for the forces over which they had no control. I wasn't shocked. I had heard my Dedo curse before, but it was the intensity of his pain, the flow of his tears of rage and despair that spilled from his eyes that shook me. What he had feared more than death was actually happening.

"They are destroying us. We might as well be dead. They took our sons. Now they are taking our grandchildren from us. Without them we have no life, no village. Nothing!"

That did it. Involuntarily, I began to shake from the sound of the painful cry that surrounded me. I looked at the weather-beaten faces of my grandparents, my aunts, my old uncles, one by one. I did not dare look at Mother. I couldn't let her see my eyes.

Father was on the Grammos front. Stefo had to remain in the village because his fourteenth birthday was later in the month, and he would be recruited by the Partizans.

I was afraid that I was going to lose my self-control. I didn't want to disgrace myself in front of the other kids. But Dedo's words, those words of his, are etched in my soul as well as my memory. As I struggled with my emotions, I was suddenly crushed against my Baba. She wrapped her arms around me.

"Oh, my child. Grandson, dearest grandson. Where are you going, my heart, my life? In which strange land will you find yourself? Will I ever see you again? Oh, Oh!"

Her tears fell on my head. I tried not to cry and I hung on to her as tightly as I could. Dedo kept patting my head, my shoulder, urging me to remember who I was and where I came from, trying to keep up our courage.

"*Haide, Sotiraki, haide*! Come on, Sotiraki, come on! Watch over the others, and if there is a just God, we will see each other again."

I looked up at him and saw tears flowing down his old cheeks. Everyone was crying. It hurt so much. The tears overwhelmed us all. I felt so much pain in my heart. I hugged him as hard as I could, to the point where he almost stopped breathing.

"*Mashala*, my goodness, you are strong!" he managed to say to me as he tried to regain his breath.

Once more he said to me with as strong a voice as he could muster, "*Da pomnish! Ti si Sotiraki. Da ne zaboravish kai si roden. Korchinata tie T'rsie. Da slushash dobroto. Da ne se lazhish! Pametvai sho ti velev za Dedoti Nitcho. Takov da stanish! Da ne go stramish imeto nashe—Nitchov!* Remember! You are Sotiraki! Do not forget where you were born. Your roots are in T'rsie. Listen and do good. Don't lie to yourself. Remember what I have told you about your forefather Dedo Nitcho. Grow to be like him. Do not shame our name—Nitchov. Remember your name, Sotir!"

Those were the last words I heard my Dedo speak.

It was almost 4 o'clock in the afternoon. The square overflowed with families, neighbors and children. Eighty-seven children—lost, confused, wondering what was going to happen to them. We kept looking at each other, storing up one last moment of emotion, trying to memorize each face, every structure. We did not know at the time that for many it would be our last memory of this village, our families, our friends, and our relatives. Even if we were to come back to T'rsie, it would never be the same village, the T'rsie of our birth. There could be no more delay. The selected *maiki*, surrogate mothers, our guardians, who would care for us, began to move toward the few horses which were waiting. The horses had straw bags hanging from each side. These were large enough and strong enough to hold the younger children, one in each basket.

Time was slipping away. The sun moved over the horizon and evening settled in. We were going to walk to our first stop, the village of Statitsa. It was time to start moving.

Several of the *maiki,* I was relieved to see, were relatives of mine. There was Maria Nichova, cousin Kotse's wife now widowed, with her 3-year-old son; *Strina,* Aunt Ristuitsa Nitchova; Olga, her widowed daughter. Another was Mikitsa Kuleova, widowed with two sons; Dana Yanchova, widowed with three children; Spiroitsa Giamova, widowed with several children; and Lika Traicova, an unmarried young girl. My mother, my stoic, obedient mother, Tsila, was allowed to come with us as far as Oshchima. Only to Oshchima.

My brother, Stefo who would be 15 on March 25, and four or five other boys were to remain behind in T'rsie because their birthdays followed so closely. The real reason they were held back was because they were big and strong for their age, and the Partizan leadership had plans for them.

Statitsa was a logical first stop because most of us T'rsiani had relatives living there. So for us kids it was still familiar territory and there would be familiar people. Even though it was getting darker, we knew the paths to Statitsa. I smile to myself, ruefully, as I remember. No streetlights. No signs to direct us. Just the moonlight highlighting our path, and the darkening shadows outlining our hills and mountains. Now, somber lookouts, our families witnessed our departure.

As we left *sred selo* we moved past Mangova *chesma*, the fountain, past the cemetery, toward Spridol, on to Tumbata, past *monastircheto,* the little chapel, past *Staro* T'rsie, Old T'rsie, which was to the right of *monastircheto,* down toward the Koriata, where the Korshenska River and the other rivers meet, past Dreno to Statitsa.

Here and there in creeks and rivers, little silvery ripples reflected the moonlight, murmured their farewell to us as we passed. The night was so quiet, so still. We didn't see or hear any animals scurrying about. Not a sound! What a group of brave, unlikely travelers we must have been on this, the first leg of our journey: 87 children, ages 2 to

14, plus horses and donkeys, the *maikis*, and the mothers who were permitted to go with us to Oschima.

This wasn't so bad, I thought. We were all *T'rsianski detsa*, children from T'rsie, going to a *panagir*! I began to perk up a bit.

Mother, my sisters Tsotsa and Mara, cousins Krsto, Ilo, Risto, Petre, Sofa and I were to spend the night at my godfather's house. The adults were engulfed in sadness. We could see that they were determined to be strong for us. The sorrow they were feeling showed only in their eyes. Strength and stoicism are a part of the Macedonian character, just as much as passion.

While we kids were sleeping, overnight word came from a friend of Father, a man named Panaiot, who served the *Partizani* in many different capacities. This time he was a courier, and he carried a vital message. The information he brought was that all of the children, my brother Stefo and the others, who had remained in the village because they were almost 15, were to evacuate the village immediately. Immediately!

This was not welcome news to the Partisans who controlled our exodus. It became clear that the Greek Communist Party, the **KKE** planners, had their own design for the 15-year-olds of the Macedonian Partizan families. The **KKE** members had no clear orders to deviate from the original plan. There was a heated exchange between the mothers and those in charge of the evacuation, but our mothers prevailed. The 14- and 15-year-olds were to join us, and word was sent to Stefo and the others to come as quickly as they could. They caught up with us by the time we reached the village of Oshchima.

That evening, our little troop of children, horses, donkeys, *maikis,* joined by the children from Statitsa, had to start on the next leg of our journey, which was to the village of Konomladi in the district of Kostur. I am not going to recount another heart-rending scene of tears and farewells—that mute outpouring of love—parents desperately trying hard not to upset their children.

When would they see us again? Would we remember them?

We had to move on. After a brief stop in Konomladi, we mounted horses and donkeys and headed toward Prespa. We passed through well-known and well-worn paths in *Lisets,* Fox Mountain, then down through the villages of T'rnaa and Rula.

By nightfall of the next day we had arrived in Oshchima. After we were fed, the leaders placed us in the homes of the villagers for the night. We were so tired from the trip that each of us slept soundly. After all, our bellies were full. The mothers who were allowed to accompany us were still with us. The beds were comfortable. We were among caring Macedonian families.

Except for the emotional greetings and farewells, in my naïve mind, this trip was not going to be bad at all. It wasn't scary. Everything was familiar; villages, mountain passes, faces, names, and *we* were the center of attention! We were V.I.P.s! We were having an adventure! The winking stars that shine brightly in our vast Macedonian skies, far from towns or cities, suggested to me that this space, this universe as we knew it, was ours. *We owned the universe.* I think there is no night sky more beautiful than our Macedonian sky, with stars hung over the mountains.

Our little flock, growing with children from the villages we passed through, had been led through familiar terrain. Many of us had roamed over the slopes of the hills and the mountains, fields and valleys, grazing our sheep and cattle. Heck, what was there to be afraid of? After all, I am Sotir, Dedo's Sotiraki. I am not going to let him down! I know who I am. I am Sotir!

Destination: Prespa

There was a tame ram, the Cheta's mascot . . . a most excellent companion on the night marches. He trotted at the head of the file, behind the voyvoda. Suddenly he would stop, give a wicked little snort and stamp a forefoot. This warning never failed. Somebody would be ahead on the trail, friend or foe.

Albert Sonnichsen, 1909

We traveled while it was light because there didn't seem to be any danger. Prespa, the Lakes area was our destination, we understood that this area was under *Partizanski* control. The Prespa area lies between the Macedonian mountains of Bigla, Gorbetz, Galitchnitsa and Suva Gora. Here we were to meet and join other Macedonian children, children from many villages, so it was very important that we keep on schedule.

Our *maikis* organized us into manageable groups. Every older child was responsible for carrying a younger child on his back. The younger children who were able to walk, were assigned an older child to lead them by the hand. We were given a stern warning: "Never, ever, let the young ones walk alone! Never!!"

The village of Oshchima was the point of no return for us. This was it, the final moment for the painful leave-taking from the mothers who had been allowed to accompany us this far. The mothers who were not *maiki* had to return to their villages immediately. This was almost unbearable. That these mothers could bear this farewell is a tribute to their willingness to live with pain, to save our lives.

The little ones were held tightly, clasped to the heart, their mothers kissing their little faces, kissing their eyes over and over again, whispering prayers for their safety. I had no interest in anyone except my mother. I looked at my brother, Stefo, and I saw him muster up his courage for this final parting. I had to do the same. My mother, usually in control of her feelings, came apart with an anguish such as I had never seen or imagined. Stefo and I clung to her, as she pressed us to her heart, crying, crying, crying, praying, and crying, repeating our names. Stefo and I tried to act like men. We tried to reassure her, "Don't worry. Everything is going to be all right. You'll see. Don't cry. We'll all be all right."

She was inconsolable.

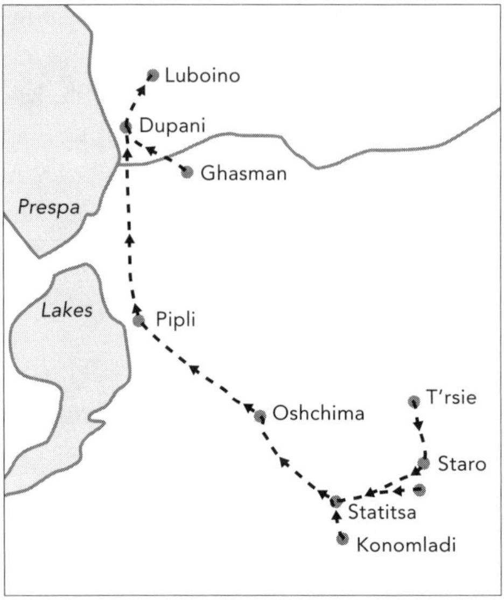

The young evacuees walked from their villages to the village of Luboino Yugoslavia.

"My boys, my boys. Stefo! Sote! I cannot let you go. They may as well kill me now!"

Stefo, desperately trying to keep her strong and to keep himself under control, grasped her by the shoulders and spoke to her with a fierceness that I never expected. My sisters and I were crying. I tried not to. Leaving my mother was so hard.

"If you don't stop crying, I will stay here and not leave Macedonia," Stefo threatened.

We cried with her as she clutched Tsotsa and Mareto for the last time. Mother covered her face. She knew there were no alternatives. She stood helplessly, her face wet with tears, trying to speak.

The mothers who had horses, mounted them, and without looking back, started the journey home, defeated in their efforts to hold back tears. The others, following on foot, Mother with them, dragged themselves away from us.

Their path would lead them back home to face their heart-breaking destiny. Our path would lead us toward places unknown, to face an unknowable destiny.

Now we felt alone. Yet, there was Stefo, my sister Tsotsa and little Mara, and my cousins. We were still together. There was a little comfort in that.

The older kids were being assigned to take responsibility for a younger child. All, that is, *except me!* ME! Sotir, a born head-honcho! Trouble-maker? Maybe. Head-honcho? Oh, yeah! I began to feel hot fury rising in my chest. They were deliberately embarrassing *me* in front of all the others! I stomped over to where Nevestata Maria was standing.

"Hey," I shouted at her bitterly, with great heat, "You forgot about me," pointing at my chest. I could not contain my outrage. Nobody could do this to me, Sotir!

She looked at me with a challenge in her eyes.

"No, we didn't forget about you," she paused for effect, "you will lead us!"

WHAT?

"Just follow the road and you will be fine," an older man suggested, pointing toward the road.

Maria hugged me, and warned, "Don't go too far ahead. Just let us know if there are holes ahead or bridges or rivers. If you see something, just call out, "*oosh, oosh*."

No problem! They had made an excellent choice. I was the best kid for the job.

How clever of them to know that. Full of confidence and pride, I started down the road. The *Partizani* assigned to us led the way to the top of the hill. I guided our little platoon of Macedonian children and *maiki* downhill into a small valley and we crossed a river. This brought us to the main road, which leads to Zhelevo, and Bigla and Lerin.

Although it had only been an hour or so since we left Oshchima, we felt as if we had been traveling for days. Some of the kids, carrying the younger ones on their backs, grew tired and asked to rest. We stopped for a while. These stops would become more frequent as fatigue overtook us. We rested where we stopped, seeking neither shelter nor comfort.

I took my scouting responsibilities very seriously, determined to keep everybody safe, staying 20 to 30 meters ahead of the group. Every time I stumbled, I shouted out, "*Dupki*, holes!" If I felt dampness around my feet, I yelled, "*Voda,* water or *dere,* creek!" Whatever I saw or felt I announced to the others.

At the top of the hill we paused. We saw something in the sky coming from Kostur. We spotted the airplanes before we heard them; they flew toward Bigla. The high mountains here were both a barrier and a safety net.

Suddenly, all hell broke loose. The roaring of the planes filled us with terror, panic. Whose planes were they? The first group of three planes didn't fire at us, but we weren't going to wait to see if they would return. The sound of those planes flying over our heads was incredible. We all knew what to do. Our leaders shouted "*Dolu*! *Dolu*! Down, down" and down we went, hanging on to our *torbas*, clutching each other's hands, scrambling, slipping, stumbling down the deep, steep ravines of the valley. We scrambled toward the crevices and ditches created by dried up rivers and creeks. There was little water in them, and they offered some protection.

The planes returned. They passed over us every 5 minutes, firing in our direction. The rounds they fired hit the sides of the hills. I could see the insignia of the Greek Royal Air Force on the planes. They never reached our hiding places.

We clung to the ground for what seemed like days, but we had been trapped for only about 5 hours. The sky was getting dark. The roar of the planes began to subside, their mission of strafing and bombing had ended. We could hear the cries of the little ones, "Mama! Mama!"

Mama could not hear them. Mama could not hear their fear, their terror. The cries of the smallest children sounded like the mewling of lost kittens. We were in Fate's hands. We could not turn back. We had to go on, to Prespa. We had to leave immediately.

With the onset of darkness, we felt the cold more acutely. It was a cold March night in our Macedonian mountains. It seemed that years had passed since Stefo and I had mustered up the courage for our separation from Mother. As we walked, it was eerily quiet. The night was pitch black. It was difficult to make out anything. The shadows around us looked menacing. I thought I heard a strange noises. An animal? My imagination? I kept on. We tried to move more quickly. After a long, long while, we began to hear different sounds. Our "pilot," ahead of me, said, "*Ezeroto,* the lake. Stay to the right." I, in turn, passed this on to the *maiki.*

We continued, and I felt dampness. The path was very close to the shoreline. The sounds were those of the waves, lapping on the shore. Needless to say, we all got our feet wet. Some cried and moaned, but I felt exhilarated. To me, this was an adventure. Occasionally, I would walk back to join Stefo and my cousins.

"You okay?"

"I'm fine. How are you doing? The old man says we'll be in Luboino in 20 minutes."

"What's Luboino?"

"I don't know. Something good, I hope."

This kind of guessing game was not enough for the *maiki.* One of them directed me: "Go find the old man and ask him."

He heard her. "In Luboino there will be trucks to take you to Bitola. Once we get to Luboino, we will not have to walk any further."

This was puzzling. No one had explained what was going to happen next. Who were these people with the trucks and where did the trucks come from? The next thought that came to me was, "When do we eat?"

Several new people joined us. Four adults: two men and two women. Someone whispered, "Maybe we're in Piple or Granitsa." I thought we were probably in Luboino, and up to this point I hadn't thought we were so far from T'rsie. We had decided to travel only at night, after our experience with the strafing by the Greek planes. Wherever we were, we were so tired, cold and wet, that we sat down on the ground and waited. There were other groups of children, children from different villages, who had already arrived and more were on the way. Each group kept together, huddled around their *maiki.*

Somebody spotted trucks in a fenced area with a locked gate. I craned my neck to get a good look. They were the biggest trucks I had ever seen. As that registered in my mind, the adults surrounded us. Some wore civilian clothes and others wore uniforms that looked different from those we were used to seeing back home. I knew they were not *Partizani* uniforms. We could understand most of the soldiers. They were speaking Macedonian! We didn't know that we were entering *Vardarska* Macedonia, which later would become a republic of Yugoslavia.

Later we learned that the men, dressed in the strange uniforms, with red stars on their caps, were soldiers from the Yugoslav army. Their job was to load and transport us. None of us realized that we were now in a different country, that we had crossed the border into the country of Yugoslavia! Later we learned that Luboino is a Macedonian village in Yugoslavia, right across the Greek border. Yugoslavia? Had I heard that word before? I thought I had. It sounded familiar.

The trucks began to move out of the enclosure, the gates had been opened. They lined up to take on their cargo—human cargo, Macedonian kids from the villages of Bouf, Lagen, Kotori, Turie, Zhelevo, Psoderi, Chereshnitsa, Piple, Gherman, Armensko, Rudari and T'rsie. We were strangers. Destiny would not permit us to be strangers for long. Together we began our forlorn odyssey. We did not guess that in a year we would be family.

We piled into the trucks under cover of darkness, listening for sounds other than our breathing. The crunch of the tires told us we were getting farther from our homes each moment. But we were so tired, so exhausted, so cold, we fell asleep at once, sitting up, slumped against each other for warmth and comfort. Worn out! And suddenly, a voice called out: "Up, up, everybody. We're here."

Here?

Questioning voices of children, sleepy children, rang out: "Here?" We awakened slowly, groggily, confused. Where were we?

I was tired, hungry, homesick. The little ones began to whimper. "Mama . . . .Mama . . . Mama".

Mothers, once constantly present to comfort, could not hear the cries of their babies, but I heard them. I can still hear them. Those high-pitched voices crying , begging to be cradled in their mother's arms.

"Mama . . . Mama . . . Mama . . . ."

The Chocolate Bar Caper

Roasted pigeons will not fly into one's mouth.

RUSSIAN PROVERB

I immediately recognized where we were. My eyes were wide open now. We had arrived at a train station! I was positive of that because I had seen trains in Lerin often when I went with Dedo to the *pazar*, or market.

While there was no doubt in my mind where we were, I had no idea where we were going, so I asked my Aunt Olga and Nevestata if they knew. All they could tell me was that they had heard something about a "Belgrad".

"But where is Belgrad?"

They both shrugged their shoulders, as neither of them knew. We were all so ignorant and so naïve.

Well, I knew where I was going to go. The hell with Belgrad. I can escape all of this, I thought. I was not such a dummy as to trust people I didn't know to take me and others to who knows where. I can find my way back home.

In my mind I would take the road leading to Lake Prespa. Once I got to the lake I would be able to see one of the hills that was easy to reach. From the hills I would see the peak of our Lundser Mountain and then it would be a piece of cake.

I would follow the river that leads to Oschima up, up and up, through the mountains until I reach Berovska Reka. At that point I would see the Vlashkite Kalivi, the Vlachs' barns, and walk past the *Golema Ornitsa*, large fallow land up toward the Lundser where the mountains seem to cross. We call it *Presekata*.

Once I arrive at Vlashkoto Bigla Mountain, the Vlachs' side of Bigla, I would be home.

It was so simple, so do-able. It would be no problem for me to reach home, I thought, because I knew my landmarks. I knew Bigla Mountain, Berovska Reka, Presekata, and Lundser, my mountain.

My home, my village, T'rsie, nestles against the slopes of Lundser. Why, Lundser could be seen from Prespa, so there was no doubt I could find my way home, one way or the other! Where there is a will, there's a way.

Man, I was pleased with myself and my idea. I had figured a way out of this ridiculous situation we had gotten ourselves involved in. No way was I going to continue any further with these strangers. The sense of adventure that engulfed me on the trail to Prespa had dissipated completely. I couldn't wait to share my brilliant plan with my brother and Cousin Risto.

I walked over to them quickly, but carefully—not arouse any suspicion or interest in what I was doing. In very low, but confident tones, as if I were explaining a new master plan for the universe, I told them what I planned to do.

They looked at me as if I had suddenly lost all of my marbles.

Stefo: "Are you crazy? There is no way you can find your way home from here!"

"Wanna bet?"

Stefo grabbed me and shoved me towards my *maika* and Nevestata. He told them what I had been hatching in my head.

Like I cared. You have to know me a little better than you think you do. I always act on my gut feeling, which in my lifetime I have learned to trust. If I feel like doing something, right or wrong, I do it, no matter what. Threats and bribes move me not at all. In fact, it just makes me more determined to act. I have always been that way, and to this day I still am. I am in your face if I feel that you are wrong. That inner voice, my gut feeling, always propels me into action. It speaks to me: DO IT! DO IT! CHANGE IT! IGNORE IT! FIGHT IT! Fear of consequences never entered my mind.

But, I did care about my family and my good friends. I would fight to the death for any of them. I have done and still do crazy, dumb things according to the standards of behavior and conduct of "others". That's the way I am.

No dire warnings of getting lost or being eaten by bears or wolves could deter me. The determination they saw in my face really scared them. They began to raise their voices at me because they knew what I was like when I got stubborn.

"You'll be killed! You know they shoot at anything. It won't matter if they are Partizans or *burandari*. Not only that, but there are land mines all over the hills—even if you could get that far."

They were yapping at me so hard, so rapidly; with such feeling that I had to get away from them. I went looking for my cousin Ilo.

"Listen," I said to him when I found him, "you want to go home? We can just take one of these trucks back. I'm sure they are going back to Luboino, and once we get there, we'll just keep Lundser in sight and make our way home!" What could be simpler? I was so certain of success; I just couldn't understand why the others didn't jump on the idea.

"I know you've always been crazy," Ilo said, exasperated, "but this is really crazy." He was shaking his head at me.

At that moment, I stopped in my tracks. I don't know what made me stop. To this day I can't figure it out. It was like an invisible barrier appeared in front of me, preventing me from going further. I couldn't move!

Had Destiny intervened at that moment, knowing what was ahead? I leaned on a post. I looked up and saw Nevestata walking toward me. "Look," she began calmly, "if you go back, we all go back, but no one is going anywhere alone. Your father, Striko Mite, made me promise him, that no matter what happens, I would take care of you. Do you understand? NO MATTER WHAT! Now, shall I break my promise to your father?"

Sullenly, "No."

Angrily, inexplicably, I walked over to where the children were being loaded on the train.

What made me abandon my plan?

What stopped me?

What made me walk back toward the train?

Who moved my limbs?

There was so much fear in the kids. Many of them had to be dragged into the train. They had never seen one before, and there was no mother or father to reassure them, to take the time to explain to them that the train was not something to be feared. As an incentive to board the train, each child was given a dark chocolate bar.

The universal bribe—a chocolate bar!

I spotted the boxes before I boarded, grabbed a bar, but by the time I sat down, I had finished it. I had forgotten how hungry I was, how hungry all of the children and adults were. It seemed like weeks since we had eaten.

At last, all of the children were finally on board, and it seemed as if they were all still crying. We were all hungry and we ate those chocolate bars quickly.

Cousin Krsto started to cry because he had lost his chocolate. Those of us who had some left broke off pieces and gave them to him, even though we were just as hungry. Nevestata and Mikitsa were talking to each other, wondering how they could get some more chocolate for the children.

Of course, I overheard them, and from where I was sitting by the window, I could see the cartons on the platform. I didn't have to think too long. I called to my cousin Ilo, and Itso-na-Linka. His name actually is Itso Malagenov, but *Itso* is a popular nickname for boys named Chris or Hristo, and since Linka was his mother's first name, we called him Itso-na-Linka.

They promptly came to where I was sitting, and I pointed at the boxes.

"Ilo, you go ask for more chocolate bars and keep on distracting them, make trouble, act like a gypsy, do anything. Itso, you wait on the other side of the train; I'll shove a carton under and you grab it. okay?"

Oh, yes. It was okay. Hunger prompts you to throw caution to the wind to satisfy the craving for food. We tried to go out the same way we came in but that door was locked.

We tried the other door and it slid open. To get to the boxes, we crawled under the train and over the tracks to where several people were still distributing chocolate. While they were distracted, I grabbed two cartons, and pushed them under the train.

It worked like a charm. Itso grabbed one. I went under the train with the other and we hopped back into the coach. We had pulled it off!

In the meantime, Aunt Olga began to miss Ilo and me. Frantic, she immediately shouted, "Sote and Ilo ran off—they are not here."

Stefo spoke up, "But they were just here! They can't have gone very far."

Nevestata ran to the door of the coach, shouting, "Two of my children are missing. Let me out! I have to find them."

At that moment, Ilo appeared, looking so innocent as he said, "Here we are."

Upset, angry and relieved at the same time, Nevestata, scolded, "Where did you go Why? You know you are not supposed to go anywhere alone! *Surdtseto mi go puknate!* You two gave me a heart attack. Where is Sote?"

"Hey, somebody help me. This thing is heavy."

"What is heavy?" Nevestata stopped. "What do you have there?"

Triumphantly, I said, "*Iadenie*, food! Get me some help!"

Stefo and the others came over to help carry the boxes into the coach. Nevstata called some of the other *maiki* over and they conferred. I could see at once that there was a danger that we could lose the chocolate after all the energy expended and risks we undertook. No *way* was that going to happen.

When one of the *maiki* did suggest giving it all back, defiantly I spoke up, "I got the chocolate for all of us. You can give yours up, but not ours!"

Nevestata, concerned about the fairness of it all, worried, "Maybe they'll be short of their supply for the other children."

"So what?" I said. "I don't care. And I'm going to go for another box!"

"No, you won't. You sit down and stay put. Don't you dare move from sight!" She spoke in words and a tone of voice I had never heard from her before.

Deflated, dejected and somewhat defeated, I made my way back to my seat by the window.

Everybody got more chocolate. At first, I was scolded, although I didn't feel I was really being scolded. I could tell by the way they were looking at me. They had to let their frustration at me come out for not telling them what I was going to do. They were afraid I had taken off for T'rsie. Now they praised Ilo, Itso-na-Linka and me, and we saw smiles on their faces. We really hadn't seen anyone smile since we had left T'rsie.

My sisters, Tsotsa and Mara, Stefo and the cousins found seats nearby, which gave us a sense of support and comfort being near each other. We were the faces of T'rsie to each other, the faces of home, the faces of caring, the faces of family. We gave each other a little hope that while we were together, everything would turn out all right.

Both Mikitsa and Nevestata said pretty much the same, chiding me, "You see, if you hadn't been here, we would not have had chocolate for the children. That's why kids seem to follow you, and you wanted to run away!"

I think it was meant to be a compliment and inducement, but all I said was, "Huh!" and settled down for the ride. I could see reflections of the other children in the window by my seat. Some of them were seated in the aisle between the rows of seats on the wooden floor. The rows of benches seated two, three and four children, depending on their size.

None of us had any blankets to cover us. Tired, hungry, fearful and confused, minute-by-minute, we were moving farther and farther from everything familiar, warm, loving, comforting.

What were we doing here, hurtling along on these foreign steel rails?

Who brought us here?

Why?

Why? Why?

Dedo, Baba, mother, father, will we ever see each other again?

Do you think about us?

I was in a kind of half-sleep for some time, leaning comfortably against my sister Tsotsa. From time to time I would awaken, not sure where I was for a second or two, and then I observed everyone sleeping, even the *maiki*. I remember thinking, "They look dead tired. They looked—dead."

I tried to focus more closely on Nevestata to be sure that she was alive. I watched her intently. Her little boy, Itso, about 2 years old was seated on her lap when I first dozed off. Now I saw him on the floor of the train, leaning against her feet.

That's when I began to wonder if she was all right. I went up to her quietly. Her eyes opened immediately, wide with concern. "You scared me. Why are you up? Where are you going?"

I looked her straight in the eye, to reassure her. "Wherever you are going, I am going, too." And I meant it. As she picked up Itso, she motioned to me to sit next to her. She began whispering to me in confidence, as if speaking to an equal. I could see her emotions were beginning to overwhelm her.

"I am not so worried about you, Sote. You can take care of yourself better than I. That's why you must help me, help us all out. The children will follow if you'll lead . . . "

I shot back at her, "I'm just like anyone else."

"You are a bad, tough boy. Everyone in the village knows that about you. But you can help us a lot now. We'll tell you what needs to be done."

"I don't know how to worry, anyway," telling her what she already knew. "By the way," I said, "a little while back you tried to fool me by telling me you promised Father something. You haven't seen Father for a long time," I accused her, "Not since last summer or maybe even before that."

She replied honestly, "I had to say something to make you listen." That made me think.

I went back to my seat. I could hear muffled sounds from the other children, some still crying out for their mothers. They all needed their mothers to hold them.

Some of them needed to relieve themselves. But never having seen a lavatory before—and certainly never on a train—they were too scared to go, so they suffered. Finally, we had to lead them one by one into the lavatories and stay with them until they finished what they had to do. There was no embarrassment, only fear.

The train from Bitola brought them to Belgrad and Bela Crkva.

From where I was seated, I spotted the last carton of chocolates we had "rescued". In my newly elevated position of responsibility, I went back to the Nevesta and pointed out the box. She nodded conspiratorially and whispered, "When the children awaken, we will give each a bar. Thank you, Sote."

Satisfied with the situation, I went back to my seat. The chill in the train began to settle in. My sisters were shivering. I took off my coat and covered them.

Turning toward the window again, I listened to the sounds of the train, the clickety-clack of the wheels; the chug-chug-chug-chug of the engine, punctuated by the sounds of the train whistle. I was lulled back into my half-sleep, barely conscious of dim lights in the distance, and then the small groups of lights. I thought they can't be *nevestulki*, fireflies. So in my mind I resolved that they had to be villages, and that the larger cluster of lights must indicate towns. My brother, now awake, confirmed my brilliant deductions. With that I dropped off to sleep.

As daylight began to break we all began to awaken. We looked and felt so tired, so beaten. We also felt dirty, unclean. Our feelings showed in our faces . . . sadness, hopelessness and that ever-present fear. It was all there.

The train never made a stop. Glued to the windows with nothing to do, we began to be hypnotized by the views that seemed to be moving past us. We saw no familiar mountains or rivers. A vast, wide plain made its appearance that made me think of the Lerinsko *polje*. The mountains looked different, though. Sometimes we crossed over rivers on bridges made of steel. Wow! But, where were we?

We felt our hunger more acutely now. Ever since we left Bitola, we had not had anything to eat or drink, except for the chocolate bars. We still had one more treat, the last of the bars we had "rescued."

It was time for the last of the chocolate bars. The *maiki* rose to give us one each. And for a moment—only until each bar was devoured—we put aside fear, hunger, chill and homesickness. But only for a moment.

Once again, we were overtaken with emotions and sadness about our pitiful situation.

Where was home?

Is anybody thinking about us?

Could they have forgotten us?

While those thoughts were going through our minds, I could feel the train slowing down. There were snatches of conversations between the adults. I could hear the word Belgrad repeated.

My ears were perking and almost twitching with the sound of the new word: Belgrad. We were reaching our destination, no doubt.

Belgrad?

Beograd?

Were these different places?

I remember asking one of the *maiki*, Mikitsa, "What is Belgrad and Beograd?"

"If I knew, I would tell you!"

A Brand New World

In a brief space, the generations of living beings are changed and like runners, pass on the torches of life.

LUCRETIUS, LST CENTURY B.C.

We were soon to find out what a different world we were going to be part of. In Bitola they said we were going to Belgrad, so this had to be Belgrad.

This was our first and only stop. I was getting restless and curious at the same time. I listened for words that I might be able to understand. *Yugoslavia, Yugoslovensko, Tito, Tsrven Krst* were some new words I heard, which meant absolutely nothing to me.

Not one word was heard about T'rsie, which I thought very strange, because my whole world was T'rsie.

There were people about in uniforms and white armbands with a cross of red on them. Others wore bands of some kind across their chests.

We were told to disembark from the train and to hold hands, including me. They were very gentle with us, steering us in the appropriate direction. I thought they were very nice. We were somebody's children.

Who were these people?

What kind of uniforms were they wearing?

Did they want something from us?

We really didn't need *them*. After all, we had our *maiki* and we knew who they were.

How curious! They were saying something to us. A word here and there could be understood, but I couldn't connect the words so that it could make any sense to me. Their language and accent was so different.

They did seem nice.

So there we were, each of our hands holding on to other hands, like little chain gangs, being led some distance from the train station. I don't know how long we walked in this fashion, but it was a little while anyway. It gave us a chance to look at this different, new world we were in.

We finally paused before several large buildings. They resembled large barns to me, but I had never seen barns this large before in my life. Nothing like these in Lerin, for sure. Now I think that they were probably army barracks. They were situated on wide grounds. When we were brought into the buildings and saw how wide the halls and corridors were and how very large the rooms seemed, it was—WOW!—everything looked *huge*!

Wow! Wait till I tell Dedo! There seemed to be a kind of 'barracks' mentality among the adults there. Looking back on the scene, in memory, it seemed that we were being handled like young, uninitiated recruits for somebody's army.

Anyway, first things first.

The adults lined us up, boys on one side, girls on the other, and then, the most unbelievable thing happened. **They shaved our heads!** We began to look at each other furtively, as if we didn't want to be caught doing it. Then we looked more openly, and we didn't know whether to laugh or cry, but some of us did snicker. I snickered the loudest.

Now we experienced the most unbelievable thing of all, at least so far. We boys were led into another area, and what did we see? Here **it was raining inside** the large barn, **water was running out of the walls!** None of us village kids had ever seen this kind of marvel. We didn't know what to do about the walls. I gawked in amazement at what I thought had to be hundreds and hundreds of pipes!

Wow! The next thing we had to do, after a demonstration by the adults, was to strip off our clothes. As we did, we were given a bar of soap. Then we were pointed to the water. They demonstrated that we were to stand under the water and to scrub ourselves clean. Oh, the water was warm! This was going to be fun!!

There was no more hesitation. We scrubbed and splashed and scrubbed some more. We scrubbed our Macedonian dust and dirt from our hair and bodies, and after that was done, we were led to another area.

More marvels!! Our eyes popped wide open, as did our mouths. There, and over there, and over there were piles and piles of clothing, all sizes, and **shoes.**

What sizes you ask? Who knew anything about sizes? You went over to a pile, tried on what you thought you liked, and then over to another pile until you found pants that seemed to fit, a shirt that seemed comfortable, and shoes that fit reasonably, and ta-*da*, you were outfitted like a dandy!

Simple, eh? We thought this was great! The clothes may not have been perfect fits, but when were our clothes in the village or even in Lerin perfect fits? Our garb was usually a hand-me-down or someone's cast-off, and we were glad to have it. But this experience, this was great fun. We had choices, and we loved making those decisions for ourselves. The little ones were helped by the *maiki*.

Gradually, we were all dressed and led outside into the open yard. I was a glorious sight. I was a unique Sotir. I was a soaring *sokol*. I was Alexander, the Great! And I knew it. I had picked out a captain's hat, or what I called a captain's hat. It was too large to be sure, but I fell in love with it. It was calling out to me in that pile of clothing. It said, "Hey, Kapitan Sotir, finally, we get together!" I stuffed it with something so it would not cover my ears, and walked out, immensely pleased with myself, to join the others.

Momentarily, I forgot everything else—home, family, hunger, Tome. I walked out into the yard as *Kapitan* Sotir. Even my friends commented to me that I looked like a *kapitan.*

"It fits your style, Sotir." I knew that! Like I needed them to tell me? This experience in the barracks was really enjoyable. My first shower, my first experience outfitting myself with clothes, brought out my good humor.

At first, when they shaved us and I saw the hair falling from our heads, I thought we looked like *golitsi,* resembling newly hatched birds and like *perlinia,* baby donkeys. The humor of this experience that we all shared brought all kinds of comments out of my mouth. We began to laugh, breaking some of the tension that had been enveloping us. Although at the time I didn't even know the word "morale", I know our laughter improved our circumstances greatly.

Now we had to be loaded into the trucks again. We were *Detsa Begaltsi* again, on the move. I started to chant out loud, "*Tsironki, tsironki. Kosturski nivichki.*" It was the way the fishermen announced their presence in the villages as they came to sell their smelt. We were the *Detsa Begalts*i, the catch of the Partizans.

As I carried on with my nonsense, with no one to stop me, now and then a word or phrase that wasn't funny would cross my thoughts. I felt like the blind leading the blind. But, I didn't say it out loud because I was supposed to be a leader for the kids. I was probably the worst possible choice for leadership, because on the stupidest dare I could lead everyone into the lake without thinking about it.

We joined the girls and *maiki* to walk to a place called *Plandishte*. To get there, we had to cross the biggest river I had ever imagined existed. Of course, it was the Danube. It was thrilling, exciting. I couldn't contain myself. I broke away and ran across the bridge, stopping traffic as I ran from side to side.

In total abandonment to the exuberance and excitement I was experiencing, I ran smack into a lamp post, which was hardly disposed to move out of my way. I must have bounced like a ball, until I hit the ground hard, knocking my head.

My hat went flying. I began to bleed profusely. I tried to get up, but I felt like a punched-out, deflated bag. Groggy, I tried to retrieve my precious hat, and, literally, began seeing all kinds of lights in my head.

Stefo and Nevestata ran to where I lay. My nose and forehead were cut. One of the Red Cross people came over, and cleaned and patched me up as well as she could.

The procession of children and adults had stopped while this was going on. Finally, they got me to my feet. My cousin Risto handed me my hat. I mustered all the dignity I could, with my patched face, and placed my captain's hat on my throbbing head. I wanted to catch up with the woman who had treated me, and as I did, I tried to ignore all the remarks made in my direction. "Once wild, always wild!"

"What's the rush? You're going to blind yourself, you crazy!"

"In T'rsie he was bad and he is bad here. He'll never change."

"He's crazy. He doesn't understand anything and he doesn't listen!" Yadda, yadda, yadda. And those were some of the better comments.

Nevstata tried to see if I was all right. "Do you feel dizzy? Do you hurt?"

"Naw, no, no!" and off I went with this strange head on my shoulders. It did hurt, but only for a while. The Red Cross woman who treated me carried a bag that reminded me of my father. He always carried the bag, loaded with medicines, bandages, gauze, and needles. I tried to thank her with facial expressions and hand motions and a lot of body motions. She really didn't understand what I was trying to say to her, but it was fun trying. In fact, in spite of my little unfortunate "pause" by the lamp post, the entire experience was great. It was really fun. It was so new.

I tried a fun game with the other kids, playing tag. You tag me. I stop. The next guy runs to tag the leader, giving everyone except the little ones a chance to run. They just watched and seemed to smile. Some of our sense of forlornness, abandonment, bewilderment and hunger disappeared.

We began to look with more interest at our surroundings: the large, long buildings; the motor traffic; everything seemed so new, so different, so impossible.

Plandishte

The heaviest baggage for a traveler is an empty purse.

English Proverb

We arrived in Plandishte under the auspices of the Yugoslav Red Cross. Like Belgrad, this place also had large, long buildings.

We were directed into a one-story building which also had large rooms. The windows seemed to be a meter high. There were cots in the room, but they did not look like the ones I had seen in the army hospital in Lerin. Each cot had an army blanket folded at the foot of the cot. I looked at the mattresses, which looked and felt as if they were stuffed with straw. Oh, well, better than sleeping on dirt, I thought to myself. Everything looked clean in this austere place, but then there didn't seem to be much to keep clean.

The *maikis* began to assign us cots. It was obvious that the authorities were not totally prepared for the number of children who had arrived. Food was scarce, we found out. Heating was inadequate, and there wasn't enough clothing for all. The Yugoslavs in charge, although overwhelmed, tried to make do with what they had. Even though it was difficult for all, they seemed to be kind, friendly, caring and very concerned about our well-being. They had to put up with a lot from us kids, believe me.

We were to stay in Plandishte for a month. I baptized Yugoslavia with my first real fight, right there in Plandishte, but my cause was a noble one and it had to do with that precious commodity, the chocolates.

Here is what happened. I remember the occasion vividly. I saw about five or six children crying, two of them from my village. I asked them why they were crying and one of them told me that someone had taken their chocolates. With the authority given to me by my *kapitan's* hat on my head, I asked them to point to the thief. They did, and it was a kid who might have been two or three inches taller than me, but I outweighed him, I figured, by three or four pounds.

Determined to right this terrible wrong—after all, we were all hungry—I approached him belligerently, with a total lack of fear. "Give the candy back to the kids!" I commanded.

"And if I don't?"

Before I could retort, "You will," I felt a hard punch land on the right side of my face, hitting my cheek and part of my right eye. His delivery was lightening swift!

That did it! All the frustration, anger and hate exploded in me, earning me another poke in the nose, a hard one. I could taste the blood dripping in my mouth, which only refueled my fury.

I hate bullies. I hated this one in particular. My hate and anger toward him pumped my strength and took control. I landed a few licks on his chin and on the side of his head, hitting his ear. I kept pummeling him to the ground. I felt a triumphant wave of joy sweeping through me and I jumped on him, straddling him between my legs, still pummeling away at him.

While the kids around us watched, cheering me on, glad to see he was "getting it," some of them began to worry. Some of the *maiki* rushed over. I could hear someone say, "Sote is fighting again."

My brother Stefo finally broke through and pulled me off. I got the usual scolding and haranguing from the *maiki,* all of which went into one ear and out the other.

Someone had apparently notified those in charge. A woman who I guess was a nurse, started to clean me up, tending to my puffed eye. She clenched her fist at me with a smile. I smiled back. It was all over. That kid never ever hit anyone again, nor was he ever tempted to take somebody else's food. I had done my duty. I was still Kapitan Sotir! I had my shiner for a week. I never knew who the other kid was, and I never saw him again. There were hundreds of us there at the time. I also never found out what had happened to the chocolates, either. *But, I won the fight!*

Things began to fall into a routine. The older girls gathered some of our clothes and washed them in the river. They spread them on the grass and bushes to dry, so we would be able to wear clean clothes again.

Our situation, though, began to deteriorate. Rebelliousness began to sweep over all of us. Those of us who were a little bolder began to demand things that were simply not possible. There just wasn't enough food to feed us. The nights were getting colder. Uncertainty and boredom with ourselves, not to mention our homesickness, overcame us again.

We didn't know, of course, that there were plans in the works, and no one seemed to see that we needed to be reassured about things.

A couple of weeks passed before we were instructed to assemble. The Yugoslav authorities, which included the Red Cross, planned to divide us into groups. If my memory serves me well, the youngest children up to the age of 5 formed one group. The next was made up of children 6 to 9 years of age. The third consisted of kids 10 to 14.

This seemed to make sense, but what did it mean?

We found out later. The little ones were to be sent to Stara Crna Gora, Trieste, Slovenia, some to Tsrkvenitsa, Dalmatsia and Hrvatsko, or Croatia. Some of these places were located in warmer climates so I guess it made some sense. Except for *maika* Tsila Kuleova, the other *maiki* were to travel with the younger children. Once we were grouped by age, we were kept separated from each other.

To keep everybody calm, the authorities were not going to allow us to say goodbye to them, nor did we know for certain when they were going to leave us.

Oh yeah? My gangsters decided that we were going to see the young ones. My kid sister, Mara, was with the little ones. Risto Bozhanin had heard that the little ones were going to be taken to their different locations within minutes. Nevestata and my aunt were going with them as *maiki.* We had to see them and that was that.

I went to the door, only to find it locked. There was someone on the other side of the door guarding it. I couldn't quite believe it. After coming all this way together, now we couldn't say our farewells to the younger ones, to reassure them somehow that

Sotir, 1948, in Bela Crkva.

everything was going to be just fine? We older kids were their last connection with home.

When I am determined to do something, nothing can stop me. Once I make up my mind, there's no hesitation. I got my guys together and told them I was going to break the window, and go head first. Whoever wanted to, could follow me out, but I was going. My brother, cousins Risto, Ilo and Petre were against that, warning me that I was going to bust my head. But they and I knew they were wasting their breath.

I positioned myself by the back wall of our stark little dormitory, picked up speed, pulled my hat down over my head, and, running as hard and as fast as I could, head first out the window. Aside from a few minor cuts and scratches, I was fine, although my shoulder hurt a bit. The guys followed me out.

I am not going to describe our farewell scene. We tried to make the little ones smile. After all, we were the men in the family here. By the time we said goodbye, though, the ones in charge of our dorm had caught up with us. I didn't give a damn! They scolded. They yelled. They threatened. But for me, it was "mission accomplished". We did what we had to do. I kept smiling through the storm of frustration around me until everything calmed down. The nurse, who had treated me at the time of my fight with that bully, cleaned me up again. I called her my *drugarka*. That means comrade. She seemed to like that, which made us both laugh and smile for a little while. My *drugarka* and I "dug" each other, no question about it.

The window was never repaired, at least not while we were there. A month later, my group left Plandishte for a new destination.

Bela Crkva

Fate leads the willing, and drags along the reluctant.

SENECA, 1ST CENTURY

Our destination this time was Panchevo where we stayed briefly.

Our next stop was at V'rshats, and then we finally arrived at Bela Crkva, Voyvodina, Yugoslavia.

Bela Crkva!

I had never seen such a city. Clean white buildings, beautiful parks, neat, well-built homes and farms, lots and lots of fields and farms. A large *polie*, or plain, with fertile fields all around the city made me think of Dedo. What Dedo could accomplish here!

The tall, white church at the bottom of a hill must have given the city its name. Bela Crkva had been a prosperous town, founded in the eighteenth century by Germans, who had established and colonized the town. Different trades developed and the production of high-quality wine helped Bela Crkva prosper, attracting people there.

In this peaceful, pastoral setting, symbols of the catastrophe called war, victims and victimizers, had left its mark on Bela Crkva over time. Prisoner of war camps holding German prisoners were a bleak reminder of the waste of war.

Barracks built for utility, not appearance, housed the Russian and Yugoslav armies. Army personnel occupied all those buildings in the fields that were three to five stories high. About 40 to 50,000 people lived there at the time we *Begaltsi* arrived—a mixture of Serbs, Romanians, Hungarians and now, Macedonians.

The *Detsa Begaltsi,* were to occupy six or seven of the buildings. These were to be known as the *Detski Dom*, the children's' dormitories. Up to 1,000 children were to be assigned to these homes.

I was assigned to the oldest group, the 14-year-olds. Our *Dom* was the *Chetverti Dom*, Dormitory #4. We were located right across from the police station, next to a very inviting park.

The older girls were assigned to the *Treti Dom*, Dormitory #3, next to one of the hospitals, bordering the front of the park. Dormitories #3 and #4 were about a block apart.

The rest of the kids were assigned to Dormitories #5, #6, and #7. Some were assigned to Dorms #1 and #2 near the church and one further east of the church, near a hospital, which we called *Shuga.* No one was allowed to go near there. I think *Shuga* meant a pox of one kind or another.

Once again we Begaltsi had to adjust to yet another way of doing things. This was definitely not T'rsie. We were going to be exposed and subjected to a new kind of regimentation. We still faced shortages of food, and we were still separated from our families. Often, thoughts of home brought on waves of frustration, depression and homesickness.

Were our families thinking of us?

Did they know where the Partizans had taken us?

Did they miss us?

What was happening in T'rsie?

When would we see each other again?

We shed a lot of tears, even us older kids. Just imagine what was happening with the younger kids. Or maybe they were adjusting better than we were?

Kopus or *zelka,* cabbage! That's what we had for breakfast, lunch and dinner for many, many days. Because of the shortage of bread, the staple of Macedonian life, it seemed as if I was always hungry. If you managed to be among the lucky few first in line, you could perhaps get a slice of bread to go with the cabbage. Cabbage!

However, after a few months, we began to see improvements. The International Red

Cross sent monitors to oversee our situation. Supplies began to come from that organization. Finally a variety of food began to appear ,and soon there was ample food for all.

What was especially surprising were the uniforms made expressly for us kids, identifying us as *The Begaltsi!* Also, the Red Cross provided us with good, warm blankets, white sheets and pillows for our army cots.

A building was designated as the shop for the production of our uniforms. The building seemed to have plenty of manpower and sewing machines. After we had been measured for the uniforms, we were wearing them within a week. We looked pretty special. Dressed in the uniforms, which were the colors of the Yugoslav Army Corps, we resembled Yugoslav Army Cadets.

And then, wonder of wonders, we were even sized for shoes! Somebody cared about us!

We were absolutely splendiferous.

We were no longer hungry, ragtag, forlorn children.

We were the *Detsa Begaltsi!*

Our Doms were equipped with showers, and, of course, we now were a little more sophisticated. We knew how to use them. We were no longer little village people.

We were given individual towels!

We were given schedules for showering, with time limits in the shower and there was to be no fooling around!

A male supervisor was stationed at the door to maintain discipline. Any noise coming from the showers was his signal to come in shouting. By this time I had had enough of him, this supervisor, and his importance. So one morning I gathered some shavings from the soap bars, wetted the shower room cement floor, and polished it with the soap shavings. Together with the other guys, we made some noise in the shower room and then we screamed.

When he came running—as we knew he would—the minute his feet hit the cement floor, he slipped and his legs went heavenward as the back of his head hit the cement with a large thud! We loved it.

Of course, I was immediately summoned to the director's office, questioned, threatened, warned, and sent back. He could find no witness to support his suspicion that I was the chief criminal! Do you see what I mean when I say I was born to be free?

I didn't face any punishment this time, but there were punishments to think about, to reinforce discipline. The possibility of forfeiting a meal, for example, was something really to think about—if you were the thinking sort. If that didn't work, you could look forward to scrubbing the mess hall on your knees, using a bucket and a hard brush; or being denied free time for shows, hikes, field trips; or being isolated from all the other kids and placed in a special area. If you were a true hardhead, you could suffer all the punishments combined.

The mess hall bore the marks of my frequent scrubbings. Rules, regimentation and conformity were never compatible with Kapitan Sotir. That is still me, even today. However, I did get up promptly at 5 a.m., which was not a problem for a village boy. I did calisthenics, made my bed neatly, smoothly with no wrinkles. We had to pass daily inspection. I washed, dressed, went to the yard, played, studied and relaxed. Maintaining the schedule and proper behavior was expected and mandatory at the Dom.

As time went on, responsibility for the beds, hygiene, and preparation of food in the kitchen was assigned to us kids. We alternated tasks weekly. Here we were, *Begaltsi* from many villages, sharing the same experiences, good and bad. These experiences together forged bonds of strong relationships among us.

We were beginning to feel as if we were from one village.

We no longer were the kids from T'rsie or Bouf. We were the kids from *Chetverti Dom,* Dorm #4, from Aegean Macedonia.

We were all Macedonian, but we were the Aegeans.

We were one for all and all for one, *Egeitski* Musketeers!!

We would become the Begaltsi Generation.

During the first several weeks, there was no formal school, but somehow we all managed to learn the Macedonian alphabet. Although at first the guys from the same village tended to stick together, that was lessening. We were able to intermingle with Begaltsi from the villages of Zhelevo, Psoderi, Rudari, Pipli, Gherman, Lagen, Kotari, *gorno* and *dolno* (upper and lower), Chereshnitsa, Oshchima and Armensko. Kids from some of the other villages played, worked and learned with us, but I have, unfortunately, forgotten, their names.

But their faces I have not forgotten. They are in my album of never-to-be forgotten memories. We learned the alphabet from each other. Whenever the older kids got a hold of paper, they would scribble letters for us. First we learned to trace our hands on the paper, and then we traced the letters that would spell out, SEE HOW BIG I GREW! We sent these drawings and scribbles to our families whenever it was possible to send them something.

We never found out if our parents ever received our letters. I remember receiving two letters from my father during the first year of our departure from T'rsie. I received one in April of 1948, and another in July, the same year. I have never forgotten those dates. In the last letter, he wrote saying, "If we are fortunate, we shall see each other within a short time. The war in China will end around September, October, and we here, back home, should end the war by November, December, 1949." That letter gave me so much hope that we would be able to return home pretty soon, and we would all be together again.

Hope. It is good to hope, but in the meantime, life had to be lived in this new place, and so all of us kids tried our best to adjust to our new life and our new routines. Of all the people who were our tutors or advisors in Bela Crkva, I remember only three. Whether they came from Bitola or Prilep is something I have forgotten. But I remember the three very well, because whenever I was called to the *konselaria,* the office, one of them acted as my spokesman, interpreter and counselor. It was the job of one of them to explain my actions and to assure his superior that I would improve my behavior after each infraction of the rules. There were many infractions for as many rules. I tested them all.

Early on, my counselor was Serbian. After several command appearances in the *konselaria,* I was told that my behavior could not be tolerated any more. Surprise! Surprise! I was threatened with severe, harsher punishments; that my privileges would be taken away, and on and on. We were expected to be civilized and act accordingly, and that I, particularly, had much to improve. He emphasized in no uncertain terms that I was to LEARN TO OBEY AND FOLLOW INSTRUCTIONS.

I always sat absolutely still during those sessions in the office. You would not have recognized me had you been there in that office with me. I gave every appearance of listening and absorbing everything that was said.

The truth of the matter is I sat absolutely still, hearing very little, absorbing nothing. When the lectures and threats ended, my tutor/counselor/interpreter would repeat in the most urgent, forceful manner everything that was said. He always ended with, "Do you understand? Do you?"

I always directed my innocent look at him, not indicating one way or the other if I had understood or not. Heck, I knew the answer to his question. I always walked away totally unmoved, and totally unchanged. After all, what could they do to me? Send me home? How I wished they would.

After a while, it was clear that I was going to be my tutor's greatest challenge. My tutor was a she, by the way, not a he. She was on me all the time, watching me, anticipating my every move. She was determined to mold me into a well-mannered, good-natured, obedient boy.

Sure! But I did like her and gave her a private nickname: *Dzhvura.* A *dzhvura* is a toy made out of wood, smoothly rounded down to a sharp point at one end. With a string tied on the small knob on the top of the rounded surface, I could spin it on a hard surface. She reminded me of my *dzhvura*, which my Dedo had made for me. It was small and plump, just like her.

I remember that she had brown hair. She was always nicely dressed and usually smiling. It was obvious she liked us kids, because she tried to help us in so many ways. Her name was Marika. I remember once when she asked me, "Why do you call me *Dzhvura*?"

"Well, you're built like one," I replied in my usual blunt way. "Second, you spin around like one, turning, running here and there, and all over."

"Dobro, taka neka bide, okay, so be it. And I will call you by an appropriate name." She paused. "*Ludo*, wild, or maybe *zaginat*, lost, sounds like either might be your real name."

I didn't much care for that, so I responded to her, impudently, "My name is Sote. Ask anybody."

"Oh, I did, and they all said, 'Oh, *toi ludio*, that wild one.'"

I decided to use reverse psychology. "Call me anything you want. I am going to be your friend just the same!"

We left it at that, not too dissatisfied with each other. I really liked my *Dhzvura*, my Marika.

Bela Crkva had some real possibilities as a place for adventure!

Iconia From Montenegro

You cannot create experience, You must undergo it.

ALBERT CAMUS

Two or three months into the school year, a lady from Montenegro arrived with her son, Ivitsa. Ivitsa was very tall for his age, and he looked like a skinny beanpole. I nicknamed him *visok Todor bes koski,* tall Theodore without bones because he reminded me of a character in a Macedonian tale about *Visok Todor.*

Ivitsa and I became good friends. Ivitsa's mother, the lady from Montenegro, *Gospozha Iconia,* widowed, and in her forties, became the second in command at the school, the assistant principal. She was a real disciplinarian, very strict, smart, knowledgeable, and very loud. She was also very kind and empathetic.

At first I couldn't figure her out, because she had the bad habit of pulling ears. Every time I did something wrong and it came to her attention, my ears were pulled, and they would be sore for a week. Sometimes, as she pulled, tears even came to my eyes.

As bad as my reputation was for being a troublemaker, and you might not want to believe me, but *Gospozha Iconia* took a liking to me! Don't ask my why. She often would share an apple between Ivitsa and me. Whenever she came back from a trip, she always brought me sports memorabilia. However, she never played favorites at the Dom, like doling out more food to one person over another, or permitting anyone to miss an assignment, or get better clothes.

Gospozha Iconia showed no favoritism to any of us, but she did see us as individuals with different needs. She liked to personalize things for me. Although I think she had high hopes for me, she always addressed me as *magarets*, jackass. She often addressed both her son and me as *magartsi*, jackasses. She seemed to be constantly on my case, threatening my ears, even threatening to have my tongue pulled. Ivitsa and I were very careful with our language in front of her or wherever she might be able to hear us.

We often got punished even when we didn't do anything, Ivitsa and I, even though I knew mischief was my middle name. She punished us both for riding the horses and getting on Drago's motorcycle.

Ahhh, that motorcycle—another true love of mine! She had no knowledge of this love affair. But even if she had known about it, I would never have been given permission to ride it. Not ever!!

I did have a bad experience with that motorcycle when I rode into the open fields. To this day, I don't know how far I had driven when the accident happened. Drago had already taught me how to ride the bike, and I was good at it. I rode that thing at will whenever the opportunity presented itself.

On this particular day, I asked Drago for permission to drive it, and as usual he gave me his consent. So there I was, perched on the bike, riding toward the Nero

River, when I decided to change direction and head for the fields. I accelerated, and then accelerated some more, hitting something and spinning around in almost a complete circle. The bike seemed to turn up and then, bamo! Down we went, the bike landing on top of my right leg.

I tried to move to get loose, to get up, but I was stuck. After stubbornly persisting, I pulled and tugged and finally got out from under and stood up on my feet. As I started to walk away from the bike, I began to smell something. I must have been about 12 feet from the bike when the explosion blew it apart. At once, I felt heat on the back of my head and back. I felt a burning sensation on my hand.

When I saw that my shirt was now on fire, I dropped and rolled on the ground to put it out. I walked for a good half hour before I got a ride back to the police station. Drago wasn't there, but Sergeant Milan was. He told me to go directly to the hospital, while he sent someone to retrieve what was left of the bike.

I walked to the hospital, where I got a severe scolding from the doctor while he treated for some minor burns. As I entered the Dom's yard, *Gospozah Iconia* saw me. Her eyes widened and, looking at me with those piercing eyes, she demanded, "Why is the hair on the back of your head so short, *magarets*? What are those patches on your back from? What happened?"

I told her truthfully about my escapade and accepted my anticipated punishment. Oh yeah, I can still hear her words ringing in my ears, "No meal tonight and, *magarets,* you will clean classrooms for 3 days!"

So, what did you expect?

Georgiadis

He that hath a head of wax, must not walk in the sun.

English Proverb

We began to see some new faces among staff members. At first a handful of *Vlachs,* of nomadic Romanian origin, from Psoderi arrived. Then, under the orders of the KKE involved in the civil war, we began to see *prosvigi,* and their numbers began to increase.

One particularly despicable *prosviga* was a man named Georgiadis, Nikolaos Georgiadis. We learned much later that the KKE headquarters selected him to ensure that we *Begaltsi* were converted into Greeks! He understood Macedonian, but refused to speak it.

This Georgiadis was a short, heavy-set man. His white hair and bushy eyebrows framed a face with eyes as dark as coals. He had the biggest hands I had ever seen, and I became quite well-acquainted with those hands of his. He hated the assignment he had been given, and hated us Macedonian kids even more. His disdain and hatred of us showed at every possible opportunity. He was presumed to be a leader among the teachers, yet he kept to himself most of the time. Never was he seen talking to children. He would stride through groups of us kids without even so much as a nod in our direction.

The first time he held class, his anger and dislike was so visible that those sitting up front could feel the spittle that fell from his mouth. He reminded us of a *bishe*, a pig. He spoke only in Greek to us. We never spoke Greek to him. All of us were certain he understood Macedonian, but he never spoke a word to us in our language. I had no personal contact with him at first because he was assigned to the older boys. My irritation began to build as I saw him insulting the boys. He tried to be cunning, but he was so obviously mean-spirited. Damn, but I couldn't stand him. I decided that there was no question but that he had to have his comeuppance, and soon.

Georgiadis had a cohort who pretty much copied him, doing everything Georgiadis did. Georgiadis, along with his cohort, took to slapping us all—even the little ones—very hard.

Why?

Why were we stuck with the likes of them?

Where were the Macedonians and why weren't they in charge of us?

Something didn't seem right.

This was the topic of discussion among us kids when we were together. The injustice of it all was what struck us. Here we were, separated from our families, our birthplaces, fleeing from the tyranny and harassment of the Greeks, living among strangers in a foreign land, only to find ourselves harassed by distasteful Greeks. We were supposed to be protected from people such as Georgiadis. Here he was, a Greek Communist, using fascistic tactics against children. Weren't the Greek and Macedonian Partizans supposedly united in the struggle to be free of terror and inequality?

How wrong we had been in our assumptions. Had the adults and the leaders of the Macedonian movement been misled? Risto Kochov from Turie was the first to voice our feelings. This is what I remember him saying with such passion, that it stirred us all:

"How is it that these Greeks can manipulate not only us but our leaders as well? It is going to get worse. Just you wait and see. We are supposed to be going to Macedonian schools, with Macedonian teachers, but these *kopili,* bastards, aren't going to let that happen, you'll see! We have got to do something and do it fast. You see how Georgiadis is trying to scare the bigger, stronger kids. He's up to something. Sote, think of something. We have to act as a group!"

We thought hard about what Risto had said. It did seem as if our *maiki* and the staff in charge of us could do very little. I felt there was only one solution to solve the problem of Georgiadis, and I voiced it.

"Let's kill him," I said calmly.

There was silence for a while. No one spoke. Then someone said that wasn't a bad idea, but, as usual, some felt the idea was crazy. We didn't act on anything because we really didn't know what to do, or how do to it.

Risto's predictions were right on, Georgiadis was up to something. He was going to get rid of the older kids one way or the other, which would give him greater control over the younger ones. My cousin Risto recalls:

"At the end of June, 1948, the kids who were in Bela Crkva, aged 13 to 15 from the villages of T'rsie, Turie, Kotori and Lagen, were sent to Bulkes. At the end of 1948, they were then sent to Prespa. Among the T'rsiani were Stefo Nitchov, Risto Nitchov, Ilo Nitchov, Petre Dimov, Yane Maleganov, Ilo Lazhgov, Goge Utovski, Mite Nanov, Risto Torkov (Temianin), Krsto Pandov, Vane Popov (Findin), Itso Chechanov, Tode Giamov and two girls, Vanga Balkova and Kotsa Karachorova.

Stefo, Vane, Tode, Krsto, and Itso were sent to fight with the Partizans because they were larger and stronger, even if they were underage. Although Vanga was selected to join the Partisans, it was decided that she was too small to carry a rifle."

They separated this group from the rest of the *Begaltsi*. They had to live alone and apart from us until their departure for Bulkes, where they were to be given new uniforms. This was the fate of the young *Begaltsi* who were evacuated from the villages and towns to bring them to safe havens, for protection against the whimsies of warfare. Instead, they were earmarked by the Greeks to become cannon fodder. I wonder how many of the Greek evacuees were selected to fight?

After Georgiadis cleaned house of the older kids, he announced the formal opening of school. We kids were not expecting the kind of education he was planning for us. The buildings he designated for our classrooms were located by the church and the nuns' home. The Yugoslav Red Cross workers—who were supposedly our hosts—seemed to have a hands-off policy regarding our education. The Yugoslavs also stayed out of our "internal" situation, just concerning themselves with our housing, food and clothing.

I don't recall how long after we had arrived in Bela Crkva that school officially opened. Until that opening, our days were spent adjusting to our new surroundings, speculating about what was happening back home, and wondering always what was going to happen to us. Most of us felt happy and eager to go to Macedonian schools. Those of us over 10 years old had already learned the Macedonian alphabet as I mentioned before.

When that first day of school came, and we walked into our classroom, we saw what looked like small table tops attached to chairs. This was different. Desks? Who knew desks? And there were little bottles or jars of a black liquid on each tabletop. All the boys and girls scurried around and picked their own place to sit and waited for the teacher. I picked a chair in the front row, to the right of the teacher's desk. I looked around the large room, which was divided down the middle by an aisle. Aisles also ran along the wall and by the windows.

Rumor had it that the teachers were delayed in transit, which had, in turn, delayed the opening of our Macedonian schools. We had been waiting about 10 minutes or so when we heard heavy footsteps. Risto, who sat to the right of me, murmured, "I bet it's that *kopile.*" Done Kostov, Goce Filkov from Oshchima and Lazo Kotev from Turie, as well as Itzo Bozhanin, and Itso Maleganov sitting behind me, heard Risto.

Then *he*—Georgiadis—walked in. An audible, collective hissing sound of disbelief and disappointment filled the room. We hated that bastard. We watched that despicable SOB walk in, and without looking at anyone, approach his desk. He sat on the corner of the desk, took out a sheet of paper, looked at it, and then counted how many of us were present. Having finished that, he sat down. Mr. Warmth he was never going to be.

For the first time, he spoke in "broken" Macedonian, asking for a volunteer to come to the blackboard and write the alphabet. I thought he was going to make fun of us and our language.

Suddenly an immense anger engulfed me and I shot my hand up in the air to volunteer. I would show him that we knew our alphabet! I got up with such determination and focus that in two steps I made it to the blackboard. Picking up the chalk, I wrote the Macedonian alphabet. Triumphantly, I placed the chalk on the ledge of the blackboard, and went back to my seat.

All this time, Georgiadis had had his back turned, reading the paper, *Phony Tis Bulkes*, which was the official Greek Communist paper, published in Bulkes. I saw the looks of shock on the faces of my friends. They were appalled.

"You're going to get it now. You better run."

I didn't hear a word. I was bursting with pride. My eyes shone with the light of the righteous pride I felt deep within me. I was absolutely elated that I had taken the first opportunity to write the Macedonian alphabet.

Now Georgiadis turned toward the blackboard. From where I was seated I could see the contours of his face become distorted. We could all sense the fury transforming his face. He mumbled something through clenched teeth and came over to my seat menacingly, thundering, "That's not what I wanted! "

"That's the only alphabet I know. Anyway, we are Macedonians, not Greeks."

Even before I finished my sentence, he whacked me so hard on the right side of my face, I didn't know what hit me. I didn't see it coming. The entire class jumped to their feet and they froze in place. Someone muttered, "Greek bastard". Others were saying something else in an undertone.

I had been hit many times in my life, but this whack was different. This hit came from an enraged adult, an enraged *mature* adult. The injustice and the shock immobilized me. It was the closest I had ever come to crying publicly. Had I a gun in my hand, he would have been dead on the spot.

My eyes burned with hot tears, as my heart raced with anger. My whole body was hot and trembling, not because he whacked me, but because I hadn't seen it coming and, so, hadn't dodged the impact of his hand!

I sat, frozen in my seat, not knowing how to vent my rage. Suddenly my eyes focused on the ink bottle on my desk, and I knew my revenge was at hand. As he harangued the rest of the class, I grabbed that little ink bottle and, with fullest force I could muster, I threw it at him, covering his face and filthy clothes with black ink. He sputtered; the class cheered. I ran to the door, turned and faced him, hurling the most vile curses I had ever heard at him.

That was a moment to cherish!

While he tried to clean off his brownish-gray suit coat—it was filthy, wrinkled, and frayed anyway—I ran like lightning out of the school, past the church, up the road, and to the top the of the hill where you could see the entire beautiful city of Bela Tsurkva.

I could see Nero, the river that was the border between Yugoslavia and Romania. I paused there, scanning the many peaceful farms and small lakes that dotted the countryside. I spotted the train station that was still beckoning to me as a way to escape all this. Sighing deeply, I walked toward a small bunker and stretched out, staring at the sky.

Ah, that sky! Relaxing a bit, I began to feel so better, so vindicated, so at peace with myself, that I feared nothing at that moment. I felt absolutely no regrets at what I had done to that *kopile*.

In that moment of triumph, satisfaction and relaxation, my 12-year-old brain started to generate thoughts again of going back to where I belonged, to T'rsie. Today, in my middle age, my middle-aged brain still longs to do that.

It was very clear to me what I had to do. I would take the train to Belgrad and once there, I would find the direction to Bitola. That would put me close to the Macedonian border. From Bitola, I reasoned, I was positive I would find my way back to T'rsie. In fact, there was no doubt I could walk the distance. I dwelt on that scenario for a while.

What a great idea. It was so simple! I chided myself for not acting on this plan earlier. I certainly was not going to remain here and be abused by stinking Greeks. So I cussed the Greeks for a while longer. It felt so liberating.

I spent the entire day on top of my bunker, daydreaming about my trip home to family. I thought of the happier times in T'rsie and Lerin. How we kids played! My memory flipped from one happy thing to another, and pretty soon I was aware that the sun had started to set.

Snapping out of my daydreaming, I willed myself back to reality. What had happened to me and why I was here on the bunker was no longer important. What was I going to do between *now* and the time I was to leave for Belgrad?

All my rage came flooding back. Georgiadis! Even if I were to go back, he would beat the shit out of me. I could almost feel his angry blows again.

I had to get in touch with my buddies, but how? Now, *this* was a serious dilemma. My mind went over the events bringing me to Bela Tsurkva and Georgiadis. I stopped trying to work out something. I knew what I had to do. I had to find Drago.

Drago

A sympathetic friend can be quite as dear as a brother.

HOMER, 9TH B.C.

Let me tell you about *Drago*, that's short for his real name, Dragolub. We met on the street the first week after we kids had arrived in Bela Tsurkva. Drago was the police captain of the station across the street from our Dom.

Drago and I bonded quickly at several levels, but our first connection was our mutual love of horses. He had the second-best horse I had ever seen in my entire 12-year old life. You know that Tome was first in my heart.

Drago's horse was a beautiful horse, with a shiny reddish coat. The hair and tail were trimmed and brushed. He was also the tallest horse I had ever seen. He was a beauty to look at. Drago called him *Kral*, Serbian for King, but I dubbed him *Tsrvenko*, or Red.

It was while Drago was holding the rein, standing in front of the station that on an impulse I couldn't control, I jumped on the horse, without permission! Drago, astonished, asked, "Are you not afraid?"

"No!"

"How come?"

With great braggadocio in my voice and manner I replied, "I had a horse back home in T'rsie. His name was Tome."

In that short simple encounter, Drago must have seen something in my face, or heard the emotion in my voice. He and I connected, just like that, and I certainly liked him on the spot. It wasn't just about the horse. There was something about the man, this stranger, I felt I could trust.

Ironic, isn't it? A Yugoslav police captain and the irascible Macedonian Sotir?

We had never seen each other before. But, from this brief encounter—seeing my absolute delight with Tsrvenko—Drago let me ride the horse whenever there was an opportunity to do so.

While I reflected on my first meeting with Drago and Tsrvenko, my thoughts drifted back to my horse, Tome. What a horse he was, the first and the best horse I ever had. Tome understood me so well, He understood all my moods and feelings quickly. How I wished he were here with me. With him I could work everything out.

Maybe Drago would let me have Tsrvenko and I could ride back to T'rsie, to home!

Again my thoughts drifted as I lay there above Bela Tsurkva. Maybe I should run down to one of the collective farms, down there near the river Nero and hide. But what if someone should see me and turn me in? The police most certainly would return me to the Dom office to face the despicable Georgiadis.

I started to make tracks toward the town. As I neared the park, I spotted some of the older girls sitting on the park benches. Pavlina, one of the older girls, saw me. She was with Tancha from Rudari, Vasilka from Gherman, Lena from Armensko and Tomka from T'rsie. Pavlina called to me and ran to where I had stopped. The others quickly followed her.

"Are you all right? How is your face?"

"How are you coping?"

"Are you hungry?"

I replied that I was fine, fine. We talked for a few short minutes. One of the girls said, "Wait here."

Two or three also left, and as they departed, I told Pavlina and Vasilka that I was going to hide somewhere. "I'll get in touch with my dorm-mates somehow," I told them, meaning Done, Risto, Goce, Laze, Yane, Itso, Vangel and Done Kuleov.

The girls returned with some chocolate bars. My cousin, Sofa, the most soft-hearted, came back with them. When she saw me, she started to cry. Finally, pulling herself together, she stopped. Then, I spoke up again and warned her and the others, "Don't tell that *Vlahinka* anything!"

This *Vlahinka,* a woman of Wallachian origin, whose first name I believe was Antigone, had a sister Cleo and a brother. Their last name was Nikiforos and they were from the village of Psoderi. Antigone had become very friendly with all the Macedonian kids, but she also was very chummy with the bastard, Georgiadis. I knew in my heart that she couldn't be trusted, so I warned the girls again. They promised not to say anything to her, and we parted.

As the girls left for their Dom, I made my way toward the *igralishte*, which are the stadium grounds. I still didn't have a clue where I would find a hiding place for the night, and as my 12-year old mind went over possible options, I had my second cogent thought of the day. I knew exactly where I was heading. No one would ever think of looking for me there.

I headed directly toward the police captain's stable. Getting into the police stable wasn't that difficult. There was no way I could go through the front gates, so I maneuvered from the houses behind the police station, climbed a couple of walls in the back and found my way into the stable.

Oh, this was perfect! I found some straw and hay, and fashioned a mattress of sorts, and lay down. Perfect! The minute my head hit the homemade mattress, it was lights out for me after my tumultuous, emotional day. I was home. I was safe.

The police station and stables were separated from the Doms by a single road, so when the kids began to awaken the next morning around 5 a.m., the noise from the Doms awakened me. Out of habit, I started to get up before I realized that I wasn't going to be able to go anywhere for a while. Goooood! I went back to sleep.

I don't know how long I slept before I felt a gentle nudge on my shoulder. As I slowly opened my eyes, I found that I was looking directly into Drago's eyes. "Don't you think you should get up and do your calisthenics? Your buddies have already done theirs." I smiled at him sleepily, and he smiled back. Then he explained that when the men began to come in to check and feed the horses, one of them saw me and reported back to the Captain.

"How come no one saw you come in? When did you get here? Why are you here? Trouble of some kind? I know you're a slick kid, but getting into the police station, with the gates closed! How and where did you find any openings?" Drago was beginning to see that TROUBLE was also one of my middle names. He was shaking his head. I laughed at him,

"Huh! I can get in anywhere, even into Tito's house."

"I believe you!"

You have to understand that Drago did not know how to speak Macedonian anymore than I could speak Serbian, but because we were both Slavs, somehow we were able to communicate with a few words. As our relationship developed we picked up words from each other. He always seemed to understand me, not just my spoken words, but my feelings and my deeper concerns and conflicts.

I remember teasing him because he always seemed to be smiling. I remarked to him, "You are a tough, bad policeman, but you always smile. Where I come from, policemen never smile. They are mean and they beat you up."

Drago kept looking at the right side of my face. "Who hit you? I can see the imprint of a hand clearly on your face. I can almost read your fortune in it."

I told him what had happened the day before and why it happened. The smile left Drago's face. He suggested gently that we go together to the *Upravnik's* office. The *Upravnik* was the director, in charge of staff and all personnel connected with the Doms. I looked into Drago's eyes and thought for a minute. I could trust this man. I agreed to go with him to the office.

Sweet Revenge

This is sweet: To see your foe perish and pay justice to all he owes.

EURIPIDES, 422 B. C.

The *Upravnik's* name was Smile, pronounced *Smileh*. He was of average height but very overweight. He looked intelligent, thoughtful, and soft-spoken. Facing him, with Drago at my side and at his urging, I repeated the entire affair, leaving out no detail.

When I had finished speaking, the *Upravnik* expressed controlled surprise. No *Begaltsi* had been reported missing from the Doms. That's what we were called now, the *Begaltsi* children who had been evacuated from Aegean Macedonia. One of the key responsibilities the *Upravnik* had was to keep careful watch over the children and our well-being. We were to be accounted for at all times.

I could see Captain Drago getting upset. I looked at him questioningly. Then the *Upravnik* addressed me. "I want you to come back here tomorrow morning. In the meantime I will investigate the matter." He also instructed me to go to the hospital for a check-up. I didn't say anything, and I didn't go to the hospital.

As we were leaving the office, Captain Drago paused for a moment and said pointedly to the *Upravnik* that he felt that Georgiadis should be arrested. The *Upravnik* apparently felt otherwise, but then he was the civil authority. Captain Drago had to accede to his authority.

The Captain felt he had to express himself a little more strongly, which sounded like "*Neches ga videt nikada.*" I think he meant that if he could arrest Georgiadis, he would never be seen again! How I wished!

Now he couldn't legitimately hide me, but both the Captain and I knew where I would spend the night. We retraced our steps toward the park across from the stables. He told me to take five or six horses down to the fields and one at a time, I could ride them through the fields for a few hours.

Oh, I was in seventh heaven! The sweet sense of freedom, feeling the horse under me, and flying through the fields, freed me—no, purged me—of everything depressing. It was almost like flying on the wings of a *sokol.*

After a while a policeman on a motorcycle came to me with instructions to bring the horses back and take out another bunch for grazing and exercise. Could life get any better than this?

With those wonderful chores finally over, I found I still had time on my hands. That's when I wandered over to the stadium again. It was then, there, at that very moment—at the age of 12—that I fell in love—hook, line and sinker.

It must have been Destiny that put her hand on my shoulder back there in Bitola, knowing that this field, and this experience, was waiting for me. I believe this. I was destined to find the love of my life right here in Bela Crkva on the playing field. My first glimpse of my love, soccer, happened just then.

I had just come upon a soccer game. It was only a practice game, and I knew from that first moment, I was hooked. Soccer was to become my life, my dream, and yes, maybe my ultimate destiny! Done, Itso, Risto and Lazo found me there.

Catching up with the events that followed my departure, they told me that a man named Kosta wanted to talk to me. I didn't know who this Kosta was, or what he wanted to learn from me. I just assumed that this man who wanted to talk to me had something to do with the bastard. I guess Risto did too.

In our reckless adolescent way, we began to plan Georgiadis' demise again. Itso Malegenov was to make the knife. Some of the guys thought about stealing a gun from the police. I flatly nixed that idea, telling them that the police were our friends. Besides, sooner or later, someone would find out it was a police gun. They would investigate and suspect us. After considering options for a few minutes, we decided to go down by the prison camps and snoop around. Who knows what kismet might reward us with?

We were obsessed with the idea of getting rid of that SOB Georgiadis. As we walked, we thought out loud, that perhaps we should follow him, see where he goes and what he does. We were in full agreement that one way or the other we would dispose of that garbage, Georgiadis.

The following day, about three or four of us went directly to the *Upravnik's* office. He motioned toward the chairs, indicating we should sit. As we did so he pulled some papers from his desk drawer. While stacking them on the desk, he scrutinized my face. "Have you seen a doctor?"

"No."

"How do you feel?"

"Fine."

"It still looks pretty bad. I think you should see the doctor."

The *Upravnik* paused. Then, with the weight of authority evident on his face and in his voice, he spoke to me in gentle, firm tones. "This will never happen again. Nobody is allowed to hit our children. Nobody," he emphasized.

"As Greeks, you have the right to have your own schools and teachers . . . ."

We heard no other words after he said "as Greeks." As if on cue, we all jumped up and started to talk at once. We startled him, and, quite flustered, he told us to quiet down.

"You will act in a civilized manner, and you will speak one at a time. Who wants to be first?"

We looked at one another and then we all looked at Risto. He spoke up courteously and respectfully. "*Druzhe Upravnik*, Comrade *Upravnik*, first of all, we are not Greeks. We are Aegean Macedonians. And that is the main reason we are here. We were sent by our families to escape from the Greeks. They are killing us back home, burning our villages, our schools, our books. Anything and everything Macedonian is either killed, tortured, burned or jailed."

Startled, the *Upravnik* replied, "But I have official documents from the Red Cross and from Belgrad that says you are Greek children." I started to speak profanely, but the *Upravnik* cut me off.

"You will be careful about how and what you say to whomever you speak." He pointed to a chair.

I sat down and my buddies, warned me to shut up and not show my anger. From the window we could see Nikoforos. I thought if only this guy could talk to the *Upravnik* in Greek, maybe then he would see the difference between Greek and Macedonian. Risto read my mind. He spoke up, addressing the *Upravnik.*

"May we bring one other person to talk to you?"

"Whom do you have in mind?"

I immediately dashed out of the office to fetch Nikoforos, the *Vlach* from the village of Psoderi, to tell him to come with me to the office.

He protested that he had not done anything wrong. I told him that if he did not join us in the office, I would smash his head just the way I smash snakes' heads. He threatened me, "You'll pay for this." I told him fine, and forced him to come with me anyway.

"Talk to the *Upravnik* in Greek. Say anything, even cuss at him. He won't understand a word." He came with me very reluctantly. He did surprise me at the courteous way in which he spoke to the *Upravnik.*

Risto addressed the Upravnik, "This young man can show you that we are not Greek children, but Macedonian. Listen to him, please."

Nikoforos began speaking Greek for a minute or so, and then stopped. The *Upravnik* got up and said, "Enough. You may all leave now. I'll check into this more thoroughly. You will return to this office in a couple of days."

Before we left, almost in unison, we said, "Sir, we want Macedonian teachers. Get rid of all the Greeks."

The *Upravnik* spoke to me, saying that I had nothing to be afraid of and that I should go back to my Dom. No one would bother me. The *Upravnik* was so soft-spoken and cool. I couldn't understand why he wasn't as angry as we were about the situation. At this point, however, I wasn't afraid to go back. I just didn't want any of Georgiadis' flunkies to try to smash my face again.

Instead, I happily went back to the stables for a couple of more nights. My presence did not present a problem for the police nor Drago because only the police were allowed on the premises. There was a point that both Captain Drago and Sergeant Milan wanted to make clear to me that evening. "In case someone else finds you or sees you, you are not to tell them that we know you are here. Don't leave any trace of food, because then I would get in trouble with the Chief. You see this?" pointing to his Captain's bars. "They will take these away, and I will become just a Milan and Milan will become just a *militsaets*—meaning I will be demoted to Sergeant and Milan will become an ordinary policeman."

I looked at Milan and then at Drago. I got the picture, very clearly. Milan had been good to me, bringing me army blankets and food every day. I hid the blankets behind the bales of hay every morning. I liked Milan as much as I liked Drago, so there would be no way that I would jeopardize the situation for them.

We were three musketeers, Yugoslavian style, co-conspirators, friends, a Serbian police captain, a Serbian police sergeant and a 12-year old Begalche, a refugee, an evacuee, a homesick boy from T'rsie, Egeiska Macedonia! An unlikely trio if there ever was one!

The next morning I made my way back to the park again and sat on a bench near the main road. This was a security strategy. Should a problem arise, I would have the option of running in any one of several directions. I was leafing through one of Drago's magazines, SPORT, which seemed to be all about soccer. I was so engrossed in it, that I didn't see the man who suddenly appeared before me. I looked up and saw that it wasn't the bastard, but a man who looked somewhat familiar. I really didn't know who he was or what his connection with us kids was.

The stranger greeted me. "*Dobar den,* good day."

"*Dobar den,* good day," I replied.

"May I ask you a question?

"It depends on what you ask," I said cautiously.

"Oh, it's a simple question," he said reassuringly.

"Do you know this kid Sote or Sotir?"

"I may have seen him around," I said, pretending indifference. "Why are you asking?"

Looking at me intently, he spoke. "I want to talk to him."

"Who are you anyway? What is your responsibility with us kids?" I shot back at him. I felt pretty cocky, but I had to listen to him carefully, because I couldn't understand him too well.

"Well, yes, I am with the children. I am helping to situate them, make them comfortable, see that they get food, clothing; education, teachers . . . ."

"Teachers?" I interrupted him. "I'll tell that kid when I see him."

I started to walk out of the park. The word "teachers" was a code word for Georgiadis to me. Maybe he was one of the bastard's flunkies. Get the hell out of here, Sote, I told myself. I got to the fence, stopped, and decided to turn around.

"Hey, what's your name?"

"Kosta."

"You speak good Macedonian," I said. "I wish I could."

"You will pretty soon. Don't worry about it," he said confidently.

I shook my head, "Not with those—*Greeks*—here."

"Be patient. They won't be here long."

Still unconvinced, I replied, "Yah, Greeks at home. Greeks here, and you want patience?"

"You should learn to trust people." He said this with a look of understanding as he spoke.

"You know, I remember my Dedo and the other Dedos saying, 'even if you could stuff a Greek in a bottle and put a cap on the bottle tightly, you still couldn't trust him,'" I told Kosta.

"The old folks are wise," Kosta agreed. "Good thing you remember what your Dedo told you. You have learned a valuable lesson, Sote."

He knew my name! My eyes widened in surprise. He smiled slightly as he continued, "Go behind the buildings. I'll see you by the i*gralishte,* the stadium, in a while."

Suddenly there was a change in his demeanor and his voice. He whispered to me, "Hurry, go on. Someone is coming this way."

"You know my name? What makes you so sure I am Sote?"

"I will tell you later. I'll bring Risto, Lazo, Done . . . get going or he will see you."

I didn't move. "How do you know those guys? Have you been talking to them?"

Urgently, Kosta again reassured me, "Yes, they told me everything. Leave now."

"Screw Georgiadis. He will have to catch me first, and I am faster. Look at that *gunische*, garbage. He can hardly walk, and with those thick window panes he wears . . ." I didn't finish my sentence, but I quickly disappeared behind the hospital, past the girls' Dom, heading straight for the fields.

Later I found out that Kosta had met with some of the kids, told them what to do and how to behave. I glanced toward the park. Sure enough, Georgiadis, accompanied by two men I didn't recognize, was leaving the post office to cross the street, heading for the park.

I walked toward the stadium. There were only prisoners working around the stadium. To the right there were three and four story buildings just like the ones we kids were occupying. These housed the Yugoslav army units. Camps were set up for the prisoners in front of the barracks. Along the Nero River, the Russian Army was encamped.

I snooped all over the fields to pass the time. Much later, Kosta and my gang met me at the stadium. He coached us on what to do. "Keep going to the *Upravnik* with your complaints. Insist on Macedonian schools with Macedonian teachers and tutors, everything Macedonian. I will help you and we'll get help from Skopje."

At the *Upravnik's* request, we met again several days later in his office. He informed us that we were registered with the Red Cross in both Belgrad and Geneva as Greek children. At that we protested loudly. We demanded that he notify the authorities at all levels about our situation. The final thing the *Upravnik* told us was that one of the Yugoslav representatives was coming to Bela Tsurkva to see us and to check up on our situation.

We left his office somewhat mollified, but still dissatisfied. If I remember correctly, the name of the Yugoslav representative the *Upravnik* mentioned was Olga.

When the Yugoslav delegation arrived, led by Olga Mihailovich, they did not speak to us. Kosta, who was working on our behalf, represented us as they met with the *Upravnik*. Later Kosta informed us that the *Upravnik* had made notes regarding our situation, our protests and complaints, particularly regarding our demands for Macedonian schools and teachers.

We were so impatient. Things were moving too slowly for us. One of the kids even told Kosta that we were determined to kill Georgiadis. Kosta cautioned us not to think about that, not even for a minute. We would just make matters worse for everybody.

This Olga Mihailovich finally met with us kids and repeated some of what Kosta had said to us. "Keep complaining and demanding Macedonian teachers, and leave the rest to us. Let us handle this. Your job is just to keep complaining about the school, or the lack of it."

Could it be that someone, somebody had been so concerned about us, that Kosta was sent to check things out, and in turn, he brought in the Yugoslav Red Cross?

We never did learn how Kosta had heard about our frustration regarding school in Bela Tsurkva. Shoot, I thought. Another day shot to hell, and we still had these lousy Greeks with us.

The younger kids were not aware of the turmoil we were in. They were like innocent little lambs being led to the slaughter. They were attending school, learning Greek, learning to forget their own language.

As for me, my time was mine alone. I did perform masterful 12-year old things like jumping in the river, swimming with my clothes on so that they could get washed. I

Cousins Ilo and Risto Nitcov in Poland, circa 1953.

was killing two birds with one stone. Clever me. I could take a bath and get the clothes washed. Life was very good.

Captain Drago had given me a bar of soap that looked and felt like a scrub brush, but, it did the job. Because the soapsuds burned my eyes, I figured I had real soap! I ate well during my self-imposed exile from the Dom. Captain Drago kept me supplied with *biscoti*, cookies, and canned foods including sardines from the Yugoslav Army Headquarters. The Russians supplied me with food, even hot food such as meat stew. Not bad for a runaway, don't you think?

After a few days had passed, Kosta contacted me to tell me that I could now join my friends and not fear Georgiadis and his cronies ever again. He said that they were going to be shipped out to *Majerska*, the Serbian word for Hungary.

Life was getting better. My trust in Kosta grew. My friends felt they could trust him also. However, even though it seemed safe enough for me to return to my bed, based on what we were told, there was still some doubt that all had not been settled. We decided to take even more precautions and be more observant. We planned to meet again the next evening by the monument in the park.

The larger, taller monument, *spomenik,* was built on the site of a mass grave for the hundreds who had been shot by the Germans. It faced the church, where the two main roads crossed. We had been told that Russians were buried there as well, and it may have been the Russians who built the monument. The smaller monument was inside the park near the Doms, and it was said that there were more people buried there.

On the evening we were to meet again, a memorial service was being held in front of the church. Kosta and my gang mingled among the crowd. Kosta was smiling at us as we walked around. He said, "Detsa, when you get up tomorrow there will be no Greek or *Vlah* left in this town. In a week's time, you'll have your Macedonian school with Macedonian teachers. It is over for the Greeks!"

With a shout of joy, we jumped on Kosta, knocking him down, hugging him, pounding his back and shaking his hand. Had the police been around, they could have arrested us for mugging Kosta because I am sure that is what it looked like.

We had won our war against the Greeks!

We finally calmed down, Risto, Done, Lazo, Goce, Yane and I. Kosta got up and shook the dust and dirt from his clothes. He slicked back his black hair with his fingers. "*Detsa*, boys, I'll never forget you."

I spoke up, "Wait a minute. You sound as if you're leaving us."

"Yes, I have to go with them. I must. That's my job." Risto spoke up,

"No, we'll force them to leave you here with us. You belong to us. We need you."

Kosta tried to reassure us. "No, what you needed, you will now have. And you will have that in less than a week, Macedonian teachers!"

Kosta hugged every one of us goodbye. When he came to me, he looked me straight in the eyes. "You are a grown man in a boy's body. You are a *losho dete, ama dobro losho*, a bad boy but for the right reasons." He laughed, "You'll be fine, no matter where you are. One thing I must know, though. Are all T'rsiani this aggressive, this tough?"

Done took the initiative to reply. "You should have been in T'rsie. You would have found out what this devil is made of. He probably would have busted your head. He has done it to practically every one in the village." Done turned to me and mimicked the older villagers in a falsetto voice: "*Ludo. Losho dete. Ne razbran.* Crazy. Bad boy. Unreasonable."

I told Done to shut up or I would hang him up on the monument. Kosta smiled indulgently, "He's fine. He'll be good. We are all entitled to be a little wild when we are growing up."

That was the last time we spoke with Kosta.

We never saw Kosta again.

I received a letter from my cousin Itso who was now in Poland. He met Kosta after they had left Bulkes. Itso wrote that Kosta talked about the kids in Bela Crkva and he mentioned my name, Sote. Seeing Itso's interest at the mention of my name, Kosta told him about our secret revolt to kick the Greeks out of Bela Crkva, and how we were successful in our determination to get an all Macedonian school personnel, teachers and tutors and, most of all Macedonian school books.

Good Riddance!!!

The sower may mistake and sow his peas crookedly.
The peas make no mistake, but come up
and show his line.

EMERSON, *Journals,* 1843

It was as if a fresh wind had blown away the dark, depressing atmosphere when the Greeks left. The evil cloud that had enveloped us with foreboding and depression, lifted. We had thought we would never to be rid of Greek harassment and humiliation.

Were it not for the actions of the Upravnik who took his responsibility for the well-being of the evacuated children in his care in a professional manner . . .

. . . were it not for the follow-through of the Red Cross . . .

. . . and finally . . .

. . . were it not for the patient, intelligent manner in which Kosta carried our grievance to the appropriate authorities—and became our advocate—we would never have been able to assert ourselves and survive as the Macedonians we knew we were.

The sun indeed began to shine on us in Bela Crkva.

The atmosphere changed for the better. Everything seemed different. We were less tense, more relaxed and more hopeful that things would work out, eventually, and that we would be home again.

Everything seemed to change. Even the staff had a better attitude; treated us as if we belonged. They involved us in as many activities as they could. Some of us worked in the kitchen, preparing food for the meals; others were assigned to the hygiene squad. I worked with the *Dezhurni*. That's we called ourselves, "those who were selected!"

As Dezhurni, our job was to see that those who cooked for us strictly followed good sanitary practices, cleanliness, and appearance. We also checked the quality of the products that were to be used for our meals. Food became more plentiful, with a fuller variety and better taste.

Some assignments of the hygiene squad included monitoring the cleanliness and order of the quarters in which we slept. The lavatories were cleaned up. The mess hall, the hospitals and the schools were included in our tasks as monitors with the adults. Daily we reported to *Gospozah* Iconia, Madam Iconia. She supervised our work.

And at last, we were officially enrolled in a school, taught by Macedonian teachers. Our teachers taught us grammar, literature, reading, writing, history, geography, and math. Equally important, we were able to participate in all kinds of extra-curricular activities—such as vocal and instrumental music, creative arts, ballet and other types of dance. We had access to our own library, which contained 800 books and four daily newspapers, *Borba*, *Nova Makedonija*, *Glas na Egeitsite*, and *Pioner*. We went on organized field trips.

Of all the activities that opened up for us, for me, the only game in town was the sports program, particularly the opportunity to play soccer!

Imagine! I could play soccer!!

We had track-and-field, boxing and volleyball teams, as well. The Yugoslav Red Cross provided the equipment. God bless that Red Cross division! They supplied just about everything we needed, except the comfort of being with our families in our own homes. The staff assigned to us was so different, so caring and so interested in our well-being.

It made you wonder if the Greeks who had been in charge previously had had some devious plans of their own regarding us Macedonian kids. Was it their plan for us to arrive as Macedonians, but at the end of the war leave as Greeks?

I was really excited when the Macedonian school finally opened for us. Oh yes, you may not believe it. I, who hated discipline, confinement, rules and regulations, eagerly looked forward to belonging to a student body in our own Macedonian school. You must remember that Macedonian schools back home were forbidden by Greek law. Now we were to experience doors opening for us to acquire all kinds of knowledge and information in our mother tongue, Macedonian! Without fear!

The thought of knowing how to read and write in our own language, to read about our history and explore geography beyond the familiar landmarks of our native villages was almost unbelievable. I remembered Father's words about how we would one day have Macedonian schools and be educated in our own language without fear. Maybe this was what our war was all about!

Imagine learning about our own heroes and heroines and of the contributions of people of Macedonian heritage!

Imagine being able to sing our songs openly and joyously like real people, and not be afraid that you would be reported to the police!

The hardships and loneliness we endured from the time we left T'rsie through the first several months following our arrival in Bela Crkva were perhaps worth it after all. Maybe that sun was really shining on us young *Detsa Begaltsi* from *Egeitska Makedonia*.

At night though, when the day's activities had ended and we were alone in our dorms, when our thoughts drifted toward home, that's when the moments of depression and feelings of abandonment gripped us. Keep in mind that, collectively, we ranged from 2 to 14 years of age. We were just babies and kids.

We needed to hear the familiar voices of the people we loved and who loved us just as much. I wondered if everyone was still alive.

Had anyone died?

Had we been forgotten?

Would they ever take us back?

Would we ever see home again?

Under the cover of darkness, when no one could see us very well, that's when the tears of loneliness welled in our eyes. Whenever a letter arrived, everyone felt a little hope, as if it confirmed that we were still connected to the world. Those who did not receive a letter couldn't help but feel forgotten or rejected and alone.

After awhile, as our lives began to settle into routine, we reverted back to being just kids, not necessarily *Detsa Begaltsi*. Kids being kids, more resilient than adults might have been under our circumstances, the heavy curtain of fear and sadness began to lift from us. The younger kids began to revert back to carefree playfulness much faster. However, if any of the children seemed to be withdrawn for whatever reason, the older ones would pick them up, and speak some words of encouragement, making them feel better.

All of us got into the practice of helping each other get over our emotional bad times. Bonds tightened among us, bringing us all closer together, regardless of which village we were from. We all belonged to one village now. We were the children from the Aegean, Egeitsi. The Yugoslavs referred to us as Egeitsi wherever we went. They recognized us by our uniforms. I felt our uniforms were our badge of honor and distinction, and woe be to anyone who disgraced them!

We had free time to go the yard or to the park with friends. We could visit other Doms to see our brothers or sister, relatives or friends. The huge gates of our compound were open at all times. Should you, by chance, acquire some *dinars*—you know, Yugoslav money—you could buy candy or ice cream in town.

I liked to walk past the ice cream parlor of Ilia Mogush, a tall, huge man who might have weighed 400 pounds. He had such thin ankles and wrists, however, and looked a little weird to me. After a while we became quite friendly, so I felt quite comfortable taking verbal jabs at him about how he looked. No matter what I said to him, he always laughed.

Done and I walked by one day. I had some *dinars* in my pocket. My uncle in Australia had sent me some money, Australian dollars, so I was rich for a day. I bought ice cream cones for Done and me. As we walked out of the ice cream parlor, there were about five or six kids looking at us. It didn't seem fair to me that Done and I were so enjoying our ice creams, licking them with great gusto in front of the kids. I motioned to the kids to follow me, and we all trooped back into the ice cream parlor.

I went to Mogush and said, "*Chicho Ilia*, Uncle Ilia, will you give all the kids ice cream cones? I'll pay you back when I get some more *dinars*." Being the good guy that he was, he gave the kids ice cream. These 8- and 9-year-olds were just delighted. They went back to their Doms and told the others that Mogush was giving away free ice cream because Sote was paying. So the rest of the kids in those Doms went to the ice cream parlor for their free ice cream. All assumed I was paying for it! Mogush dished it out as fast as he could until he ran out of ice cream.

The next time I strolled by the parlor, Mogush ran out and said to me, "Sote, you owe me over 800 *dinars*!" My jaw dropped. I told him that I didn't have that kind of money, but I would pay him back. He had to wait a while, but he did get paid.

I said to him, "Next time, I am not paying for your carelessness."

He protested. "You told me to give all those kids ice cream cones, so I did."

"When I told you to give them the ice cream there were only five or six kids with me. That's what I meant, not 800 kids!" I pointed out to him. Chicho was not to be denied. "You said all the kids, so be quiet and pay me. Go earn 800 *dinars*!"

School Days

Knowledge is the true organ of sight,
Not the eyes.

PANCHATANTRA, 500 B. C.

The kids that I remember were eager to learn everything. Knowledge from books which had been so long denied to us, now beckoned to us: *Come, unlock our mysteries.*

Our teachers were not only good people, but they were good teachers. They displayed a respect toward each of us that was so encouraging. Not only that, they extended a reassuring personal kindness and friendship, strengthening our resolve to learn.

Our classes were large. There were at least 50 or 60 to a classroom. We had some very smart, very intelligent guys that were quick to grasp, absorb and learn. We all got to know our teachers well enough so that we could kid around with them.

As you can imagine, I was not one of the "brains" in the classroom. I excelled in practical jokes and hijinks. Although I wasn't the only one involved in pulling off pranks, you can bet I was always in on them. I remember with some remorse now, as well as fondness I must say, the day I varnished my teacher's chair.

My punishment for that prank was to kneel in the corner, which was sprinkled with salt, for an hour. The director brought the bag of salt to the teacher, saying, "He will learn one way or another!"

I didn't get a beating!

We also loosened the legs of the teacher's chair another time, so, of course, when she went to sit, she hit the floor instead, her feet pointing to the ceiling. Things like gluing her books together, watering the chalk, mixing her ink with different colors, were some of the fun things to do. It's not that I'm proud of myself but, then, these seemed like inspired things to do.

Of course, girls did not escape my attentions, either. I'll only relate one other incident at this point that happened in the park during our free time. I tied together the long hair of two girls, Pavlina and Tomka, who were sitting on a park bench, totally unaware of my presence behind them. When they started to get up to go on their way, they were yanked back together, screaming. Great screams! Poor things!

I solved their problem quickly with a pair of small scissors that I had borrowed from the lab room. I paid for that prank, too, on my knees in a pile of salt for a while. That burned like hell!

There wasn't a teacher who didn't experience my creativity at one time or another, and some of them more often than others . . .

. . . I exchanged the signs on the men's and women's rest rooms.

. . . I lent my touch to the directional signs in the hallways, so that they inevitably led to dead ends. We were taught to follow directions and pay attention to the signs, no matter what. So you can imagine what happened when about 1,000 kids were in the halls.

. . . Unnoticed by our target teacher, we tied his shoes to the desk with a thin wire, as he sat.

. . . We set a trap for a rabbit, using an entire desk to do so.

. . . We put sugar in soup and salt in milk

. . . I coerced a guy named Yane to write love letters from one teacher to another. Yane was a good forger. We almost fooled our grammar teacher into believing the letters were from the geography teacher. The staff traced the handwriting to Yane, but I couldn't let him take the blame, so I admitted that I forced him. He received a light punishment for not telling the appropriate authorities.

Although I tried to keep the fun within certain boundaries of "good taste," I may have stretched it a bit. A kid has to have some fun, right?

On the more serious side, we were finally getting our own Macedonian grammar books. The trouble was, we could get them only in this foreign land, not in the land of our birth. It brought back the realization of how far from home we were.

On the first day of school, we were lined up, two-by-two, like little soldiers in file formation, column after column. We had to walk for about 15 minutes to get to our schools. Someone started to sing a popular *Partizanski* song, which begins with, "I am going to be a Partizan on *Vicho* Mountain . . . ." Others joined in and then all of us in unison began to sing, even though we did not know all of the words. But we sang one song after another.

One would start singing a song sung by our parents in the village about our heroes, and others would join in. The townspeople who saw us and heard us, waved, smiled, and cheered us on. It made for a wonderful start on that first day. We were so elated.

Once we arrived at the schoolyard, we were arranged into age groups. Each of us was assigned to a classroom and a desk, and we were given supplies of paper, ink, pen, pencil and a beginner's Macedonian language book.

The book at first was in short supply, so three or four of us had to share. I was so impressed. I had no idea how much easier it was to learn when you are taught in your own language. Our teachers spoke clearly, so that letters and words became alive to me. There were some words that I did not understand, but I understood the teacher's explanation. Ha! School was going to be a breeze! No doubt whatsoever!!

I cannot stress enough how genuinely interested our teachers were in us. What were our names, our family names? From which village did we come? How much schooling did we have? I guess it was just a normal opening day, but when I think of our experience with that *kopile*, that bastard Georgiadis, it seemed like the difference between day and night.

Each teacher discussed rules and schedules, including breaks or recess. Our schooldays started at 8:00 a.m. and ended at 4:00 p.m. We were given 1 hour for lunch, which was served at the Doms. We walked back and forth to school, six days a week. From 4:00 to 6:00 p.m we had supervised homework and tutoring time. After 6:00, we had free time until 7:15 p.m., when we were expected to have washed and tidied up, presentable for dinner, which was served by 7:30 p.m.

Following dinner, we had free time until 9:40 p.m. for play, study or visitation. We were expected to walk quietly to wherever we were headed, unless we were told to remain in the mess hall for some kind of failure to observe a rule or two. I had that experience a few times, when I had to assist in the cleanup of the mess hall.

At 9:45 p.m. the bell would ring, signaling that we had to prepare for bed, which meant washing up, brushing teeth. By 10:00 p.m., we had to be ready for bed and lights out. Staff checked every room to be certain everyone was accounted for and lights were out.

We found ways to have lights on after check-up to talk. We managed to get some black sheets of paper from the Yugoslav army barracks. We cut these to size, covering the windows as snugly as we could, so that no one could see from the outside. This was because of my brilliant mind. It was great while it lasted, but later, I paid for my brilliance—again.

At 5:00 a.m., shrill whistles woke us up. By 5:15 a.m., in shorts and T-shirts, we went to the yard for our morning calisthenics. In the winter we wore heavier clothing. At 5:45 a.m. we had to have made our beds perfectly and had to wait for bed inspection, or we would miss breakfast and be placed on KP duty for a week.

We were not in T'rsie anymore!

Everything had changed.

This had become home!

My Passion, My Sport

Love knows hidden paths.

German Proverb

All this time it had existed, and I never knew it. However, Destiny was in charge and I was its captive. As all kinds of extra-curricular activities began to develop it was the game of soccer that drew me. My competitive, aggressive nature would at last find its inevitable outlet—SOCCER.

Although we had no balls, shoes, socks or shorts, we played with heart. There were inter-village competitions and these were great experiences for kids. Soccer rules and regulations were loosely enforced. For example, if a village did not have enough players to form a team, then two village teams would merge for a game.

The way the inter-village competitions were set up, I was allowed to play with the older guys. Eventually we formed one team that we christened Borets, fighters. The best players from each of the village teams were selected for Borets.

First, we competed against ourselves, among team members. Eventually we developed a schedule to play other schools in Bela Crkva as well as from surrounding communities. Even without uniforms or shoes with cleats, we were formidable, great at strategy. Our soccer balls were formed out of rags. But, when we played other school teams, we played with their balls.

Enter Drago, Drago, our savior; Drago, our guardian angel; Drago, my friend. It was Drago who played another important role again in my life. It came about this way. Whenever the police had free time, they played soccer on their grounds. I watched them play whenever I had the time. During one of those times I mentioned to Drago that we were going to play an orphanage team in the city, called Internal but we really needed a soccer ball. He was listening to me intently.

When I had finished, he looked toward his roster of balls and pointed at one. "How would you like that one there? It's almost new."

I looked at the ball hungrily, "Oh, boy, would I!"

This is what Drago proposed. "Here is what we'll do. You go over there and tease or dare one of my guys to kick a ball out of the grounds. Put this ball back with the others. I'll go outside and get some of the kids to pick up the ball as soon as they see it and hide it. By the time you and your gang come looking for it, my men will be gone. I'll see to that."

I let out such a yelp. I jumped all over Drago and hugged him. Normally I am not a huggy-kissy type. The only other time I remember hugging anyone was the time we had to say our final goodbyes before we left our village, and then when Kosta left us.

With the confidence of a seasoned co-conspirator, I began to challenge Drago's men to see who could kick the ball the highest and farthest. And the strategy worked! After about 10 or 15 minutes of play, the police tried to kick the ball over the roof. Our gang, in the meantime, was waiting to seize the moment.

When the ball went over the roof, one of the kids picked it up, and Drago's men ran after him into our field across the road. The rest of us, of course, went to look for it, and surprise, surprise! No one could seem to find that ball, but we played out our charade for a little while longer, searching between the roofs, back around the yard and the field. No ball! Too bad! So sad!

Drago also acted out his role superbly. He came to us and asked what had happened. We told him that we were puzzled too. Darned if we could figure out where it went. We shrugged our shoulders, shook our heads, and looked as perplexed as we could. It was an Academy Award performance. We all surmised that the ball was just lost, because all of us looked everywhere it could have bounced or rolled.

Drago walked away, trying to look as angry as he could, without making a comment. Whoever had kicked that ball would have to pay for a new one. Sergeant Milan told us that he had never seen Drago so angry. Our reaction was very appropriate. Yep, it was too bad, and off we scampered, cloaked in great innocence, to join our own team, which had already started kicking the newly acquired ball. Now, I think you can understand why to this day, I love Drago.

As soon as I walked toward our huge gate, Done informed me, "Hey, we got us a soccer ball."

In a serious tone I replied, "I know. It belongs to the police, so we better hide it for a while."

That's how the ball was turned over to me for safekeeping, and I promptly violated two key rules of the *Dom*. They were:

1. Do not go into your sleeping quarters without permission from one of the staff or committee members.
2. It is forbidden to bring anything into the sleeping quarters, not even study books.

Ha! I thought, no supper for me tonight if anybody catches me. Who cares? I nicknamed the soccer ball *Baba Mara* and hid it in a basket-like affair I made from a burlap bag. I tied the ends of the burlap, and then tied it to the mattress under my bed. That way, there would be no lumps in my bed to make anyone suspicious. And, it worked. There was only one person from the staff who knew about it, but we worked a deal so she wouldn't report it. That was Marika.

I want to tell you about Kanachki, too. He was an employee who played for the Granichar team. He was one of those soft-hearted individuals who always interceded for us kids. Kanachki tried to help in so many ways. He enjoyed watching us play soccer with our rag-tag ball.

Kanachki was the supervisor of the sewing shop that made our school uniforms. He gave us pointers on the art of soccer playing, and it was Kanachki who interceded for us with the *Upravnik* to get us some uniforms, shoes, soccer balls. To this day I don't know if he played the key role in getting us uniforms, but I do remember the day he made us a proposition, which could have been a daunting one for us.

This is what he he had in mind. "Look, suppose your team challenges Granichar for a game of soccer. I think they would like to take you kids on. If you win the game, you'll get complete uniforms. But, if you lose, you lose!"

He stood before us hunching his shoulders and hands outspread. There was no hesitation. We struck a deal. Our team, Borets, would challenge Granichar!

The game was advertised all over the city. Posters appeared everywhere: Granichar vs. Borets From Aegean Macedonia! The advertising captured attention in the town and word-of-mouth stirred curiosity among the townspeople. Our team practiced very hard with Kanachki as our coach.

Days of intense practice brought us finally to game time, Sunday, at 4:00 p.m. Granichar versus Borets. Waiting impatiently for the starting time, we had been told not to eat later than 11:00 a.m. After that the only thing we were allowed to consume were just liquids, and those rules were strictly enforced. We were told to report to the stadium promptly at 3:00 p.m.

Were we primed?

Were we pumped? Were we ready?

Do you have to ask?

About 15,000 soccer enthusiasts had paid to see this match-up. The fans who had paid tickets filled all the available seats. The *Egeitsi* kids stood around the stadium throughout the game. The Granichar team was considered a semi-pro team and was competing in the *Voyvodanska Liga,* Voyvodina League, which ranked below the Yugoslav Third League. In retrospect, I think it was probably an amateur club in the Voyvodina Banatska Division. They were good experienced players and, of course, older than we were.

Capturing the imagination of the spectators was the notion of a David competing with Goliath. Had we had the smarts at the time, we might have caught on to what this was all about. We didn't have a clue, except that we were going against an experienced team, and people paid to watch us play. Who needed more?

As we came closer to starting time, the Granichar team came onto the field, dressed in uniforms and regulation shoes. Then we made our appearance, barefoot; no uniforms. You should have heard the shouts and the applause!!

After a brief warm-up, Kanachki reviewed the game plan with us and threw in some last-minute pointers. He designated Vasil and me as co-captains, giving us the authority to make substitutions. In short, we were player-coaches. He left us to go to the dressing room. Shortly, we saw Kanachki emerge dressed to play in uniform for the Granichar team!

What was this? We thought he was going to coach us all the way! Apparently not. What was going on? It was 4:00 p.m. and game time. The official referee signaled for the captains of each team to come to the middle of the playfield for the official introductions, toss-up, and selection of sides and so forth. We won the toss and elected to kick first.

Moments of waiting were over. This was it. The Granichar team had a player named Baraba, a born clown but an excellent player. He always wore his shorts so that they fell below his knees, almost to his calves. He made everybody crack up. Baraba was so comical that he was able to make people laugh so hard to the point where they felt their sides would split. He was hilarious. Baraba could make players forget that there was a game ongoing.

As the game was about to start, we were very nervous. Granichar scored in the first 8 minutes. We began to get discouraged and disorganized, losing our focus. Kanachki tried to bolster up our courage, even though he was playing against us. No matter what we did, Granichar scored again. Now it was 2 to 0!

Kanachki came to me, and challenged, "When are you going to wake up? Think about what you are losing. It's not just the fame, but uniforms and shoes. Just think about that and get going. What's the matter with your tongue? Are you scared?"

Scared?

SCARED?

SCARED?! That did it. That was all I needed to hear. I said,

"Never!

NEVER!

NEVER!" I began to shout at every player who came near me. I even cussed to upset them, to make them madder than hell.

"Don't get mad at me," I yelled at my team. "Get mad at them. This is embarrassing. What kind of name is Borets if we are not fighting like *Bortsi*?"

My team got the message. We settled down and started to play with a little more organization and focus. Before the first half had ended, we scored. Delco was the scorer. Now it was 2 to 1, with 12 minutes left. Kanachki came over and talked to us again. He reminded us of our strategy and positions. He reminded us who should be playing against who, but he got on me very hard. Now, that irritated me and it embarrassed me as well. I didn't like it one bit.

"Hey, I'm not used to this. I'm not alone! What more can I do?"

Kanachki replied, "I know you. You can do better. Dribble a little more, shoot more. You know you are the fastest one on the field, except for Bato. Use your speed and use your head. You're much smarter than what you have shown here."

I piped up, "Am I the only one here?"

"Quiet! When I coach, you just listen."

I never said a word to him for the rest of the game. I couldn't wait for the second half to start, to get out on the field. I was furious. I'll show him! Kanachki will regret what he said, knocking me like that; degrading me in front of everybody. Just wait, I'll show him!

It was the second half now, and we ran out onto the field, charged up with anger and frustration. Granichar started slowly, and we managed to tie the game. Then we scored again, taking the lead. Granichar tied it up, 3 to 3, with about 10 minutes to go. Granichar scored again, up 4 to 3. We struggled back again and managed another goal, tying it up again.

All the kids in the stands and on the ground began to go wild, cheering us on. One more! One more goal, and only 3 minutes left. Now the ball was Baraba's near their goal area, and he had control of the ball. He started to tease us, dribbling cutesy, fancy all around the area.

I was reaching my boiling point. I chose a different strategy. I was going to knock him down and get the ball from him. I got close to him, which enabled me to pull him by the shirt, slowing him down a little. Then I gave him a semi-friendly kick just below the calf muscle. Baraba dropped down. As usual, he acted out and really overplayed his pain. But he wanted us to win.

I kicked the ball and went a few yards, pulling the goalie to my left, sliding the ball to Goce. Goce just directed the ball into an almost empty goal area, making it 5–4 in our favor. Just a few seconds later, the final whistle blew, signaling the end of the game.

We had won, 5 to 4!

The fans exploded and the kids went wild over our victory. None of us had ever been as delirious as we were at that moment, not in all the time since we had left our homes.

For a while we even were able to forget that we were so far from home. But only for a while.

A short time later we discovered that Granichar had planned the game so that we would win. They just tried to make it into a real game for us. When they wanted to score, they did. When we needed to score, they let us. It was really Kanachki's idea to make it difficult for us, but also to make it fun for everyone. He did tell me that the strategy was to make it intentionally frustrating for me, to make me a better player. He emphasized that this was just one experience and that I would experience more. He felt that I could become a very good soccer player some day, and maybe even an important player.

I looked at him hard and long. Was he making fun of me? My eyes searched his face intently. There was nothing but sincerity and belief in his face and his eyes. I was filled with emotion that I tried to control, but I think Kanachki understood what I was feeling.

You might accuse the Granichar of fixing the game. It wasn't a fix. It was a fund-raiser. The Granichar team wanted to raise money to buy us uniforms—and give us an opportunity to have some fun.

The realization of what Granichar did hit us later, when we received brand new uniforms. The game had really been about us and for us. Our gratitude ran so deep, to think that these former strangers and foreigners could care enough about a rag-tag, inexperienced team of foreign kids who wanted to play soccer. When we thought about the effort they made to organize a *bona fide* soccer game with spectators and all, we could not even express ourselves adequately for their gesture of kindness and caring.

You never forget that, ever.

From that day on, from that special episode in our forlorn young lives, we gained more confidence in who we were, and we were filled with hope. Maybe there was a world out there and it had not forsaken us. We had been blessed to have been placed among these strangers in a foreign country who had shown us nothing but kindness, caring, and support.

As a team, we became more successful and competitive. We gained support from the city and the Red Cross. Everybody helped to make our dream of having a fine soccer team possible. We even formed a younger team called Borets II, our version of a farm system.

We Aegean kids, we *Begaltsi,* had carved out a niche for ourselves among the townspeople in a place called Bela Crkva, with the help of strangers, in a country called Yugoslavia.

The Gang from 309

A gang has many heads, but no brain.

ANONYMOUS

The gang from Room 309. What a group of boys we were then—Done, Lazo, Risto, Yane, Goche, Itso, Vasil and I.

Oh, yes, there was T'rpo, too. T'rpo, the sleepwalker who we watched over constantly. Every night, one of us was responsible for him and had to monitor him closely. On a couple of occasions, he did manage to get away from us, and that was only when someone overslept or just nodded off to sleep. Then T'rpo would strike out. The chef's crew found T'rpo once in the yard, so we had to invent our own foolproof wake-up system. We managed to get a long rope to tie to T'rpo's foot. The other end was tied to whoever was assigned to watch him that night. T'rpo never got past the door after that. The idea came to me as I remembered how we kept the horses from running away back home in T'rsie. We used to tie the front legs and ankles of the horse. The legs were about a foot apart, which allowed them to graze or feed in the fields. Owners could sleep somewhat more peacefully.

I should mention that we had two other companions in Room #309 and they were Mischief and Trouble. They were both with me one evening as we were going to our mess hall for our evening meal. The *piski*, straws, next to the milk seemed to have a fascinating attraction for me at the time. Of course, we used these to drink our milk, but my hard-working brain thought of a better use for the *piski*. I decided to demonstrate this other use to the kids without any fanfare.

I sucked up as much milk as I could with the straw and sprayed as far as I could around the mess hall. To my delight, all hell broke loose as the kids followed my brilliant creative display for the alternative use of the straws. We had a glorious spray caper that evening. Can you picture hundreds of kids spraying milk all over each other? It was great! What a show!

Of course there were consequences, as there usually are when I become so innovative. But this one consequence I certainly could not even imagine. It seems that some of the guys did not wash out all of the milk from their heads. That which was left in their hair and on their scalp dried. Now the medical staff checked us regularly, and each of us had a schedule for routine checkups. When the kids were examined during their appointed times, their scalps seemed to have some kind of "condition" needing medical treatment, and if not treated properly, the "condition" could lead to loss of hair. In Macedonian, the "condition" is known as *lishai*, dry skin. The treatment was to put the patient under the ultra-ray machine for about 10 minutes. The hair usually fell out, too.

There were many kids with the "dry scalp," as you can imagine. As the kids began to lose their hair, the novelty of the milk *piski* attack began to be replaced with their

The Nitchov 'bulog,' a few of the cousins. In front, young Risto, in back left to right, Sofa, Mara, Sotir, Krste and Sofa Dimova.

anger, focusing on me. Well, I deserved their anger inasmuch as I was the one who started the whole mess. Fair is fair.

To make them feel less hostile, I sprayed myself with the milk and went straight to the hospital without the doctor's authority. I just sneaked in, got the treatment, lost my hair, and had my scalp painted with this awful green, smelly solution, twice daily. They kept me in the hospital for about a week before they finally sent me back to the *Dom*.

Because I returned hairless, I was one of them again, and everybody was happy. No additional punishment. This time, I lucked out! Eventually, my hair started to come back in, kind of nice and wavy.

The gang from #309 came up with lots of innovative ideas to stretch the rules a bit. When we wanted to stay up a little later or go to a movie, two or three of us would tie our sheets, end to end, and secure the loose end to the bed. We dropped the loose end out the window, and that served as our ladder. When we were ready to return, one of us would toss a stone at the window, signaling that we were ready to climb back into the room.

Another little device that worked for us was a dark tarp, which the Army used to make window shades. I came across a discarded tarp, which I thought we might be able to use. As I rolled it up and placed it under my arm, walking back to the *Dom*, I had an idea for it. We could use this to cover our window in the evening, so that we could keep our lights on after curfew. The guys thought it was a workable idea, so we set about trimming the tarp. We made a perfect fit for the window, and we got away with it—for a while. Of course, the monitors, the tutors and *Gospozah* Iconia caught on to our "window drops" and our darkened window. A trap was set for us.

Buddies, 1949, Bela Crkva: Sotir, Yane from the village of Zhelevo, and Mitse from the village of Lagan, Macedonia.

They waited for us on the side of the grounds, just under our window where we usually landed. Lazo and Goche went down first. First down; first caught! I was supposed to be next, and I was just about to start my descent when I heard Lazo and Goche cough loud and hard. It sounded as if they had suddenly caught a terrible cold. That was the signal for me to get back in, but it was too late. There was Todor's voice shouting in my direction, "Get down now!" I got down.

With not a little sarcasm in his voice, he said to all of us, "The next time you want to go to the movies, just tell me, and we'll not only drive you there, but we'll pay for the movies!" He waited for a reaction from us. The other adults chimed in with their comments with a lot of sarcasm. Well, we all took our turn telling him that we had been doing it for a while. Of course!

The punishments handed to the #309 gangsters—that meant all of us—were scrubbing assignments in the bathrooms, wall-washing, and no dinner, for 2 weeks! For whatever reason, this time I was not singled out as the leader, nor was I accused of hatching the plan.

You figure it out.

The Great Grape Caper

When an elephant is in trouble,
Even a frog will kick him.

HINDU PROVERB

It was now September, *Grozdober. In* Macedonian Grosdober means grape harvesting month.

As time permitted, we explored Bela Crkva and the peaceful countryside that surrounded that beautiful town. We didn't hear the sound of gunfire or bombs exploding nearby. We didn't have to deal with Greek xenophobia.

On this one particularly beautiful autumn day, Goche, Done, Lazo and I took off for the vineyards in the peaceful valley on the outskirts of the city. Earlier we were truly turned on by the sight of someone eating grapes in the park.

Back home, many villagers had vineyards not only for the sweet taste of grapes, but especially for the juice of the grape, you know, wine. Everyone made their own homemade wine, and Dedo always had wine with his meals.

I remembered that particular ritual of Dedo's with great nostalgia. The grape juice which had not turned into wine yet, or ***most****, was such a great drink. Both Mother and Baba used to make a wine pudding from the* ***most****, called* ***mostopiti****.*

The sight of that man in the park eating his grapes with such obvious pleasure, spurred us into action. Don't ask whose idea it was to seek grapes. Fresh grapes, right off the vine! As village kids, we knew what freshness really was, so we spent at least 2 hours in the vineyard, savoring the fresh fruit that hung temptingly on the vine. We ate and ate until we were totally satiated and couldn't put one more grape into our mouths.

Having had our fill of grapes, we did what came naturally to me and my gangsters. We started to throw grapes at one another. I think we did more damage lobbing grape missiles than we did just picking the grapes and eating them. Does it surprise you if I tell you that we were caught red-handed by the *poliak,* the field guard, right there in the middle of the vineyard and in the middle of our grape wars? There was no way we could hide or disguise ourselves. Not only had we gorged ourselves to the point of not being able to move very quickly, but our uniforms, of which we were so proud, identified us as the culprits.

The *poliak* himself was not harsh toward us, but he had a job to do, and that was to take us to the *Upravnik's* office. That prospect didn't appeal to us at all. I pleaded with him. This unfortunate, unwise incident would never happen again, if he would let us go. He sighed, good man that he was, but regrettably indicated it was his duty to turn us in to the authority at the *Dom*. This was not good.

Without changing the look on my face, I muttered to Done that we could get away without getting reported. Done, without any expression on his face, muttered back, "How?"

"We can hit him, knock him down and run," was my ready reply. Still expressionless, Done answered,

"Then we will be in double trouble."

Lazo, eager to avoid the *Upravnik*, out of the side of his mouth, muttered, "We can deny it was us."

I had another brainstorm. "Here's another idea."

Goce, disdainfully, but carefully, "Yeah, another stupid one?"

"Listen," I said earnestly, "Let's jump him and tie him up. Someone will find him and untie him."

All caution aside, Done said, a little skeptically, "That sounds a little better to me."

I turned to Lazo. "Lazo, drop down on your knees and pretend that you are sick or something. And don't any of you guys help him at all."

Done, "Then what? Oh, I get it. When the *poliak* bends down to see what the problem is with Lazo, we'll jump him then, right?"

"You got it!" Nothing ventured, nothing gained. We ventured. Lazo went down dramatically. On cue, as the unsuspecting *poliak* bent down to see what the trouble was, we jumped on the *poljak* tied his hands and hauled him to the gate with his belt, scarf and some vines.

We left quickly for the *Dom* and acted as if nothing had happened. We were the most innocent-looking pack of gangsters you could ever hope to see. We had washed our sticky hands, faces and heads near a fountain. We went very quickly to the *Dom* to change our clothes. With that completed, we went about our way as if nothing unusual had happened.

Of course some of the kids knew, but nobody squealed on us. As we were eating breakfast the next day, an announcement came over the p.a. The announcement had to do with an incident yesterday near the vineyard involving four of our boys. Apparently, the boys had ended their caper in the vineyards by tying up the *poliak*. The four boys were asked to step up to the podium.

There was no question that my guys were an honorable bunch. I was very confident that they would keep their mouths shut. Goche was next to me, Lazo across from me, and Done was about four or five seats behind me. Goche whispered, "I'll go up." I almost panicked. I hissed back at him,

"Are you crazy? They don't know who it was. Don't be stupid."

Lazo, now with a guilty conscience spoke up, "We all better go up there, before they find us out."

I nearly went nuts. "Keep your mouths shut. Mind your own business. Don't say anything." I used some profanity as well to emphasize my point. Done looked up at us. I signaled with my head, *no*! I had just completed one punishment cleaning and scrubbing floors, and I wasn't quite ready to do it again.

One of the monitors started to walk down the aisles, looking intently to the right and to the left. He passed Done. Nothing. He was getting closer. I deliberately dropped my fork and bent down to retrieve it. He stopped by Lazo, Goche had somehow moved. The monitor pointed at Lazo.

"This one," he said. This looks like one of them." The *Upravnik* and *Gospozah* Iconia motioned to Lazo to follow them to the office. Now we were all beginning to feel uncomfortable and started to sweat a little. Lazo wouldn't tell on us. We were certain of that. But how would Lazo get himself out of the jam? I told Done and Goche to get lost until the man left.

I went toward the office with the excuse that I was looking for Ivitsa, Iconia's son, because he had my book bag. I knocked on the door of the office, walked in and there was *Gospozah* Iconia. I asked her if she knew where Ivitsa was. The *poliak* was standing there. He looked hard at me and said quite positively, "This one. This looks like one of the kids."

I, innocently, asked, "One of the kids what?"

Gospozah Iconia, whom I could never fool, said sternly, "You know."

Still playing dumb, I said, "Know what?"

The *poliak* again pointing at me replied with conviction, "Yes, he started it. That is him."

"I don't know who he is," I kept on insisting. "I never saw him before. Besides, yesterday I spent my time down at the stadium with Kanachki."

The *poliak*, even more emphatically, "Yes, this is the one. I am very sure."

With the most pained expression on my face and injurious tone, I whined, "How come all of a sudden he recognizes me when the man in the mess hall did not?"

The *Upravnik* had had enough. He spoke to Lazo and me. "Both of you leave. I'll call you back when we finish with this gentleman."

Still keeping up my act, I asked, "Where is Ivitsa?"

Gospozah Iconia, mad as hell, stepped in quickly, "He should be outside somewhere. Go look for him." You should have seen the look she gave me!

Lazo and I walked out gravely, and as soon as I could, I sneaked out of the window in my room and made a dash toward Kanachki. I told him the truth. He knew I was trying to get him to cover for me. He quoted me something from the Bible, regarding right and wrong, truth and lying. He sighed, for he knew I liked being with him. "I guess boys will be boys. Go on, get out of here."

As I moved toward the door, he spoke up again. "Don't worry about it," and his deep voice cracked. Was I safe? I didn't know at the time, but I never heard anything further about our great grape caper. We were never called into the office again on the matter. However, 2 days later, *Gospozah* Iconia met me, and pulled me over to the side. She eyed me directly. "Ok. If you will tell me the truth, I'll forget everything and you will not be punished. If you don't tell me the truth, and I find out later . . . " she didn't finish her sentence, but I read her implication clearly from her eyes. This woman could read me inside and out. I knew she would persist until she got the truth.

"I'll tell you the truth, but I won't tell you who else was involved. You can punish me all you want, but I gave my word to the others that I wouldn't squeal on them. Yes, it was me." I looked up at her.

"I see," she said with no expression on her face.

"Well, then, no more will be said. Just don't ever, ever do that again!" I nodded meekly, gratefully.

She pulled my ear, but in a kindly manner this time, as she said, "Between you and my son, I don't know how I am going to live to be 100 years old! *Bozhe, Bozhe, dai mi pomosh,* Lord, Lord help me! I need all the help I can get to deal with these two *devotinia*, monsters."

And so, the great grape caper ended in a prayer—of sorts.

Titovi Morinari

Ridi, Pagliaci . . .

GUISEPPE VERDI, PAGLIACI

Ah, the pain and the pleasure of the performing arts! I am proud to say that we had a very good dance group, all boys, dressed in sailors' uniforms. We were the *Titovi Morinari,* Tito's Sailors, and had the opportunity to perform in several cities.

Unfortunately for the performers, I was selected to be part of the first group. This was definitely not by choice. I have to confess that I despised it like hell, and did everything I could to get out of the group. It took me 6 months, but I did get out, and I think by now, you might be able to imagine how and why.

I felt this dancing was for sissies. My preference was to dance in and around a soccer field, playing soccer. At this point, the choice was not mine, so there I was, for a while, a *morinar*, a sailor, one of Tito's *morinari*. I schemed and schemed, trying to think of how I could pull out of the group when a golden opportunity opened up.

There was one kid who thought he was some hotshot. He acted up all the time. Boy, he got on my nerves. I waited for the moment to teach him a lesson and take him down a peg or two. As all good things come to he who waits, the moment came. I capitalized on that moment.

Done, one of my gangsters, and I found the kid's costume. We cut four or five slits, 2 inches apart, in his pants. We were scheduled to perform at the city auditorium, so we knew it would be a full house. The time came for us to get dressed and be ready for our entrance on the stage. The lights dimmed and the curtains parted and, one-by-one, we pranced on stage, doing different steps, and made our entrances.

We started our routine that contained jumps and stretches. Mr. Hot-shot, whose name was Lazo, started his star-quality routine. He began to jump higher, stretch farther, and twist like a top. Little did he realize what a star he would become that night. As he was literally twisting in the wind with all his might, we heard a tremendous roar coming from the audience. His tight pants had come apart, and there he was, center stage, bare butt and all.

The sucker was so embarrassed that he left the stage crying. Being the professionals that the rest of us were, we continued our performance with great dedication and innocence. Done and I savored the rest of the performance with a wicked sense of self-satisfaction.

The end of the performance was not the end of the matter as far as our director was concerned. She gathered all of us together and demanded, "Who cut the pants?" Silence. Only innocence prevailed in the room, from one end to the other.

She demanded again, "I know someone did it. It was quite obvious." More silence. Again, innocence prevailed, but touched with perplexity this time. I could see that everyone was getting a little uncomfortable and that someone was going to be blamed.

I didn't want everybody to get punished, and since I got the greatest satisfaction out of doing the terrible deed, I spoke up, "I did."

"Just as I thought," she snapped. "I'll tell you what. You have been trying to get out of this group for a long time. Well, as of today, you are out, *out*, OUT!" Hooray, I achieved two goals! I was so happy, I almost kissed her, but I said nothing and left the stage without a look backwards.

But it still wasn't over. There was a final act to the 'dancing' Lazo incident. A few days later, Lazo and I had one of the bloodiest fights I had been involved in for some time. I wound up with a cut lip, black eyes and a torn ear. It gives me great pleasure to tell you that "dancing Lazo" wound up in the main hospital for about 10 days. Glorious! It was worth it, even though I was punished big-time. First I had to scrub the mess hall for 7 days. For 1 day I had no breakfast, and had to go without dinner for 2 days. For 5 days I had to remain indoors in the study room. As for outside privileges, forget it! They were taken away until "further notice." That was like forever.

Yet, where there is a will, there is a way, and I found some ways to sneak out. One way was to hide under the cart on which the kitchen workers (or *Dezhurni*) transported the dishes to the kitchen. The carts were large enough that a short adolescent to curl himself into a ball in one and not be seen. The other way was through the mess hall window in one of the corners. Some furniture and plants by the window made it quite secluded. In fact, the window could barely be seen. Climb up on the furniture, open the window, and I was outside.

I used that window exit for quite some time. Of course sometimes staff would look for me when they discovered I wasn't where I was supposed to be. Heck, the only consequences then were some additional penalties, with which I became very familiar. I was assigned to the principal's office, sorting out papers or sharpening pencils, penalties like that. They tired of me very quickly in the office, so the additional penalties began to slack off after a while. Satisfaction! It was worth every penalty I deservedly received.

Call me a *paliacho,* or anything that comes to mind, but Sotir is my name. By the way, I don't know how *paliacho* became another word for clown in Macedonian, but it did.

A Christmas Tale

Holidays have no pity.

EUGENIO MONTALE

It was December, the month of *Sznezhuk* in T'rsie.

Gospozah Iconia wanted to do something special at Christmas for the kids, something memorable. For the occasion she planned an original Christmas play and she chose the actors with great care. The mess hall was where rehearsals for the play were to take place. As luck would have it, the person originally chosen for the leading role was banished. No reason was given as far as we knew. I don't recall who that banished individual was. Still remains a mystery. I received a summons to see *Gospozah* in her quarters.

"Good afternoon, *Gospozah,*" I greeted her with a curious look. I hadn't done anything recently, I thought. What's going down?

"Sit down and listen carefully. I do not wish to repeat myself."

"Yes, *Gospozah.*" I sat down as she indicated.

"You have been selected to play *Sneshko Belich,* Father Snow."

I started to laugh. "No way am I playing *Sneshko*. Get someone else who fits the part."

"*Chuti,*" she cut me off. "You are *Sneshko* and here is the script. The most important part of your role is this poem which you are to memorize."

"No, I will not play any part . . . "

She cut me off again and in her most severe, no-nonsense tone she told me, **"I will not, I will not, I will not repeat myself. Do you understand me? You are *Sneshko Belich.*** You will show up for rehearsal at 8:00 a.m. Saturday. Everything is settled. You are to report to me from now on. You'll be given a schedule tomorrow."

I tried to scream, "No, no, no!" but she kept on giving me instructions.

Ivitsa tried to intervene. "Sotka, you better do what she tells you or she will make things very difficult for you, especially regarding soccer."

I turned to him. "Soccer? What has that to do with this," I paused to whisper the next word, "*crap*?"

Of course, the *Gospozah* heard. "I know how crazy you are about soccer, but don't worry. You won't miss much time."

Still trying to protest, "This poem . . . it's so long. There is no way that I could memorize it in 1 week!"

Her reply, "You will. I will help you."

Trapped!!

I was stuck with this stupid thing and had to attend the rehearsals. She saw to that. I just couldn't seem to memorize the entire poem, I hated it so much. In spite of my resistance to it, I managed to memorize some of it. *Gospozah* assured me that she would be able to help me during the play, because she would position herself in the half-moon box on the stage to feed us lines. Ugh!

Christmas Eve seemed to come much too quickly. Every kid from all the Doms arrived. They were packed in, like sardines in a can. On stage was one of the most gorgeous sights I had ever seen. There was a tree decorated with all kinds of ornaments. I had never seen anything like it.

Back stage, they dressed me up with a long, white beard, a white mustache and a red coat with white trim, just like the pictures of Father Frost I had seen. On top of that I had to carry all the crap that *Sneshko* is supposed to carry.

The play opened with a song or two, followed by some announcements about the program, etc. Now it was time for the entrance, my debut as Sneshko Belich. I began reciting the poem, walking in and around the front of the tree, reciting as *Gospozah* guided me from the half-moon. Well, I thought, so far, so good, although it seemed to me that the kids were getting kind of restless. Why shouldn't they? After all, the poem was in Serbian, and Serbian was Greek to us. I had tried to warn her that the kids wouldn't like it and that it was far too long. However, she insisted.

You have to remember she wasn't Macedonian. She had come to us from Montenegro, so I guess she assumed that we would understand her Serbian. After all, weren't we all Slavs? Well, yes, but we were Macedonians! Let's continue.

When the second page of the poem came up, I went blank and could not remember a single line. She began to get upset, making all kinds of noises and gesturing emphatically to me. She began to get quite emotional, but, figuratively speaking, I turned off my hearing aid. Now the audience really got restless. In another minute or two, a revolt seemed imminent.

At that moment, I decided to improvise. Whatever came to my mind, I voiced it. I started telling them that I forgot the rest of the poem, and that Gospozah was fuming in the box. I asked the audience if they wanted to see both of us do the rest of the program. They screamed their approval and began to chant, Iconia, Iconia—so she had no choice. She came out and stood next to me. At that very moment I whispered to her, "I'm getting even with you, don't you dare pull my ears!"

"Just you wait," she muttered to me.

I turned to the audience. "This is Sneshko's mother. So if Sneshko forgets his lines, blame the mother. She has pulled my ears so much that she has also pulled out my brains through the ears. Those are not ornaments on the tree. They are my brains scattered all over. That is why the tree is so beautiful. Before I leave tonight, I know I'll get punished for this."

On and on I rambled. I made fun of the teachers, the tutors and the directors. The audience went wild. Whatever I knew about the staff, I incorporated it into my performance. All in all, if I do say so myself, once we safely got beyond the poem, things seemed to go on much better.

After an hour or so of the performance, everyone in the audience had to pass by Sneshko to receive his or her present, which consisted of a bunch of hard candies and a good bar of white chocolate. Believe it or not, I played my part so convincingly, nobody recognized old Sneshko except Vesa from the village of Turie. When she came by, she said smiling, "*A bre, Sote. Da puknish!* Oh, Sote. May you explode! You were so funny. My sides hurt from laughing so hard."

Muttering, I threatened her, "Don't tell anyone or I'll . . . " Off she went, laughing.

After the performance, dressed now in our own clothing, *Gospozah* Iconia came toward me and got me by the ear. She was not pulling hard. In fact, she was pulling me to her side to hug me. She kissed my forehead. She was so happy that the kids had some good laughs and enjoyed the evening. Some of the other staff people were congratulating me for a job well done. That's what they all said. You know, it turned out to be a fun thing for me too. I enjoyed myself thoroughly. In fact, I was only slightly embarrassed when word got around and the kids found out who *Sneshko* was.

The Vesa who recognized me as *Sneshko*, was Vesa Novachkova, who always stood behind me when there was roll call. Novachkov came after Nitchov, which is me, Sotir. When we were given shots, sometimes in both arms at least once a month, when my name was called, I would shove her ahead of me. She got my shots. Then when her name was called, she had to go up again. She tried to tell them and show them that she already got her shots. Most of the time they wouldn't believe her, and frequently she would get a double dose of shots. She finally, came to me one day, crying, "Sote, please stop. Don't do this to me. I can't get my arm up. It hurts."

I believe that was the first time that I ever apologized to anyone. I never shoved her in front of me again.

The next day, in the yard, somehow I got into another fight with Risto Mizhorko from the village of Lagen. I can't remember why, but I spent one of the Christmas holidays scrubbing the mess hall for 3 or 4 days, on *Gospozah* Iconia's orders!

Yes, Sotir, the star, scrubbed the mess hall for 4 days, but Ivitsa pitched in and helped me.

What a guy! What a buddy! What a Christmas!

Motivation

There is a destiny which makes us all brothers; none goes his way alone.

EDWIN MARKHAM, 1900

Not too far from our Dom were several small lakes that attracted many of us. In fact they were too attractive to resist. Giving in to the temptation, a group of us sneaked out one day to go swimming. Oh it was so inviting!

As soon as we got there, some of the kids jumped into the smaller lake. Vasil and I stayed out because we were going to go over some plays and strategies for an upcoming soccer game. We were so engrossed in planning that it was several minutes before we realized someone was yelling. The urgency of the tone made us turn toward the direction of the sound. "Help, help! I'm drowning!"

Thinking that the guys were up to their usual hijinks, I ignored the plea, saying to Vasil, "Ah, they're just fooling around. Don't pay any attention to them." We resumed discussing our strategies.

Just as we were about to make some decisions, we heard shouting from some of the guys from my own village, T'rsie. I recognized their voices immediately. First Itso, then Yane from Zhelevo were calling for help. Both Vasil and I jumped up and ran to the lake's edge. I could see bubbles of water coming up from the lake, which made Vasil and I realize that it was fed by an underground spring, an *izvor*. At that moment we saw also the warning signs:

DO NOT SWIM IN THE MIDDLE
CRAMPS
COLD WATER

As we scanned the lake, we saw that the water was flowing from lake to lake. Urgently, Vasil pointed toward the center of the lake, "Look. Those guys are too close to the center. That's where the cold water is coming from."

One of the kids apparently tried to swim across the lake when he began to cramp in the legs. Realizing he was in trouble, he called for help. One of the kids jumped in to help him, when he also began to cramp. Then another jumped in, and the same thing happened to him. It was a chain reaction with one jumping in to help the other.

Vasil couldn't take it, so he jumped in, and swam over to where the last one was. Vasil extended his arm and shouted out to each to grab an extended arm from the guy behind him. Since Vasil was on the edge of the bubbling water, he was not affected by the cramping. Just remembering the incident now, still makes my heart pump a little faster. It was a frightening sight, three kids cramping in the water, while three others were trying to help them. Finally, they were able to pull themselves out and swim to safety, thanks to Vasil's quick thinking and action. Had it not been for him, the first three would surely have drowned.

Who it was that alerted the police is still a mystery to me, but the police did come and saw that everybody was out of the water. Everybody was rescued in one form or another, except me. I had hidden under a bush and didn't go into the water at all. At first, I really thought the swimmers were just kidding around, playing games with each other. Then, because soccer was the most important thing in my life, I was totally engrossed in figuring out strategies and plays. And, I had not moved when the police arrived, so they missed seeing me.

That evening, no one was punished at the Dom when they were brought in by the police. No one, except me. I not only got hell, but I went without dinner. My nemesis, Vangel, apparently informed the authorities that it was I who had the idea to go to the lakes. Vangel was one of the bigger boys, and probably the oldest as well. I don't think he was much liked by anybody. He had the annoying habit of slapping a kid on the back of the head, no matter who the kid was. He had been doing it to me, as well, and I hated it. It drove me nuts. My blood boiled for quite a while each time it happened, but I restrained myself. I kept telling him to stop, damn it. His taunt to me was always, "What are you gonna do about it, cut my hands off?"

This Vangel was getting to me. He was so sure of himself. I always displayed my hatred toward him, determined to have my payback time on my own terms. For some time, I had been fuming and planning my revenge when I wasn't thinking about soccer. Even in my sleep, I dreamt about how and where my revenge would express itself. The opportunity came after he had squealed about our swimming expedition, targeting me as the ringmaster of that little water circus. My fury had reached its peak and would not be controlled any longer. It was Vangel himself who gave me the opportunity to vent that built-up fury.

The day after the lake experience, Vangel happened to pass by me and, as usual, he slapped me on the back of my head. I exploded.

"You may kill me, but I am going to get at least one good punch in, and that is all I am going to need; one good punch. Then you can kill me if you want. I don't care."

Vangel, the bully, laughed at the challenge. As tall as he was, he could only bend down and grab at a shorty like me. Playing soccer had helped me to develop my strategy as my anger against him was building. I got closer to him, and then I gave him my best soccer kick into his privates. He howled and grabbed himself in pain. I started punching him, and punching him harder than I ever had hit anyone. By this time we were surrounded by the kids. Teachers and tutors who had seen the action, immediately tried to break us up, but the kids blocked them. I just kept on punching with a fury and vengeance that knew no bounds or rules. I wasn't even aware of anybody or anything else. The release of my anger gave me a strength that even I didn't know I had. I got to him before he could recover from my kick. He couldn't get up. Those punches I landed on him had been waiting to be released for some time. Finally, one of the teachers was able to pull me off of him.

I was panting, but I was triumphant. In spite of all the fury and hatred, I suffered only some bruised knuckles. As for Vangel, the bully, he lay there, eyes closed, with a broken jaw and cheekbones, and fewer teeth. I wasn't sorry. I felt good about it. He had asked for the fight, and I got satisfaction.

My victory was short-lived, however. I earned a new package of troubles. As a result of my inglorious drubbing of the bully, other, tougher bullies, of various sizes and ages wanted to take me on. The thinking was, so you beat up Vangel, but let's see if you can beat me! That's all I heard daily. I used to have one or two fights a day for a very long time. Not only that, but the consequences of fighting were punishment after punishment. My reputation was that of the resident bad boy, the Dom troublemaker. No one seemed to believe that I wasn't the one starting the fights. Regardless of who the instigator was, I was the one who took the blame. I hated the situation in which I found myself. I felt that I had to go to Todor, our principal.

As soon as I entered the office, he stopped what he was doing and sat back in his chair. Physically and mentally, he seemed to brace himself as he waited for me to speak. I didn't hesitate.

"I know you are sick of us, I mean of me. All these fights are not my fault!"

Todor responded reasonably, "No, I suppose the fault is mine." He paused. "All of these kids come over here to fight you? And you did nothing to them, except break their noses and knock out their teeth."

"I know it looks bad for me, but you have got to understand that I haven't started these fights, except for the one with Vangel, and he had it coming!"

"Well, what do you want from me? Are you expecting a small medal for that fight?" Todor leaned toward me again. "Listen to me. If you don't stop all of this nonsense, you'll be sent to a special place for kids like you."

I saw that I was getting nowhere, so in desperation I pleaded, "Look. Just have someone, and I don't care who it is, just tell that person to follow me for a week or two. Don't even tell me who it is. I know you will find out who really starts the fights and who the real trouble maker is."

With a stern look on his face, he pointed to the door, "Get out of here. I don't want to see you in here again, understand?"

Rejected, dejected, despondent, I left his office.

A month passed by. Tudor called me into his office. "Sit down. Can you see with your eye like that?"

"Yes. Things look a little foggy, but it's getting better." I really had a good shiner.

Tudor twirled his pencil between his fingers, looked at me again, and then spoke. "We owe you an apology." I almost dropped to the floor. An apology? To me? From him? What's he up to? Just then *Gospozah* Iconia came into the office.

Todor continued, "We found out that you were telling the truth. We did not believe you nor the friends who were trying to defend you."

"My friends? Which friends?"

"Risto, Done, Lazo, Goche and *Gospozah* Iconia." I truly couldn't believe that anybody would willingly speak up on my behalf. I know my mouth was half open, undecided as to whether I had anything to say.

"From now on, just stay out of trouble. Don't retaliate against anyone. Don't try for revenge. We will do the penalizing because that is our responsibility."

I didn't know if I could agree to that.

"Sir, I can't run away. If someone sneaks a punch, I have to fight back. Believe me, I have tried to ignore the taunts and jabs, but I can't."

"Then try harder."

"I tried today, and look what I got. I let the guy give the first punch today, but look at my face, my eye. I have to protect myself."

Gospozah Iconia spoke to me, "It's time to go to the hospital and get that eye checked." It was clear that she was taking charge of me, and there was no room for discussion. The two of us left the office and headed toward the hospital.

This wasn't the final curtain on the fighting, but there was less and less of it. Eventually, the fights were few and far between, as when guys from the other Doms would come over, looking for action. Some came to show off. Without fail, whenever a new bully appeared on the scene, everybody let me know.

Nevertheless, as time went on, and as my interest in soccer began to consume my time and energy, I had less and less leisure time to spend in the yard or to go on field trips. In fact, I decided to forego field trips. The one I really wanted to go on was the trip to Ohrid for a month. All of the kids from Dom went as well as the girls. Another trip I would have liked to go on was a 2-week boat excursion on the Danube during summer vacation.

I decided to spend as much free time as possible going over soccer plays and strategies. 95% of my time was spent on training for soccer and reading anything I could find that related to the game. I suppose it was no surprise that my grades had fallen to twos and threes, from the fives and fours I used to get. Five was the highest mark and two the lowest. I was given 4 weeks to bring my grades up or forego soccer!

Forego soccer? You might as well have taken my life! It wasn't that I hadn't been forewarned by teachers and friends. I just didn't take the warnings seriously until I was threatened with the loss of soccer. This was a challenge of a different kind. I understood that, and I intended to meet the challenge. Soccer meant everything to me.

I began to buckle down, following a regime of hard study during every minute I could. You can be assured that my impulse to sneak out to practice my soccer skills was not curtailed. I made up for time lost on the field by staying up late, after 10:00 p.m., which was a serious violation of rules.

Rules! We had to be in bed by 10 o'clock and lights out! The only lights on during the night were in the halls and bathrooms. There was a patrol and room check at 10:15 and if you were not in bed by check time, you faced punishment. Obviously, spending time concentrating on soccer strategy and plays, meant that I had to have more time for the school assignments. I talked to Risto and Yane because they were the smartest and most serious students. They agreed to be my tutors, tutoring me in the bathrooms for an hour each night. This went on for a while, until someone noticed us and warned us. So we stopped our sessions in the bathroom for a night or two.

Exams were coming up shortly, one for each of the subjects. The geography exam would present no problem for me. I loved it. The grammar exam would be a little tough, but I felt I could handle it. Now history could be difficult. I just couldn't get interested in it. I hated it from the very first day. It didn't seem to have anything to do with my life. I can remember challenging the teacher with comments like, "Who wants to know about Cleopatra or the Pharaohs or a Caesar? Teach me about today and tomorrow."

I always ended up with a three minus in history. Obviously, the next 3 weeks were going to be pretty rough for me. All the guys tried to help me through my dilemma. I pushed myself very hard. In fact, my room mates were telling me that in my sleep I was saying something about good marks, good soccer; no marks, no soccer.

Soccer was my obsession; my addiction, my motivation for living. I didn't care about food, as long as I could spend my time on the soccer fields. I never felt tired, either, but give me a book, and 20 minutes later I would be exhausted with boredom. Everyone who cared about me urged me to study more, study harder.

Even though I had a *tikva*, a pumpkin for a head, and many thought I would remain that way for the rest of my life, I guess I was destined to prove them wrong. I was destined to learn, but learn the hard way. I had to go back to my night-time study in the bathroom after hours, alone. I didn't want any of my buddies to get into trouble. Rules were rules, for everyone, I guess, except me.

I must have fallen asleep as I was cramming for the history exam. My books and papers were strewn on the floor around me, when *Gospozah* Iconia spotted me—our bathrooms had doors that were open on both the top and bottom. She came over to me and shook me awake. I had to have been in a very deep sleep, because she had to shake me several times before I came to.

"Do you know what time it is? It's two in the morning. What are you doing here?"

Groggily, still half asleep, I said, "Who knows? Who cares? My right side is hurting right now."

"You fell asleep on that side. Get up and come with me. Don't make any noise."

She led me to her quarters, just around the corner from our room. I fell asleep on her bed. Ivitsa, her son, had his own bed, so she must have slept on the couch. I fell asleep so deeply, that at 5:00 the next morning, I couldn't awaken. Everyone else was going through the morning routine, including Ivitsa. About quarter to eight, *Gospozah* came to wake me up. She said that all I had to do was get cleaned up and go for breakfast.

I asked her, "What will happen to me? I missed roll call and gymnastics."

"Not to worry," she replied. "Everything is taken care of." I did exactly as she told me, and nobody bothered me, except my buddies. Everything seemed to go well even in my classrooms. And my exams so far seemed pretty easy. In fact, better than good, I felt. I had survived another day.

When we returned from school that day, I went straight to *Gospozah's* office and asked her, "Why wasn't I given any punishment for violating the rules?"

With compassion in her eyes, she said to me, "When a youngster is trying to improve himself, there have to be exceptions to the rules. So you keep trying, do you hear me? You know, don't you, *magarets*, that you could say 'thank you', or haven't you reached that level of civilization yet?"

I looked at her with gratitude. "Thank you very much, and I will repay you one of these days." By that I meant that I was going to make her proud of me. "I'll give you free tickets to the Yugoslav National Stadium one of these days. Just you watch!" *Gospozah* was a loyal PARTIZAN soccer team supporter—and the PARTIZANs played in the stadium in Belgrad.

"I would be the happiest person in the world to see you play for the PARTIZANs, but I will pay my own way. The best way to repay me is to become a good person. Learn, become something; don't just be a footballer. You and Ivitsa scare me at times. Neither of you seem able to do the right things. You must think before you act. Consider, whether an action is right or wrong for you. To you, if it is something you want to do, then it is right. In your life there doesn't seem to be any wrong. That is why the two of you get into trouble. *Sotka*, I am talking to you as if you were my own son."

I knew she meant what she was saying to me, because she was speaking softly, sincerely to me, not in the gruff, demanding voice I was so familiar with. I don't know if all that she had said really registered in the *tikva* at the moment, but later, in the yard, I began to mull over what she was telling me. I knew she was on my side and trying to help turn me around. I was grateful for that. On reflection, all the adults were trying to make us better people. They were all trying to motivate us to do the best.

For me, the greatest motivation was to be able to play soccer. That was the motivation that helped me set some goals in other areas as well.

I smiled to myself as I thought of something the *Gospozah* had said. She'd called me by name, *Sotka*, not *magarets*.

Is It Better to Be or Not?

Do not plan for ventures before finishing what's at hand.

EURIPIDES

British and Yugoslav film crews had arrived in Bela Crkva to make a documentary about us kids. At first, we were pleased with the idea. But when we started hearing them speak of *Grtsia*, Greece, the genuine interest in the film that had been generated among us degenerated into protest.

They started filming us, but we protested so loudly that the filming stopped. The crew wanted to sort out what all the protests were about. They talked to the staff and finally began to understand that we were not Greek refugees from Greece, we were Macedonian refugees from Macedonia. The general English public did not know that. This was a learning experience for the entire crew.

Once that point was settled, quite a few from our *Dom* were chosen to have speaking roles. I wasn't the least bit interested, because it would have taken too much of my soccer time. However, I piqued the crew's interest in our soccer game, which was scheduled for the coming Sunday.

They came to watch us play. The woman with them seemed to be either the producer or the director—I didn't know the difference. I heard that one of the British crew was an ex-soccer player. He and I became friends a little later, when I learned he had played for the British team called Hot Spurs.

On the Sunday they came, we played a very aggressive game, and afterwards, the British lady asked to see me. Coach took me to a building near the ice cream parlor. I didn't know what a hotel was, but he told me that this building was called a hotel.

She met with us and, through the interpreter, she told me that she liked what she saw and had asked Dobrila, our director's assistant, for permission to use me in the movie. She told me that they were going to film at Nero, and that I would go with the other kids.

I refused, but Dobrila and *Gospozah* Iconia strongly urged me to participate. What was there for me to lose? I thought silently, "Nothing, except soccer time!"

I did join the other kids. My role was described as a kid who was gutsy, fearless, and courageous. They gave me directions to do this, and do that; jump this way; roll over that way; run here and so forth. Whatever they told me to do, I did, and with gusto, figuring out that the faster we finished the sooner I would be able to get out of there.

Not so!

We spent about 2½ weeks with the film crew. I was itching to get away. What a waste of time! I couldn't stand the make-up they were putting on me, nor the constant changing of clothes. They made us up to look as if we were wounded. I hated all that crap. It was so phony. But *Gospozah* and Dobrila insisted on my participation—my *cooperative* participation!

So I stayed. That's when I got to meet the ex-soccer player. Most of the time he was behind the camera. I wish I could remember his name. It might have been Matt.

I called him Met, which in Macedonian means honey. My very private name for him was "footballer." Met must have been 40 to 45 years old then, but, oh, how he could dribble the soccer ball. He dribble-controlled the ball like no one else I had ever seen up until then. He was full of tricks. When everyone was resting or eating, he and I played soccer, one-on-one, juggling, heading, shooting! Let me tell you, this was heaven. My time with Met was the best fun-time ever.

Even though we were filming and sleeping in Nero, we were still doing school work with our tutors. The next Sunday I was scheduled to play with one of the two city soccer teams, either Borets or Granichar. Met was such a soccer fan that he came with the team to Zrenianin where the game was scheduled.

Met could speak neither Macedonian nor Serbian. When he was filming, he had the services of interpreters. Here at the game, we could only use body language and hand signals to communicate with each other. Our team played a terrific game. Met thoroughly enjoyed it, and you could see that soccer would remain forever in his blood.

After several weeks, when that film had been completed, the film crew started to prepare for another one. This one was to be about a famous pre-war Yugoslav soccer player whose name was Matosic, playing for Hyduk from Split, and the National Yugsolav team as well. I have to tell you that I was thrilled to be chosen to play Matosic as a youngster up to the age of 20. I was told not to worry about the age, because they could do magic with makeup. I'm sure that the idea for the film came from Met because, after we returned from Zrenianin, he talked to the boss-lady, pointing at me.

A schedule was developed for the filming. Five days later, when some of the crew started talking about making still another film, I really tried to get lost. I definitely did not want any more filming. But everybody pressured me. The crew began to film the background in town. They went to Panchevo and Belgrad to shoot scenes and then back to Nero and the Granichar stadium.

The title of the film was *PLAVA 9TKA*. The only time I saw it was a few months after its completion, when they were editing it in the Belgrad studios. On the last day of filming the director/producer lady came to me with several papers. The interpreter explained to me that she was holding adoption papers for me and she wanted me to sign them.

I was stunned. I couldn't comprehend for a while that she really wanted me to sign the papers. Maybe she was joking. No, she was quite sincere. The interpreter told me she had learned that I had two sisters, and she had included them in the adoption papers. I couldn't believe what I heard. She was going to adopt the three Nitchov children.

No!

No, no, NO!

Dobrila and *Gospozah* Iconia were very much in favor of accepting the offer. They both told me that she promised to send me to school for acting and that I could play for a Liverpool soccer team.

NO!
NO!
NO!

I walked away quickly, shaking my head.

I wanted to say goodbye to Met.

He, too, tried to persuade me to sign the adoption papers. He added that I could probably play for any soccer club in England within 2 or 3 years. He had that much confidence in me.

He tried, with the help of an interpreter, to paint an enticing future for me in England. It was too much for me. I was just a kid, a Macedonian kid, a *Begaltche* from T'rsie.

What did I know about a future?

What could I plan for when all I had thought of was returning to Macedonia, to T'rsie and my family, when we all would be together again, to live our lives—hopefully in freedom and equality.

I could not think of a future. I only knew of yesterday, and today.

What could England possibly mean to me?

What about my mother?

My father?

My brother?

Our property?

There was no question or hesitation on my part. The answer was "No" to England, "No" to adoption. That was final.

Should the answer have been different?

All's Well That Ends Well

When angry, count four.
When very angry, swear.

MARK TWAIN

I remember a Sunday when the Granichar team was scheduled to play in Panchevo. Both Kanachki and Bato, who played for the team, wanted to take me with them. My heart leapt, and then sank—for this happened during one of those times when I was restricted.

Persistently, Kanachki urged me to ask for permission to go. Kanachki, of course, didn't know why I was restricted, and I wasn't about to tell him. "I'll ask, but I know they won't let me go."

"I'll go with you," Kanachki offered. That was just fine with me. We walked together to the director's office. The door was open and he looked up to see us at his door. I always felt that director Todor braced himself whenever he saw me in his office, ready for the worst.

Kanachki took the initiative to explain our presence. "We think this kid has some talent, and we would like to break him in with our team, Granichar," Kanachki began. "If you would be so generous as to give us permission to have Sotir come with us, he will be the first Aegean Macedonian to play on our team."

"It is very nice that you think this highly of Sotir, but did you know that he was failing in his grades?" asked Todor, rather kindly, I thought.

With genuine surprise, Kanachki responded, "No. He has never mentioned anything about his studies to us, and to tell you the truth, we never thought of asking him about that."

I felt that I had to risk breaking in or lose the very thing I wanted to do so very much. "Sir, my grades are improving. . . . " *Gospozah* walked in. I continued, "I, um, my grades are improving and, *chesna rech,* I give you my word, that I will keep on improving."

The director looked at me with concern, but with interest as well. "That is the first time I have ever heard you give your word, but do you mean it?" His eyes stabbed mine with his look.

Before I could answer, *Gospozah* Iconia spoke, looking at me directly, right down to my soul, "When this *magarets* gives his word, he does keep it. I can vouch for that." I gulped. Her look was speaking volumes to me in contrast to her brief statement to the director. As I waited to hear what the verdict would be, the three of them, Todor, Kanachki and Gospozah Iconia moved to a corner of the office to discuss the issue among themselves. It seemed like hours of discussion—but it couldn't have been more than 10 or 15 minutes. They kept glancing at me.

Finally they stopped. They looked at me for a minute or two more, without a word, and then came back to where I was standing, one on each side of me with Todor in front of me.

He folded his arms across his chest, and looked into my eyes for a short time. Then he said, quite slowly, and thoughtfully, "Well, Sote, you may go this time, but you must report back to me or to *Gospozah* Iconia as soon as you get back."

He turned to Kanachki. "And you, Mr. Kanachki, will be responsible for him for the next 2 days."

Back to me, "Now go, and pack your things."

He was going to let me go! I couldn't believe it. I was overwhelmed. I was thrilled. I wanted to jump up and down. I wanted to hug him. To this day, I haven't been able to find the words that can describe my complete joy, my total happiness for this unexpected gift. To be able to do the one thing in the world that I ever really wanted to do—to play soccer—it was a dream come true.

I kept repeating thank you, thank you, thank you, until Kanachki put his hand on my shoulder to usher me out of the office. I told everyone I saw that I was going to Panchevo to play soccer. I must have said it over a hundred times before I got to my room. My roommates were as happy for me as I was.

For the first time since we left our homes I began to feel happy, totally, totally happy, fulfilled. I hadn't felt this way in such a long, long time, in another life, when Tome and I would ride with the wind up to Lundser, feeling the warmth of the sun on my head, knowing the *sokols* were envious of our flight.

All the Granichar players were good to me. They really enjoyed teasing me, and tried to put some fear in me by talking about a guy nick-named *Grobar*, grave-digger, who played for the Panchevo Dinamo soccer team. Each of the guys had something to tell me about *Grobar*, how deadly tough he was and tricky. One of them told me how *Grobar* liked to pick on *golo bradi,* beardless players, younger kids.

They all described him as a very vicious player, and said that when he talked, he sounded like a barking dog. I learned from our players that he ate dirt and cursed all the time, and so on, and so on. I loved it. Nothing they said about him fazed me. I was in seventh heaven. "You can't scare me about *Grobar*. I don't care if he eats rocks for breakfast, lunch and dinner. You can tell me all the horrible stories you want until doomsday. They don't mean diddly to me!"

Much later I learned that the Partizan players were called *grobari,* gravediggers, too.

We boarded the train that would take us to Panchevo for the game. I could barely contain myself, I was so eager to play. We arrived in Panchevo and went to dress without wasting any time, and then I saw who this famous "gravedigger" was. Let me tell you that the core of what my team had been saying about *Grobar* was true. This guy was a maniac. He didn't "play" soccer. His game was kill-or-be-killed! He *crunched* soccer players.

In the first few minutes of play I was almost decapitated. He pulled some cheap stuff on me, kicking me a few times. That surprised me. How could he get away with it? The referees called no fouls. What I couldn't understand was why the older players let him get away with that. During a break, I complained to Bato and Kanachki and the others. I threatened to break *Grobar's* legs if he kicked or punched me again. Some of the guys laughed, while others wished me luck, wisely.

The second half of the game started. *Grobar* was really of average size, about 5 feet, 9 inches, weighing maybe 160 pounds. He never stopped cussing and trash talking. Now, I was only about 5 feet, 8 inches tall, weighing 148 pounds, so the inevitable was going to happen. We came close together reaching for a high ball. I was going up for it, and so was he. He came at me and landed his fist on my face, hard! Finally, a foul was called on him, and we got a free kick. *Grobar* got a warning.

Kanachki came over to me and cautioned, "Stay away from him, do you hear? I was beyond warning. "Oh yeah, I'll stay away all right. You had better get a stretcher for him." Was I ever ready for *Grobar*! I was dangerously furious, ready for action. I was *so* ready for our friend, *Grobar.*

The play started. Just minutes later we made contact again, but this time I was more than ready for him. I punched him so hard that he spun around and fell to the ground. The referee did not see the punch, so he did not call a foul. I bent down as if to help him. I stuck my two fingers up his nose, one in each nostril, and pulled as hard as I could, causing one of his nostrils to bleed. All during this attack he was holding his face and muttering something. To me it sounded like noise.

His teammates close by tried to see what was going on, but the fans and some of the other players thought I was being a good sport, helping him up. His cheek had a pretty good gash, so he was bleeding nicely. He was like an outraged bull, spitting, cursing and yelling at me, which made the referee give him another warning.

I loved it. His teammates dragged him over to the side and patched him up. The game was ready to resume. I realized that now I had to watch out for him even more closely. My very shadow was a challenge to this maniac, this *Grobar*. I had the most beautiful sneer on my face you could ever hope to see, just to make him crazy. He began to threaten me. He was going to break me in two. He was going to kill me. I would never play soccer again. With every cheap threat, I felt stronger and stronger. I was in my element now. Every aggressive tendency that I had building in me throughout my short life came together now, ready to explode. I just kept saying and nodding, "*Da. Da*," yes, yes, to everything he was spitting out of his mouth.

He charged toward me, as if we were playing hockey, and tried to cut me under with his hip, but I had seen him get ready. He charged with a run. I braced myself, balancing my feet, raising my knee high enough for him to run into it. I maneuvered in such a way, that when he impacted me, his right collarbone bore the brunt of it. Down he went. There was no question that he was in great pain, so they had to take him off the field and straight to the hospital.

Bye, bye, *Grobar*. I didn't regret it one bit. I still don't.

By the way, we won the game! My team looked at me with a new respect. I could meet any challenge now, that was the consensus among them. When we returned late Sunday night, I reported immediately to *Gospozah* Iconia, even though I had to wake her up. She gave me a thumbs-up. I smiled and left to go to my room, lucky #309. As soon as I hit the sack, I fell asleep, exhilarated but totally exhausted. I was allowed 2 extra hours of sleep.

All in all, I had the first terrific couple of days of my life. All's well, that ends well, they say. I relived the joy and triumph of the whole experience for days. My team treated me with affection. What gave me even greater pleasure was remembering how some of the opposing team players, *Grobar's* team-mates, had patted my back, remarking how good my plays were and that I should keep it up. That was the kind of praise I had seldom ever received.

The next day, the papers had a picture of both *Grobar* and me. The write-up was a favorable one for me. I was happy about myself and everything and everybody around me for a long time. I got lots of hugs and approving smiles. That game proved to be the beginning of my real soccer future. I was going to be playing with young men, 19 to 30 years of age, and let me tell you, there is a world of difference between them and playing with and against 15- or 17-year-olds.

Things started to improve in other ways. My grades improved to the point that all those who had been concerned were no longer worried. That made me happier because I had more free time for soccer and less time for fights, pranks and mischief in general. True to my nature, I couldn't resist a prank or two from time to time, but nothing serious enough to incur penalties. I didn't miss any dinners, nor did I have to scrub the mess hall for a while. Believe it or not, I had become a little wiser, a little cagier. I loved sports. Still do.

I joined the boxing club and, to my surprise, I proved to be a lousy boxer. Everybody was able to ring my bell. The boxing instructor advised me to quit. As he put it, "Son, you are a street fighter, not a ring boxer. I don't think we can change that." He was right. Every one of the kids I had fought outside the ring I had beaten the daylights out of. In the ring, though, it was just the opposite. They were able to punch my lights out. Don't ask me why. I guess most everybody was as surprised as I was. I tried harder, but the reality was that I was usually counted out, or just out, seeing rainbow colors and stars.

I tried out for track and field, short distances. In running 50, 100 or 200 meters, again I didn't do too well. Interestingly, anything beyond 200 yards, I could usually hold my own or move ahead of the others. I enjoyed vaulting, javelin and hammer throwing, the triple jump, and the high jump. All of these activities were the fun part, the positive part of being a *Begaltche.*

That label never left any of us. We were enshrouded with the term regardless of where we were or who we were with. We were all still Begaltsi, evacuees, refugees, and for the time, homeless.

From among the boys, some excellent athletes emerged. I remember Gavre Kuslev became the Macedonian boxing champion and competed in the Yugoslav elite competition. Gavre remained on top for several years. Risto Shishkov, also an excellent athlete, became one of the better actors in Yugoslavia. There were many among us who became soccer players, track and field athletes and went on later to prove themselves exceptional in competition.

What is as awe-inspiring is that so many Begaltsi eventually became doctors, lawyers, engineers, professors, actors, musicians, singers, teachers, poets, journalists, writers, and members of academia with advanced degrees. Can you imagine that possibility had we remained in our villages during the disastrous civil war and the aftermath under Greek occupation and tyranny again? And if it had been possible to survive the holocaust of Macedonia, would any of us have had the opportunity to achieve our individual goals without having to deny our Macedonian background, language, heritage, history, and culture?

Stefo, my Brother, Standing Tall

I have loved badly . . . withdrawn my words too late;
and eaten in an echoing hall alone
and from a chipped plate
the words that I withdrew too late.

EDNA ST. VINCENT MILLAY

He was 3 years older than I. No two brothers could have been more different in every imaginable way. My brother Stefo was my complete opposite—quiet, gentle, courteous, thoughtful and reflective. It was not in his nature to get into trouble.

For Stefo, rules, regulations, guidelines were to be followed. I must have been an embarrassment to him because of my careless concern regarding rules. My wild, untamed nature overturned every obstacle in my path that might have prevented me from the consequences that befell me. He was a conformist, and I was anything but.

Stefo, trying to make me reflect on my behavior and willfulness would ask me, "What are you doing? Aren't you ashamed of what you did? Think, Sote, your behavior is shaming our name. Why can't you be like the rest of us? Look at our cousins Itso, Ilo, Petre, and Krsto. Do you see any one of them getting into the kind of trouble you find yourself in?"

Stefo's birthday was March 25 and, initially, he was earmarked to be evacuated with the younger children. That changed and, like the other almost-15-year-olds, he was held back, targeted for recruitment by the Partizans. As I mentioned earlier, had it not been for Mother's intervention—and that of the other mothers who notified a friend to get word to my father—Stefo would have become a recruit. So, with the others, he joined us younger *Begaltsi* in the village of Oshchima.

A sense of fair play and self-sacrifice characterized my brother throughout his life. One incident remains vivid in my mind—I want to tell you about it because it shows the sense of fair play and self-sacrifice that characterized my brother throughout his life. It also shows clearly just how different we were.

I think it was early 1947—in Dreno, bordering Gorna Statitsa and T'rsie—on a cold snowy day that Stefo and some of the older boys found a new toy. It was a rifle—either Italian or Russian—I didn't know the difference. The boys started experimenting with the rifle, shooting at some target or other. Ilo and I were in a place called Koria. When we heard the shots, we immediately started to investigate. As we reached the Dreno area and saw Stefo and the others, I knew that I had to have a turn with the rifle. When I asked if I could try the gun, they all refused vehemently.

"No! You're too young to hold this gun!"

Now they knew that I had held many guns and shot them off, too, but this time, they were not going to let me do it. I never could take "no" for an answer, so we stuck around for a while. I kept watching for an opportunity to grab the rifle. In a split second I saw the opportunity and grabbed it. It was mine now, and that was that. All of the guys demanded that I give up the rifle. I had gotten about 20 yards away from them, when Goge Shipinkov, one of Stefo's buddies, started toward me to take the rifle.

"Don't come any closer or I'll shoot," I warned him.

He took a step or two before I fired and he backed off.

They appealed to Stefo,

"He's your brother. Maybe he'll listen to you."

"Stay away or I'll shoot."

Stefo at first didn't take my warning seriously.

"Don't come any closer. . . . " I warned him again, but he kept coming toward me. All I wanted to do was what *they* were all doing, firing a new kind of toy—this foreign rifle—and I *was* going to do it!

I pulled the trigger and fired. To my horror and everyone else's as well, the bullet grazed Stefo's right shoulder. Everybody scattered. I don't know if anyone took the rifle. Stefo tried to clean up his shoulder the best he could. I didn't know what to say or do. We all left in a hurry. Stefo said not one word to anyone, until that evening when Father came home.

Stefo eyed Father as he said, "I hurt my shoulder a bit."

Father took a look at it.

"That's not a scratch or even a cut. Tell me, what happened?"

I could see that Father was preparing himself to hear about some kind of encounter.

"Who shot at you? What really happened?"

Reluctantly, Stefo started to tell him that it was an accident, when I piped up. I had to tell the truth.

"I wounded Stefo with that new rifle they were shooting. They wouldn't let me hold it or shoot it." And I told him the whole story from beginning.

Stefo tried to protect me from my own stupidity, but it didn't do any good. I was severely scolded, lectured, warned. I got the message clearly.

Later, Stefo hissed at me, "I tried to protect you up there."

I hissed back, "I protected you from lying!"

He shook a fist at me, threateningly, but that was it. He never laid a hand on me.

There are so many memories of Stefo. There's another story about my brother that is such an example of his character. During the early days following our arrival in Bela Crkva, when food was still somewhat scarce, Stefo was in the very first group of the *Begaltsi* scheduled for the mess hall. He would often go hungry, so that those who followed him in line would have a little more food to eat.

In those early days, whatever amount of bread was rationed for us had to be cut into small slices and placed in baskets, one basket per table. Each basket was equal in content, one slice per child per table. Hunger was our constant companion. Some of us, including me, would take bread from the baskets as we walked down the aisles to our seats. Frequently, by the time the middle of the line was seated, the breadbaskets were empty! Even I went without bread for 2 or 3 days.

For a Macedonian, young or old, bread was more than a staple of life, it was our means of survival. Stefo never picked up an extra slice. In fact, he often gave his portion to someone who didn't get any. I can't understand why the staff in charge did not immediately see what was happening.

Having gone without bread for a couple of days, while in the yard one day, I told my best friend, Done Kostov, from the village of Bouf, "Done, I just made myself a promise. I won't ever go hungry for bread again!"

Done, while sympathetic, laughed. "And where are you going to find the bread? And if you do, save some for me, will you?"

"Go ahead, laugh. But tonight, I'll have lots of bread. Just you watch."

Seeing that I was seriously hatching a plan to sneak some more bread, Done said, "Good. I'll have some of yours. Hey, Lazo, come over here and listen to this!"

"I am listening to my stomach making noises. Do I have to listen to you, too?" Lazo replied plaintively. Lazo Kotev, another one of my friends, was from Turie.

"Are you planning to steal from the *kuina*, kitchen?"

"I already thought of that, but I couldn't figure out a way."

Both Done and Lazo laughed and snorted. They shook their heads, half believing that I would.

"You guys can laugh and joke all you want, but you'll be begging me for a slice," I taunted.

That evening during roll call, as the lines were beginning to form for supper, and as my name was called, I turned and quickly stepped up front, as close to the bigger boys as possible. That was the procedure: step forward and follow the person ahead of you when your name was called. The line started to move into the mess hall. As we entered, I began to grab slices of bread from the side of the aisle, between the tables, stuffing the bread in my shirt. Nobody noticed. I must have accumulated about a dozen slices before some of the kids saw me and began to protest. As usual, I didn't care. I had made a promise to myself never to go hungry again.

For about 3 days I went undetected when my brother found out. A couple of the kids complained to Stefo. He scolded me and tried to make me put it all back, but I refused. He tried to talk some sense into me, not with anger, for that was not his way. He tried to reason with me, to appeal to my sense of fairness.

"Listen, little brother. What you are doing is wrong, very wrong. What about the other kids? They have to eat too, and they are just as hungry as you are."

Smugly, impudently, I answered him, "I am not going to worry about anyone except myself."

Still Stefo persisted. "You just don't want to understand, do you? What do you suppose it will take for you to understand how selfish and wrong you are?"

Defiantly, patting my stomach, I replied, "See here? A full stomach every night. Maybe if everybody takes more bread, they will have to find more bread for us."

Itso and Petre joined Stefo, trying to convince me to stop my bread thefts.

Stefo turned to the others. "I think we are wasting our time with him. Let them catch him and lock him up. Maybe that's when he will learn his lesson."

Even more impudently I said to them, "You mean they will lock me up for trying to stay healthy?"

Stefo and the others left, thoroughly disgusted with me.

Done, Lazo, Goce, and my cousin Ilo joined me outside. I gave each of them one extra slice of bread, but warned them, "If you guys laugh, you forfeit the bread. You will have to get your own after this."

Ilo laughed, "I knew you would do it. I even told my brother, Itso, that you would do something stupid. What if they catch you?"

I challenged him, "If what I did was so stupid, why did you accept the bread from me?"

"Because I'm hungry, that's why!"

We all munched away on our precious slices of bread, hunger somewhat abated.

A few minutes later, Stefo came back and asked me if I had any more bread on me.

"Yeah."

"Will you offer me a slice of bread?

Now I was thoroughly disgusted. "You know, Stefo, you are one of the first ones in line, and yet you go hungry. That's a shame! Go and get your own!"

I refused to give him that slice. Stefo left without saying another word.

After thinking about what had just happened, my conscience began to bother me. I consoled myself by rationalizing that Stefo had to learn to take care of himself first. He had to look out for himself. It wasn't that Stefo was weak or cowardly. Stefo was very strong. He could bend you in two just with his hands, but he refrained from doing that. It was just not in his nature to take the offensive.

That's what bothered me so much about him. He was quite able to defend himself against anyone, yet he never hit anyone nor did he try to hurt anyone. He always went out of his way to help someone, unasked. I remember my father scolding me, "Why can't you be more like your brother? Learn something from him." Then I thought about how arrogantly and impudently I had acted toward him. After all, it was only a slice of bread.

As badly as I began to feel about my behavior at the time, it is nothing compared to what I feel today at that memory. Every time I eat a slice of bread, I am reminded of Stefo, and it hurts. Sometimes tears come to my eyes. I can never make it up to him.

You see, no matter what uncivilized thing I did, no matter how arrogant or impudent my behavior; no matter how thoughtlessly, how brutally, how stupidly I carried on, my brother never rejected me.

In spite of our different temperaments and personalities, Stefo and I were very close. I always felt very close to every member of our family. If anyone tried by any means to hurt my sisters, cousins or my only brother, I defended them vigorously, with every ounce of strength in my body.

And yet, I denied Stefo one slice of bread.

I was in denial of so many things in my young life then. Time was of no real importance. One day flowed into another as routine began to set in. What further plans were being made involving us weren't announced in advance. I wasn't aware of a place called *Bulkes* or how it would affect our lives.

There was a lot we didn't know. That gap in our information regarding Bulkes was soon to be revealed to us, unhappily. We had no clue, no inkling—with the exception of a select few—that our older *Begaltsi* in the *Doms* were targeted to be shipped out, surreptitiously, without the knowledge of their siblings in the *Doms.* They were not going to be permitted to say their farewells. The boys were simply to "disappear."

One late afternoon, while I was milling about in the yard, a very pretty young nurse approached me. I stopped whatever it was I was doing and waited for her to speak. Very quietly she told me her name was Nada, as she took me aside. Her message was brief and to the point, because there was so little time. I looked at her without comprehending what she was starting to tell me.

"I have a message from Stefo. Please go to the Russian memorial to see your brother off."

See my brother off? Off where? Why? I kept looking at her, this pretty dark-haired young woman, waiting for some kind of clarification. Seeing that I was not getting her message, she motioned to me to come with her. I followed her to the memorial in front of the church, and yes, there was Stefo! What was this all about? Stefo looked at me carefully, searching for the words, and in his quiet way he began to explain.

"Sote, we are being sent someplace, but I don't know where we are going. I want you to promise me that you will look after Tsotsa, Cousin Krsto and Cousin Sofa. And Sote, you must behave and stay out of trouble. Do you understand me?"

Did I understand him? No, I did not understand.

"Why are you going? Who else is going? Do you have to go?"

In his calm and clear manner he answered, "Our cousins Petre, Itso Ilo, Vane Popov-Findin, Kosta, Tode, Goge Nanov and some others from our village are also going to go. They will be taking some of the older girls, too. So listen carefully. I don't know if I'll ever see you again. It is important that you find a way to bring our little sister, Mara, back here. One other thing, Sote," he put his hands on my shoulders, "if anything should happen to me, you must promise to take care of our Mother and Father."

Why was Stefo talking like this to me, as if I were his equal, and not his younger brother? I was trying to absorb what he was saying, but I wasn't making any headway.

Stefo continued, "I'll write to you as soon as we get to where they are taking us.

Also, I want you to know that I just got a letter from Father yesterday. He is in some place called Olympos. He says he is fine. You can write letters and give them to Nada. She'll know what to do."

"Can I see the cousins?"

Nada interrupted. "No, they are not permitted to come out. In fact, Stefo, we better get going or they will miss us and come looking for us."

We had to say goodbye, but I didn't know how. Stefo reached out to take my hand for a manly handshake in farewell. Instead he reached out to put his arms around me and hugged me tightly. I couldn't think. I simply couldn't understand!

And that was it! That was our final goodbye. A speechless parting from one who was the strongest tie to everything that was familiar and important to me in my young world. We had never had to say goodbye to each other before. I stood, dumbfounded, watching Stefo and Nada walk towards the *Dom*, hand in hand.

Was this some nightmare, some dream I was having? We had only been in Bela Crkva for a couple of months. Why this?

I watched until they disappeared from my sight, and then sat at the base of the Russian memorial for a few minutes, to think, to reconstruct what had just happened. What the hell was going on? Something had to be terribly wrong. My stomach was beginning to react as the thoughts circled around and around in my head. I suddenly felt ill. It felt as though a sudden chill wind had blown away all my ability to reason, leaving only a terrible sense of foreboding.

One question after another, over and over again.

Why?

Who?

Where?

I felt like a helpless baby. I wanted to see my family, Mother and Father. I wanted to be back home with Dedo and Baba. I wanted to go back to T'rsie and ride my horse, Tome . . .

I needed everything and everybody familiar to me, so that I wouldn't feel so abandoned, so burdened with responsibilities—the dimensions of which I couldn't even begin to comprehend then.

I never got a chance to say goodbye to my cousins or anyone else. I had the unhappy task, the next day, of telling Risto that his brothers Itso and Ilo had left with Stefo to go someplace—but I didn't know where.

Poor Risto. He cried for a little while and so did my sister, Tsotsa, and cousin Sofa when I had to tell them that Petre was also leaving. What was there for us to do, four young *Begaltsi*, so far from home, but cry together? We were a pathetic, hapless group, weaned unwillingly from the comfort zone of family love and support and hope. This moment was truly an awakening to the fact that neither we nor our families had any control over our lives or our destinies.

About a month later, we learned that Stefo and the older boys were sent to the camp in Bulkes, near a village called Maglich in Serbia. Much later, we discovered that the camp was operated secretly, hidden from everyone—including the Red Cross—who was supposed to oversee our well being and security.

Little by little, the letters we began to receive informed us that many of the boys selected to go to the camp were 13 to 14 years old. They were from the villages of T'rsie, Turie, Kotori, Lagen, as well as a few from some other villages.

Some of the others from T'rsie who had left with my brother Stefo, were cousins Risto and Ilo Nitchov, Petre Dimovski, a cousin on my mother's side, Tode Giamov, Vane Popov-Findin, Krsto Pandov, Yane Maleganov, Risto Torkov-Termianin, Goge Utovski, Mite Nanov, Ilo Lazhkov, and Itso Chechanov.

They lived and worked apart from others at the camp, enduring 8-hour workdays and daily night school for 4 hours, where they were forced to study Greek only. Vanga Balkova and Kotsa Krachorova were two of the *Begaltsi* girls who were also sent to Bulkes to work. They must have sent more girls to Bulkes, but Vanga and Kotsa were the ones I personally knew.

The Greeks needed several types of workers. Some were designated to cultivate and work the farms, some were assigned as carpenters, and others were assigned to make uniforms for the Partizans. So these young adolescents, still children, provided the manpower to keep the Partizan war-machine going.

The living conditions were poor. The biggest complaint there was the lack of heat. It was always cold in the camps.

Vanga Balkova told us many things about Bulkes and what had happened to so many of the *Begaltsi*. We learned that around September, 1948, some of them were given Partizan uniforms and sent to Prespa. Among those were my brother, Stefo, Tode Giamov, Vane Popov-Findin, Risto Pandov and Risto Chechanov. Vanga was also selected to be sent as a *Partizanka*, but she was returned to Bulkes because she seemed to be too weak to carry a heavy rifle and too small to be a *Partizanka*! The others were loaded into freight trains.

As time permitted, she managed to keep us posted of other changes among the *Begaltsi* in Bulkes that we didn't know about. In early Spring, March of 1949, a year after we had set out on our long *trail of tears*, the rest of the kids who had been sent to Bulkes from Bela Crkva were shipped to Poland.

My cousin Risto also remembers that phase of his life very well. He was given Stefo's pants, but was not allowed to see Stefo to say goodbye before he was shipped out. Apparently those who were to be shipped out were separated from the others who had not yet been scheduled for deployment.

The rumor circulating among the Macedonians was that Zahariadis and his band needed the young bodies to inflate their guerilla quotas. It didn't matter whether they could fight or not. The guerillas needed a slaughter machine to keep their movement active. That *kopile* Georgiadis, in the company of some KKE, had come to Bela Crkva to select some of the taller, stronger boys, some of whom were only 13 years old. The oldest boys were 15. These were the ones to be sent to Bulkes. The selection was made by the end of June, 1948. The rest of the *Begaltsi* in Bulkes eventually were sent to Poland in the spring of 1949.

Of the boys who were recruited into the Partizans, only two survived: Krsto Pandov and Risto Chechanov.

Stefo was killed at Malimadi, July, 1949. Tode was killed at Ramni Vir, T'rsie. Vane was also killed at Malimadi One report the family received was that my brother and his cousin, Nase, Kotse's brother, ran into each other at Malimadi. This had to be soon after Stefo had left Bulkes. They were sitting and talking near a water hole when the shelling started. Nase had been drafted in 1948. He was one of the more educated of the Nitchov bulog. Nase had gone to school in Porodin, a village near Bitola and finished high school there. He was able to complete 1 year of college before he returned to T'rsie just before we kids left the village. When he was drafted by the Partizans he was immediately made a sergeant and very shortly he was elevated to captain.

We eventually learned that Nase was killed in 1948, and Stefo in 1949. They had been killed almost a year apart at Malimadi.

Krsto Pandov survived the civil war because he happened to run into my father near Kostur.

"Were it not for Numkoto Mite, I would be dead now. When he spotted me, he immediately rushed over and grabbed me by the arm. He told me to pick up my coat, leave my gun and head for home. 'Don't stop or talk to anyone. Just go home and hide. Don't speak to anyone,' he warned, 'or go anywhere with anybody. Whoever sent you here had no right to do so. Just go now!'"

Krsto left at that moment and never looked back. In a day and a half he was home and somehow managed to survive. Itso Chechanov simply ran back to Yugoslavia. That was the last word we had about him.

Father kept on looking for Stefo and any of the other *Begaltsi* forced into uniform, but the KKE commandants hid them well.

We also learned from my cousins and some of the other kids in Bulkes, that they had met the man who helped us get the Greeks removed from Bela Crkva. His name was Kosta from Rudari, and it grieves me that I cannot recall his last name. He told all the kids, and adults as well, how we in Bela Crkva stood up to the Greeks and demanded Macedonian schools and teachers. He was so proud of our actions, and he was more than happy to have supported us. My cousins became especially interested when Kosta mentioned a boy named Sote. Risto asked a number of questions, whether it could have been a boy named Sote Nitchov. Kosta wasn't sure of the last name, but he remembered that the boy was from T'rsie or Turie.

In Bulkes, when Kosta learned of the plans to send him to Poland as well, his comment was, "Boys, I am going where there are no Greeks!"

It was so tragic to learn that the hated Georgiadis and his assorted devils had identified all the tall, strong kids in Bela Crkva to be sent to Bulkes. He undermined the authority of the Red Cross and got away with it. Had the Red Cross known the *Begaltsi* were being selected to fight as Partizans, they would have put a stop to that "recruitment" immediately. The Communist leaders, secretly and illegally, violated their own laws by sending these young boys and girls to the war zone.

Stefo, my brother, and the hundreds of other young Macedonian boys and girls who were sacrificed by the Greeks and Communists will always remain in our minds and our memories, *standing tall, like the poplar trees that grace the forests around T'rsie.*

When a gentle breeze flows among the leaves of those trees, it most likely will be the gentle spirit of my brother, Stefo, moving across the familiar Macedonian landscape, upon which a vibrant, passionate people staked their claim, born to live and hope and die so that Macedonians could be free.

Stefo and his generation of boys—as well as generations of Macedonian boys, men and women before them—returned to the land they so dearly loved. The price for that return—paid in blood—was too deadly.

I see him in my mind every day:

Stefo, my brother, standing tall.

1949

The human being as a commodity is the disease of our age.

MAX LERNER, 1959

When American General Van Fleet replaced Livesey as head of the AMM upon his arrival in Athens, he announced that Greece was going to be a laboratory experiment.

The AMM experimented on the Partisans with the new incendiary and chemical devices, using the latest techniques in warfare. The resistance by the Partisans revealed the depth of their commitment to change in Greece. Even though the huge rocks in the Macedonian mountainswere plastered with blazing jelly, the Partisans, who had been trapped for a week, repulsed the attacks. All food had been exhausted. More of the Partisans succumbed to the hunger and cold than to the napalm, because to have broken out of the trap would have meant abandoning the sick and the wounded.

When August came to a close, one of the bloodiest battles of the war in Greece ended in defeat to the Partisans. Without America's role in the war, the ending might have tilted the entire region into waiting Soviet hands.

January:

- Zachariadis ordered his guerillas to attack Naoussa again, which they held for three days, retreating along the Pisoderi valley with additional recruits.
- At the Fifth Congress of the Bulgarian Communist Party, Zachariadis, Ioannidis and Vlantas revived support for the national claims of the Macedonians, which were now opposed by the KKE.
- NOF was given a wider leadership role to blunt Tito's efforts at division and subversion in Greece. NOF reported 1,200 Bulgarian 'brothers' arrived in Greece.
- American and British representatives gave Greece assurances that the establishment of a Macedonian state would be viewed as contrary to the tenets of the Truman Doctrine.

February:

- Thousands of Partisans attacked Lerin (*Florina)*, headquarters of a Greek Army Corps, in their effort to reach Solun (*Salonica*).
- Greek government reinforcements were delayed by heavy snowfall.

March:

- The meeting of the NOF Second Congress on Grammos called on all militants to support the Democratic Army's struggle. NOF restated its position that the Macedonian people would be able to decided freely their own status after the victory of Communism in Greece.
- KOAM indicated that the KKE was relinquishing its authority in Greek Macedonia.

April:

- The Greek cabinet was purged and reshuffled due to a number of embezzlement scandals and inconveniences to the American forces.

May:

- The Greek Provisional Government in the mountains issued 26 peace proposals to the Greek Government which were rejected.

July:

- Greek government forces launched an attack in the Kaimkchalan Mountains along the Yugoslav border, east of Vicho (*Vitsi*).
- Tito formally closed the Yugoslav/Greek frontier to the the Greek guerillas, which confirmed a growing suspicion among the Greek guerillas that Tito was an undercover agent for the British all along.

August:

- On August 2, commemorating the 1903 Illinden Uprising, in Skopje,Tito reiterated his support for a united state of Macedonia.
- Bulgaria immediately accused the Yugoslavs of traitorous intents against the Greek guerilla movement.
- Zachariadis had 8,000 Partisans fighting at Vicho (*Vitsi*), and 5,000 Partisans high up on Grammos, resisting strongly among napalm-blackened crags. For a brief time Albanians tried to help in the resistance.
- Partisans withdrew from Vicho (*Vitsi*) leaving hundreds dead and reached Grammos.
- The Greek Third Government Army Corps deployed its entire air force at

Beles Mountain. After 4 days approximately a thousand survivors crossed into Bulgaria.

- The Americans reinforced Greek air power with planes, ground support aircraft, machine guns, cannons and tons of bombs.
- KKE slogans began to appear: THE ENEMY SHALL NOT ESCAPE VITSI (VICHO). GRAMMOS SHALL BECOME THE GRAVEYARD OF MONARCHO-FASCISM.
- Grammos fell.
- Kamenik fell. Thousands of Partisans reached Albania.
- August 27, Grammos fell.
- The entire guerilla force of the KKE, its leadership, and the members of the Greek Provisional government escaped into Albania.

October:

- Accused of being Yugoslav agents, NOF members were arrested in the Albanian refugee camps.
- Macedonia remained partitioned.

The Letter

The Moving Finger writes; and, having writ moves on: nor all your Piety nor Wit shall lure it back to cancel half a line, nor all your Tears wash out a Word of it.

Omar Khayyam

From time to time, a letter would arrive from Father postmarked either Albania or Yugoslavia. I had no idea how the letters found their way to us. We had no relatives living in either country at the time.

In one of the letters Father explained the mystery to me. Because there was no way to send mail from the battle zones, he would give a letter to one of the wounded Partizans. Wherever the wounded soldier was sent to recuperate, he would see that it was mailed. This could mean weeks, months, years before a letter reached its destination.

The last letter I received from Father was dated late August, 1948. In it, he wrote about the war in *Kina* or *Kitai*, meaning China. I had no idea what he was referring to, but I do remember he wrote that when *that* war ended, then ours would end right after that. He would see us as soon as possible after the war.

I did not hear from him at all during 1949, but in April or May 1950, I received a letter from my Cousin Lena in Skopje, which was now the capital of the People's Republic of Macedonia. At first I had thought it might be a letter from Father. By now—reading the Yugoslav newspapers—*Politika* and *Borba*, we all knew the Partiszans had been defeated. And since the war in China had ended, maybe Father would be coming home.

Holding the letter in my hands, the thought crossed my mind that perhaps Father was in Skopje with his niece, Lena. I was uneasy, though.

There was something about this letter in my hand, this unopened letter that made me pause.

We were all getting letters more frequently, and we usually opened them right on the spot. Something was holding me back, though. I needed to be alone.

Walking toward the stairway leading to the second floor of the *Dom*, I started up, then stopped on the landing near the window. I stood by the window, still hesitating about opening the letter, feeling suddenly a paralyzing sense of fear. But I couldn't understand it.

My hands began to tremble as I stared at the envelope. This sudden emotion, this fear, felt so alien, so strange, but I finally opened the letter, and spread it before me on the window sill. I found myself quickly skimming the lines of the letter.

Nothing made any sense!

I had to get a hold of myself.

Start over, read slowly.

"Dear Cousin Sote,

"Please don't hate me, but you must be told. It will hurt, but what can one do? This is Fate. Whatever is written shall come to pass. I guess we were born to suffer. First my brother Kotse was killed in 1944, in Gostivar-Debar with the Partizans. Now we have more tragedies."

The letter slipped out of my hands. I bent to pick it up. The first page contained no other name. It just referred to past tragedies. Lena wrote about everything, mentioning how quickly life flits by. I was getting more and more confused. Why was she writing these things to me?

The letter was about two pages long. She was trying to prepare me gently for devastating news, trying to cushion the inevitable shock that was about to engulf me.

I turned to the second page of the letter, again skimming to the names she had written near the middle of the page.

"Tatkoti, your father, Stefo, Nase were killed . . . ."

Something struck me hard. Was it a sword cutting through me? Who struck me? I dropped to the cement floor, dazed. All I could remember was that I was on the floor, tears streaming down my face like rain.

I looked toward the window, but saw nothing.

I heard nothing, no noise of any kind.

I began to swing my arms as if there was a phantom gloating over me, challenging me.

I got up and looked around again, and blindly swung at the window, breaking the glass, cutting my hand.

I felt no pain.

My head was spinning and my stomach churning, churning, churning. All the while, my chest seemed about to cave in.

I was so weak. No more energy left in me.

I raised my hands—or was it my foot? It was as if they were not a part of my body.

I had no feeling whatsoever.

I felt disembodied, numb, and I couldn't stop trembling. Was I breathing?

Some of the kids passed by on their way somewhere. They stopped when they saw me to ask what had happened. Was I hurt? My hand was bleeding.

I couldn't say a word. I just started to sob harder, mouth open, nose running.

Word got around swiftly. Cousin Krsto heard that I was on the landing, crying and couldn't talk. He ran to me and tried to get me to tell him what had happened. I couldn't form a single word.

Done, Lazo and Risto came as soon as they heard. Here I was, the tough, fearless kid, known to have more energy than 10 kids combined, more energy than the sun, always on the go, never standing still for long. Here I was, crying, unable to move.

"Sote is crying!"

"I can't believe you are crying! What's wrong with you?"

They were all crowded around me on the landing, wondering, talking anxiously, trying to find out what had happened.

Finally, exhausted, I found the strength to get up and shout, "Leave me alone!" I ran down the stairs, into the yard, and out the gate, running toward the big mulberry tree by the Nero.

I leaned against the tree. All I could think of was Father, Stefo, Nase, all killed . . . all dead, dead, *dead*.

I slid down the tree and remained slumped there on the ground for I don't know how long.

I must have fallen asleep, because I heard a voice—someone gently speaking to me—trying to get me to open my eyes. That voice began to sound familiar, and I opened my eyes slowly. Drago? *Gospozah* Iconia? What did *they* want? They were saying something to me.

Gospozah Iconia spoke again. "Risto read your letter and told me the sad . . . ." But she couldn't finish her sentence.

Drago, equally moved, tried to speak philosophically, "Sote, these things happen in war."

I just kept quiet, and let them talk. They kept on talking, trying to ease my pain, but I just couldn't say a word to them.

"Let's go over to the jeep and go home," Drago urged.

Gozpozah took my hand, and we walked over to the old jalopy. We rode off and, as we neared the *Dom*, she turned to Drago and said, "Drago, please turn around and take us to the hospital."

He made a quick turn and stopped at the hospital. Inside, *Gospozah* called Nurse Ruzhitsa to tell her that I was to spend the night there. She would return in the morning to check on me. Both Drago and *Gospozah* said their goodnights to me, and then drew the nurse aside. The three of them discussed the situation, and after they left, Ruzhitsa led me to a bed in one of the hospital rooms. As soon as my head hit the pillow, I was asleep.

When I awoke around dawn the next morning, Ruzhitsa was asleep in the next bed, still in her uniform and cap, leaning against the back of the bed. I covered her with a blanket from the next bed and put a pillow behind her head. She didn't awaken.

Around 7:30 in the morning, another nurse, Lutata, came to take my temperature, check my nose, ears, eyes, and pulse. She listened to my chest and declared that I was fine. Then she nudged Ruzhitsa awake. Chagrined, Ruzhitsa declared, "I must have fallen asleep. Who covered me? I am so sorry. I was on duty and I should have been on my feet."

Lutata didn't say a word. She seemed to be the meanest nurse in the hospital, but I must acknowledge that she was a very good nurse—though very strict, a rule-follower, and not very friendly. I had originally nicknamed her Serta, bad-tempered, and then nicknamed her Luta, hot-tempered. The kids picked it up and the name stuck to her.

Gospozah and Dobrila, the head of the girls' *Dom*, both came to see me. They agreed with the nurse that I was probably strong enough to come back to the *Dom*. We walked through the park, where Kanachki was working on our uniforms. He had not heard about my terrible news, so he asked me why I had missed practice. After I told him, he immediately changed the subject to clothes.

"You know, Sote, you have outgrown your uniform, so I think I had better measure you again. In a few days you'll have a new one."

Good old Kanachki. He was trying to make me think of something else.

From there, we proceeded toward the *Dom*. I went directly into the study room, and sat by the corner window, staring, seeing nothing. My buddies started to come in; they brought me the letter I had dropped. They started talking about all kinds of different things, trying to make me feel better. I just couldn't respond. I tried, but felt empty. I had no more tears. There was nothing left in me.

"I just want to be alone, guys."

"Well, fine, but we'll be right back if you don't come out soon," Lazo said, as he and Done left.

As I plunged more deeply into my pool of sorrow, I felt like drowning myself, anything to escape this emptiness, this numbing pain, this indescribable sorrow. I felt that every anchor for good who had tried to stabilize the wildness in me during my short, hectic life—Father, brother, cousin—everything good in my life was gone.

I would never see them again.

I would never hear them again.

I couldn't believe it, nor could I accept it.

A large part of what was deepest in my heart was gone.

I couldn't take it. I kept shaking my head from side to side in disbelief. No, no, no.

After wallowing in my sorrow and loss, I felt I had to leave, move, run.

I opened one of the windows and jumped out.

In truth, I wanted to jump out of my skin and return the rest of me home, back home to T'rsie. Maybe if I could do that, surely Father, Stefo, Nase, and Kotse, too, would be there, and my world would be whole again.

I had to run away from where I was, from this place where the unacceptable news reached me.

The window was not very high from the ground, so when I jumped I landed, unhurt—physically unhurt. Nothing could never hurt me physically as deeply as the pain I was feeling. Not then; not now. Thinking about that jump now, even if I had hurt myself, I probably wouldn't have felt it, I was so numb.

I walked toward the main street, over by the church, toward the small hills above the church. I know I passed people who spoke to me, but I didn't see or hear them. I just kept walking. I had no sense of time or place.

I found myself by the Russian memorial and sat on its edge, by the iron fence, staring at the marble monument. The inscription read: *In Memory of the Heroic Soldiers Who Gave Their Lives.*

This was where Stefo and I had met for the last time, and his last words to me began to echo in my head, over and over:

If something happens to me, you must promise you will take care of our mother, father and sisters.

Oh, Stefo, did you know you were going to die?

Did you ever figure out what purpose our lives served, or even if there was a purpose?

What is going to become of us?

What are we doing here, in this different world, so far from home?

There were no answers. I needed to get back home, to T'rsie. There was no meaning to my existence here.

Try as I might, I could not make any sense of the puzzle of our lives, and the tears began to roll again. I couldn't hold them back. Loss and emptiness again overwhelmed me and imprisoned me.

After a while, I had to get up and walked up the road leading out of the city, toward the vineyards and fields. When I reached the top of one of the hills, I turned left toward a small road that cut across the vineyards and fields to the other side. At the fork in the road, which separated the city from the farming communities, I arrived at a small grove of trees and paused there. Not able to go further, I sat down under the shade of the trees, staring, unfocused, straight ahead. I couldn't pull myself together yet, so I stretched out on the ground, to stare at the blue sky. Pretty soon, I closed my eyes and drifted to another place, a happier time.

Lundser, T'rsie, Home, Father, Stefo, Kotse, Nase.

How were they killed?
Were they shot point-blank like Gilo?
Were they left to die, or were they buried?
Where were they buried?
Who buried them?
Did anyone pray over them?
What were their last thoughts?
Did they feel any pain?
Were they afraid?

I had seen bodies rotting on the mountains before we had left Macedonia. I remembered the cold-blooded shooting not only of Gilo, but the two others, the one from Bouf, and the other, shot in the cemetery of St. Nicholas Church in Lerin. Unspeakable memories of killings, murders, which I had buried in my mind, came floating back.

Why?
Why?

Memories of Father came floating back. The times when we worked in the fields surfaced, like the opening of a movie. Father had talked to me about so many things, trying to teach me about life, fairness, morality, duty, responsibility, honor. At the time, I didn't fully understand, but I was beginning to.

"Son, maybe soon you will go to school. You will be able to learn a *zanaet,* a trade. Maybe even become a professional, an engineer, a doctor or a lawyer. No matter what you decide to do, or what you *have* to do, be the best you can. Always use your head and your mind. Treat people in the way you want to be treated."

Father had wanted to become a doctor. He would have done anything to get into a school. However, he would not denounce his Macedonian heritage or language. He would not change his name to Greek; therefore, he was unacceptable. My grandfather had the means to provide for his education in Greece, but refusing to denounce all things Macedonian, the door was closed to Father.

Yet, he was recruited to serve in the Greek army on the Albanian Front. That's where he became a *giatre,* a medic. At the time of the fighting on the Albanian Front, I remember how he described being buried alive in his bunker for several hours. How he and the others were dug out, unhurt.

After that war, he treated the ill in our area, vaccinated most of the kids in the village, and treated all kinds of wounds and broken bones. Villagers would come to him for medical advice. He clung to the hope that one day it might be possible for him to continue his medical training. Perhaps a medical school might even accept him.

Father also served as *psaltar,* a chanter, in the church, hoping to become eligible for the priesthood. If he were accepted he could study theology and medicine as well. On the advice of a couple of doctors in Lerin, especially a Dr. Adjitase, he was urged to apply.

Just thinking about this, I found it strange that he was encouraged to become a priest, for Father at this time had a bounty on his head. I wondered, was it a ploy by the Greeks to capture him? Or was it just the usual Greek bureaucratic paper shuffling? It is ironic that Father's application for the priesthood finally arrived in 1951.

"Don't steal, lie, cheat or kill. Keep your word and always tell the truth."

That was Father's constant refrain to us, especially to me.

I recall that, working with Father in a small field in Lenishche, I asked him why he didn't go to school.

He replied, "I went for a while, but you are too young to understand. When you are older, you will understand better. You see, we were not allowed to have our own schools. In a way, we are at home here, but without our houses."

Puzzled, I remember asking him, "Why do you mean by that?"

"The *Grtsi*, Greeks, won't let us be free. They rule, and right now we have to obey their rules. Perhaps soon we will be able to have our own rules, our own schools, our own independence. As you know, Kotse left Mara and Itseto, the baby he never saw, to fight for freedom and independence, and he died for that. That is the highest price a man can pay for his freedom. Others also died for the Cause."

What he had said went to my heart. "When I grow up, I'm going to be a *Partizanin*, too!"

Unexpectedly, the response from Father was, "No, you won't! You are going to go to school to learn how to prevent death. Son, I will never forget Kotse. He was not just my nephew. I felt like he was my brother. I shall mourn for him as long as I live. The pain of losing Kotse will remain in my heart forever, but I try not to show it. It is a personal, private thing.

Staring up at the sky, I relived the many moments I had spent with Father.

My thoughts leapt from him to my brother and my cousin. How we Nitchov kids loved to play. The villagers referred to us as the Nitchov *bulog*, the Nitchov herd. We always looked out for and stuck up for each other. And now, what was left of the *bulog*?

Stefo, Nase, dead.

Itso, Ilo, Petre sent to Poland.

And Goge, where was Goge? He had left to join the Partizans when he was 14 years old. Was he dead or alive? Petre and Goge were my first cousins from my mother's side.

Uncle Risto and Uncle Ilo? Then I remembered that Uncle Risto was shot in Kostur early in 1947; we never learned where Uncle Ilo was killed.

But where was Uncle Krsto, Mother's brother?

Mother!

Her stoic face seemed to be staring at me, saying something to me, but what?

How is she surviving? I couldn't bear to think of Dedo or Baba. How could those two survive their losses at their age? But if they hadn't, where would Mother be?

What happened to my Cousin Dina and her husband, Ilo? He had joined the Partizans in 1943. Cousin Dina joined in 1948. Are they dead or alive?

How are we kids going to survive here in Bela Crkva? With strangers shaping our lives, what kind of life are we destined to live and where?

As my thoughts spun around, I began to feel rage building in me, so strongly that I found myself breaking branches from the trees and bushes around me. I wanted to hurt something, someone. The tears had stopped, but anger overtook me. I couldn't hear, see, or think straight.

Lundser, T'rsie, home, Stefo, Father, Kotse, Nase, Uncle Risto and Ilo! Gone.

No!

I couldn't accept it.

It was a while before I became aware of the sound of a motorcycle. I didn't bother to see who it was. Eventually, I became aware of Drago.

"I knew I would find you here. I searched first at Nero, and when I couldn't find you there, I went toward Livadia and the lakes." He paused. "Are you hungry? Do you want something to eat?"

I murmured something.

"Listen, Sote, you have a right to be angry with the world and even with me. You can say anything you want to me, but I have something to say to you, now."

Drago was speaking to me in such a personal way, with so much emotion in his voice, struggling for the right words—so that I would hear him. I tried hard to focus on what he was saying.

"What has happened cannot be undone. It is a shame they had to die. Sote, these are not good times for anyone, especially during a war. You must know that war means death for those we love as well as for those we do not. Now you have to get a hold of yourself because you cannot bring them back. They are gone, gone forever. You will never forget them. No one forgets his own. There will always be a special place for them in your heart, and that is where they will stay. It will always hurt. It will remind you at times of even greater hurt. But you must go on. You are too young to let yourself get sick. You are going to have a great future, Sote."

Words! I couldn't listen. I couldn't hear him just yet.

We slowly got up and walked over to the motorcycle. I started to walk away. He didn't start the motor, but began to push the motorcycle toward the main street. Like a robot, I helped him push. Drago stopped, still trying to find a way to penetrate my shield of shock.

"Everyone is looking for you, Sote. They are all worried about you. There are many who care about you. Don't turn your back on them. Don't walk away."

Wearily, I turned to Drago. "Believe me; I don't want to cause anyone any trouble. I just don't know what to do yet. Right now, I still feel dazed. I'm sleepy and tired. Something in my head is going round and round, and I can't let go. I don't think I can even explain it to you."

"You don't have to explain anything. Come on, let's go."

As we were talking, I saw Nada coming toward me. She, too, had been looking for me since she heard the terrible news. As she drew closer, I could see tears streaming down her face.

"I have been looking for you for 2 days." She ran toward me and hugged me for a long, long time, both of us crying harder by the moment. I couldn't find a word to say to her. What could I say?

We were standing and crying about 15 feet from where I had that last talk with Stefo, and said goodbye. I knew she was remembering, too.

Finally, Drago spoke to Nada, quietly, telling her that he would inform the staff that I had been found and that she was with me. As Drago left, Nada and I went to the church steps to sit down. We talked for a while. She told me of her feelings for Stefan, which is what she called Stefo. She confided that they had had plans to marry. She was planning to live in *Ageiska Makedonia*. I listened to her intently, feeling sadder and sadder by the moment. I was moved and depressed at the same time.

Afterwards, she walked me to my *Dom*. Dobrila, Todor and some of the teachers were waiting for us. They all came toward me, each trying to say something to comfort me. They were so concerned, and all I could say to them in return was, "May I go to bed?"

Had I the strength then to look at them, I would have seen how concerned they were for me, how much they really cared. I couldn't look at them and went directly to my room.

In this foreign land, the only familiar article that was mine was bed, *my* bed. I lay down on it and fell asleep. I heard the boys come in around 10:00 p.m., but I couldn't open my eyes or get up. Some tried to talk to me, but when I didn't reply, they eventually left me alone and quieted down.

The next morning, they told me that *Gospozah* Iconia checked on me quite a few times during the night. I thought to myself, why?

I went through the morning routine as if I had been drugged, moving slowly, without any energy. I skipped gymnastics. Although I hadn't spoken to my cousin, Sofa, she knew. I knew that other kids had been receiving the same kind of bad news about people in their families. Everyday, someone had been getting one of those letters. As I thought about that, I wondered how they coped.

I met Sofa in the park, and when she saw me, she started to cry and couldn't stop.

She has always been a very soft, kind-hearted person. Some of her friends were passing by and tried to help her to stop crying.

It was so sad. Here we were, practically orphans, just kids; kids trying to comfort and console other kids. What kind of world was this?

I couldn't handle any more crying, so I took off for Nero again. On the way, I met some Hungarians I knew from the soccer games. They offered me a ride in their horse-wagon.

What happened next is a complete blank in my mind. All I remember is that I awoke the following day in a hospital bed with Luta standing by and staring at me. What had happened with the Hungarians, how I arrived back at *Bela Crkva* was a mystery. Not only that, but no one could fill in the blanks.

Luta took my pulse, not saying a word to me. As she was doing that, the doctor walked in. He stripped off my shirt, checked my chest, listened to my heart and lungs: checked my eyes, nose and throat. He pinched me here, and tapped me there. All I could hear from him was, "Uh, hum, aha."

He instructed Luta to give me a shot of that, and a shot of the other, to cure what, I didn't know. He asked me when I last ate, and I told him I couldn't remember.

To Luta he said, "He is to stay in bed for 3 or 4 days. I will come in every other day to check him out."

Later, I was given something to eat, followed by a very bitter pill. This was to be my daily routine for the next several days.

As I lay there, all I could think of was home, back home in T'rsie, but I just didn't have any strength in me to try to escape. Lots of visitors came to see me the second day, but my regulars were Nada, *Gospozha*, Done and Risto.

How I hated the pills. True to my nature, I started to get rid of them. When the doctor came to look at me, checking my eyes in particular, probing with a small light, he called for the nurse, Rushitsa. I was fascinated with the small probing light he used.

"Nurse, why isn't this patient getting the pills I prescribed?"

She checked my chart. She informed the doctor that indeed, the appropriate medicine had been given, and gave him the days and times it had been administered. Then, she looked at me.

"What are you doing with the pills? Do you know how hard it is to get medicine these days?"

I gave her a hard look, and being the insufferable, arrogant nut that I still was, I hauled myself out of bed, not saying a word, walked over to the waste basket, dumped everything out on the floor, and pulled out the three or four pills that I had contemptuously thrown away. The doctor picked them up. He came up to me very closely, and in a calm, but firm, no-nonsense voice spoke.

"Those pills are to make you feel better. You will take them when they are given to you!"

He had raised his eyebrows, emphasizing his authority. In a way, he reminded me of Father when he was making a point. No screaming, yelling or threats; just plain, clear, firm, emphatic directives. There was no room for question or argument. I nodded my understanding to the doctor. He instructed the nurse to chart that I was to take pills with a full glass of water, and that a nurse was to stand there until I had completely swallowed the pills.

I guess they worked, because after 4 days I was released and sent back to the *Dom*. I still felt a little foggy, a little dizzy and very sleepy. I still wanted to be left alone.

I shunned my friends. When cornered, I just listened and then walked away to be alone. This went on for about a month. I had been instructed to report to the hospital once a day to take my pill. Sometimes I skipped days, which prompted *Gospozah* Iconia to finally take me by the arms and march me to her quarters.

Her quarters consisted of a bedroom, a little kitchen and a small space to accommodate a chair or two. Ivitsa was there when we arrived. She instructed him to go out and entertain himself for a while because she had something very important she wanted to discuss with me. He left. Then she sat me down on one of those chairs. She brought me a glass of something to drink before she sat down to talk to me.

"I am going to talk to you like a mother, so I want you to listen to me. I am going to tell you something about my family and myself, first."

Talk to me like a mother? Yes, I had a mother. Stefo told me to take care of Mother if anything should happen to him. The thought of that moment cut across my heart with greater pain.

Mother?

How was she?

How is she dealing with this terrible loss?

Was she even alive?

I didn't even know that much. I had been thinking only about myself and giving in to my feelings.

Who is comforting her?

Damn, I never had thoughts like this before. What was happening to me?

Gospozah Iconia picked up on the conflict going on within me.

"Come now. You have to snap out of this. You shouldn't be as weak as you are now! Listen to me, Sote, because I, too, have a terrible story. I have kept this close to my heart because I must go on for Ivitsa, as well as for myself."

I looked at her a little more closely. She had paused, eyes closed for a brief moment, and then took a deep breath, sat up straight and squared her shoulders.

"Sote, my husband, my two sons and a daughter, aged 11 years, were killed."

What followed after that was lost on me because when I heard the word "killed" I was unable to hear anything more, but I had to go on. I still had Ivitsa. You must realize, you have to understand, that no matter what you do now, neither you nor anyone else can bring them back. They are gone forever. All you will see of them will be in your memories, that's all."

She paused again, then, watching me carefully, took both my hands in hers, forcing me to look into her eyes. She stroked my face gently with one hand, trying hard to reach me.

"Now is the time for you to be the strongest you have ever been, to stand up and say, yes, they are gone, but I will go on for them, for my mother and sisters, and yes, even for myself. Sote, you have to embody the strength, the valor, the faith of your father, brother, cousins and uncles, and make it possible for you and the rest of the family to go on.

"Because of this hateful loss, Sote, you will have to grow up faster. You have to prepare to take their place because you, you are the one man who is left to be in charge. I know you are still a child, but you will start to think like a man soon. That is the way of life, Sote, the way of nature, the direction of your destiny. You will never forget them. You will remember them for as long as you live, and you must take courage in that.

"There will be many times when you will hear others speak of father, brother, uncle or cousin, and it will remind you of those you hold in your heart. It will hurt. The pain will never totally leave you. It will come back sometimes stronger than others, when you least expect it, but you will learn to control it. And that, Sote, will be the greatest accomplishment of your life, when you are able to do that.

"Had anyone ever even hinted that I would see you like this, Sote, I would have laughed at them. You have a strong will. You are persistent. You have the kind of energy that you can put to better use to help you control your thoughts and actions; to help you achieve your goals, to be the man your father wanted you to be. There is only one person who can help you now, Sote, and that is you!"

She stood up, still holding my hands, her eyes fixed on my face, trying to reach deep down into my very soul, my *dusha*. Slowly, kindly she smiled at me, encouraging me to smile. No, she was beseeching me to understand what she had been saying to me. There were no words in me.

I finished my drink, looked at her and left, her words ringing in my head. As I left, thoughts of Father began to drift through my head again. At first I just felt his presence—nothing that I could see. It was just a feeling. And then, little by little, words that he had often said to me when he was trying to set me straight, came back to me:

"Be yourself. Do what is right. Help others."

And then, like an echo, my brother's words filled my head: *"In case anything should happen to me you must take care of our mother and our sisters."*

If I let myself go, how will I be able to take care of her? Who will do it, if not me? How was I going to be able to help anyone? Despair and depression don't just disappear because you want them to. Why did these terrible things happen to good, innocent people?

Going through this private hell pushed me to the point of realization: being sick was not going to help anyone. Not only was I miserable, but those around me who cared about my well-being were being made to feel miserable, too. I stopped to think of the many other kids who had faced and lived through losses; but it's difficult to think of others when you are still coping with your own despair.

It took almost 2 months before I could feel that I was climbing out of my deep abyss. I was beginning to sort things out in my mind, what was best for the family—what was left of it—as well as what might be best for me. At least, I felt was making attempts in the right direction, to think more about today and less of yesterday. I could not change one second of the past.

Much later, I learned a little more about *Gozpozah's* life. Her husband, two sons and her 11-year-old daughter were killed, their throats cut. This happened in Montenegro near Sutjeska. The *Ustashi*, Croatian Fascists, had slaughtered the entire village.

Evil enters like a needle
and spreads like an oak tree.

Catching Up

That which does not kill me
Makes me stronger.

NIETZSCHE, 1888

I found my friends again and they seemed happy to have me back. I started training for soccer and track. Slowly, in small increments I began to gain back my full weight and strength. Apparently I had lost 12 or more kilos.

When I had my checkup, the doctor pronounced me healthy for all physical activities. That visit made it all worthwhile because I did not have to take any more medicine, nor did I have to report daily to the doctor. Having received the go-ahead to continue living, I gathered enough courage to go to the Red Cross and inquire about my mother. I had not heard from her in almost a year and a half. I had assumed all that time that she must have been surviving because I had not heard otherwise. However, the visit to the Red Cross clarified the situation for me. When I had filled out the original search papers to reach my mother, I had written her name as Tsila Nitchova—which, of course, was her name—and her village, T'rsie, Lerinsko.

When I discovered that the papers had come back to the Red Cross with a short statement saying that there was no such name nor village, town or county in Greece, I was dumbfounded. I knew instantly what the Greeks had done. Arbitrarily, the Greeks had renamed Macedonia, the counties, towns and villages and "re-baptized" all Macedonians with Greek names! There was no such country as Macedonia and therefore, there could be no Macedonians!

There was northern Greece, though. I could resubmit the papers. As it turned out, I did not have to resubmit them, because I received a letter from my cousin, Lena, in Skopje. It was she who updated me about the family, the whereabouts of my mother, my grandparents and other relatives. At almost the same time, I faced another separation, that of my sister Tsotsa, Sofa. She was going to be sent to Skopje to live with Lena. My youngest sister, Mara, had been sent to Stara Gora in Trieste when we were separated in Plandishte in 1948. I would not see either of them for some time, and so I would be alone again.

Was this my destiny, to be alone forever, separated from those closest to me? I could not fight Fate, and so I turned more and more to the guys around me. I talked and played with them more than before my misery, although they treated me as if I might break down again. They were still concerned about me, speaking to me in a manner that would not hurt my feelings. In short, they were all trying to be nicer, and I didn't appreciate that!

I did not realize how truly disturbed I was. These friends of mine, though, could see what was happening, and they tried to support me as I tried to cope.

I wasn't even sure how to react to my friends. I kept sending mixed messages: I told them, no special treatment, but they couldn't be sure how I would react. They could see that I was becoming more and more stubborn about things. They kept reassuring themselves that I would come out of it and be my old self again.

In my own mind I think I must have been just acting like Dedo Vasil who was well-known for his stubbornness. That justified my behavior to me. Even if I was wrong, and deep down in my soul I knew was wrong, I wouldn't admit it—just like Dedo.

Just like Dedo! I had to pull myself out of my misery. If Dedo was able to face life, I *had* to. *He* would expect me to. *He* is going to be able to count on me to be strong! *He* was my life-line. If Dedo was able to survive his losses in life, I could too.

That was to be my personal battle cry. IF DEDO COULD DO IT, SO CAN I. Although I still suffered from the emotional trauma of my loss, I tried not to let it control me. To do that, I began to play mind games with myself. I pretended that I was the good guy and my bad feelings were the bad guys. I was not going to cave in to depression. I was a fighter, and I would not go down!

Before, when I had been hit hard physically, I usually came back twice as hard, with a vengeance, rage, and plain meanness. I was able to overpower whoever or whatever my target was. My feelings of depression were challenges to my strength, and I decided that Sote was going to win. It became easier and easier to win, to overcome many obstacles—or things I thought were obstacles.

IF DEDO COULD DO IT, SO CAN I.

I began to struggle back to being me. I resumed my pushing and shoving so that I could repeatedly sent to the office for my behavior. Somewhat relieved, Todor, the principal, began to sigh and say out loud, "Well, Sote is back, so now we don't have to worry about *him* any more. I'll just have to buy bigger buckets, new brushes and new mops. We will have the cleanest mess hall and lavatories in this town. Sote is back to his old tricks. Welcome back!"

One evening in our room, after lights-out, I spoke up, "Listen, you guys. I appreciate your concern and kindness, but I liked it better the way it was before between us. I don't want special treatment. I don't want you to go out of your way just to make me happy. No more! Just forget that stuff! Let's be the way we were, got it?"

Right away Done spoke up, "Fine. Do you want to fight right now? Do you think you have the guts for it?"

Disgusted, I said, "Oh, shut up. Go to sleep. You can't fight anyway. Remember when we first met on the wall, by the nun's dormitory near the monastery?"

Done, "Yeah, I did good, too. I gave you a black eye and you were bleeding, too. You do remember that, don't you?"

Lazo, interceding, "Yeah, Done, but you got the worst of the deal. I was there and I saw it."

Yane, agreed. "Me, too. I have to give Sote that fight by seven rounds and only three to you!"

I nodded at Yane, "Thank you, Yanko. May you be the judge for the next 1,000 years!"

Risto chimed in. "That one fight was the stupidest fight I ever saw. Two jackasses on top of the wall, standing up and just punching each other."

I had to reply, defending myself, "I didn't want to hurt him. I just gave Done a chance to get even. He can't hit for shit. He hits like he is wearing gloves."

"Oh, yeah? Then how do you explain the black eye, the bleeding nose and the other stuff that landed on you?"

Magnanimously, I gestured, "I told you. I wanted to make you feel good, so I decided to bleed a little." The guys laughed.

There was a soft knock on our door, and one of the monitors opened it to warn us, "If you kids don't shut up, I am going to report you. So be quiet and go to sleep."

In unison we replied, "Yes, ma'am. Good night." And it was a good night, the first in quite a while for me. I was back. Sote was back.

The Apples of Contention

No real friendship is ever made without an initial clashing, which discloses the metal of each to each.

David Grayson, 1907

That fight with Done had been a good one . . . .

A particularly fertile apple orchard in Bela Crkva yielded delicious, succulent apples. It was located near the nun's home, right next to our school. High walls reaching perhaps 8 to 10 feet high surrounded the orchards. It looked as if the top of the walls were wide enough for one person to walk on. We had our eyes on the mouth-watering apples for a while.

A couple of my gangsters and I met Done in the school yard one late afternoon, just hanging out, when those apples caught our fancy again. We had previously discovered that there was only one entrance from the front on the north side. The temptation had dangled before us much too long. I had found a way to get into the orchard by climbing up to and over the wall, using the drain gutters from the school building to support me as I climbed. A person could walk a few yards on top of the wall and jump over to the closest apple tree. *Eto*!

When we needed fruit, I was the bold one to scale the wall. On this particular day, unfortunately, we made enough noise that the nuns were alerted to the possibility of trespassers in their orchard. It was no wonder they heard noises; I was tossing at least a bushel of apples over the wall to the kids on the other side. They were having a ball, catching the apples.

When the nuns saw apples going over the wall, they ran from their house and saw me—just as I caught sight of them. They shouted at me.

I seized the moment to jump from the tree and run toward the juncture of the two walls. Spotting the broken stub of a tree near the wall, I grabbed it and placed it upright against the wall. Then I stepped up on the tree stub and started to move toward the drain gutters.

The nuns were still shouting at me. A couple of them had thin poles with which they tried to reach me—as if I were an apple that would fall into their hands. They couldn't touch me! I made all kinds of terrifying faces at those nuns, which irritated them much more than my pilfering their orchard.

As I reached the middle of the wall, I saw this other guy coming toward me. I kept telling him to turn around and go back, but he ignored me and kept on coming. In the meantime, quite a crowd had gathered in the school yard. They could see a glorious confrontation about to come to a head, and weren't going to miss it.

Some adults also came on the scene, urging us to come down. Come down? Oh, yeah? The two of us met face to face on the wall. "Why don't you go back? Are you blind?" I asked.

He answered, "You go back! Stubbornly we both stood there, challenging each other, eye to eye, nose to nose. We exchanged challenges and taunts, but neither of us would budge. I was determined that he go back; otherwise we would have to jump into the school yard, so I swung first. It connected with his nose, which immediately squirted blood.

I stopped, waiting for him to move. He looked at me and said nothing. Instead of swinging at him again, I told him, "Go ahead. Take a shot at me. Punch me!"

He did, and connected with my left eye. It was a direct hit, which fogged my vision. I couldn't see him clearly. Then he stood still. I took another swing and cut his lips. Then he swung; then I swung. This went on for about 5 minutes. We did a marvelous job, bloodying our faces with some good cuts and bruises. Finally, I hate to admit it but, kind of exhausted, we both said, "*Stiga*, enough!"

We stopped the punching. The crowd on both sides of the wall had gotten larger and all were shouting at us. I told the guy to turn around and go back. I would follow him. He refused.

I said, "Don't be so stupid. Do you want to start again? There is only one way down, and it's by the gutters, unless you want to jump and break both legs." He thought for a second, and then conceded. We both made our way down. We had quite a reception committee at ground level. The principal, teachers, and a crowd of kids were all waiting for us, and watched as we were marched into the office.

After some very brief inquiries, we both were sent to the hospital to repair the damage we had inflicted upon each other. We were cleaned up, patched, repaired and returned to school.

And that is how Done and I met! We became inseparable friends from that time on—after we had spent 3 days cleaning the latrines and the yards at the school and the *Dom*. Yech!

Marika

A thing of beauty is a joy forever . . .

JOHN KEATS, 1817

To me she was the epitome of beauty. At the time, she may have been about 25 years old; 5 feet 1 or 2 inches tall, about 120 pounds, strawberry blond hair, green eyes, a beautiful, full round face. When she smiled—and she seemed always to smile—you saw a row of nice white teeth. Her smile was the sweetest thing I had ever seen. She was what I would describe as *kulturna,* a cultured lady, smart, with a pleasant, easy-going nature, and very kind. Her manners were exceptional. She was a lady, and liked by everybody.

Marika was one of the very first people from Macedonia to join us in Bela Crkva. She was assigned as a staff member to our *Dom* # 4. Her name was Marika Mihailova. Many, many years later I learned she had come to us from Bitola. We were supposed to address her as *Gospozah.* I took one look at her and I knew of a more appropriate name for her—from here on—to me, she was *ubava Marika, Bitolchanka,* beautiful Marika from Bitola.

When I first saw her she was talking to one of my best friends, Done. I just stopped and stared at her, and then to Done, loudly, I said, "Who is this *Bogoroditsa,* this Madonna?" I said that deliberately, to test her out, to see what kind of temperament she had.

After I made my remark to Done, I took off. I couldn't hear what she was saying to Done, but I heard Done replied apologetically, "Don't pay any attention to him. He is always saying something stupid," pointing to his head to say that I was mentally off balance.

Stupid? Heck! I think that, once again, I had fallen in love at first sight. First Tsrvenko, then the motorcycle, soccer, now *ubava Marika, Bitolchanka*! Why not? I was an adolescent now, 14 years old. I looked back to see Done still making gestures, trying to explain my foolhardy remark. I thought she might show anger or disgust, but she just smiled, and that ended *that,* which was just fine, because my other love was pulling at me.

My routine for sneaking out to my secret getaway, the soccer stadium, was well-established. Many of the guys knew about my sneaking out, but no one ever squealed on me. Occasionally, one or two of the guys would sneak out with me to watch me practice with the Granichar soccer players.

Granichar was recognized now as the official city team competing in the Voyvodina League. Wouldn't you know? It was during one of my getaways that Marika met me officially! As Marika was exiting the post office around the corner from our *Dom*, I had stuck my leg out of the window without checking the area out, when I heard a soft voice. "*Ah, bre momche, kade so zdravie si trgnal? Nema li vrati za tebe*?"

My God, I was so surprised. I wasn't certain who it was who had spoken to me. I was looking out of the window from the inside. I turned a bit and saw her. She smiled at me and said, "*Eto Bogoroditsa pristigna,* look, the Madonna has arrived."

I didn't know what to say or do. I kept thinking, "Stupid, say something quickly, don't just stand there." So I played it out as foolishly as I knew how. With as much over-the-top drama as I could muster, I replied, "Young lady, I waited for you an entire hour, and when you didn't show up, I decided to see for myself what, if anything, had happened to you." She played along.

"My goodness, how clever you are! Does your mother have another even more clever than you?"

"No," I modestly answered, "I am an only child. All the cleverness has been allotted to me!"

"It's amazing to me that such a clever chap as you would not know where the doors are. Well, maybe it's so, but who can believe you?" I had no answer to that one. I asked her if I could go back into the Dom.

Her reply was simply, "No." I had to get down. "We will both walk to the principal's office. By the way, what is your name?"

"They call me Sote."

"Do you have a last name?"

"Sotir Nitchov, from the village of T'rsie, Lerinsko, Egai . . . "

She cut me off saying, "If I want to hear your full biography, I will ask for it. I just need your name to report to the principal that you have been sneaking out. By the way, quite a few people have warned me about you, and now I can see why."

I had to disarm her somehow, so I tried at first to have her tell me her name, and she sensed it was a pretense, and said to me haughtily, "I'll be asking the questions and you will just answer them."

I wasn't intimidated in the least. "Oh, I don't think your are so mean. However, whatever you say! After all, you are the Madonna. No, come to think of it, you are God!"

Gruffly, she said to me, "Let's go."

"But what shall I call you? You didn't tell me your name. I could call you *Gospozah,* but that's for old women. You're too beautiful to be called *Gospozah."*

"Marika, call me Marika."

"What a beautiful name. But the name goes with the person, beautiful name; beautiful girl." I kept repeating that over and over like a mantra.

"That is not going to get you anywhere. We are going to see the principal," she insisted, shaking her finger at me.

"Let me tell you something about the principal, Marika. He and I are so close; we fit together like *gus i gastche,* butt and pants. He knows me better than anyone else."

"Then you have nothing to worry about, if he knows you so well. Incidentally, who is doing your homework while you are roaming around?"

"I do all my own homework. I told you, I am so smart, I sometimes sell my brain to other students. Would you like some?" She ignored that.

"Where were you going? Were you going to the *pazar* to buy some more brains? You need them!"

I pretended to be deeply hurt at this remark.

With pain in my voice, I told her, "Marika, you just crushed me. How can you say that? Here I am, standing in front of you, begging to you to let me go. Do you have any idea how hard it is for me to beg? If you could see into my heart, you would see that you have struck me with two large *peroni*, nails, which have pierced my heart."

"Ok, stop that nonsense. You still haven't told me where you were going."

I sighed deeply and with resignation in my voice I told her, "I suppose I have to tell you, but don't spread it around. Please keep this a secret. I was going to meet my girlfriend. She is probably worried, wondering what has happened to me. I am so late, why don't you let me go?"

Marika, still playing along, leaned toward me and whispered, "You have a girlfriend? What else do you have?"

"Yes, I have and we're going to be married soon. You'll be invited now that we have met!"

"When is the wedding and what is your girlfriend's name?"

Now, *that* caught me off guard, so I stumbled about for a moment and then blurted out, "Pavlina. Her name is Pavlina. Wait, no, it's Fanche. Really, it's Vasilka. The other two are bridesmaids."

"For a fellow who is getting married soon, it's a pity you can't remember the name of your bride-to-be."

It was time to give in. "You win. I was going to the stadium to practice soccer. *Zhimi tebe*, I swear to you."

"Ah, yes. I forgot. You are the soccer player everyone is talking about. Now I know why you don't have any brains. The ball has been hitting your head too much. I know what I am talking about. I have a young brother who is as crazy about soccer as you are. It's no wonder you kids have no brains!"

"How can you say that? There is nothing better than soccer for me. You know everybody likes something and I just like soccer. Listen, Marike, will you please let me go? I'll do anything you want, if you will just let me go." I was quite sincere about this.

"Anything? All right, I'll let you go this time, if you promise, if you give me your word that you won't sneak out again."

"No, no. That's asking too much. Here, take this little knife and cut my throat. If I can't practice and play soccer, I might as well die, right here. I'll never agree to this kind of bribery. I can't give you my word."

Marika made the sign of the Cross and sighed. "Lord, Lord, how silly this young boy is."

Seeing this, I said to her, "Marika, you have just confirmed that you are *Bogoroditsa*. Do that again. Cross yourself again. It's so interesting when you do that. Now can I go? We have wasted a lot of time here, which I could have spent on the field, practicing."

Shaking her head, Marika murmured to herself, "Oh, Mother dear, what can a person do with a kid like this?"

I moved closer to her and whispered, "Oh, my daughter, Marike, since you asked, I'll tell you straight. Let the boy go and play a little." That made her burst out with laughter.

"So now you have become mother, too? Oh, you're going to be the death of me yet. Come on, now, stop this nonsense. We are going to see the principal."

We started moving toward his office, which was on the other side of the building. When we were about 20 or 30 yards from the gate, I moistened my eyes with saliva, discreetly, so that Marika wouldn't notice. That made me look as if I had been crying. I stopped her and said, "Marike, I understand you have your job to do. So you go ahead and do it. I won't hold it against you. In fact, I feel that I like you even more for doing your job."

She looked at me intently, trying to figure me out. Was this real? I quickly wiped my eyes and face. I wasn't sure if she had noticed my eyes, but I had a feeling I had gotten to her.

She put her hands on my shoulders and said, "Does it really mean that much to you?" She paused, searching my face, and then, "I'll tell you what. I won't tell a soul, but neither will you. So go, go, before I change my mind."

I whooped and jumped with joy. Mission accomplished! I planted a kiss on her forehead. This really was a first for me, kissing a female who wasn't a relative. She just stood there, saying nothing, but motioning with her hand to go, go.

I went, went. No, I flew, *flew* like a *sokol,* winging my way to the stadium.

My next encounter with Marika occurred after several days had passed. She asked me if I told anyone. "Marika, if I give my word, I keep it. It's my bond. Just ask anybody here. They'll tell you. Besides most of the guys here are my friends. They know about me sneaking out, but they don't talk about it. We cover up for each other. You see, you already have won our trust."

"Well, thank you. I do want to talk to you about something else. I hope you're not in a hurry about soccer. Are you?"

"Not until 4:00 this afternoon. Until then I am as free as a bird. Do you want me to fly out of those gates?" She smiled, and then spoke quite seriously.

"Listen, Sote, I have been talking to others, some of the kids, the people in the kitchen and mess hall, even with the director and *Gospozah* Iconia, as well as some of the girls in the other *Doms*. What they say about you is quite unpleasant. You have been labeled a troublemaker, a practical joker, a brawler among other things. I can't seem to understand how you get away with such things. Some even called you a wild animal, crazy, stupid—don't you get tired of all that? Are there supposed to be special rules for you only?"

"Marike," I began to reply, "is that what you think I am? Do you think I am an animal or stupid or both? If I am, maybe it's the environment or the situation we find ourselves in. Don't believe everything you hear. If you were to get to know me and the reasons for my actions, you might be able to understand why I do what I do."

"But what about all this fighting? Do you have to fight all the time?"

"Maybe you won't believe me, but I tell you I don't look for a fight. I only defend myself. Maybe you are just like the others. You have got to understand why I fight when I do. You have to make the effort to get to the reason for the fight. It's an easy excuse for the authorities to say that I am guilty because I fight all the time. If I were to tell you that I am responsible for having started only two fights since I have been here, would you believe me? I tell you, the reasons for the fights were that we were being threatened and shoved around by others—who were also taking stuff from the younger and weaker kids."

"Then why didn't you go to the authorities and tell them?"

"Who would believe me? With my reputation, who would believe the truth? I know I have an attitude problem. I am a rebel. I have had run-ins with the Greeks here, but once you get to know me, you might begin to think differently."

She told me she had learned that I recently got news of my father's death and how it had shocked me. Iconia and my friends told her about the letter. When she started to talk about my family, I had to cut her off. I hated talking about deeply personal things, so I ended our conversation by telling her I was going to the park.

Sensing my mood change, she urged me to meet my friends. "We'll talk another time." I said nothing and walked away.

A couple of days went by with no fights. When Marika and I crossed paths in the yard, she shouted to me, "I am so proud of you. You have been behaving."

I turned around and looked at her, yelling back, "You have been standing under the sun too long. Get into the shade. You'll feel better." Whatever that she said I couldn't hear her. We both went on our separate ways.

That same week, Kanachki took me and his soccer club to a town called Zrenianin for a scheduled soccer game. It was a rough game. I wound up with cut lips, black eyes, one closed, as well as facial bruises, most of which I deserved. I learned a lot in that game. It was a terrific lesson. When we returned on Monday, and my friends saw me at breakfast, they laughed and joked, "You finally found someone meaner than you. You must have met your match, eh?"

When Marika saw me, her usually pleasant demeanor, disappeared. She came directly to the table where we were sitting and snapped at me, "You football–crazy kid! You stay behind. There will be no school for you today. You'll remain here until I return. Do you hear me? Stay right here!"

"Yes, your Highness," I answered. I had no idea why she was upset with me. Oh, well. As she walked away the guys started in on me.

"What the hell did you do to her?"

"Did you fill her shoes with mud or something?"

Done spoke up. "No, he didn't. But I know why she's upset. You all know that big gorilla and Slono are making bad remarks about her. They said the remarks came from Sote."

I looked at all of them. I told them they were all crazy and so was she, and left with the guys. We had lined up to start for school when the director yanked me out of line.

Furious with me, he scolded, "You can't obey an order, can you? Weren't you instructed to stay behind?" Oops! I had forgotten that Marika told me to stay put. I apologized and told him that I got carried away with the regular routine.

That did it. He shouted at me and told me to get back to the mess hall and stay there. I couldn't understand what all the anger was about, I hadn't done anything, but I went back to the mess hall to wait. My conscience was clear, so what was going on? After about 15 minutes I heard footsteps coming from near the podium in the hall. Coming towards me were *Gospozah* Iconia, Marika and the principal, Todor.

I remarked out loud to no one in particular, "Here come the Gestapo...Hitler, Himmler . . . and . . . ."

I didn't finish my sentence because the people cleaning up the mess hall heard me and started to laugh. One of them said to me, "Boy, you're in trouble again. What did you do this time? Kill somebody?"

I protested, "Nothing, nothing! I don't understand this, unless I was sleepwalking and did something. I'm wondering, too, what this is all about."

As the trio reached me, *Gospozah* Iconia shouted angrily at me, "Get up, *magarets*." I was her personal *magarets*.

I stood up. She placed her hands on either side of my head and started to murmur something. Finally, she put one hand out and asked me how many fingers were up, and I correctly answered three. Then she directed me to read a sign hanging on the door on the other side of the room, about 12 yards away.

"Ivan Lola Ribar, *Yugoslavenski Heroy*, Yugoslav Hero." That was correct. Then she asked me if I had seen the doctor. I told her that I had seen the club doctor.

Impatiently she snapped, "No, I mean our doctor."

"No." Then she asked Todor, the director, to fetch Kanachki for clarification. Wow, I was really getting the third degree. What had I done? This is the way it went:

"Why do you look like this? What happened to you? Is it for this that we let you go with the club? Can't you behave for once?" On and on she went. I listened as she continued her harangue, accusing me of setting a horrible example for the rest of the kids. Finally, she stopped. "What have you to say?"

"Well, it's my face, my eyes, and I am not complaining. What are you people so angry about? It happened. It's done and it's over. Can I go to school now?"

Gospozah Iconia ignored me and turned to Marika, directing her, "He's going to the hospital and after that he is to come and see me. Take him to the hospital now." The director had gone to get Kanachki. *Gospozah* Iconia left for the office, and Marika and I went to the hospital, which was only about 8 minutes from where we were.

That was the longest 8 minutes in my life. As we started to walk, Marika started on me again. "Look at you. You are not normal. Cut lips, bruises all over your face. I don't even think you can see out of that one eye. Who knows how many bruises you have on your body. Are your feet and legs all right?"

Now I was getting angry. "Marika, will you stop it? What's the big deal? Yes I can see. Yes I have cut lips. I have bruises on my body and legs. Do you want me to strip and show you right here and now? Why don't you people leave me alone? I have had black eyes, bruises and cuts before. I am not complaining! So why is everyone so concerned? It's my body and I'll do whatever I want to do!"

As we were walking past the park, she suddenly pulled toward a park bench. "Now sit down and listen. Listen to what I have to say and let's see if it can sink into your head. Open your mind, that is if you have any mind left. Look, football is acceptable to play for fun. However, education is the number one thing in life. It should be your number one priority. You have an opportunity here to learn, which you would not have had if you had remained in the village—if you were even still alive. Now are you crazy, stupid or both?"

I interrupted her with, "Thanks, thanks."

She interrupted me. "I am determined to make a good young man out of you. And you will be one; just you wait and see, even if it kills me. You will be a decent student. You are to forget all about soccer."

"I am a good person. I really don't bother anyone. But you people . . . ." I didn't know how to express what I wanted to say. "I do have brains. I am not stupid." I was building up steam. "And by the way, you might want to kill yourself now. I am not giving up soccer. My school marks are very good and," I snorted at her, "how can you make something that is crazy and stupid and brainless into something good? I wish you all good luck. I am going to play soccer no matter what!"

"Stop it, and listen to what I am saying to you . . . ."

"I am listening to you but, as you say, I have no brains. Everything goes right in one ear and out the other." Then, to annoy her even more, I began a little rhyme in singsong fashion: *Oh, lele, lele! Popo rodi tele, go krstie Gele. Oh, lele, lele!*

"What is that supposed to mean?" She didn't get it. I repeated the rhyme over and over again, which was ribald, peasant-like, rhyming nonsense, and eventually she started to laugh out loud. At that I stopped, and told her that I liked seeing her angry, because she usually she was all smiles.

"Sote, I don't know what to make of you." She tried to tell me of her concern for me after she had seen my name in the director's book. "You probably have spent more time in his office than he has."

"Well, I am his assistant, because somebody has to be in the office at all times in case something important were to happen," I answered impudently. She poked me in my ribs.

"You have an answer for everything, don't you?"

"Do I? But you have accused me of being dumb and stupid. How come?"

She stood and pulled me up from the park bench. "Let's go see that doctor and maybe he will put some brains in your head."

I faked being hurt by her words. "You're not starting that again?" Because she had poked me, I pretended I was feeling pain in my ribs. For just a split second I think I scared her before she recognized that I was still trying to put one over on her.

"*Abre, aman*, oh, please! Can't you be serious? Everything is a joke with you. You are not a little boy any more."

We resumed walking toward the hospital. Marika began to talk about her brother and how involved he was with soccer. She conceded that I was probably crazier than he regarding the game. Her brother played for Bitola, the Pelister League, and because I read as many sports magazines as I could lay my hands on, I recognized his name. He went on to play for Vardar, Skopje, in the first division. He had to be a very good soccer player.

We finally arrived at the hospital, but the doctor wasn't there. He was expected any minute. Wouldn't you know, the meanest nurse around was who I ended up with. We had many nicknames for her, one of which was *chushkata,* hot as a jalapeno, the meanest of the mean. She was very strict in every respect it seemed to me. Some of the other kids referred to her as *farmak* or *luta,* meaning poison or hot. As soon as she saw me, in a loud voice, addressing everyone there, including the walls, she started to describe what a terrible thing I was—that I belonged in a sanitarium—that I needed a brain transplant. And that was only the beginning of her tirade.

I asked her for some cotton. Without asking why I needed it, she gave me a handful. To irritate her further, I stuffed the cotton in each of my ears, and shouted at her, "Now you can shout all you want. I suggest that you shout louder and wake up the dead if you would like." If she could have struck me, believe me she would have, but she took out her frustration with me when she began checking me over and cleaning out some of the cuts and bruises. She was rough! She pinched, pushed and squeezed a lot harder and deeper than was needed, to hear me complain, to beg her to stop and tell her it hurt.

No way was I going to give her any satisfaction, however. I really didn't feel that much pain. I called to Marika. "Marika, tell her to be a little more gentle."

Like a cobra, *chuschkata* snapped. "I am the nurse here, not you. You take care of your business. You know nothing about nursing, so shut up." When *chuschkata* wasn't blocking my view of Marika who was sitting a few feet from me, I'd wink with my good eye at her. She would raise her eyebrows and smile. I tried to motion to her to relax, but she put her finger on her mouth, suggesting that I stop irritating the nurse.

Finally, the doctor walked in and, placing his case on his desk, came toward me and my least-favorite nurse saying, "Oh, it's you again!"

"Well, I missed you so much, Doc, that I decided it was time to see you again. This was the only way they would let me in!"

He looked me over. "What did you do, run into a wall? What happened?"

"This was the situation, Doc. Granichar and Proleter had a rough match, and I got caught in between. That's what I get for being nice," I told him, an injured expression on my face.

With a trace of sarcasm in his voice, the doctor replied, "Where would you find the *niceness*? Did somebody drop it so that you could find it? I thought you were allergic to that sort of thing." Nevertheless, he began to check me out and, finding nothing of any consequence, he told me to see him again in about 3 days.

He told Marika that there were no broken bones or vessels, no damage to the eyes. As we were leaving the hospital, I turned back and made an un-nice gesture to my favorite nurse. She started toward me, teeth clenched, fuming with anger. I swear I saw fire coming out of her nose, mouth and ears. By the time she came out of the hospital, we had already crossed the road. She was ready to commit murder.

Marika was appalled and asked me what I did to make her so angry. "You really don't want to know because you are nice," I responded cryptically. "But, maybe I *should* tell you. I told her I loved her, but I had decided she was not for me, not my kind of girl, but I know who is."

Playing along, Marika said, "You're very popular. I suppose you have lots of girlfriends. And what is your kind of girl?"

"Well," I began dramatically, "I was going to keep this a secret, but if you really want to know, I will tell you. You can't tell anybody else. She nodded.

I started to laugh, "Now don't get angry and don't faint on the cement. It's too hard, you know. Marika, it's you. I am in love with you. From the moment I laid eyes on you, my heart jumped in my chest. Every time I look at you, you melt my heart like a candle. Your eyes, your hair are so beautiful. I cannot live without you any more . . . . Let's get married now."

Where did those words come from? I knew I had shocked her. But I was good. She was looking wide-eyed at me, and then the absurdity of it all hit her.

She didn't laugh, but she was trying to control her smile, "You little nut. Where did you learn such romantic language?"

I smiled, pleased with myself. I told her that a couple of months ago, Done, Lazo and I were returning to our *Dom* from the *kino*, the movies. Passing through the park, we heard voices, and decided to check it out. One of the guys thought that there were two Serbs talking, but I recognized who the two were.

"Serbs, my eye," I whispered to them. "It's Dragi and Dragitsa."

"What?"

"Yeah, that's them. They're speaking Macedonian, you dummy. Can't you hear?"

We crept closer. As we listened, we punks thought that the romantic crap they were saying to each other was silly. I became impatient and somewhat bored. "What time is it?" I asked Done.

"It's ten to twelve."

"Let's go before somebody sees us."

"Weren't you out late?" Marika asked. I smiled but didn't tell her about our little system. Curfew was 10:00 p.m., of course.

With the silly smile still on my face, I said, "That's where I heard that romantic stuff. I was just repeating Dragi's words, as much as I could remember, anyway."

Marika shook her head, her eyebrows forming a frown. She knew the two people. They were both teachers. "I didn't think you kids were old enough for that kind of language. Did you tell anybody?"

"No, you are the first one. I trust you. Once, when Dragitsa made me remain after class, I wrote something on the blackboard. At once, she saw that I knew something about her and Dragi."

I was comfortable with Marika and felt I could tell her anything. I felt as if she were family. She understood me pretty well, but like an older sister, she did try to discipline me from time to time. I always took her disciplinary efforts as a joke.

Marika was curious about the relationship between Dragi and Dragitsa. I didn't want to talk about it anymore. I told her what I felt, that if it had been her and her boyfriend, she wouldn't like having me discuss them with others. She patted my head approvingly. "By the way, I have no boyfriend."

"I'm available!"

"Get out of here," and smiling, she went on her way. I was teased a lot about Marika, but it didn't bother me. She was my buddy, so I ignored them and everything else.

I was never bothered by anyone again regarding my appearance or the game in Zrenianin. Things seemed to be going great for some time, and everything seemed back to normal for us. My bruises and shiners were all but gone—though not for long.

A couple of big *gorillas* were looking for some action, so they decided I was to be their target. You see, things were beginning to be too quiet, no action anywhere. I began to hear comments from them about me. I wasn't bothered a bit. I simply didn't care, and went along with them, returning tease for tease. This was not what they had anticipated. During one afternoon, Goce, Risto and I were spending some leisure time together, and some of the kids began to drift over to where we were, until a little crowd had gathered.

Risto began to sense something was afoot. He said to me, "Lets get out of here. Someone is looking for a fight. Don't be a fool. Let's go." Goce grabbed my arm, pulling me out of the crowd. We started to move out of the circle of kids, which parted to open a path for us.

When I had taken about three steps, Vasil, one of the *gorillas* tripped me and made a nasty remark about Marika and me, and kept yapping and yapping. I tried to hold back, saying nothing. The kids were picking up on the possibility for some action. They were getting boisterously loud. We could see a crowd mentality take over. I could hear the taunting. "Are you going to take that?"

"Go get him. Go on, get him."

Insults didn't bother me. I was used to them. Risto and Goce were encouraging me to get out of there, not to fight. However, the goons must have seen that talking about Marika was what was getting to me, so they kept up their trash talk. I could feel my anger building, the blood rushing to my face, and my heart pumping faster.

Having taken about as much as I could of their trash talk, I stopped, turned and asked, "All right. Who is going to be the first?" and before I could finish the sentence, I was punched hard on my injured eye. That was all I needed . . .

Later, the guys told me that I looked as if I went berserk. For the second time, I paid Vasil in full for what he had been asking for. The other goon, Slono, the elephant, couldn't help Vasil because we all adhered to a certain rule. Nobody jumps into a fight when it is one-on-one. If anyone attempted to break that unbreakable rule, all the kids would swarm over him like wasps. I went at Vasil hard. knocking him to the ground. I hit him so hard, he couldn't get up.

As usual, Vasil ended up in the hospital, I in the principal's office. As always, I politely greeted the principal and asked about his health. His head was bent over what he was writing; he had not looked up as I was speaking to him. "What can I do for you today?"

"I am reporting, sir."

Still not looking up, "Reporting what?" I guessed that he had not heard of the fight, and like the fool that I was, without thinking, came to him on my own. I was just programmed to do that. He finally looked up at me and immediately stood up. "Now what happened? There is no game scheduled."

A high school photo of Sotir's class in Bela Crkva. Sotir, still flaunting rules, is the one with his cap worn sideways.

"Sir, there was a fight, and I was involved in it."

"Naturally. Who else do we have to fight but you? I would like to know when you intend to stop fighting? Who did you fight with this time?"

"Vasil."

"Vasil?"

"Vasil, yes."

"He is twice as big as you. He will break every bone in your body. Have you lost your mind?" He was upset and it was building to an explosion. He made a visible effort to control himself. After a minute or two, he told me to get checked up and treated and to tell Vasil that he was to report to him immediately.

"Vasil was taken to the hospital."

"What? Is he that badly hurt?" Now the principal was shouting.

"Not any more than I am. Well, maybe a little more. Can I see Marika?" Pointing to the door he said,

"Get out of here. I don't want to see you anymore!" Later that day, in the study room, Marika came to get me. She told me to follow her to the park. We approached one of the park benches.

"Sit here." I sat, not knowing what to expect or why we had to be in the park. "Now listen, I have had it up to here." She pointed to her nose. "You'll obey the rules that apply to all of the kids. There is no special rule or category for you." She continued to chew me out very hard, pointing out that I was doing a lousy job as a human being, and on and on. I finally interrupted her.

"Marika, if I am causing you this kind of concern, I am really sorry. I didn't mean to cause you any trouble. Why don't you wipe your smile off when you talk to me this way. I can't tell if you are angry or what?"

"It's my nature to smile. Right now, I am so angry with you, I think I could kill you right here, on this spot!"

"What can I do? Trouble comes to me. I don't go looking for it."

"Risto told me what happened and how the fight started. Don't you realize that somebody will always make remarks about *someone*? So what? Let them. You don't need to defend me or anyone else. There will always be someone looking for a fight, and if you always take the bait, you are the one who will be punished again and again."

"Hey, I always am, even when it's not my fault." Wasn't that the truth!

Marika the Goalie

Hold a true friend with both your hands.

NIGERIAN PROVERB

Time moved on and all of us were maturing in one way or another. Perhaps the uniform rules and regulations forced us to see things differently. The discipline of those rules gave us some insight into what the outer world was like and what our role in that world could be. I felt that things began to ease up, and each day saw some improvement in our new situation. All of us were talking to each other more, discussing a lot of different things. We found that we could joke freely, as we developed closer ties with each other. And we could do it in our own language, without fear of being spied upon and reported to a hostile adult. We felt more and more like our own unique family. Thoughts of home and family and the onslaught of homesickness seemed to recede farther and farther—though we weren't forgetting them.

We were hitting our mid-teen years, my friends and I, and we were beginning to deal with emotions and thoughts that both confounded us and surprised us. There was one incident that occurred at the stadium, that perhaps illustrates this.

We were scheduled to play a soccer game with the team from one of the large schools from, just before the feature game that Granichar was to play. Our team got on the field a little bit earlier for our warm-up. As it happened, Marika came out on the field to join the gang, pretending to be a goalie. The guys thought that might be fun and began to take shots at her. When I came closer, she shouted so that everybody could hear, "All right you big, bad boy. I bet you can't score on me!"

"What are you betting?"

"How about ice cream?" she responded.

"Fine. If I score, you buy ice cream for the whole team. Is it a deal?"

"It's a deal, but what are you buying if you miss?" We agreed to a five-shot round. I was so positive that I would score, I didn't even think of the possibility of losing the bet. I thought for a second or two and then I knew. Stockings! Every girl seemed to be crazy about those things. The players in Belgrad were always buying those stockings for their mothers or sisters or girlfriends.

With a pleased expression on my face and a gleam in my eye, I said to Marika, "In the next couple of weeks, I'll be in Belgrad and I'll surprise you with something. Deal?"

"I don't know if you can be trusted. You'll probably bring some toy, knowing you. You have to name it." She wasn't kidding either.

I got closer to her and whispered, "How about stockings? Do they come in sizes? Or how about underwear, huh? Let's see." And I strolled behind her. "Ah, yes, big, big, size!"

As I started to walk away from her, she turned, angry and embarrassed that I made what she considered an out-of-line comment. She tried to take a swing at me with her hand. "You jackass. You should be ashamed. Get away from here. You will never become a decent person."

"Just joking. I'm only fooling around," I tried to pacify her.

"Get lost you . . . you . . . . Go take your shots. I hope you miss every one of them."

"I haven't missed one in 2 years and I don't intend to now. You better have enough *dinars* for the ice cream. Chicho Ilia sells only for cash."

I was to take five penalty shots. On the first shot I scored. It was one to one. "Marike, you better give us the money now. You don't know how to save. You're not a goalie," I teased.

"Shut up and take your second shot." I did, and it was two for two.

I told her, "You're not a goalie. Don't try catching the ball or you'll break your fingers."

"Shut up and shoot!" I took a few steps back, with my left foot this time, and hit the ball. It was a pretty hard shot, which hit her directly in the chest. Both she and the ball fell backwards. Marika lay unconscious. Some of the guys ran for help, while the others and I ran to where she lay. Out came Kanachki and the club doctor, who immediately began attending to her injury. After a few minutes she was up, a little groggy, a little unstable.

Her face at first turned yellow and then sort of bluish. She had difficulty breathing, which devastated me. Later some of my friends said to me, "You actually looked worried. We had a hard time believing it. You must be mellowing."

Kanachki chewed me out real good for not using common sense. Nothing new on that point, I thought. Gesturing with his hands, shaking his head, Kanachki, ranted, "She's a woman. You don't shoot that hard at a woman!" As he was trying to pound some sense into my head, Marika recovered somewhat, and felt strong enough to come over to where Kanachki and I were standing.

"Don't scold him. This is my fault. He does shoot that ball, doesn't he? It felt like a cannon hit me." She turned to me, "Did I save that ball?"

"No, you didn't. You both went into the net. You know what that means—ice cream!" I retorted, only a little relieved.

"Only if you score today and win the game!" I began to feel better, so I resumed our teasing, but very much subdued,

"Reneging again! You never follow through on your bets." She gave me a smile and walked off the field with Kanachki.

Several days later, when the team and I returned from Belgrad, I did bring her a couple of pairs of nylon stockings. When she opened the brown package and saw what was in the package, she was so surprised and very excited, just like kids are when they receive something totally unexpected.

"You really remembered! But I lost the bet."

With my deepest heartfelt sincerity, I told her, "You could never lose. You're a winner, especially with us kids. You will always be the champ."

She must have believed me because for the first time I saw tears in her eyes. "Hey, I thought you were tough, like steel. So stop that, or I'll start too."

I tried to change the mood a bit, further remarking to her, "Sorry, I couldn't find any silk pants. I forgot the size." That did it. She scolded me again. I told her that sounded more like the Marika I knew. We were in the yard now. Marika told me that she had to go to Dom #2, which housed the 9- and 10-year-old children. To get there we had to go through the main street that also housed the ice cream parlor.

I said to her, "Come on. I'll buy you a cone."

"I should buy because I lost the bet," she countered, "but I don't have my purse with me." I shrugged that off and walked into the parlor. My friend, Chicho Ilia greeted me. How many today?"

"Two specials." The specials were equal to three small cones. The regular cones were so small you could barely see or taste the ice cream. I told Ilia that I would pay him when I had the money, which by this time was no problem for him. I had already established a pretty good credit line with him. I was his best customer. He had never lost a *dinar* from me.

Outside, Marika commented, "I thought you had money!"

"Don't worry about that. You're with Ilia's best customer and he hasn't lost any money because of me yet."

"My goodness, have you conquered the entire city?" Marika laughed. She added, "My father is coming to visit me. He is from Bitola. I would like to have him meet you because I have written to him about you."

That gave me pause. "Who knows what bad things you have written about me."

Thoughtfully, she said to me, "You have an unusual quality and quantity of goodness in you. You just don't realize it yet."

"Yeah, yeah. That's why all of you people are down on me. I am what I am, and I can't help it. You know, I forgot to tell you that I am leaving for Belgrad on Friday.

The Partizan professional team has sent for me. We are going to a tournament in Spain. Kanachki tells me that this will be my challenge and test in international competition. I probably won't play much, if at all. These players are just under 21 years old."

"You? Not play? They know what you can do. I'll bet you'll be in the line-up right away."

"Don't bet if you can't pay up," I teased. "But, I hope you are right, Miss Coach. I certainly don't want to let you, Kanachki and the rest, down." I paused. "I think I can tell you this confidentially. The only thing I fear is embarrassment. Nothing else. Like Kanachki says, this is my big opportunity and I certainly don't want to blow it."

Marika put her hands on my shoulders and shook me a little. "I really think you are actually worried. You, of all people, worried! I can't believe this. You are a good actor. I have just realized it. Listen, you will not fail, because you love the game so much. Besides, Kanachki says you can't miss, and he knows better than anybody. Watching you play, I think you are very good. If the Partizans didn't think highly of you, they wouldn't waste their time to send for you. I guarantee you that. Remember when I told you about my brother? Well, he made it, and so will you, although you're still very young."

"I hope you're right. I understand the tournament in Spain will feature the best teams in Europe, like Real Madrid, Juventus, Inter Benefica, Ajax." I confided further, "After graduation this year, the Partizans want me to move to Belgrad."

"Ah," she replied. Now it was her turn to tease. "That's good news for the director and the staff. You won't have so much trouble in your life for a while."

"The only thing I will miss is my friends, and you the most, whether you believe it or not." At that, she gave me a hug, not saying anything. Marika and I had bonded. I was able to tease and joke with her, as well as irritate her. She talked to me freely, as I did with her.

On the Friday I was preparing to leave for Belgrad, Kanachki and Drago drove up with a police jeep to take me to the station.

Just at that moment, Marika came rushing up. "You can't leave without saying goodbye. I want to wish you good luck and not to worry about anything. And, stay out of trouble!" With that she planted a kiss on the side of my face. Drago and Kanachki were eager to get going, but I stood by the gate watching Marika walk away.

She turned once and shouted, "We'll see you when you get back. Be good! I'll save the *sliki* for you." *Sliki*? I was to learn that the word meant pictures. It was a new word for me. I shouted back, "Yes, Mother."

Finally, Drago and Kanachki dragged me into the, jeep and we left for the station. They also wished me all kinds of luck, as they said their goodbyes.

Once I got on the train, I settled down, and started to think. Strangely enough, I wasn't thinking about great achievements in the soccer arena, which truly had become my life's goal. I got to thinking about friends and friendship, who my friends were and who were among the best of them. This was a weird thing for me to do. I had never entertained such deep, almost philosophical thoughts before. What were the qualities that made some friends stand out from the others? There were Done, Risto, Lazo, Goce and Yane, but it was Marika who jumped out in front.

I trusted her totally. As a female, she was mother, sister, adviser, teacher and mentor. I could communicate with her on any level. I could be an upstart, a wise old man or a jackass with her. She was still my friend. I know I didn't always take her advice, nor did I necessarily listen to her. Like Kanachki, like Gospozah Iconia, Marika kept trying very hard to make me a better person. She was always honest, truthful and impartial. She, like the others, recognized that I needed personal attention, so she spent more time with me.

However, if there was someone who needed her more, she was there for them. I did not have romantic thoughts about her then, but, certainly, for the adolescent boy I was at that time in my life, she was the romantic embodiment of the ideal girl. A few years later, I learned that she had married an army officer. I lost touch with her.

She was such a positive influence on me that she still lingers in my memory after all these years.

1950–1952

Cloud 9

Obstacles cannot crush me.
Every obstacle yields to stern resolve.
He who is fixed to a star does not change his mind.

LEONARDO DA VINCI, 1500

I felt that I had come full circle, that I was going to be me whether that meant likeable or despicable. Whatever I was, whoever I was, I was going to be the best. My determination to be the best I could be, channeled my focus, energy and emotion into the game of soccer. Having decided that, I was also determined not to neglect my studies or violate any rules in this reincarnation or reinforcement of the me who was Sotir Nitchov.

I *am* Sotir Nitchov! I was proud of my name and my heritage. Whatever I was going to try to achieve, I would give it all I had to do it legitimately and with the approval of whatever authority governed me. Because, at this point, I was the only male in the family to have survived, I was determined to make the most of every opportunity.

My transition to the reinforced, reinvigorated Sotir Nitchov included a few minor setbacks. I *did* get into minor mischief occasionally, but nothing equal to the uninhibited, thoughtless wildness of my previous years. I was making headway, I believe, because I overheard the adults running the soccer team making remarks like, "Sote is maturing!"

Exposed now to the company of adults more often than not, I was beginning to modify my behavior, by talking less, running more errands and, most importantly, listening! In fact, I liked being around adults. It was 2 years since we had left our old world in 1948. We had adapted to this new world in which we found ourselves, Bela Crkva. We had met new people from different countries and were exposed to different languages and cultures.

The fearful, bewildered, naïve, homesick children that arrived in 1948 were now growing into more secure, respectful and respected young people. Our new lives, shaped by the discipline of education, the schedule of field trips and the opportunities to participate in creative and physical activities, had laid the groundwork toward self-expression in positive ways.

Interaction with the community revealed to us opportunities beyond anything we might have dreamed back home. We had begun to adjust to this new life. With the learning and educational experiences in a formal school, in which so many of us had spent little time back home—with the opportunity to question and discuss openly all kinds of topics in our own language—we had begun to relax. We were now happier than we had been in a long, long time.

As the *Detsa Begaltsi*, we formed close bonds with each other, sharing not only the fear and worry of the past, but also the hope of a better today and all the tomorrows to come. We did many things together.

Nero, as I have mentioned frequently was a favorite place. It was a resort area for the wealthier people. Located in a wooded area, there was a waterway leading to the Danube, a wonderful, natural attraction for all. There were plenty of play areas. It was in Nero where we Macedonian kids performed our dances and our songs for an audience. Looking back, in contrast to what had been happening at home, we were leading carefree, idyllic lives as *Detsa Begaltsi*. We had access to the creature comforts of life, plenty of food, clean clothes, clean dorms and beds.

The most important thing, though, for all of us was that we had, for the first time in our short lives, our Macedonian school. It was a true blessing, a gift. Back home, with all the wars and guerilla attacks, school was practically non-existent. Here, the ignorance that had accompanied us from home, was being replaced with skills, knowledge and information in our own language. We were learning about our heritage, our country, our language, our history, our identity.

No one tried to humiliate us or beat us.

We weren't questioned, fined, jailed, tortured or killed because we were Macedonian and proud of it.

We did not have Greeks to fear anymore.

None of us adopted the Greek version of our given names and surnames. Right from the beginning we gave our Macedonian names. I hear those names in my mind. I speak them out loud, and it is like poetry to me.

There was Risto Kochov from Turie; Vangel Angelovski from Dolno Kotari; Goche from Oschima, Done Kostov from Bouf.

All of us knew our names and the names of our key towns, our villages, and our extended families. When we identified ourselves, we would say, for example, I am Sotir Nitchov, son of Mite Nitchov, from the village of T'rsie, Lerinsko. Whether we had to fill out papers, or were requested to sign something, that is how we did it, and nobody questioned it. To us, that was such a wonderful thing. It represented, somehow, that we existed and were respected in this world after all.

There were unhappy times, but we had been learning to cope with our initial loneliness and separation from our families. We did feel like orphans. We could not see our mothers or fathers, not to mention grandparents and relatives. We had lost our homes and our meager belongings. We shared tears and loneliness with each other, but we grew stronger each day. With the Greeks gone, we had staff members and other adults who really cared for us and about us.

There were about 30,000 *Begaltsi* spread out into so many different places and countries who received a good education and became skilled craftsmen, professionals—and many entered the political fields at different levels.

Had we been in our homeland, in Aegean Macedonia throughout the civil war period in Greece, under the many unstable Greek regimes, we would never have had the opportunities that were open to us elsewhere, if we had survived the killing and massacres.

My goal by this time, my dream, was to play some day for the great Yugoslav soccer team Partizan in Belgrad. The name Partizan was emblazoned not only in my mind as my goal, but I think it was even emblazoned on my heart.

I guess it was the name that got to me. The minute I had heard of the club, I knew that was where I belonged. I identified so strongly with the name. Father had been a Partizan, as had so many Macedonians.

The Partizan soccer team had been formed by the Yugoslav army. At first it was just called the army team. The team got its name from a Yugoslav general who was watching them play, and he commented, "Look at those partisans play. Bravo!"

Ever since that moment in 1945, the team has been known as the Partizan soccer team. I read everything I could find about the Partizan team. When the radio broadcast their games, I glued myself to the radio, my heart beating to the rhythm of the game. My adrenalin was always high, just listening to the commentators. I drove myself hard. I slept, ate, dreamed soccer. By Spring, 1951, I was playing for our team, Borets, as well as the local city team, Granichar. Later Granichar would be called Radnichki.

Kanachki was both player and coach for the team, while working with the kids. He spent much time coaching our team, so we got to know each other well. He was like a close relative to me, more than a friend and coach.

In the fall of 1951, Granichar was scheduled to play Dinemo Panchevo. As the teams were warming up, Kanachki came by to tell me that there were two scouts present for the game. One scout was a man called Bato, from Granichar; the other was Vasko from Dinamo. Kanachki informed me that these scouts worked for the Partizan club. Hearing that, my heart nearly leapt from my chest. I secretly thought that maybe one of these days those scouts would come out to see me play. It was such a sweet thought. I wondered who they had come to observe today. Maybe Kanachki was just teasing me, because he knew how much I hoped to be invited to join the Partizan club. Seeing the disbelief in my face, he came over to me and pointed in the direction of the scouts, describing what they were wearing. "Do you see those two guys now? They're sitting right above the gate, close to the bench. Do you see them?"

The man called Bato was coming towards us so I called to him, "Have you heard about the scouts?"

"I don't think they're here."

That confirmed for me that Kanachki was just joking, so I decided to play along.

"Kanachki, do you see those two scouts?"

"Yes."

"Well, right behind them, if you really look hard, you'll see *Ristos,* Christ, and behind Him, are St. Paul, and the *Bogoroditsa*, the Holy Mother of God, scouting you out as a coach for the *angeli*, angels. They are looking for the clown of the team for that matter, as well as for the whole town," I deadpanned.

Kanachki got the point. He started laughing so hard that everybody gathered around us. I'm not sure what he told them, but they reacted with laughter and we all enjoyed the moment.

When the game was over, and after showering and dressing, I came out with Baraba, Kanachki, Milan, and Ivo. The two men that Kanachki had pointed out to me before the game were standing right in front of us. I kept on walking, knowing I was not the one they were interested in.

As I was passing them, one of them grabbed my arm. "Hey, *mali* (meaning young one), we would like to talk to you." What? What did he say? I stopped, unsure, and looked at him. I must have looked pretty dumb. Kanachki immediately saw my bewilderment and came over to me, nodding his head affirmatively. These guys wanted to talk to *me*. Was the unbelievable, my hoped-for dream and fantasy going to come true? Nah! Without another word, the two scouts, Kanachki and I walked toward the players' bench.

We sat down. They faced me. The first man spoke. "So you are from *Grchka,* Greece? How did you learn so much 'football' there? We hear they are pretty weak when it comes to soccer."

As politely as I could, I informed him, "Sir, I am not Greek. I do not come from *Grchka*. I am Macedonian, an Aegean Macedonian."

The second man spoke to him, "I told you that in the first place. These kids are the *Begaltsi* from Macedonia."

Kanachki picked up at that point. He explained our situation, the children from Aegean Macedonia, how, when and why they were here now in Bela Crkva.

The first man spoke again, "Anyway, we came here to take a look at a couple of other prospects, but your performance in the game caught our attention. We've talked with some of the players on both teams, and they gave you a lot of praise. Kanachki did not want us to talk before the game. He thought that we might have been originally interested in another kid. He didn't even mention you."

The other scout added, "But we are definitely interested in you. We know it will be hard for you to leave here, but you don't have to plan to leave just yet. You're still very young. All we want from you is a commitment that you would be willing to try-out for us. By the way, our team is Partizan."

Was I hearing him correctly? Was this happening to me? Naw, they can't be serious. They're only playing with me, I thought, as my heart began to pound, louder and faster with every breath. Their words were beginning to sink in, though, and I was beginning to think I was going to explode.

I don't recall what I said, if anything, that made any sense. To this day, the only thing I actually remember was a stuttering response that sounded like, "I . . . aaaaaa . . . I'dddd . . . ummmmm . . . aaaaa . . . " I had never, ever stuttered in my entire life, but at that moment I couldn't find my tongue or think of words or look anything but dumbstruck. I felt my jaw slacken as I looked from one to the other. My mouth must have been wide open. As I struggled to say something, one of the men said, "We understand, *mali*. Go get a drink while we talk to Mr. Kanachki for a few minutes."

I don't know if I flew or walked to the water pump, but I knew I pumped vigorously until the water started flowing. I splashed some water on my face to cool my forehead and just stood there by the pump wondering what the hell was going on? Was this really happening to me? I pinched myself four or five times to see if I was awake. I was! I just had to pull myself together, since I really was awake. I had to be a little more controlled, more mature. Wasn't this just what I had been dreaming about, working toward, and wishing for every minute of every day and night for almost 2 years? Wasn't this my chance to find out if I really had the stuff for a real soccer career or not?

As I struggled with these thoughts, Kanachki called me back. Nervous as hell, I went back and stood facing them. We were now standing near some tall grass, which I absent-mindedly pulled out, one at a time, to chew on the stems. All three of the men tried to relax me by just chatting away about absolutely meaningless things, switching back and forth to different subjects.

Feeling that I had had enough time to get over the shock and surprise, one of them turned to me and asked, "If Vardar were to ask you to try out for them, would you be interested?" Vardar was the all-Macedonian team, and they were very good.

I had to be honest, so I looked at them both and replied sincerely and earnestly, "Only if I fail to make Partizan one day, and that's it."

"But with Vardar, you would be among your fellow Macedonians."

"Yes, but it doesn't matter. Everyone knows that my one and only ambition is to play on the Partizan team one day, and that's that!"

The other scout, obviously pleased, slapped his knees and said, "That is what we want to hear." They both stood up and pulled out papers for Kanachki and me to sign, and we did, right then and there!

I was told that in about 3 weeks, someone from Partizan would get in touch and arrange everything. They shook hands with Kanachki and me, commented on my playing again, encouraging me to keep on doing what I was doing. Their parting words to me were, "You have great promise, *mali*, and one day you will do great—very, very well! See you soon in Belgrad!"

I watched them leave, excited, exhilarated, humbled. After a minute or two I realized that Kanachki was telling me something, so I tuned in to what he was saying. "I really didn't tell them about you. I didn't even make a recommendation that they observe you, because I was sponsoring you, and maybe they wouldn't be as interested.

"It's much better that they observe for themselves without any recommendations to bias them and make their pick on their own. Once they do that, you're in, and they owe nobody any favors.

"As it happened, Sote, they came scouting someone else on somebody else's recommendation. The scouts didn't even mention him, when they saw *you* play. I knew you would be the one they liked! I am 100% certain that you will be playing for the Partizan team in the very, very near future. But you had better keep your head straight on your shoulders, do you understand?"

"Kanachki, I am too dumb to be anything other than what I am. I can not be anything else, I can promise you that."

He gave me a real bear hug. "Let's go, before Drago and his men come looking for you."

By the next day, word got around and just about everyone knew what had happened. Our Macedonian grapevine was working. Just about everyone was happy and excited for me. The kids, especially, made a big thing out of the whole situation. I can't ever remember being as excited as I was then. I didn't think I would ever be able to simmer down.

The next 3 weeks went by so fast, that the day I was to leave for Belgrad loomed before I knew it. I quickly gathered up my few things and was ready. Kanachki was coming along as my guide, protector, advisor, lawyer, father—everything.

It was the month of summer vacation, and the kids were scheduled to go to Ohrid, me included. I gave that up willingly as well as many other recreational, fun things just to play soccer. For me it was no sacrifice. The older guys on our team had always said, "To be a good player, you have to sacrifice some good things in life. But you also have to be a little crazy, too."

Well, I knew I met the second criterion, but I still had no idea what the best things in life were. All I knew was that I had to be one of the best, if not the best, player on Partizan.

Our arrival in Belgrad marked only the second time I had been in this huge city. The first time, of course, was when the train had brought us in from Bitola, 3 years ago—when I was still thinking of running away to get back to T'rsie.

Now, in 1951, the city seemed different. Things had changed. Was it better, cleaner? There certainly were more people on the streets. They seemed to be more relaxed, friendlier, happier, or was it just me? I couldn't wait to see the JNA the Jugoslovenska

Narodna Armija stadium. I had heard and read so much about this stadium that I felt I had already been there. The truth is that I had seen the stadium in films.

A team representative greeted us at the train station and drove us straight to the stadium restaurant. There were more people to meet, introduction after introduction. I can't remember how many or who I met except for one person, and that was Kiril Simanovski, a Macedonian, and one of the stars of the team.

Kiril was rather short, dark-complected, and bow-legged—and such a nice, soft-spoken, polite, natural person. He was very interested in us, and we talked steadily for about 15 minutes. Then, he and a few others showed us around before we walked into the stadium proper.

I stopped.

Wow!

It was huge, humongous!

Was I really here?

As we walked onto the field, my knees wobbled, and my body trembled. That playing field was something—even just walking on it. I felt such a thrill. This was the greatest thing that had ever happened to me! This had to be Cloud #9 that I was on. No, not #9, but #90.!

I felt higher and higher with a happiness I had never before experienced. Here I was, a naïve, ordinary kid, straight out of a remote Macedonian village that few people outside of our section of Macedonia had ever heard of, being escorted onto the great soccer field of the Partizan Soccer Club of Yugoslavia.

It was a glorious moment.

I felt like a prince—no, like a king.

This long-dreamed-about place had such a hold on me. The emotions it stirred now gripped me and I was overwhelmed. My eyes teared up, and I found that I could not stop the flow streaming down my face.

The men around me were moved and tried to get me through my emotional moment. Simanovski, especially, helped me by diverting my attention. He began to explain things to me in Macedonian, emphasizing that if I worked hard, one of these days I would be playing right here in this stadium.

He took me to the dressing rooms, the lockers, the reserve playing fields, and just about every place he could think of, giving me time to absorb my experience more comfortably. He spent about 2 hours with me and Kanachki, who stayed with me throughout the time we were there.

Kiril also showed me where I would stay in the complex. I knew that I would have to make adjustments. Although the arrangements being made for me would only be for this short period, I had to develop new friendships among these guys. I was determined not to worry about it and do my best.

The officials had everything planned and the schedules had been set. There were a lot of guys, big and small, different age groups from 14 to 18. We were divided into groups for the tryouts. These were to be held on the outside playing fields—not in the stadium. That was a bit of disappointment.

The tryouts for the 14-year-olds didn't present any challenges to me, for I had already mastered the skills involved at this first level. The following week, I was placed with the 15-year-olds. Here the challenges were mixed. The specific skills were pretty much the same as in the first group, but the tactics were somewhat more difficult. I felt that this was to be expected because we had never played together before, and we all came trained in different styles or systems. So, the coordination and the creativity on the fields were not as smooth as might be expected had we had the opportunity to play together prior to this tryout.

To my delight, though, by the end of the week, I was placed with the 18-years-old group. What a difference! This group seemed like men, not only because they were bigger, but also because they were stronger and better skilled. It was a great challenge for me because these guys were very good.

About six or seven coaches watched us play. Each coach had his particular area of expertise: skills, speed, tactics, vision or physical and mental readiness. They watched us like a *sokol* watches its prey as it wings its way across the sky.

The coaches looked for offensive and defensive skills as well as courage, strength and technique. We were drilled harder and faster, which increased their demands and expectations of us on the field. I thrived on their demands. That was no problem for me, and I adapted quickly.

I thought to myself, "This is *my* game. Yes!" Having played with Granichar as much as I had, I felt prepared for all of the challenges I had to face.

Up to this point, I felt a satisfaction in the way I was playing. I enjoyed the roughness of the scrimmage; the tempo, the body contact—everything.

We were put through many scrimmages, involving different positions of the players, and changes from playing offense to defense. Little by little, guys were being eliminated, until there were about 13 of us left, which left me with the feeling that we were the team. Wrong!

The next day, we dressed in the brand-new uniforms we had been given and were led to the main stadium. As soon as we reached the track, there on the opposing side of the field was another group of guys about our age. This had to be the regular 18-year-old junior Partizan Team referred to as the Podmladak. No one had given us even a single clue that we were going to play against them!

It dawned on me that this was going to be the final tryout. I either had to make it today or plan to go back to the *Dom.*

Our escorts gave a little speech. They told us what they would be looking for in this game. One of them put it this way, "From A to Z, whatever you know, whatever you can do, show us. That's it!" And with that advice, the game started.

Our team, which I will refer to as the Tryouts, held up pretty well in the first half, even though we were behind in the score 1:0. As soon as the second half started, the Podmladak team kicked in the ball, scoring 2:0. The superior coaching of the Partizans was very obvious. It showed in the movement of the ball, the passing and the deployment of the players without the ball, and in the set of plays and their execution.

I was thinking that if only I could play this game as an individual, I could do more, because I spotted some weakness in their play.

Should I take advantage of the situation?

Would I be criticized as being too selfish and not a team player?

What would they say then?

What should I do?

These questions ran through my mind, as instinct began to assert itself; then I stopped following up on it.

I went over to the side bench and asked one of the coaches if I could play a little more individually and aggressively. His reply was to the point, "As we said, show us anything and everything you know and can do!"

That was all I needed to hear. I went back, ready to play in earnest. One of the guys I had spotted playing defense on the opposite team had a habit of passing kind of soft and blind—not really looking. I knew what to do, so I timed him and myself, waiting for my chance. It came soon after I intercepted the ball. I broke through their defensive line and went in on the goalie. I faked him out, placing the ball in the net. Now it was 2:1.

And 15 minutes later, we tied it 2:2.

We talked it out among the three forwards on our team and made a quick set play. Their center was a little slow and could not turn easily to the left. I told my wingers to come into the middle, quickly speed up and out to the wings' side of the field, criss-crossing. I was going to go to the right and cut left. Hopefully, their defender would try to follow me.

Our midfielder had the ball and was to push it into the window—through the open space. Then I would turn from my right, cut to the left, crossing in front of the defender, taking the ball and going on to goal.

We executed the play in full and scored. However, in spite of our effort, we lost the game 4:3. The coaches and players were impressed with my movements, strategy and ability to read the opposition. I got a lot of satisfaction from hearing the coaches remark that I really understood the game and had the vision to see what needed to be done.

After the game, our plays were discussed. The coaches directed questions to me, and really, my answers to some of the questions were quite simple. I commented that if we had an opportunity to play the Junior team again, our team would do much better because of our experience of playing together as a team. Our coordination would be vastly improved. I talked about how we could eliminate #9 and #10 on the opposing team, and made some observations about what we could do on our side.

The coaches expressed pleasant surprise that I could discuss strategy. The head coach, Ilia Spic, was watching and listening closely. When I had finished, he spoke up. "You will play them three more times," and with that he walked away.

The next game we played with the Partizan Juniors, we still lost 3:2. The following game, we held them 4:4.

The next game they blew us away, 6:l, but the fifth game was the best, the fastest and the roughest. There were a couple of fights and I, of course, was involved. I had been hit, pushed and held constantly by the center half. I had taken so much abuse and general shit from this guy, that I wasn't going to hold back any more. I simply lost my cool, which I hadn't done in a long time.

I clobbered him with an uppercut, cutting his chin and lip. He was bleeding, and the game was stopped. The trainer came on to the field to check him out. He packed the chin and decided to take the player off the field.

None of the coaches admonished me or even said anything to me. A short time later, the center came back into the game and started doing the same routine on me. He kept it up and wouldn't stop.

Well, that did it. I started kicking him, knocking him down at every opportunity. If he was going to go for the high ball, he was going to get punched. Whatever I could do and get away with, I did. Then he punched me hard, right in the face. That stunned me temporarily, and it was a good thing he didn't follow up on the opportunity because he could have made mincemeat out of me.

As soon as I recovered I went after him with such anger and rage, he started to run from the field. I caught him and began to pummel him hard. Believe me; the momentum was really with me.

Finally, I don't know what took so long, the coaches pulled me off and told me to sit on the bench. Sitting there on the bench, my head down between my hands, elbows on my knees, bent forward, staring at the ground, I was still seething with rage.

I enjoyed the feeling of satisfaction, though.

Now my thoughts spun . . .

OK, stupid, you screwed up good, you dummy! You just had to lose it, and on the last day, too!

What now? Back to Bela Crkva as the laughing stock of the whole town? What is the matter with me?

My one chance to make my dream come true, my hope for a professional career and I blow it.

For 3 weeks everything was going great guns; everything was coming up roses, and then, BOOM! Nothing. Gone!

How could I do this to myself? I could have taken the abuse for just a few more hours!

On and on my thoughts went.

Someone said to me, "Get in for #9 and finish the game. You should be feeling fine by now. Have you cooled off?"

I don't know who spoke to me, but I thought to myself, *Mister, you don't know how lousy I feel. My insides are eating me up alive.*

But I did as I was told, and played. I played with a vengeance, mad as hell. I didn't care any longer who was in front of me or who had the ball. I was going to get the ball.

I didn't even know what the score was now. All I wanted was the ball.

I stole the ball a few times, made good scoring passes, but we didn't score.

The bench was trying to get my attention. When they finally did, they told me to dribble and shoot more for the rest of the game. There were only a few minutes left. I asked a team mate what the score was, because I had only been concentrating on the ball, just the ball, I had to get the ball.

I was told it was 1:0 in favor of the other team. I said, "Let's get the ball and see what we can do!"

With less than a minute to go, we got the ball. I got to about 30 yards from the goal. This was going to be our last chance; our last shot. The goalie was a little out of position. I made as hard a shot as I could with that ball. It had to be *better* than good.

Swing! The ball took off, right over the goalie, into the net, under the cross bar. Score: 1:1. Seconds later the game ended.

That was it. I was drained. The end of the game was such a letdown. I thought I would get a comment from someone, but no one spoke to me. I went to my room. Two other guys were there. We didn't speak. I picked up my clothes, stuffed them in the bag, ready to be sent back to Bela Crkva.

I sat, waiting for my ticket.

That's when one of the guys spoke up, "What are you doing, packing? Where are you going?"

Dejected, I answered, "Home! Where else? I blew it." I could hear the bitterness in my voice. One of the guys, Chedomir, who was very good on the field, was also a very nice person, very polite and soft-spoken. He invited me down to the restaurant for a soda. It seemed like a good idea, better than sitting and waiting, so I went with him.

While waiting for our sodas, we talked about things in general and soccer in particular. He pointed to the corner table. My eyes widened. There they were, just about every coach involved in the tryouts. They had papers spread out on the table-top. I asked Chedo what they were doing there.

"They're evaluating us. Each coach has rated those players that got his attention. Whoever left an impression is being tallied," Chedo explained. As he was explaining, Bobek, Brozovich and Cholich walked in and sat down about three tables from us. This was the first time I had ever seen Bobek in person—or any of the others. I worshipped Bobek. I idolized him. For me, he was the best soccer player in Yugoslavia. He had been voted the number one player in Yugoslavia for several years. I kept looking at him. In fact, I was staring at him, open-mouthed, which I am sure was embarrassing to him. I didn't care. This was *Bobek!*

Kiril Simanovski walked in from another entrance and came straight toward our table, greeting the Bobek group.

"Aha," I heard Kiril say to us, "you guys have been hard to find. And you, *Makedonche,* how are you?" I couldn't answer, so taken was I being so near to Mr. Soccer, *Bobek*!

I heard Kiril say, "Come on. We'll go over to Bobek's table and shake hands with them. You can talk to all of them if you want. Come on."

I could feel myself trembling all over again as we started to move toward his table. Kiril began to introduce me, "Hey, guys, meet the future of *Crno-Beli,"* Black and White, the Partizan club colors. And you know, they stood up to shake our hands.

Then my idol, the Master spoke, "Is this the kid that wore the #10 jersey?" Then they shook hands with Chedo.

"Of course, we know who Chedo is," smiling at him.

Kiril, pointing at me, "For your information, this kid is your replacement. You're getting to be an old man, you know. Not only that, he is a *Makedonets*, as well."

Bobek, looking at me, "It would be a privilege to have such a young talent to take my place, and yours, friend."

The thrill of the moment, the embarrassment I felt, almost choked me. I couldn't say a word. I didn't even murmur a thank-you. I just stood there with my mouth open and eyes lit up with joy.

They tried to relax me by joking, laughing, kidding one another. One of them pulled up a table and chairs and we all sat down again. The talk naturally turned to soccer and the upcoming game. Eventually they came around to the game we had just played. Kiril pointed toward me and said, "This Macedonian not only showed them how soccer is played, but he showed them that he can box. Did you guys see that?"

One of them replied, "Yah, that was entertaining. Good thing there was no regular professional referee. You would have been thrown into the Danube!" Everyone chuckled. I was still star-struck, silent, looking from one to the other. Bobek was full of compliments as were the others. We had not realized that they had watched most of the five games played.

Cholich asked, "Did you know that Zlatko Chaikovski picked this kid from the beginning? He told us to watch that kid. He will be the one at the end to make it!"

I was melting away with embarrassment! How sweet it was to hear these soccer stars talk about me. Chaikovski was another tremendous Yugoslav soccer player. He was like a motor when he got going. Nothing got through his side. He was short, gutsy and just excellent. He never paused in a game from start to finish. On the field he was like a coach, talkative, advising his teammates how, when, where . . . here, watch this, look out for that! He was a human machine.

When we finally broke up for the night, Chedo and I went to our quarters. I wanted to know more about him. I asked him how he could remain so calm. He revealed to me that he was a member of the under 18 team. There were four other players selected to play on our side. He also told me that the guy who got to me and pummeled me so hard was instructed by the staff to agitate me. It was a test the coaches put recruits through.

According to Chedo, I did very well. He knew, though, I had gotten a little out of hand. "Where did you learn to fight like that?"

"I think life taught me how to fight ever since I could walk!"

We were interrupted by a knock on the door. One of the coaches had come up to get me. I was wanted downstairs.

Well, I guessed, this was goodbye again to Belgrad. I grabbed my bag and was about to say goodbye to Chedo. I knew this was the end, in spite of the good comments and compliments that had swirled about me.

The coach looked at me, puzzled. "What are you doing with the bag? Leave it here."

I put the bag back on the floor and followed him downstairs. About five or six of the coaches, including the first team coach, Ilia Spic, were seated, and they gestured for me to sit down with them.

Mr. Spic said, "*Mali*, all the coaches and players who saw you play were very impressed with you and, frankly, so am I. We would like to have you commit to this club. You will be assigned to the under-16 team to start. Then we will see where to place you. I think you could play with the under-18. You are, what now, 15 years old?"

I replied, "I am 15." My heart began thumping again. I thought everybody could hear it. I think I went into a stupor again. Could this really be happening to me?

It was.

I tried to absorb and understand the instructions for the week. And what a week it was. For me it was unforgettable fun to train and learn to do what I liked to do best—to do it better. The training and the drills went on for a couple of weeks that seemed to fly by. I had no sense of how much time had passed.

Before the end of the month, I was promoted to the under-l8 group. By this time, I had already met every player, and I was looking forward to playing with Chedomir. It was not going to happen, though, for apparently he felt that he had had enough exposure here and had become homesick. After some time passed, I heard that he was playing for his home team.

Although I tried to be more creative and a better overall team player, my style and effort, which were all hustle, remained pretty much the same. I was able to determine what the coaches were searching for, so I tried to accommodate them to the best of my ability, determined to give my all, whatever I did.

I know this probably created some resentment among some of the players, but the coaching staff handled that. In fact, one of those players was released outright, which taught the other two or three to shape up.

A problem of a different dimension was looming for me. Everyone was going to school except me. I was put on the spot when someone suggested I go to a Serbian school. I evaded the issue a bit, asking the coaches to give me some time to think about it. I certainly didn't want to jeopardize my future in soccer.

I concentrated very hard on training with the A team because they trained both mornings and afternoons. The training focused on set plays, execution, timing, changing temp and styles, and conditioning. Those 4 weeks of the summer vacation were some of the happiest times of my life—both before and since then. I became a part of the team in very real sense.

Those tremendous players taught me so much. Their names still run through my mind: Chaikovski known as Chiko; Zlatko known as Shtef, Stjepan Bobek was Boba; Kiril Simanovski was *Tsrna Tigra* or Black Panther; and Minda, Lazar, Branko, Chole, Vuka, Brozo.

I still hadn't made a decision regarding school. I was sitting on the bench one morning, so lost in my thoughts that when Kiril and Zlatko saw me and walked over. I wasn't aware of them. Seeing the look of concentration on my face and the tension in my body, Kiril asked, "Something wrong?"

I sighed, deeply, "I am getting behind in school, and I don't know what to do about it."

For Zlatko, the answer was quite obvious, "Then, go to school."

"There is no Macedonian school here in Belgrad," I answered worriedly.

Kiril understood the problem at once, of course, and sympathetically suggested, "If you want a Macedonian school, then you must go back and finish your gymnasia. After you have decided on a vocation or profession, then you can come here to Belgrad to study."

Zlatko nodded in total agreement. I wasn't so sure that was the solution to my problem. "But once I leave here, would I be able to come back later?"

Reassuring, Kiril replied, "Of course. You're just a baby, but you are a part of this club. Certainly you can come back." Having given me that assurance, they left me to mull things over.

I decided that I had to talk to Mr. Spic. I left a message for him. Later in the day, he called me to his office. When I explained my dilemma to him, he also affirmed that there would be no problem whatsoever if I returned to Bela Crkva. "I would rather have you stay in Belgrad, but education is an absolute priority, especially for young people like you. I will see that tomorrow afternoon you go back to resume your education."

I appreciated his support so much. He knew how much I loved soccer, and I knew by now that he was anxious to groom me for the future of the team. Yet, he helped me make the only decision I could make under the circumstances. It was probably the most important decision I had to make.

I wasn't entirely convinced that I really wanted to go back.

How do you weigh, how do you measure the importance of reaching your life's goal—against your life-long responsibility to be the man of your family, when you are only 15 years old?

Could I do both?

Photo taken in 1972. Sotir is pointing to the JNA, the Jugoslav Narodna Armija Stadium, where he was recruited and played with the Partizan soccer team.

If not, what should be my highest priority?

If I were to be happy I had to play soccer.

I hated to leave. I felt that I was so near my goal, so near to achieving the dream of a lifetime, that to leave now would be giving it up forever, in spite of assurances that that was not the case.

I began to feel the familiar pangs of anxiety. I felt I was turning my back on my destiny.

To this day, I don't know why I made the decision I did. It wasn't that I was such a great student. But deep down, wherever it is that memory and conscience dwell, the words of Father came to me, "*Da se izuchish po Makedonski nekoi nauka.* Learn a skill in Macedonian."

How could I ignore what he had written to me and spoken to me often: *"You must learn a vocation or a profession in the Macedonian language."*

Could I in good conscience. live having ignored those words? His face, his words, as well as Stefo's, Kotse's and Nase's were always with me, and I never knew when they would surface to remind me of something important.

Sometimes an incident or some conversation or a scene would come into view, and I would think of them. This was one of those moments. I had to act on my decision.

The next morning, I went to the field to take my leave of the players there. They had become my friends. It really was a sad time for me, but they tried to cheer me up, giving me encouragement. As I left, I heard, "Don't forget to come back. We will be waiting." Shouting their goodbyes, they gave me a thumbs-up salute.

The coaches, each one, encouraged me to continue playing and training with

Granichar. They informed me that they would make any necessary arrangements with the club. I could see now that Granichar served as a kind of farm club for Partizan. It was going to be quite an adjustment to play for Granichar and Borets now. I had given my heart to Partizan, and they had never let me down. The team had made me feel that I really belonged to them. I felt so humble and so proud to have had the privilege of playing with the finest players in Yugoslavia.

I went back to Bela Crkva. You know, it was fun to see my friends and be with them again, and it just took about a week to adjust to my old life. Kanachki came over to talk to me and my friends. He also spoke with the principal and the staff. Since he was the liaison between Partizan and the authorities of the *Dom*, he discussed with them Partizan's expectation of me. They discussed the educational program that was suggested. *Gospozah* Iconia was so happy to oblige in any way because she knew me well—as well as my mother did. There were not going be any problems coordinating my education and training schedule.

During the evening hours, the gang asked me all sorts of questions about the players I had met and spoken with. How big were they? How did they talk, walk, eat, and dress? How fast was so-and-so in shooting, heading and so on? Whatever they had heard or read about the players spurred their questions to me.

Sometimes we fell asleep, half talking, not hearing. It was comforting to be back among my own. I had obviously missed some key events and activities the kids had experienced while I was gone. The one thing I missed most was the month-long trip to Ohrid. My buddies rubbed it in, telling me what a good time they had in Macedonia, how beautiful Lake Ohrid and the city were. All I could respond with, remembering my own unbelievable time in Belgrad was, "I'm really glad you had a great time. Someday, I'll get there, too."

Alone

The earth is a beehive; we all enter by the same door but live in different cells.

African Proverb

Whenever the Partisan team played in a tournament or the under-21 cup games, I would be called a week ahead of the date to the JNA stadium. I had a tutor most of the time, because I was going back and forth from Bela Crkva to Belgrad quite often. From 1951 my playing time was split between Podmladak and the under-2l team. The difference between the two teams was that the under-21 team was allowed three 21-year olds and the rest had to be less than 19 years of age.

The Partizan Club had worked out a schedule that allowed me to attend all Cup games and tournaments, which meant that I would be away from school for more than 14 days. It was a perfect setup for me. In 1952, I was fortunate enough to attend most of the tournaments with the Partizan team. I played in what we called friendly games, which did not count for league points or international competition. The Club was breaking me in and bringing me up slowly. There must have been over 50,000 fans there that day.

Why did I feel like the loneliest guy in the world on this first Sunday in May, 1952? The fans generated wild excitement all around the stadium. The most prestigious trophy in Yugoslavia, the Marshal Tito Cup, was waiting to be claimed by the winning team today—and two of the best teams were competing for it, Partizan vs. Zvezda. The high intensity of anticipation building in the stadium, pierced with the whistles, screams and shouts from the spectators, was fueling a spectacular game destined to explode into a frenzy of celebration.

It was going to be almost impossible for us to hear each other on the field. The fans viewed the players on both soccer teams as the future stars of their clubs. We were being groomed to replace some of the older players. These games gave me the greatest personal satisfaction, because they were fiercely aggressive, physically tough, and mentally stimulating. Both teams wanted to be the winner of the Marshall Tito Cup, so this game was going to be especially competitive. I thrive best on that kind of competition, where everyone really wants to win!

The first half of the game ended scoreless, so at halftime the coaches began to make positional changes. My position was now forward, striker, with Iule playing right full-back, and Vase center-half. That position is called "sweeper". The coaches drew some diagrams on the blackboard showing us the strategies they wanted us to put in play, and went over them a few times. We nodded and were ready, heading for the field.

Early in the second half we scored once and kept the lead. Time was running out for the other team. The players had to open up and try to even the score. Now we may have had a few skirmishes before but. at this point, we were really into brawling—and then some! The crowd felt the intensity of the fury on the field and reacted to it.

The referee stopped the game and called the on two captains to warn the teams to cool it. The crowd went ballistic! The game restarted.

Our coaches instructed us to drop one forward back in the midfield and play with only two forwards. I was to play mid-center and to defend 80% of the time and attack only 20%. The coach yelled 15 minutes plus! With every stoppage of the game, minutes are added. Usually the referee tacks on from 2 to 4 minutes extra.

Zvezda aggressively pushed and attacked with more men, which only made them more vulnerable. We had to exploit the situation to make it work for us. We immediately stripped the ball from them in our own end. Quickly one kicked the ball to the left, midfield, and another one passed to center midfield. One more pass of the ball to the right wing and we had three on one. We played the ball quickly for two more passes and the ball swooshed into their net! 2-0! One big roar filled the stadium with sounds of celebration, shouting, and everyone, including our team, jumping up and down.

About 4 minutes were left, but 3 more were added, so we had 7 minutes to kill. But, as luck would have it, Zvezda scored and now it was 2-1 with 2 minutes to go, 2 of the most furiously competitive minutes of soccer I have ever lived through.

Zvezda attacked with everything they had, and we defended likewise. In all the pushing, kicking and cussing, somehow the ball was pushed behind their last defender. Luck was with me at that moment and I ran as fast as I could, outrunning the defender. I broke away and all I could see was their goalie. From that moment on, it was just one-on-one, him and me!

As I kept running, the net seemed to be getting bigger and wider, so I faked in one direction and pulled toward the other, leaving the goalie lying on the ground. I walked in with the ball over the white line and kicked as hard as I could. Don't ask me why! I had never done that before. Well, a minute or so later, the game officially ended, 3-l. The Partizan team had won the game, the Cup and the whole country!!

There was bedlam in the stadium. Everyone went absolutely wild. It took about 15 or 20 minutes before both teams could be reassembled on the field.

We began to hear announcements coming over the loudspeakers. I had no idea what was coming or what the next event was going to be. I was just feeling the absolute joy and happiness of the moment with my teammates and the coaches, when I suddenly heard my name coming over the speakers. I looked at my teammates, not understanding what was said. They were smiling at me.

When they saw my confusion, they started to push me toward the small platform. I was shocked. I had no idea. I was named the most valuable player of the team, and was given a gold watch and a great trophy. Me, Sotir Nitchov! Unbelievable! I was so thrilled, so happy, so humbled. Then the Zvezda team players each received a medallion commemorating the game.

Following that presentation our team was lined up again. The guys pushed me up to the front of the platform. Once again, the Master of Ceremonies made a few congratulatory remarks and handed me the Marshall Tito Cup. How can I describe a moment like that? It felt like I was somebody else. Like a member of the crowd, I watched the whole event play out, enjoying, thrilling with each moment. The Cup was a heavy one, but I lifted it to the sky and passed it to the other players on our team. Then we made two or three runs around the field.

The fans were noisy and as happy as hometown fans can be. I can still relive that day and those moments, but I can't find the words to describe the absolute euphoria of the moment. I felt as if I were floating on a cloud. Never had I ever felt like this before.

The celebration ended slowly. We started toward the dressing rooms on the south end of the stadium. I brought up the rear and, as I approached the area that was crowded with the players and their families—mothers, fathers, brothers, sisters and others—I stopped. There, in the midst of their happy personal celebrations, I stood alone, and I couldn't hear the joyful noise of the crowd anymore.

I don't know what happened. It was as if I had been stunned by something so powerful that it separated me from everyone and everything around me.

I felt absolutely, coldly, alone, as never before.

I didn't belong in this circle of happiness and togetherness.

The victorious Partizan soccer team defeated the Dinamo team from Zagreb and won the prized Marshall Tito Cup. Sotir is third from left.

I was alone, again.

There was no one from my family to share this moment.

The memory of this occasion was to be mine, alone.

To talk about it would only make me seem like a jackass.

I gave my trophy to someone; I don't even remember who it was.

I don't know how long I had been in the shower room, still dressed in uniform while the shower was on, before the equipment manager, Chichko, another word for uncle, saw me. He had kind of adopted me, always looking after me. He got to know me and my moods quite well.

Right away he sensed something was wrong. He paused for a minute or two, looking at me closely, and then spoke to me, gently. He felt my loneliness.

"Now and then, you will feel unhappy, maybe a little pain, like today." Then he turned, walking past the benches, paused once more, and said to me, "Here are the towels. Your clothes are by your locker. Why not shower and dress? Come on and join me in the restaurant. I'll meet you there."

Then he emphasized, "Don't let your teammates see you like this. You are their leader. What kind of impression will they have of you, to see you like this? It's a time for celebration, so get going . . . ."

Another pause, and then with so much compassion in his voice, he said to me softly, "Push your thoughts aside, son. It won't be the last time you'll have these thoughts, but to live, you must go on and meet the next challenge, and often you will have to meet and conquer each challenge alone."

None of us knew very much about Chichko, whether he had a family or where he came from. Those last words to me were a clue that he also understood loneliness from his own life's experiences. How wise Chichko was, but at that moment of celebration when my teammates were with family and friends, I was alone.

The memory of that sense of isolation still sears my heart.

The End of a Beginning

The world is round
And the place which may seem like the end
May also be the beginning . . .

IVY BAKER PRIEST, 1958

Late in 1952, I was oblivious to the fact that our civil war had ended disastrously for the Macedonians. I was oblivious of the fact that some of the families of the *Detsa Begaltsi* were making efforts to find their children to bring them back home, and even that some of the *Detsa* had started to leave under the auspices of the Red Cross.

I was in my own little world, totally immersed in soccer, untouched by the active forces at work, which were about were about to knock me for a loop that would keep me reeling for years.

As the *Detsa* who had been contacted by the Red Cross realized that they were about to leave their home away from home—and that it was final—strangely, the prevailing mood seemed much the same as when we had prepared to leave our *real* homes, so long ago. We were about to break up. We *Begaltsi* had bonded to each other so closely, we were truly a family, closer than brothers and sisters, solid in our identity with each other through our experiences as *Begaltsi*. That would remain with us all our lives.

We were the *Begaltsi* generation. Nothing in life could have pulled us apart, except for the one certainty that no matter how many years it would take, we would be reunited somehow with our families—or what was left of our families back home in Macedonia, Egeiska Makedonja, our birthplace and that of countless generations of Macedonians over the centuries.

As each one left in tears—of happy anticipation or in fear of an uncertain future—heartbreak overtook us *all* as we faced the reality that our lives as we lived them for the last several years were ending. Major decisions had to be made and each of us knew that, ready or not, we had to take on the responsibilities of adulthood far too early.

The *Begaltsi* generation was about to be turned around again. The boys—and that's what we still were—who had lost fathers or older brothers, had to become the men in our families overnight. The mantle of manhood is heavy. Girls also faced the uneasy

Action shot of Sotir.

prospect of what it would mean to return home. If there was no man left in the family, betrothal and early marriage were possibly the only solution for her future.

Early in 1952, the Red Cross headquarters in Geneva had sent us documents to be filled out and returned to them. After a number of days, Red Cross representatives from Belgrad and Geneva arrived in Bela Crkva, concerned that so many *Detsa* had not acknowledged receipt of the documents. It took only one meeting with them to clarify the situation. We had returned the documents, completely filled out in Macedonian, naturally, and signed with our Macedonian names.

Our identification problems again rested with the Greeks. They wouldn't accept any information written in the Macedonian language. After the Red Cross straightened out that matter, the documents, which stated that our mothers wanted us to be returned, were finally processed.

Conflicting and equally devastating emotions had me in a bind. I was heartsick trying to deal objectively with both my moral, ethical dilemma and my deeply passionate desire to carve out a soccer career.

I decided that I had to go to Belgrad to discuss my situation with the Partizan officials. Kanachki came with me. Again, I was treated with a genuine friendliness. They listened sympathetically, but were very negative about my returning to Macedonia, and I was offered an alternative. "We could arrange to bring your mother to Belgrad, or if she prefers, we'll make all necessary arrangements for her to travel to Skopje."

I looked at them, thinking what a wonderful solution. Kanachki agreed that was the answer to my dilemma. Everybody seemed pleased. As we left, I met some of the players. I explained why I was in Belgrad, and what the Club had offered. Hearing that, the guys thought I had solved my problem, and counseled me to remain in Yugoslavia. In fact, they strongly urged me to stay. We shook hands and Kanachki and I left to go to the Red Cross in Belgrad to tell them of my decision.

But in life, timing is everything. Life can be capricious when timing is not in sync with opportunity. I was 1 day too late; the documents had already been returned to Geneva from Greece. I didn't remember signing the document, but when they showed me a copy with my Macedonian signature, there was nothing more to say. I was a day too late.

The reunion process had begun. Papers had been signed. It was a done deal. The final nail in the coffin that buried any hope of staying in Yugoslavia to pursue a sports career in soccer was the information that my little sister, Mara, was on her way to Belgrad from Stara Gora in Slovenia to join me. My other sister, Sofa, who had been in Skopje several years, was meet us at the train station in Skopje for the journey to Solun on the date specified.

We had to return home the way we had arrived in Belgrad—together. Was I a man or a boy? There were no choices. I had to be the man of the family and return with my sisters. They were going to be under my care; my responsibility. The reunion process was moving forward, convenient or not.

Once again, the direction of our lives was in other hands.

We were like puppets, pulled in several directions, by an unseen director.

The changing scenario made it impossible to make long-term plans. I was beside myself. I didn't want to return home, not now. The Club had offered to bring my mother to Yugoslavia. All I could think of was the possibilities if mother and my sisters were here, and I would be able to continue to develop my career. I argued with myself that my mother and sisters would be safe and close by in Skopje. Mother would be eligible for my father's veteran's pension, and she would be with Lena. Then, too, she would be among many T'rsiani as well as other Macedonians who now lived in Skopje.

The Club told me they would cover her housing and financial needs. My heart pounded stay, Stay, STAY!

What if mother would not agree to leave T'rsie, or if she could not come for any number of possible reasons; my grandparents, if they were still alive; the Greeks' horrendous bureaucracy; illness?

If I decided not to return, what then? Would Mother feel totally rejected, that I did not want her, or worse, that I had forgotten her? Her husband, killed. Her first son, killed. Two young daughters to care for.

Could I walk away from my responsibilities to the family?

Could I abandon my mother to live her life on the charity of others?

Could I really do that?

Stay! Stay! Stay! I can't stay.

I heard Stefo's words pounding in my head over and over as my heart beat heavily in sorrow in my less-than-manly chest:

If anything happens to father or me, you must take care of our mother and sisters always. Give me your word here and now.

And then, like a refrain, I heard:

Never leave your mother. Always take care of her. There is only one mother and one father in your life. Your brother, you and your sisters must care for each other. That is the way of life.

Why was Father's voice ringing in my head?

If only I could talk to mother, she would understand. Everything will turn out fine when she understands.

Would she understand, and still be hurt with my choice?

Soccer?

Mother?

Stay. Stay. Stay.

What about my little sister, Mara, whom I hadn't seen in 4 or 5 years? She was just four years old when we left T'rsie. Would she recognize me? I thought I probably would recognize her.

What was I to do?

I had to think, to plan, to think of a plan for everyone, but I discarded plan after plan after plan. There was no plan, no strategy. You can't escape the force of destiny.

You must take care of our mother and sisters always. Never leave your mother, care for your sisters always.

Kiril, Boba and one other official from the Club came to my quarters to talk to me. The official repeated that they would bring Mother to Yugoslavia. Although it might take a little time, she would join me there.

"We don't want to lose you. You are the future of our Club. The reports we have received about you are excellent, top-notch. Whenever there is talk about soccer, eventually the talk centers on you. As you well know, there are many other clubs scrambling for you, so don't give up now. You are one-in-a-million, born with such football talent, drive and true desire . . . "

Kiril cut in, "He is right. You should pursue your goal. You're almost there. In 3 or 4

Team passport picture of Sotir.

years, you will be leading us, doing great things on the field. Don't throw your chance away. We all know how hard it is for you, but it will be better for you and your family after a while. That's guaranteed!"

Didn't they know that with each word uttered, they were driving *peroni*, nails, railroad nails, into my heart?

I listened, crying on the inside, and finally murmured something that may have sounded like, "Thank you very much. Let me think about it."

As they left, each one touched me in some way, a pat on the head, on the back, the shoulder. I tried to think.

As a last resort, I tried to telephone my cousin Lena in Skopje, but I couldn't contact her. I could only guess that she and my sister Sofa had already left.

That night, there was no sleep for me. When morning came, I was still dressed in the clothes of the previous day and I still had my shoes on. I got up very early and headed for the stadium. Kanachki knew that I had to struggle through these moments on my own. He returned to the Club office. I headed toward a bench and sat down to think. But I couldn't think. I only knew that any decision other than going back home with my sisters would be unforgivable, unthinkable, dishonorable.

Chicho saw me. "What's the matter? You look sick. You . . . " he didn't quite know how to say it, "I have never seen you look like this. What is wrong? Do you have an ache? Any pains?" He paused.

I didn't, I couldn't answer.

"Let's go see the doctor. Come on."

Aches and pains? I had lots of them, but I answered, "Chicho, these aches and pains aren't physical. They are mental. I have never missed my father and brother more than I do now. If they had been alive, this horrible dilemma would never have had to be faced. Why do these things happen? I don't know who I am or what I am or what I should do . . . " I didn't finish. I put my head in my hands. The pull to stay was so strong.

A couple of hours later everybody showed up for the practice session. One of the coaches saw me and came over immediately. He would not allow me to play, and ordered me to rest. I must have looked awful. I left to go to the restaurant, but I couldn't eat. I was supposed to meet Mara at the Red Cross building, the point of arrival for all the *Detsa Begaltsi* who were coming from different directions.

All decisions had been made. That was that.

Reunion

Pain makes man think.
Thought makes man wise.
Wisdom makes life endurable.

JOHN PATRICK, *Teahouse of the August Moon,* 1953

I recognized her at once, and felt the years had vanished.

My eyes saw a little 4-year old Father called Mare or Mareto, the diminutive for Mara.

But the little girl I was looking at wasn't a 4-year old. This young sister of mine was more grown up, walking toward the mess hall in the Red Cross headquarters, one of a column of youngsters.

The Red Cross personnel began to check the children in, confirming their identity and their destinations. It felt like *déjà vu*—it was just as it had been when we arrived 5 years earlier, following our long journey from Macedonia. We had showered here and received new clothes, marking the official entry into Yugoslavia as the *Detsa Begaltsi*, although that was not how the Red Cross knew us. So much had happened to all of us between the time we had first arrived and this, almost the moment of our departure for home, to T'rsie.

The memory of our arrival had faded in my mind after all the emotional highs and lows I had been experiencing so recently. But this was here and now, and I waited for the most opportune moment to speak to Mara.

After the children had been checked in, they were given instructions to go into the yard and enjoy some free time together before they were called in for dinner. Now, I thought, is the time to introduce myself.

I approached her slowly, and called her gently by the name my Father always used, Mare.

"Mare."

I waited. When she heard that name, she stopped what she was doing for a second or two, turned around and looked toward me. I waited for a sign of recognition. None! After another minute or two, she turned back to her little friends to play.

I went a little closer to her, but I didn't want to frighten her. I could see that I was no more than a stranger to her. She didn't remember me, but then how could she? When we had been separated, I was 12 years old. During the years of our separation, each of us had changed in so many ways, physically, mentally and emotionally. The 4 years of separation—minus the strong influence of family—was bound to make us different people than we would have been, had we remained at home.

We, ourselves, would not become aware of how much our attitudes and outlooks had changed—until we were home again. Would we be strangers for the rest of our lives, or could we become more closely bound together because of our lives as the *Detsa Begaltsi*?

I decided to try calling Mara again.

"Mare?"

Again, she only looked at me, but, this time, before she ran off, she gave me a quick, but furtive smile. Oh, boy, what do I do now?

My attempts to get Mara's attention attracted a couple of staff members from the Red Cross. They decided they had better check me out. When I first arrived, prior to the arrival of the children, none of this staff had been here.

"What is your interest here, young man?" I explained the situation, gave them my name, and informed them that we were scheduled to leave for home from here. They still had the lists of the children's names and the related information, but they couldn't find my name on the list. I told them to check the list from Bela Crkva. They did, but still, no such name, and that's when they got a little suspicious because the Bela Crkva arrivals were not due until about 8:30 p.m.

I had to explain that I was staying in Belgrad, and that I had been in my quarters at the JNA Stadium for awhile. They were not ready to believe me and escorted me to the office. On the way, I passed Mara and told her that I would be back. She smiled again and then skipped off again. This time I felt that there was a hint of recognition in her eyes.

As the staff checked their information sheet, they found that the names of my sisters appeared in Macedonian and in Greek as Sofia and Maria Nitsou. No data on Sote or Sotir Nitchov appeared anywhere on their lists.

Then it dawned on me. If they had a list for Bela Crkva, Stara Gora, Crkvenica, Brailovo, perhaps they might even have one for Belgrad. "Would you at least look and see if there is a list of names from Belgrad?"

I persisted. The man who was earnestly searching through the list said, "Here it is, I think. Let's see. There are only two names here, Goce Stavrevski and Sote Nitchovski."

Oh, jeez! "Listen," I said patiently, "my name is misspelled. It should read Nitchov."

"Are you certain that is you?"

"I think I know who I am," I replied. "This is not the first time there has been confusion regarding our names. My name is Sotir Nitchov. It has always been Sotir Nitchov. Sometimes I am called Sote by friends and relatives. My Dedo used to call me Sotiraki. But my name is Sotir Nitchov. The Greeks tried to change my name to Nitsou. Here, in Yugoslavia, they put the "ski" ending to all the Macedonian names, so that somewhere they have written my family name as Nitchovski. But my family name is Nitchov. It has always been Nitchov and no one has the authority to change my legal and given name. I am and always will be Sotir Nitchov."

In spite of what I had been telling them, the staff insisted that I remain there in the office. Instead, I rushed out the back door to see my little sister. I called to her, but she did not speak. Again, no response at all, not even a smile. Adding to my overall frustration was this additional situation. There was nothing more I could do, so I left the grounds of the Red Cross building and went back to my quarters.

The next day, after practice on the field—which can only be described as a stinkingly poor performance—I felt that I didn't have the ability to do anything right. My teammates were great. They understood what I was going through, so my poor effort on the field didn't worry them. Zlatko called to me, motioning me to come over to the side.

"Sotka, don't leave here. No matter how hard it is for you now, stay. I know what I am talking about. I know what I am saying. Your talent for soccer is such a natural thing. You have a good head on your shoulders. I know you won't let success spoil you, I can tell. Sotka, this only comes around once in a lifetime!"

Sotka! Chico and many of the older players called me *mali shtef*, Kid *Shtef*, as well as *Sotka*. That meant so much to me. As he spoke, his eyes were beseeching me to stay.

I could only look at him with tears in my eyes. A deep sigh of regret escaped from his lips. The only thing he could do was to give me a big bear hug in farewell. Then he walked over to where his wife was waiting. They turned to look back at me and waved goodbye for the last time, calling out, "*Do Vidzhenia*, until we meet again!"

I couldn't say another word, just waved back at him, with tears flowing down my face, as a terrible sadness gripped me. That was the last time I saw Zlatko Chaikovski, one of my all-time idols and my great booster. I admired him so much, not only for what he was able to do on the field, but also for the character of the man on or off the field. As with Bobek, Zlatko was like a god to me.

Mareto. I had to deal with that situation and resolve it. How to handle this initial hurdle of winning her confidence and acceptance as her brother? I decided on a strategy that usually works with children. I bought some ice cream cones and, with those in hand, I headed to where Mara was—on the grounds by the Red Cross building. I offered her one, but she wouldn't accept it. She was still unsure of this stranger who had been trying to make friends with her.

The ice cream was melting fast, so I offered the cones to a couple of the other little girls, and they eagerly accepted them. Casually, I asked around to find out if there were others from T'rsie who might have been with Mara. Having befriended a few of her little friends to a degree with the ice cream cones, I could see that Mara was beginning to be less fearful. She seemed a little more relaxed and became a little talkative as she saw the others unafraid to talk to me.

On the third day, I asked one of the Red Cross staff if I could take Mara and five or six of her friends for some ice cream. Now that the staff had been informed that I was legitimate—the real Sotir Nitchov, brother of Mara—I was given approval.

With these little *Begaltsi* with me, we walked about three blocks to the ice cream parlor. At that time, in the early 1950's at least, there was no air conditioning and very little refrigeration in Yugoslavia. I bought the ice cream and we went outside immediately. As we licked our ice cream, walking down the street, nonchalantly, I started to talk about the village and some of the people in it. But these children couldn't relate to anything I was saying. They didn't remember a thing! They only knew that they had parents in T'rsie, but nothing else.

Then I asked if anyone remembered their parents. One or two of the children said yes, but the rest shook their heads, no. Of the "yes" group, none could really describe their parents, but in their mind they felt they knew them.

Then I asked the children about the *maiki* who had been assigned to them in Stara Gora. I particularly asked Mara about our Cousin Kotse's wife and son, and I hit gold, sort of. Yes, she knew Nevestata. "I think I knew some other kids, but now, I don't think I know who they are any more," Mara said.

I felt we were making some real progress. At least we were *talking*, as we headed back to the Red Cross building. The *Begaltsi* from Bela Crkva had arrived and they knew who I was. I felt that I knew most of them, and tried to demonstrate that to Mara. She was still hesitant, unsure that I was really her brother. I thought it was time to ask her about our mother. I was so caught up in what she was saying that I can't recall now how she described her. She had not forgotten her at all. She described her to a "T".

"I can't remember what Father looked like, but I do remember a little bit. I remember a man bouncing me up and down and singing, "Mare, lichno, pretty Mare" and laughing. I remember that. I remember Baba, too. But Dedo, Dedo was very mean, always hollering at Baba."

I smiled at that recollection and wondered if Dedo would appreciate her memory of him. "Do you remember any animals, Mare?"

"Ooh, yes, there were lots of sheep."

"How about Vesko or Tsotseto?" Those names didn't mean anything to her at all.

"How about Tome? Do you remember Tome?"

She almost jumped. Wide-eyed, smiling, "*Koncheto, sivo, so tsrni damki*" was her description of my beautiful Tome, the gray horse with the black dots. "I remember Tome!" I told her I used to take care of Tome and that I took her on a ride with me on Tome, mentioning some places. She couldn't remember the places, only Tome. We were conversing more easily now.

One by one, as Mareto and I were talking, her little friends joined us where we sat. They just listened at the beginning. Eventually, one of them spoke up, "I have a brother. He is in Kotori."

Another, "I have a brother in Lagen."

Another, "I have one in Chereshnitsa."

A few confided that their mother had sent for them, happy to think that they really belonged to somebody. I didn't pry or ask questions of them, but I said something pleasant and encouraging to them, letting them think that they were really special. I told them, "When you join your families again, you'll be able to play just like you did when you were babies, crawling around, but, now, you'll be running instead of crawling and everyone will say, 'how you have grown!" That seemed to make them feel very good.

When I got up, Mareto grabbed my arm, I took her hand in mine, and we started walking toward the mess hall. When I felt her grab my hand, I felt as if a heavy weight had lifted from my chest. We had finally bonded after several days of trying! It was four days since the children had arrived in Belgrad.

I was informed that we were to leave Belgrad for home the next afternoon. Everyone was to be ready to board the train. Everything was to be ready for travel. That announcement made me realize that I had to voice my final decision, to stay or to leave. My time was up.

Real physical and mental agony overwhelmed me again. Mareto immediately sensed something. "Why are you so sad? Don't you want to go home again?"

What in God's name could I tell her?

"Yes, Mare, I want to go home," I told her. "We have to pick up our sister, Tsotsa, who is going to come with us when we get to Skopje."

"Sister?"

"Ya. Remember you mentioned the name Tsotsa when we were talking before. That is our sister."

Even as I was reminding her, I realized that all she remembered of her sister was her name. She had no image of her at all. Five years away from everybody and everything familiar almost erased the first part of her life. Who could we fault for that? Was there anyone or anyway they could repay the children for their lost lives?

Early in the morning of the next day, I received word that the officials at the Partizan Club wanted to see me. They had the Red Cross staff in the office by the time I arrived. I was so full of emotion—my head and chest so full of pain and throbbing—that I thought I would explode.

Eyes bleary, struggling to keep tears from spilling, I thought, this is too heavy. Inside my head, I heard myself crying out, Mother, Mother, Mother, why me? Why now? My cries were not helping. Nothing could help me now. I had pounded the walls the night before. Bruises and cuts were visible on my hands, but I felt nothing.

One of the staff of the Red Cross said, "We really have to go. There is much work to do yet." But one of the Club officials interceded and told him that someone from the Club would bring me in time.

"Give him time to say goodbye to the team and his friends," he urged. The Red Cross Staff agreed and left. I went to the restroom to pull myself together enough that I could go for my bag, which was still in my quarters.

We all went to the field for the final, final goodbye. I was given a brand new Partizan sweat suit with name, emblem, and number emblazoned on it. I packed it in my bag, along with my soccer shoes and a few other things. This was a terrible moment for me. I had experienced many bad moments, but none like this one. I felt as if someone was cutting me up from the inside right down the middle. I felt actual burning and pain in my stomach. Most of the older players knew exactly what I was feeling, and they gave me such encouragement and sympathy. Everyone went all-out to try to make me feel better, but there was nothing anyone could do to make this parting less painful.

The final words were about to be said, and I don't even remember who spoke, but these words are engraved in my heart:

—

This kid, Sotir Nitchov, was so adaptable, so likeable, besides all the other abilities he has shown for such a young person, that I feel I am losing a part of myself, a part of all of us.

At one o'clock in the afternoon I was dropped off at the army barracks where we were scheduled to gather. Mareto looked quite worried because she hadn't seen me. She had been looking for me since morning because I had told her that I would be there early.

When she saw me saying goodbye to the two men who had brought me there, she ran to me and hugged me. As she hugged me I thought to myself, well, I didn't bungle this up for Mareto. She had accepted me as her brother, the only one she would ever know.

I felt most of the little children were feeling somewhat abandoned. Maybe that was just me thinking like that. It was good to have my little sister with me. Mareto made me feel less melancholy for a while. As we waited, some of the *Begaltsi* from Bela Crkva began to talk enthusiastically about going home. I didn't feel like talking. I didn't want the guys to think I was snubbing them, but I explained a little of my situation regarding the Partizan Club. That was now a part of my past. I had to put the past behind me and concentrate on today and tomorrow.

Characteristic of most plans and schedules in Yugoslavia, we didn't leave as planned. It wasn't until about midnight the following night that we boarded the train in Belgrad for Skopje. When we arrived in Skopje it was still dark and Mareto was asleep next to me. As I looked out of the window, I saw my sister Tsotsa standing on the platform with our Cousin Lena and her husband, Jordan. I stood and waved from the inside as hard as I could, until they eventually saw me, waving back excitedly.

We couldn't leave the train. I watched while Tsotsa hugged Lena and Jordan so hard, kissing them over and over again. Greetings and partings among Macedonians are always heart-wrenching. We lived in a time when no one knew if they would ever see the other again. One more tearful goodbye! For a minute I lost sight of them, but they reappeared again right by my window. They were motioning to me to go outside, for we had not seen each other for so long.

I could hear the shouting, "Where is Mareto?" I woke up Mara and pointed to a cousin she couldn't remember, but she waved at them anyway with one hand, rubbing her eyes. Still crying, Tsotsa finally boarded the train and joined Mara and me. Lena was crying outside; Tsotsa was crying inside as the train finally began to pull away. Would we never stop crying, we Begaltsi?

As Lena and Jordan began to fade from view, Tsotsa looked at Mareto and recognized her immediately without a second glance. However, Mareto pulled away from this stranger. I urged them both to go to sleep. The only thing I remember about this portion of the trip to Solun was something Sofa said, "Are you sick? You look terrible!"

"No, I'm just tired. Go to sleep, why don't you?" The train whistled, shrieked, and

Mareto's group of young Begaltsi.

the familiar clickety-clack of the wheels began to lull us to sleep, Sofa, Mareto, Sote, Nitchovs all, together again.

As I dropped off, my last thoughts were, where was I going? Where had I really been?

Reunion in Solun

There is no slave out of heaven like a loving woman;
And of all loving women,
There is no slave as a mother.

HENRY WARD BEECHER, 1887

By the time we arrived in Solun the next morning, a large crowd had gathered. Nothing interested me, neither the preparations for our arrival, nor the strange-sounding language. Nothing here existed for me; nothing seemed real. My eyes did take in the sight of priests and nuns. Who cares? I had other thoughts in my mind, such as my responsibility for my two sisters.

As we lined up near the train doors to exit, I saw buses parked near the platform. Guessing that the buses were for us, I led my sisters and a few of the children with us toward the first bus. Other children started to follow me into the bus. A couple of nuns hurried into the bus to tell us in the Greek language, that we had to leave the bus and remain outside. They were gesturing to us to go outside. While in Belgrad, Tsveta Yanchova from T'rsie and I got to know each other quite well. She was very helpful because she understood Greek and was able to interpret for us, especially for me. Replying in Macedonian to the nuns, I said firmly, "We are not leaving this bus!"

I told Tsveta to tell them, "I know what they are up to. There are photographers here and they are preparing a formal reception to show the world that their "Greek" children have returned home to Greece. We want no part of that phony stuff. We are not Greeks. They want to continue fooling the world."

I don't know how much of what I told her she repeated to them. Telling the children in the bus to remain where they were, I stepped outside to look for a Red Cross representative. They wanted to use us for their shitty Greek propaganda. Spotting a couple of people wearing Red Cross armbands talking with some very well-dressed people, I stormed toward them burning with hostility and directed my verbal blast at them.

"While you are here chatting away, totally bamboozled, the damned Greeks are going to use us for their propaganda. Somebody has to stop them!"

I didn't care who heard me. In fact, I hoped everyone did. One of the Red Cross representatives, a Yugoslavian, understood what I had just said. She pointed toward the buses as we walked away from the others. As the children boarded the buses. I shouted to them in Macedonian, "Stay inside. Don't come out."

I boarded the bus immediately and, in a few minutes, the buses began to move toward the large gates of a church. Once inside the gates, the buses parked and we were told to disembark. As was the usual pattern with large groups of children, they formed columns and followed the nuns who were now in charge. Tsveta and I were at the end of the line, just to be sure that nobody got lost. It had become an ingrained habit with the older ones to look out not only for each other, but for the younger children as well. We were wary and distrustful of the nuns and the other adults, particularly now that we were again in Macedonia but under the authority of the damned Greeks.

I could not allow my personal emotional pain and the burden that had depressed me so deeply deplete my energy nor sidetrack my concern for the immediate problems of this reunion. Where were they going to take us now? It was obvious that the Greeks were preparing something, and that we were to be involved in it. Tsveta's perceptive mind figured it out.

"They're going to take us into the church to preach to us about something!"

As we were led into this beautiful, awe-inspiring church, we all gaped at everything we saw. When we had all assembled, a priest came from the altar and crossed himself three times. Then he began his—I don't know—maybe a sermon? A lecture? Whatever it was, it was mumbo-jumbo to me. If I sound sacrilegious, I don't care. Here was a Greek priest addressing Macedonian children and young people in the Greek language. Few of us understood any Greek. Tsveta was one of the few who did. I couldn't take more than 5 minutes of this before I took my little sister's hand and walked out, with a few of her friends following her.

Someone in the rear tried to stop us. He started to say something, as he blocked the aisle. I pushed the man aside and led the kids out. When the others saw us, they, too, began to follow. There was a small open area, surrounded by a wall. I perched on the wall, with the younger ones around me, waiting for the next step in the little plot that was unfolding.

Sure enough, about six adults—including some of the nuns—came over to me and, with great intensity, began their diatribe in Greek. I understood about five words, so once again, I called to Tsveta to translate.

"They are telling you that you are in Elada, in your own country. They are going to teach all of us Greek, how to make the sign of the Cross and how to pray in Greek. She said that we should be happy now that we are out of the dungeon that is Yugoslavia. Now you are free and there will be no more suffering. . . . "

I exploded, directing all my emotion at the Greeks. I tried to start out with a better vocabulary than what was in my heart, but this is the way it came out:

"As usual, you Greeks are stupid. What you are doing and planning here today shows what ignorant, selfish, egotistical, dumb, self-centered idiots, imbeciles, bigots you are—and you are also the biggest hypocrites in the entire world."

That was just for openers. I said a lot more. I used every vulgar expression I knew. I felt sorry for Tsveta, for she began to blush, unable to translate my vulgarity.

I ended with, "How can you even think of speaking Greek to us, when we don't understand you, nor do we even want to try? You Greeks will never be able to find and enjoy the kind of respect, care and freedom we Macedonian children experienced these past 5 years in Yugoslavia, not in your entire lifetimes!"

I saw the priest come toward us. That was all I needed, and with all the audacity I could muster, I said, "Greeks are so stupid you will never be able to realize how deep your stupidity goes. Any history you try to teach us will be full of deceitful, revised history, suitable only for the purposes of your stinking Greek politics. We are not in Elada. We are in Macedonia, and we are Macedonians. You label me and others who speak out as being evil, but you are the evil ones because you have done us much evil for too long. You are not concerned about our well-being. I am going to speak to either a Swiss or Yugoslav Red Cross representative!"

They mumbled among themselves about the United Nations. Apparently giving up, they crossed themselves and walked away. As they left, I yelled at them as loud as I could, "Crossing yourselves won't help you. Only a gun can put you out of your miseries, you miserable bastards!"

As I was spewing out all of my hatred for everything they stood for, the children had encircled me, listening with eyes wide. I don't know if I had exhausted myself, vented all my anger, but at this point we were all hungry. None of us *Begaltsi* had been fed since we left Belgrad. We had not had breakfast even.

Much, much later, we were given some food that was supposed to pass for breakfast. We also learned that we had been in the former Macedonian Church of *Sveti Dimitria,* which the Greeks call St. Dimitrias.

This was where we stayed for a couple of days, primarily for Greek indoctrination, before our mothers were able to claim us. I say mothers, because there were only about four men that appeared with them. The absence of the fathers meant only one thing. They had been killed, wounded or jailed on one of the Greek islands. The more fortunate were the ones able to escape fled to Eastern Bloc countries, and anywhere else they could.

On the second day, the nuns tried to organize some games for the children, followed by some dances. Some of the younger ones participated good-naturedly, enjoying the activity. Tsveta, her two friends—one from Kotori and the other from Turie—and I watched from the *bunar,* the well. I sat on the edge of it, while the girls leaned against it. As I looked up, I said, "Uh-oh, here comes trouble. What do you think they want?"

The "they" I was referring to were two nuns, looking for all the world like two ghosts, *samovili* or *vesthtits*i. The girls laughed, but covered up quickly, straightened up, and tried to put a respectful look on their faces. One of them said to me in a very low voice, "Sote, please don't cuss at them. They just don't understand about us."

"Well, don't you think it's about time that they begin to understand? Piss on them!"

"*Lele, Maiko, ke ne ostramish pak.* Oh, Mother! You're going to embarrass us again."

"Then you go. You don't have to stay here, " I replied, but the girls stayed where they were.

One of the nun approached, saying something. Tsveta translated.

"The nuns want to know why we are not dancing."

As sarcastically as I knew how, I said, "There is no band to play for us, and they can't sing for shit. We are waiting for the well water here to call them over, get them to jump in and drown them!"

Tsveta did not translate the last sentence relating to the *bunar.*

"Fine, don't. Just tell them to leave us alone. Tell them to get the hell out of my sight, " I snapped at her.

One of the nuns left, but the other was most persistent. She took Tsveta and her friends by the hands and, one-by-one, incorporated them into the dancing group. Then she came back for me, trying to pull me by the arm. She was saying, "*Pigadi, pigadi. Gerakina kinise*," referring to a Greek folk song. I think she was saying that she was going to teach me how to dance. She wouldn't let go of me. I tried to shake her off, to tell her to let go, but no, she had made up her mind. Did she think I was so shy? I was strong and far more stubborn than she could ever be, so I yanked my hand from her so hard, that she fell flat on her bottom. Her legs went up, as did her robe, almost to her hips. Shocked, she got up, brushed off her clothes and went crying into the church. I think she was more embarrassed than hurt. I didn't care one whit about her embarrassment, but I didn't want her hurt physically, either. She just wouldn't take no for an answer.

It was no more than a few minutes before four or five people came up, mouthing words at me, saying who knows what. I couldn't understand them anyway, so I didn't react one way or another. I do remember one word, though. It sounded like *thirio*. Whatever.

The dancing had stopped by this time, and the younger ones surrounded me again.

My little sister came up to me and held my hand, somewhat fearfully. She knew there was anger in the air, and that the anger centered in and on me. Finally, a couple of the Red Cross staff approached me. I couldn't wait to speak to them.

"If the Greeks continue with their bullshit attempts to brainwash us into believing we are Greeks, not Macedonians, before we even see our families," I complained, "we just won't accept it. We won't tolerate it—not for 1 minute."

One of the staff tried to explain, "By law, we have to turn over our responsibility for all of you now to the Greek Red Cross. Those are the rules. Each of you will have identification cards, and if you have any complaints, or if any abuse occurs, you are to notify either the Greek, Yugoslav or Swiss Red Cross."

I was tired of explanations. "All we want from these people is to be left alone and have our parents notified that we have arrived. We are waiting for them to come for us and get us out of here. We are supposed to be going home."

One of the Red Cross representatives seemed puzzled. She spoke to us, "Your parents should have been here already."

She left our group, determined to find out why there was a delay. The others still with us were left to wonder, too, what might possibly have happened to the parents. As they were discussing the possibilities among themselves, the lady returned.

"What is your name, young man?"

I wrote my name on a piece of paper, which she put in her purse.

"There will be some parents here tomorrow, I am quite certain."

So instead of being home, we were still going to be in Solun. The nuns and the priests stayed away from us, and for this we did say, "Thank God!"

Would it surprise you to know that the parents, mostly mothers, had already been in Solun for 2 days, in hotels, waiting, but nobody had notified them that we had arrived 3 days prior? The parents had been told to contact a certain office regarding our arrival, but when they did, the parents were informed that we hadn't arrived yet! There is no doubt in my mind that the Greek strategy was to indoctrinate us upon our arrival; to turn us away from our parents, our language, everything Macedonian.

The next day came, and again I made my way to the yard, facing the gateway entrance, not knowing what it was I was looking at. A little distance away, the silhouette of a woman in black appeared. My heart leaped in my chest. I knew that silhouette, even though it had been years. I recognized her instantly and raced toward her. At that instant she too recognized me and came running to me. This figure, encsed in black from head to toe, reached out to me as I reached out to her, and we clasped each other as if we would never let go of each other again. She kept squeezing me tighter and tighter, trying to bridge that physical gap of separation we had endured.

Mother. It was Mother, this figure, encased in black, who clutched me so lovingly, crying, saying my name over and over, mumbling something, murmuring, kissing my head, my face, touching my hair, standing back for a moment, and then clasping me to her again. Our tears mingled as our faces pressed together. Then she looked at me hard.

"Sote, Sote. How are you? You look so thin. Are you all right?"

I couldn't get a word out. I choked. I just hung on to her. Finally, I was able to say, "I'm fine, Mother."

This was not true, but I repeated it. "I'm fine. This is the way I am supposed to be. I have to stay in shape," but I couldn't say any more.

I felt a tug. It was Mareto.

Pulling away from Mother, I said to my sister, "Mare, this is our mother."

An agonized cry filled the air as Mother opened her arms to her youngest, her baby. Mare jumped into her arms. She had not forgotten her. How could she have? That indefinable tie between Mother and child is stronger than any other force in the universe. How many kisses were exchanged? Who counted?

Then Tsotsa, my sister Sofa, ran to us, crying, "Mother, Mother". We all sobbed and clutched each other, the four of us. Four Nitchovs pressed together as if nothing could ever part us again.

But no, it wasn't four, it was the six of us, because within our tight little circle, as we hugged and cried, we were pressing the memory of the two who would be with us always, Father and Stefo. They had joined our reunion, too, our bittersweet reunion, mingling their tears, their laughter with ours.

While we were together, other parents had been coming into the churchyard to reclaim their children. Some came in groups; others one by one, alone. I could describe the entire scene as one of happiness and excitement, but the truth is that it was one of the most heart-wrenching moments in our experience. Among the younger children, there were those who didn't recognize their mother, and ran from outstretched arms. Five years ago they were just 3- or 4-year olds. Now, all around them were these black apparitions. None of us, not even the older ones remembered our mothers like that.

There was one little *Begalche* who could easily break your heart. Her eyes showed such confusion as she looked at her mother. She pulled herself away from her. I could see that the mother, though saddened and pained, understood why here little daughter refused to accept her.

All of the children wanted to believe that they were looking at their mothers, but how could they be sure? How could they be certain that these persons hadn't just abandoned them or discarded them and left them in the hands of strangers? They had been in a safe place. The little ones hadn't seen the horror of a particularly bloody civil war.

Regardless, the little toddlers who were now young children, had been separated too long. They had adapted to different people, in different countries, to different disciplines. The memories of home and parents had receded deeper and deeper in their little memories.

No, the reunion was quite difficult for many.

One of Mareto's young friends, Pavlina, had become more and more comfortable with me. She had begun to talk to me freely, even sometimes—as little girls do—about some of her thoughts and fantasies. I remember asking her what she remembered about her village, Gherman, about her parents. Until this point little Pavlina had also rejected the black-clad woman who claimed to be her mother, I saw the look on her mother's tear-stained face, as she stood absolutely still, not knowing what more to do. I wanted so much to do something to bring them together.

I gave her mother a nod of reassurance, and knelt by Pavlinka. I began to ask her gently what she remembered from before. She started to tell me about a bridge, and a river, a walnut tree and some animals.

"When you were playing with your friends in those places, who called you home to eat or to do something in the house? Do you remember who put you to bed?"

Her little head was nodding yes to my questions. She answered, "It was this woman with the white *shamija,* scarf, on her head and a white *pregach,* apron."

I nodded along with her and then said to her, "That was your mother."

I knew, after hearing Pavlina's description, what the problem was. The woman, her mother, who had approached her, dressed in black like the other mothers also wore a black *shamija* on her head. All the widows wore this dark, depressing color, which revolted me then, and revolts me to this day. It was no wonder Pavlina rejected the person she saw. No child wants to have anything to do with these frightful, black apparitions, with the mournful eyes and face. These were unwelcome strangers.

When we had finished our little conversation, I told her to go over and join Mara for awhile. As she did, I went over to the mother who was surrounded by the other mothers, who were trying to comfort her. She was in such anguish, not knowing what to do.

She cried, pleaded to God, "May I be turned into stone. My baby does not know me or want me. It would have been better to have been killed by a *kurshum*, a bomb. It would have been better if I were dead, if my own flesh and blood does not know me, her mother. Oh, oh, I don't want to live."

As she wailed in agony, she struck herself several times on her chest, bent over as if in pain, then raised her head again to rail at the heavens.

There had to be something that someone could do. But what? Pavlinka wouldn't accept the woman no matter how much she cried and pleaded. I searched my mind for some kind of answer, when suddenly, an image popped into my mind—that of little lost lambs and the mother sheep trying to find her own. It reminded me for a split second of the winter I had spent in Lerin, herding and grazing the sheep; watching the birthing of the lambs. I remembered how the little wobbly lambs would bleat for their mothers, who bleated back at them. I remembered how they would reunite, when the sound and smell of each brought them together. I felt I knew what might work here. It was worth a try.

I went to the mother and took her by the hand, moving her away from the others, about 10 or 15 feet. I asked one of them for a white *shamija*. They looked at me as if they hand no idea what white was. White? No one had worn white for years. Seeing the reality of the situation, I gently pulled off her black *shamija*. This surprised her, somewhat shocked her, and for a minute she stopped her wailing.

"Stop what you are doing and listen carefully," I said with as much kindness and sympathy as I could. "Forget the *shamij*a. Don't say or do anything crazy now. No one wants to hear you. If you want your little Pavlinka to come to you, you are going to smile, and try to look and feel as happy as you can. Your little girl only remembers this woman with the white *shamija* and a white apron. She remembers you milking a cow, and she remembers a bridge and a river. That is why you must put on white and tie the *shamija* like you used to, above and around your head, with part of it hanging like a braid. Talk to her about those things that you did together. Remind her of walnuts, the river and the bridge, of eating together, and putting her to bed."

Believe it or not, as I was talking to her, one of the nuns brought us a white *shamija*, and the mother put it on slowly. Someone else found a white cloth that could serve as an apron. I instructed the mother to come over to Pavlina and me in a few minutes, but she had to be smiling and looking happy.

The poor soul looked at me, still mournful, unhappy, desperate, ready to give up. "Oh, my boy, how can I smile, when my heart cannot?"

"What choice do you have? If you want your child back, this is what you must do. You have to put on the best act you can. It is critical for both of you!"

I rejoined my mother and sisters to explain what I was trying to do. Mother encouraged me to do what I could, so I knew she approved. I kept my fingers crossed, which was quite an unusual because I don't believe in superstition.

I went back to where Pavlina was, and we sat down on the ground together. Again I asked her to tell me everything she could remember about her mother, just her mother. I maneuvered Pavlina, so that she would be facing her mother, but for the moment, I intentionally blocked her view. So Pavlina began her little sing-song way of sharing her favorite memories, as I prodded her. After a few minutes, I moved aside a little, so that when Pavlina looked up, she would have a full view of her mother. As we were drawing something in the dirt with our sticks—with Pavlina giving her full concentration to her little recital and her markings in the dirt—out of the corner of my eye, I could see her mother coming toward us, on cue.

"Look, Pavlina, your mother is coming for you. She is right behind this lady coming toward us!"

Pavlina looked up to see where I was pointing. Suddenly, there was a change of expression on her sweet little face, that of shocked recognition.

In a quivering little voice, Pavlina cried out, "Mama! That's Mama!"

As the woman drew closer, Pavlina sprang up from the ground and ran to her. She literally flew into her mother's waiting arms. They remained glued together for a long, long moment. The mother was murmuring softly to her. Nobody knew what she was saying to her little girl, but with their arms around each other, and Pavlina's legs locked around her mother's body, they spoke volumes. Nothing would ever separate these two again in this life.

Later in the day, Pavlina told Mara how happy she was that she, like the others, had found her own mother. Her mother looked for me, and when she saw me, she gave me whatever squeeze she had left over, so grateful, so overjoyed, that she was beyond words. I knew what she was feeling.

We traveled together—our family and Pavlina and her mother—as far as Lerin. We had lots of time for conversation and tears. I promised we'd go to Gherman to visit them one day, but the chance never came.

That reunion in Solun was the most bittersweet moment. At least it took my mind off my own problem.

For my mother's niece, Sofa, one of the 200 *Begaltsi* who had returned to Aegean Macedonia in May, 1954, her reunion with her mother was almost unbelievable, due to the incredible byzantine bureaucratic bungling. She was part of the 12 to 17-year-old Macedonians who had arrived in Solun and had been housed temporarily in the military barracks in the city. They had remained there for 4 days. Naturally, they arrived under their own legal Macedonian names by which they had been known since their birth and baptism in the church. However, their parents had been forced to change their names to Greek, the spelling of which was different. Consequently, the parents were not notified that their children had arrived and were waiting to be reunited with them.

After 4 days, when the parents did not show up, Sofa and the other unidentified children were placed in the orphanage in the town of Kozhani. While there, Sofa and a 12-year-old boy from the village of Konomladi were interrogated over and over again. In a rude, arrogant manner and tone,. They were asked . . .

What kind of education did you receive?

What kind of language were you taught?

Were you fed regularly and well?

Were you treated well?

Whether the unidentified children ended up in Solun, Kozhani, Lerin, Kostur, or Voden, the identical questions were asked.

Sofa's mother and aunt finally went to Solun because they had heard from others that the children had arrived. But on the day of their arrival, Sofa had left for Kozahni, where she spent the night. While there, the next day she met a woman, Hristina, who worked at the orphanage. After the interrogation, Hristina got permission to have Sofa spend the night with her at her house. The next day they left for Lerin.

As Sofa and Hristina left for Lerin, her mother arrived in Kozahni.

As soon as Sofa and Hristina arrived in Lerin, she was taken to the *astonomia,* the police station to be interrogated again. Just as in Kozahni, they treated her rudely, as if she were interfering with more-important business. They didn't like to deal with Macedonian riff-raff.

Who are you?

Where did you live before you were sent to Yugoslavia?

What is your name?

How long were you gone?

What is the name of your village?

Y our mother's name?

Your father's name?

She spent hours at the station, interrogated over and over.

In the meantime, in Kozhani her mother and aunt were informed that Sofa had left for Lerin. Once again, they went in pursuit of Sofa.

One of the reasons for the continuing interrogation of Sofa was that she had brought all of her Macedonian schoolbooks with her—grammar, geography, botany, history, literature and books—all in the Macedonia language. Both in Kozahni and in Lerin the police examined the books very carefully, but did not confiscate them. Sofa had told them straightforwardly that the books were hers and that she was going to keep them forever.

Sofa was asked, "Do you want to go to the village of T'rsie or someplace else."

Without a moment's hesitation she replied, "T'rsie."

Permission was finally granted.

Just as Sofa left the station and started on the road to T'rsie, her mother and aunt appeared on the same road. And there, in the middle of the road, the unbelievable, joyous reunion of mother, daughter and aunt after 5 years apart and much bureaucratic delay, finally, lovingly, tearfully took place.

All of us Begaltsi tried to readjust now that we were home again. But the paranoia and hostility of the Greeks who had been empowered by the Greek authorities to harass and intimidate the remaining Macedonian population was continuing.

In 1955, it was not unusual to hear the church bells ring urgently at midnight when villagers were asleep. The Greeks in jeeps, revving their motors up and down the village created deliberate chaos. They pounded on the doors and through their megaphones they would shout, "Go to the village square now!"

Rousted, bewildered, fearful, the villagers obeyed, leaving their houses in the middle of the night. Sofa's mother's first concern was to hide the Macedonian books. Quickly, they hurried to their basement and actually dug a hole in which to bury her precious books. Her mother worried, "If they find these books, they are going to punish us and put us in jail in the islands."

They reached the square and saw every villager standing there. The Greeks announced that they were looking for draft dodgers, which would have been hilarious, had it not been so tragic. The Greeks knew damned well that there were only old men and women, widows and young children left in the village. This was simply an excuse to harass and intimidate the people. It was a typical Greek ploy, which they used several times a year and always at midnight and always for the same reason: they were searching for draft dodgers!

That same year the Greeks kidnapped Tode Yanchov and took him to the village of Neret. They kept him all night before he was released. No one was able to find out why he was taken, nor what had happened in Neret. Tode did not say a single word to anyone regarding who kidnapped him or what he was asked or what he said.

After all these years, Sofa still expresses the fear and harassment she experienced during that period in her life. Her story has a happy ending, though. She is married to another *Begalets*, and enjoying a most comfortable and happy life with her family and grandchildren.

The brutality of the Greeks still sears the soul of the Macedonian Diaspora. The unanswered questions linger in the mind. Why won't anyone make the Greeks acknowledge their grievous behavior and make them accountable for their harassment, and their ethnic intimidation of the Macedonians?

"On 3 March, during a Belgrade Youth Conference, the Cominform countries took a decision to offer refuge to Greek children between the ages of three and fourteen who were living in particularly exposed districts. By the end of the year, according to Red Cross reports, there were l0,000 in Yugoslavia, 3,801 in Rumania, 3,000 in Hungary, 2,660 in Bulgaria, 2,235 in Czechoslovakia and 2,000 in Albania . . . The UN Inquiry Commission . . . reconvened in October of the previous year without Soviet participation . . . It began compiling a dossier on the 'kidnapping of Greek children'. These unhappy victims, torn from their families and forced to absorb Slavic ideology by intensive brainwashing, would surely illustrate the true extent of the pan-Slavic intervention in Greece. . . . ***When interviewed by the Greek security services, parents showed a natural reluctance to boast of having chosen to send their children to the People's Democracies rather than to Queen Frederika's camps. . . .*** *Colonel A. W. Sheppard, former chief of the British economic mission in Northern Greece wrote: 'Propaganda never sinks so low as when it seeks to exploit the natural affection which everyone feels for children. . . . And was the Greek Provisional Government wrong to evacuate the children from the regions it controls to save them from the British and American bombs used by the Royal Hellenic Air Force? . . . All war is cruel, civil war especially so. Mr. Tsaldaris had admitted that the Athens government was in the habit of exposing severed heads in village squares. . . . I should perhaps mention here everyone who has seen both sides is unanimous in rejecting the stories put out by the Government in Athens. . . . In chatting with Mrs. Levinsohn of Save the Children organization in Stockholm, she said that after carrying out searing inquiries among the mothers and children of the children's camps in Hungary, she is convinced that they*

all left Greece with their parents' consent and that they are being looked after in a way that leaves nothing to be desired . . . Agents of the Athens government had enough influence to PREVENT the publication of all, or very nearly all of Mrs. Levinsohn's personal statements."

From the *Kapetanios* by Dominique Udes

Past/Present

Buffaloes are held by cords, man by his words.

MALAY PROVERB

We had traveled about 4 hours by train. Never once did we mention Father or Stefo. Mother could not speak about our terrible loss—not then, nor ever since. I had neither the courage nor the wisdom to ask her if she knew how they died, though I had discovered how and where Father had been killed.

I was to learn many years later from my cousin Risto that Stefo had sent Mother a letter from the training camp at Prespa. Risto recorded in his memoirs that it was illegal to write from a training camp. Everything would have been censored because the 'civil war' was at its peak. Apparently Stefo found a person going to the village of Statitsa and it was this person who personally handed the letter to Mother. Stefo was informing her that he was back in Macedonia at the training camp in Prespa, and if, God willing, he passed through the village, he would see her soon.

Mother received the letter after Stefo had been sent to Malimadi, where he was killed in action in the very first battle. Several weeks later, Risto's sister, Dina, was in a regiment that moved toward Lerin in 1949, which gave her the opportunity to meet with Mother.

"I have the last letter from Stefo," Mother told Dina as she reached into her bosom to pull it out to show her. Dina was expecting Mother to ask her to read it to her.

Instead, as she unfolded the letter, almost in pieces and torn at the folded edge, Mother began ' to read' the precious words. Dina was stunned for Mother had never learned to read. Mother had asked a villager to read it to her, a man by the name of Laze Mishovski. She had memorized every single word. With every word Mother 'read' aloud, a cry or a moan of anguish would escape from her mouth. This last piece of paper, the only item she had now to remind her of Stefo, she could place close to her heart.

Risto recalls that, when he met with Mother in Detroit in 1963, he asked her about the letter, she replied, "Before I left to come to America, I buried what was left of the letter in the stone wall of the foundation of our burned house.

As we reached Nausa, I almost started to speak because this was where Father was killed. But I caught myself quickly before I blurted out the horrible knowledge. It was best to leave that alone. It would not change our situation, only rekindle the deepest pain and hurt in all of us, which could never cease or be erased.

The train continued to roll noisily along and then, at last, we arrived at Lerin. Could it really be possible that I was back in Lerin again?

With baggage in hand, we started to walk to our home, which was a little distance. Going through the center of town, I stared at the familiar sights. The buildings looked so old, worn out, almost uninhabited. As we began to reach *T'rsianska Mala,* the quarter of town where many T'rsiani had homes, everything began to look even worse. Houses, roads, the bridge showed neglect, no sign of any maintenance. The river looked muddy. Peeling paint mocked the passersby. These places that used to thrive with the energy of the Macedonians who lived there were now grubby, dirty or abandoned. People greeted us, but I recognized only a few of the older ones. Even some relatives who stopped us to welcome us back, were unfamiliar to me, but I responded as politely as I could.

We passed the school, and I called to Mara to look.

"Mare, this is where I took Tome home from that yard. No one was able to stop me. There were lots of Germans around then, but Ilo and I got Tome out, and I rode him home!" What a sweet memory that was.

Mother nodded her confirmation to Mara, that what I was telling her actually happened.

"Your Dedo still talks about it, how they took our money and sheep to get Tome back, but it was Sotiraki who brought our horse home."

Turning to me, Mother said, "Dedo always asks about you when he is not talking about you, Sote."

"Do you think he will recognize me?"

With such sadness, she replied carefully, "Dedo is not able to see any more, so I can't say."

I dwelt on that for a bit. Dedo blind, not able to see his beloved land and animals—after having spent so much of his life working to acquire the property and stock—was such a shock. We walked on silently.

We were now by Pelopida's Café, which I remembered well as the scene of some of my infamous shenanigans. From that point, we passed the houses . . . Tane Arnautinot's house . . . the Mishovtsi house . . . Teta Tana's house . . . Tsila's place . . . this one belongs to Uncle Sotir . . . the Dimovski house . . . then Goga . . . Elmazoite . . . Turkovite Dulioto . . . across the creek where Pando lived . . . then Teta Traianka's . . . Filipoite . . . I had to congratulate myself on my memory. I remembered it all.

We came to the fork in the road. One road leads upward to the main road to take us to T'rsie, Turie and Kalugeritsa. The *putcheto,* little straight road, leads to our Lerin property further up. The road that turns slightly downward leads to St. Nikola Church and the Kondopoulo. Whether you were headed for St. Nikola or toward Kondopoulo, it was necessary to cross a bridge.

Mother led us toward Uncle Sotir's house to greet him first. After a few minutes, we headed for home, the Nitchov's "palace", the *kaliva.* We crossed the *dere,* the creek, and we were home. It was there waiting for us.

There was Dedo, sitting at the end of the *kaliva* facing the river and the church. It was the place he always enjoyed, just taking in the view, breathing the clean, fresh air, and relishing the pleasure and pride he felt in those moments. He would never admit that, though.

I sneaked up close to him and greeted him loudly, "*Zdravo*, Dedo"—the Macedonian universal greeting, meaning *good health.*

Dedo whipped around in the direction of my voice. "*Sotiraki! Si diode doma!* Sotiraki has come home!"

Before I could reach out to him to help him up, he was upright so quickly. The surprise of that sudden movement caught me off balance. He could not see me, but he recognized my voice, even though it surely had changed. There was so much I wanted to say to him, but I couldn't get a word out—I was too caught up in the emotion of the moment. He knew I was struggling inside.

He had begun to run his hands over my chest, arms and hands, and then his hands caressed my face and lingered there. "Let me see how much you have grown! *Mashala, poraste tsel mush! Mashala, mashala, na Dedo mush! Malko slab si, ama, ke se zgoesh.* Bravo, you have grown into a man. Bravo, bravo, Dedo's man. You're a little thin, but you will fatten up."

How could he tell that I had lost weight? How could he tell so much without his sight?

"Dedo, you can't see me. How did you recognize me? My voice has changed."

"Ah, that is the secret of the old. Your voice, your face, your body may have changed, but I have not changed. You grew up in my mind all these years away from us. I pictured you in my mind and I imagined the kind of changes that I just felt with my hands."

He asked about the girls. As I was telling him that they had arrived with me, I signaled to the girls and they ran over to him, hugging and kissing his hands and face. I went inside to look for Baba.

She was sitting in a wooden rocking chair, swinging back and forth with ease, her feet on the dirt floor. I called to her, "*Babo, kako si?* Grandma, how are you?"

She stopped rocking. "Who are you?"

I stood before her. "I am Sote, Baba."

She must not have heard me clearly, if she heard me at all. She slowly came and peered at me, and then instantly her arms went out to embrace me. "*Mite, chedo!* Mite, child!"

She thought I was Father.

"No, Baba. I am Sote."

Arms still around me, she looked up at me, then rocked me side to side, as she murmured, "*Sote, na Baba. Chedo, ne te poznaf.* Baba's Sote. Child I didn't recognize you!"

Could she always have been so small, so short, so beaten down? She was much thinner than I remembered her, and a little . . . different. She could not reach up to my face to kiss me. I had to lean down so that she could cover me with her wet kisses. She was Baba, loving, caring, kind. She was always concerned with our well-being. From that standpoint, she was unchanged.

A flashback came to me . . . of the time I was in a fight and had come home with a black eye and some scratches. When she saw me, she scurried around the kitchen to make a poultice of wet bread and salt for my eye. The way she bandaged me, you'd have thought I'd have died without it.

And here she was, now as before, peering at me to see if I had been hurt, so that she could do something about it. Some things never change.

"Let's go outside. I want to see clearly what you look like. *Aman, bre chedo.* My goodness, my dear child. Where have you been?" She turned her face to the sky. "Look, God, you brought Sote back home to me." She had raised her arms in gratitude talking to God, grateful that I had returned.

Then she saw my sisters for the first time since our fateful departure years ago. "*Gospo, ami ova e Tsotseto*? God is this Tsotseto? She looks beautiful enough to be a bride. And Mare? *Lele,* oh my! How did this good fortune find me, that I should see my grandchildren one more time?"

As she started to lament, invoking Father's name, "Where are you, Mite, to see your children . . . ," I cut her short, afraid that we would all end up in an orgy of crying, drowning in our own tears.

"Baba, what are we going to eat? What do you have for us?"

"I have everything, dear child," and turned to Dedo, taking him to task for not telling her that we were coming home.

We spent a good part of the evening and night inside of the *kaliva*, talking about everything from we could think of. We went from subject to subject, jumping back and forth, trying to bridge the gap of our separation, until my sisters fell asleep sitting in their chairs. It was then that Mother told me I would be sleeping at my Uncle Sotir's house. That seemed a little strange to me. Why? Everyone else was here.

"Isn't this place good enough for me? I am staying here. I'll sleep here with all of you, the way it used to be, and that's it!" I insisted.

Not sleep at home? That upset me. I went outside to control myself and started to walk toward the *kladenche* . About half way, I met my Uncle Done. He was coming from Kalugeritsa, and really didn't see me until I stepped out in front of him. He stopped dead in his tracks, as if he had seen a ghost. Although he and the others knew we were coming home, he did not realize it was going to be today, so he was quite surprised.

"Sote, is it you? *Abre, dete na Striko, ela tuka!* Oh, uncle's boy, come here!"

He almost picked me up as he grabbed me and hugged as hard as he could. I was much bigger now and a little heaver. He seemed so much older to me and not as strong as I remembered.

"Uncle, I am not a kid anymore. Don't try to pick me up. You might hurt yourself."

For the first time in my life, I saw Uncle Done burst into tears. They spurted out of his eyes and rushed down his cheeks. I tried to comfort him, because I was afraid that if he kept on crying, I would not be able to control my own feelings.

"Uncle, men don't cry. Remember telling me that when I was a kid? So stop. Everything is going to be fine."

He cried out to Father, "Where are you now, brother, to see . . . "

I stopped him before he could finish his sentence. I knew how deep his pain went and where his words would take both of us. There was nothing his words could change. This was not the same man I had left 4 years ago.

The image I had of Uncle Done was of a big, strong man, without a care in the world. He used to say, "Be happy. Why worry? Have fun in your life because everything will fall into place anyway, the way it was meant to, no matter what we try to do differently."

It was depressing to see him look so defeated, so much older and worn out. Stress and depression were etched into the lines of his unshaven face. How could they not be? The destruction, pain and suffering, the murders and the killings took their toll on him and everyone else. He spat out a curse so vulgar, so shocking, it cannot be repeated word-for-word in front of women, children, the elderly—or even on this page. The curse was aimed at heaven, hell, earth and the evil Fate that destroyed the lives and hopes of the Macedonian people.

In less than a week, I clearly understood the scope of our collective tragedy. Before I had arrived home, I thought I had a sense of what our people, my family in particular had endured. But the reality was much worse.

There was a ragged, depressed, undernourished look on the people's faces everywhere I went. It was the look of grief, loss, and hopelessness—colorless faces, and personalities changed forever. The people were more closed, less talkative, very cautious, almost secretive in their conversations. There was little eye contact—perhaps for fear that the eyes would betray a feeling or thought that had to be hidden from the curiosity of others. People were careful as they went about their affairs—perhaps to avoid offending others.

Why these changes? The answer is simple. Everyone had a new, uninvited, unwanted, family member—named Fear. It was part of the family structure and thinking now.

Fear was the constant companion of those who had witnessed, experienced, lived with the bestiality of man's ability to inflict one horror after another on other human beings.

Our people had gone to Hell, and then back to another kind of Hell.

If only I had had a camera then—and mustered the courage to record what I saw—hearts would have broken throughout the civilized world, and a cry of outrage would have been heard throughout the universe.

I could see and feel fear pulsating even at the *pazar,* the marketplace on Saturdays. Even trying to start a conversation was like pulling teeth. No one wanted to show any interest in anyone, or if they did, there would be a careful glance around first, to see if anyone was looking or trying to listen. Then the response would be very brief, spoken in an undertone, and the individual would move away quickly. There were spies everywhere, even spies spying on spies it seemed, waiting to catch someone speaking the forbidden language, Macedonian.

I met some villagers from Turie. I was naturally curious about some of the kids who had been in Bela Crkva with me, particularly about one of my best friends, Lazo. Their reaction was just like that of the others. I spoke to them quietly, with civility, and immediately each looked around to see if they were being observed or overheard. I got a quick and somewhat hostile response.

"Oh, you are one of those kids."

"Yes, I am."

"Well, you have a lot to learn, boy."

"Why? What did we do?"

"You kids don't know about life here; how much to say to people, or what to question. Don't you know that here we are watched all the time?"

"All I am asking is about is Lazo. How he is, that is if you know him. That's all. Besides, who is watching?"

"We have to go before we are seen talking to you. Lazi is fine," and with that, they walked away from me quickly, leaving me by myself, puzzled. Who is watching?

This was the typical behavior from everyone, whether I spoke to someone from Lagen, Kotori, Banitsa, Belkamen or Bouf. Sometimes, I would get no response at all, as if they had not seen nor heard me. For them, I was invisible. During those first few days, Uncle Done and I just sat by the *Kladenche*, talking by the hours, catching up with each other, filling in the gaps of the last 5 years. He asked about his own children, Risto, Ilo and Dina.

"Uncle, we were separated very early after we arrived in Yugoslavia, and I never saw them again. Dina used to write now and then. Krsto [the youngest] was returned with the first group of kids to Lerin."

Uncle wanted to know why my brother Stefo had left Yugoslavia. "Why didn't he remain in Bela Crkva?"

When I explained how Stefo and his age group were selected by the vile Greek Partizan leadership to be sent to the Partizan front lines, Uncle Done erupted.

"I will shit on their Greek blood. They sucked our blood before and they are still looking for fresh blood, those *pezeventsi,* pimps," and he broke down sobbing. I cried with him.

He turned to me, "Why did you kids return? I just don't understand. We did not know what your situation was like there, whether it was good or bad. But I know that no matter how bad it might have been where you were, it could not have been the hell it is here! This place is not for you. I can see your father in you right now. I haven't welcomed you properly, but I must tell you that things here have changed for the worse. You must . . . " He stopped, couldn't finish his sentence.

"Don't worry about that, Uncle, or about anything else. We're going to be fine. I am here now, and I'll try the best I can."

"You don't know these Greek dogs," he protested. "They are sucking our blood still and we don't have much left to give."

Krsto, who had been with me in Bela Crkva for a while, came to look for him. He had left Bela Crkva when I had been in Belgrad, so we didn't have the opportunity to say goodbye to each other. He was as surprised and happy to see me as I was to see him. Hugs and shouts and more hugs! There we were, almost as in the old days, trekking back to the *kaliva*, happy to be together at home. But not quite. There were too many of those most important to us who would never come back home.

When Dedo heard us coming, he started to say how good it was to be together again, that it had been too long since we had been together as a family, and suddenly, he couldn't go on. He broke down and cried, those sightless eyes, crying for what he would no longer be able to see. I walked away quickly, heading for the river.

I felt the unbearable weight of such painful thoughts swirling around in my head. I knew I had made an horrible mistake in coming home. The despair of leaving Belgrad and soccer was unbearable. This overwhelmingly smothering atmosphere of suspicion, repression, secrecy and loss was so destructive. I tried to persuade myself that things could change now that I was home. I just had to decide on a plan, on a goal, on some strategies to create change. I had to pick up the pieces of our lives. Remember, I told myself, you are in T'rsie, right here where you were born and lived so freely. I had to start being Sotir Nitchov again and get reacquainted with my land and my country. I vowed to myself that I would follow through on that goal. It was time to return to the house.

It was already getting dark. The sun had gone down and the green mountains began to take on their shades of black. The moon was beginning to shine, as if to reassure me that life does go on. Nature continues her seasonal cycles regardless of what we humans think we can hold back or change here on earth.

Everyone was getting ready for bed. There were no more individual beds for each person as there had been in the Dom. Just a *postela,* bedding and a blanket. It was up to you to find a spot to sleep.

Dedo and Baba had their own *postela.* I knew I was home again because I could hear Baba nudging Dedo, "*Abre, aro, ne ke se nagurchish nikoi put. Tsel zhivot gurchish.* Hey, you donkey, you're never going to snore enough. All your life you have snored!"

There is no doubt about it. In any snoring contest, I know that Dedo would receive the highest award. I whispered to Baba, "Leave him alone. He is not going to stop now!"

"He is going to awaken the girls," Baba whispered.

"No, they won't hear him. Don't worry."

Upon rising in the morning, water for wash-up had to be brought in pitchers from the river or the Kladenche. I thought to myself, I am going to miss those showers. I wonder who is enjoying that luxury in the Dom now? Here we had a *kazan,* a tub, we filled with cold water. To take a warm bath, a couple of buckets of water had to be heated, and then tossed into the *kazan.* Jumping in quickly to take advantage of the warmer water was a must. Primitive? Oh, yes, but there was always plenty of water!

In Bela Crkva I routinely ran at least 5 miles every morning. I needed to continue that routine for my own mental health, if for nothing else. Where would I run? It wasn't a difficult decision. The road to T'rsie was an easy choice. So, even on my second morning home, I was running down the road. Not many people were out this early. Had they seen me, I'm sure they would have thought that I had truly lost my mind.

I ran all the way to the Chaulata, which is perfect for running, a straight road up the hills, and then lots of bends and curves. Here I was again, only this time there were no horses. Perfect. I stopped, stretched out on the grass just off the road. It was a picture-perfect moment . . . .

. . . In my mind, I was a younger Sote again. Gazing at the sky, looking for the sokol, my thoughts drifted off to that incident with the Germans and the Partisani, shooting at each other, with me in the middle of the action. I could almost hear the frantic shouting from Donevitsa Mangova warning me of the danger to which I paid no attention at all. It's a wonder I wasn't killed that day. Why was I spared? The bullets were whizzing by me from every direction. The mare had been wounded. Her bridle had been struck three or four times. The road sign had been punctured by so many bullets, it could have served as a sieve, but there wasn't even a scratch on me! On that recollection I thought to myself, would I have been better off dead? I shook off thoughts that were heading where I didn't want to go, and decided I had better get up.

As I headed for home, I saw two villagers from Kalugeritsa rounding the bend in the road coming into view. I greeted them, and they returned the greeting but kept on going. A few moments later, one of them stopped and turned back.

"Aren't you Mite's boy? Which one are you?"

"I am Sote, the younger one."

The other man came back and greeted me again. They were from the Kuslai family. He thought he had recognized me, but wasn't certain.

"What are you doing here this early? If the police see you they will take you in.

"Why would they do that? I am not bothering anyone. They wouldn't bother you, would they?"

"No, but then we have an *adia,* identification card, from them."

"I don't need anyone's permission!" I scoffed.

I alarmed them. They both warned me, "It's not safe here. There are lots of wild animals around. You must be careful."

Their warning—in code—was very clear. There were certain kinds of people they urgently wished I would avoid. I thanked them and walked on. I was beginning to feel a little sweaty and chilly at the same time, so I decided to start running again.

When I returned home, the family wanted to know where I had been and what I had been doing. The one thing I detested most was to be questioned closely like that. I knew that they wouldn't understand my determination to maintain my fitness regime. It would take too long to explain and it would be painful as well because it would bring up a difficult subject. It was the subject I wasn't ready to confront yet.

"What are the plans for the day?" I asked, hoping to change the topic, without specifically answering their questions.

My mother answered, "It's a good plan. We are going to visit your Teta Traianka and some of the other relatives." She knew I would like that. Teta was my mother's first cousin, and they were about the same age. They had grown up together, very much like sisters. Teta Traianka had always been my favorite aunt. I was ready and we started out, my mother, sisters and I.

As we entered her yard, Teta came flying out of the house. She hugged me for all she was worth. I hugged her back, tightly. Teta!

"*Na Teta koren, srce, ubav na Teta,* Teta's root and heart, Teta's handsome boy."

If I hadn't cut in she probably would have gone on and on to the point where nobody could possibly recognize me as the boy she was describing.

"*Nemoi, Teto, tolku. Ke me pochudish, pa setne ke barash nekoi sho baye!* Don't, Teto, too much. You are going to put a hex on me, and then you will have to find someone who brays!" I kept hugging her as I answered her.

It was so good to see her again. I knew that she, like so many of the Macedonian women, had gone through hell and back because her husband, *Tetin*, Uncle Traian had joined the Partizans early in 1946. The "brave, heroic, stinking" Greeks found it great sport to beat the Macedonian women whose husbands had joined the Partizan movement. The Greeks beat them not just with fists, but with rifles, guns, wood, anything hard that could produce howls of pain.

In spite of what had happened to her, her face was glowing with tears and smiles. My Teta Traianka!

Past Still Present

Conformity is the jailor of freedom and the enemy of growth.

JOHN F. KENNEDY, 1961

Time was dragging its feet. For the past month or so, I had been trying to adjust to being at home. I made every effort to keep occupied with family matters, but it felt like such an empty, meaningless existence, conforming to the wishes and expectations of the family I loved with all my heart. I wanted to fill every void in their lives, but I felt like a stranger, doing and saying things automatically. The only thing that sustained me through my misery was the memory of my soccer experience. Whenever I let loose those thoughts of the opportunity that had opened for me in Belgrad, try as I would to stay strong, those unbidden tears would stream down my face. I couldn't help myself. Even today, a grown man, hot tears spring to my eyes when I look back. I never could have imagined myself capable of such painful heartbreak.

I hated to have anyone see me in this self-pitying state. It was such a sign of weakness. Weakness or not, I was caught with my emotional pants down, so to speak, by none other than my Teta Traianka.

That morning, I had left rather early to get some wood. The wood supply was always being depleted. After I had chopped for a while, I sat down to rest. Usually I brought something to read relating to sports. I was making attempts to read the Greek newspaper which had a section on sports. Lost in thought, I didn't notice Teta coming, until she was right there in front of me. She caught me as I tried to wipe my eyes. I was so embarrassed.

"Are you hurt? Did you cut yourself?" Her eyes were taking in every aspect of me.

"No, no, nothing like that. I'm sorry you had to see me like this. It won't happen again, I promise."

Gently, she spoke to me, "You know, dear one, I can sense that something is not right. I have been watching you, and something is very wrong. What is it? You pretend to be the same old happy-go-lucky Sote, but you can't fool me. I have something I want to talk to you. Tell me. What is bothering you?"

How could I tell her? How could I tell someone I trusted and loved so much that I hated being here, that I wanted to return to Yugoslavia? She wouldn't understand, and worst of all, she would have to tell Mother, and we would all be devastated, destroyed. It would make their worst suspicions a reality. People, including family, were certain that we *Begaltsi* had been converted by the Yugoslav Communists to reject our families and relatives and our birthplace. What was the point of going into this discussion, even with Teta?

"Ah, forget it, Teto. It's just this fantasy of mine, and it is gone now."

She moved toward me and stood in front of me, very close, and put both her hands on my shoulders.

"Look at me, Sote. How long have we known each other? You do trust me, don't you? Whatever it is that's causing you so much unhappiness, you can tell me. If you feel that whatever this is must be kept secret, it will remain a secret between us. You know that. Now, tell Teta."

This was the moment for absolute truth between us. I looked down at my feet to think for a moment, and decided to share with her the burden I was dealing with.

"Teta, I'll tell you. I know you will understand. No one else understands as well as you. You must know that I don't like being back home. I never thought I would ever say such a thing. It is making me so miserable for lots of reasons, and I could kick myself for coming back. I had such an unbelievable opportunity to make something of myself back there in Yugoslavia.

"But here, I feel so guilty, because all I can see is misery, and I can't do anything to change that. Look at the people here. They are afraid to speak freely, even in the open air. They hide their true feelings, and feel and look lost, lost in their own land! Their heads are always down, so they don't see anybody, afraid to look anyone in the eye!

"Nothing is the same. The village is not the same, with so many houses burned down. And the Greeks, it is even worse now than before. I can't stand their arrogance and their stupidity and their treatment of us Macedonians. They should be looked at as the strangers in our own country. Instead we have allowed them to make us the strangers. What kind of future is there here for anyone?

"Teto, what has happened here, we can not forget, nor can we change the reality. The past is past, yet, no one seems to think of planning for tomorrow. There will be a tomorrow for those of us still alive, Teto, but will there be a future for us, something to look forward to?"

I kept yakking and yakking because I could see she was not only listening, but hearing every word, when she suddenly interrupted me.

"Sote, for most of us here, the world has ended, especially for your mother. Where is her world? Can she plan a future for herself when she has you to worry and wonder about, or for your two sisters, both girls, with no father around them to protect and guide them? Can you not imagine yourself in her shoes? What if you had been your mother, instead of Sote, and saw the terror we lived through? Would you be able to live through every attempt to crush our spirit with beatings, torture, imprisonment, humiliation, and fines, Sote, if you were allowed to live? The enemy sucked the life out of any hope for tomorrow. First your brother, Stefo, still a boy, dying like a man.

"And your father—your mother's husband—her life's *drugar* as we say in Macedonian—a man, equal to any other man, with compassion in his heart. He believed in honesty and fair play. He loved all of you and wanted to protect his family. He really believed the Partisans were the only chance the Macedonians would ever have to be free and equal to any man, so that his children could grow up proudly, intelligently. Your mother and you, Sote, have lost that man, that guardian. Could you, if you were your mother, forget all that and, instead, plan for a future, Sote?

"As I said, for most of us here, the world has ended, but not for you. Her world is buried somewhere in these mountains. You must see that she needs to be helped to rebuild what may be left in her world. There is probably no future here. You will need to begin to find another path that can lead you to a better place, a better time, but not to go back where you have been before. It is foolish, a waste of time and energy, to think that you can go back to what you think you had before. Sote.

"I am sure you know we do not want to walk around like chickens, with our heads bowed. No, we are Macedonians. We know what we are capable of achieving, but we went through so much. We can't go through it again.

"I know this is not what you want to hear. My heart aches for you because your heart aches, too, dear Sote, but something else will come along. Some kind of luck will change things."

There was so much compassion in her voice and eyes. There was nothing I could do or say that would prove her wrong.

"Teta, I understand so much. But good luck doesn't just come along like that," I said, snapping my fingers. "You have to make your own luck. I don't want to hurt anybody, least of all Mother, but I must go back. I know that in a couple of years, I will be able to send for her and Tsotsa and Mara. I'll have some money by then, somehow. Soccer is on my mind all the time. It is my life. Try as I can, I can't erase it from my mind, nor pull it out of my heart."

"How can I be somebody here? There is nothing for me to learn here. In Yugoslavia, I was able to study any subject. I was Macedonian and it didn't bother anyone. No one felt threatened, but here . . . !"

I shrugged my shoulders. There was nothing more I could say.

Teta was incredulous. "That bothers you so much, this football? Sote, football is for kids, bums, fools. As for school, Sote, or some kind of education, forget about it. Start thinking about working the fields. Make some money from that and then leave. Why not think about Australia? We have relatives there, and many of our people are trying to go there."

She confused me a bit.

"First you tell me to stay here, and then you tell me to go to Australia? Why not go to Yugoslavia?"

"*Isto laino se i devete,* because the same shit is there as here."

She paused, "Your uncle is in Canada. If we are able to join him, I will send for you if you are still here."

I smiled at her.

"Laugh," she said indignantly. "Go ahead, laugh!"

"Teto," I reminded her, "you know these Greek dogs won't let you go. You **know** that!"

"They let your uncle go. Why not us?"

I felt I knew the answer to that. "Because they are afraid of people like Uncle. They are happy to get rid of them. They don't want ex-Partisans here, but they will string **you** along and milk you for your money, pretending they will get the papers you have to have, that's all. The Greeks know how to make you bleed in many different ways."

"You're wrong!"

"I hope so, Teta. I hope you will leave here. If anybody deserves to go, it's you. You have suffered more than enough for any three people, not just one."

Teta wasn't giving up yet. "Sote, don't you have an uncle in America, your father's brother?"

"I don't know. I do know I have an uncle in Australia. He wrote to me regularly when I was in Yugoslavia. He did want me to go there, but I turned him down. He sent me some pictures, but I have no memory of him at all."

"Ah, you are a *magare*, Sote. Write to him and tell him you would like to go to Australia. Leave this forsaken place."

"Teto, if I leave here it will be to go to Belgrad. Nowhere else!

"Why Belgrad? What is there that pulls you so?"

"First of all, that is where the football team, the PARTIZANS, are."

"Shit on the *Partizans*! It is because of the Partizans that we are suffering now. What did we gain? We just filled our fields, our mountains and valleys with our bones!"

This was not good. She was really getting upset. We found ourselves sitting on the rocks in the middle of the Lokmata Mountains. Both of us forgot what we had come for. Whatever thoughts were going through our minds, she suddenly asked, "Why were you at the police station. What did you do? Did you swear at somebody?"

"It was just a misunderstanding. There's nothing for you to worry about."

I couldn't stop her from advising me on how to behave, what I shouldn't say, and what I could talk about. Her final words were, "Sote, it would be best if you would keep your mouth shut and tend to your own business!"

Wrong! That did it!

"Teta, if some asshole tries to intimidate me or humiliate me for no good reason, like the kind of clothes I wear, or because of who my father was, or because I am Macedonian and proud of it, then the hell with them and everything else. I am not afraid. I will not stop speaking freely or defending myself. So what are they going to do, shoot me?"

I didn't say out loud what I thought, that they probably would shoot me if I drop my guard.

She shook her head slowly, from side to side. "I can not believe you at all. It's been many years since I heard that kind of talk from your father and your uncles. What did they accomplish? You can see for yourself what has been accomplished. We are the dead and the dying now. All their energy, their plans, all of their words have brought us to this end, just more suffering, depredation and no hope."

Still shaking her head, "How did you take on your father's nature? These times are different now. Everything is much worse, harder than before. Sote, get it through your head. To the Greeks we are nothing!" Her angry voice was full of sorrow. She hugged me, and held me for a moment, saying in my ear, "What am I going to do with you? You are not for this place. You refuse to understand anything."

I said, with a muffled voice, "You see? Already I have made you upset and sick of me. Why not let me go back, without offending everybody else. You do understand, Teta, don't you?"

She let me go, and we both moved toward the wood I had cut, to load the horses. As we walked, she said to me in a resigned voice, "I understand nothing. You are the one who has to understand, not the rest of us."

As we loaded the horses, other *drvari*, wood-cutters were coming down with their loads and stopped to help us. We walked home silently, thinking our thoughts, without having changed anything.

That evening I went to the stadium, knowing that Teta, Mother, and Uncle Sotir were going to discuss me and my nebulous future, providing I survived long enough to have a future!

Greek Crime and Punishment

If men and women are in chains anywhere in the world, then freedom is endangered everywhere.

JOHN F. KENNEDY, 1960

I could not believe my eyes when I saw *Teta* again.. She was smiling at seeing me, still strong as ever, in spite of what she had lived through and what so many Macedonian women lived through. I want to tell you about her courage and her determination to survive in spite of everything.

Teta Traianka was imprisoned in Lerin for 6 to 7 months at a time. Her baby, Kostaki, was less than a year old when she first went to prison, nursing him during her imprisonment. Kostaki's grandmother, Baba Vana, was also imprisoned in Lerin, while *Teta's* other children, 10-year-old Tsila, 7½-year-old Goge, and 5-year-old Tsanda were left to fend for themselves.

At first the entire family had been imprisoned, but later the children were released, all except the baby. That put 10-year-old Tsila in charge of the household, taking care of her brother and sister. She also did the cooking, and prepared food for her mother and grandmother in prison. Anyone caught trying to help this family was in danger of punishment.

A serious problem arose when Tsanda developed an ear infection. No matter how hard Tsila tried, medical treatment for her sister was not available from any doctor in Lerin. Doctors refused to see her, and they would not make any recommendation for treatment. The doctors did not dare to treat children or any member of a Partizan family because of the fear of the police. For a doctor to treat any known Macedonian raised suspicion.

Tsanda's ear became so badly infected that maggots began to crawl around in it. The only treatment possible was a medicine the villagers used to treat their animals. It was called *tsrliva bilka.* That was the only solution for little Tsanda. Tsila treated Tsanda's ear with this *bilka* a few times. It eventually cleared up her infection. However, as a result of the treatment, Tsanda lost 50 percent of her hearing in that ear.

While in prison, *Teta* Traianka befriended another prisoner, a young woman about 24 years of age, who helped her with Kostaki. She made some clothes for the baby, and they tried to keep up their spirits during their imprisonment. Just before *Teta* was to be released for deportation, the police executed the young woman. They gave no reason for her execution, and there was no trial. This was simply a strategy of intimidation the Greeks were fond of using in their determination to destroy the spirit and morale of Macedonians. They chose to murder this woman as an example to other young men and women. In other words, this can happen to you if you resist or object to Greek authority. All the Greeks needed were informers or spies to accuse someone of a crime against the government. The accusation was all that was necessary. Evidence was irrelevant and so, apparently, were witnesses.

Tsila thought her name might have been Antigoni or Evdokia.

After about 7 months of their last incarceration, Baba Vana, Teta and the children were taken out of Lerin and dumped in the village of Moteshnitsa. They were not wanted in Lerin, the Greek police told them. The Greeks abandoned them at night, without food, warm clothing, or even blankets, so they would have to travel in the dark. Baba Vana was 73 years old. Why should the Greeks care if six more Macedonians died, an old woman, a mother and her four children? No one would hold the police responsible. After all, the police were Greeks, weren't they? Besides, there was no one around to act as witnesses, no photographers or journalists to record these inhumane acts and arouse the conscience of the world. Their victims were "only Macedonians". Greece could cover herself with the ancient mantle of myth from the past as "the cradle of democracy."

All through the night this sad little column of defenseless civilians, a woman nursing a baby, an old grandmother aged 73, and three children, aged 10, 7, and 5½ walked. They were shivering with cold and abandoned to the elements. You can see how dangerous they were to Greece.

They walked for hours and hours, a long treacherous trek over Bigla Mountain, until they reached Psoderi.

My father, in the meantime, had received word about *Teta's* ordeal. Father would never allow *Teta* and the family to be abandoned if he could help it. He and *Teta's* brother-in-law, Tsande Panov, reached them and brought them back to T'rsie.

After about 3 months in T'rsie, Baba Vana and young Tsila, her granddaughter decided to go back to their home in Lerin. They did not want to leave it abandoned. When they reached Lerin, an informer had already let the police know that they were back. The police were dispatched to the house immediately and warned them if they did not leave, they would have to report to the police station in the city daily! As Tsila remembers it, even though the police denounced them, berated them—including name-calling and vulgarities—they decided to let them stay, reminding them of their daily duty to report to the police station.

In late 1948, *Teta* and the other children decided to take a chance and return to Lerin to be with Baba Vana and Tsila. As you can imagine, the police had been informed and again Teta had to suffer all kinds of threats and intimidation. However, the jails were packed full at the time, so she was allowed to stay at home, kept under 24-hours surveillance, until the fighting ended in 1949.

Sotir as a professional soccer player by Alex Gigeroff.

During the war, no one knew where my uncle was—let alone whether he was dead or alive. Suddenly, in 1950, released from prison, he showed up in Lerin. There had been no word of any kind.

Tetin, my uncle, had been captured as a Partizan fighter in action in the Peloponesus in southern Greece. He was fortunate in that he was not captured in Macedonia, because Macedonians were usually executed on the spot. What had also saved *Tetin* was that he could speak Greek fluently.

Once released, *Tetin* was put on a train for Lerin. He was traveling home. The war was over. Maybe there was hope that a somewhat normal life could begin again. In that frame of mind, he began to sing. He sang Macedonian songs, patriotic Macedonians songs. He sang every song he remembered. After all, he was a free man now, a free man in Greece. Greek police patrolled the trains and stations, and when they heard him singing in this outlawed language, *Tetin* was charged with treason and was immediately arrested on the train. In addition to his charge of treason, he was accused of making undesirable propaganda, creating a public nuisance and "other crimes against the state."

At the next stop he was taken off the train and put on another one, destination Salonica. There he was taken before a military tribunal to face charges of treason and engaging in Communist activities.

Tetin asked if he could speak in his own self-defense, which was granted. He spoke to them, "Sirs, I ask you, under this blue sky, is it only Greeks that are allowed to live? I sang in my mother's tongue. If that is a crime, then I am guilty!"

He was released, with no comment, and was sent home to Lerin.

Back in Lerin, *Tetin* was arrested again before he even reached his house. The same charges were leveled against him, which kept him in jail for two nights. He was finally released, with the stipulation that he report daily to the police. He was also warned that if he was seen on the streets after 8:00 p.m. in the summer, he would be imprisoned again, only this time it would be a life sentence in one of the island prisons.

The Greek government did not want people like Tetin to remain in Macedonia. The Greeks wanted Macedonians swept out of their native land because they still feared

Sotir and his beloved Teta Traianka at her home in Toronto, Canada, reminiscing.

the Macedonian spirit, even though the war had ended—twice! If at first you don't succeed at the process of ethnic cleansing, try, try, and try again!

There is a happier ending to this woeful chapter of Greek injustice.

Tetin's sister in Canada eventually brought them to one of the free and democratic nations of the world. She applied for and filed papers for Tetin to emigrate to Canada. Three years later, in 1954, he was able to send for the entire family, reuniting with all of them and settling in Toronto, Canada, happily in freedom and prosperity together, speaking their own language as well as English.

Teta died in Toronto. The torture and beatings she endured resulted in broken ribs and collar bone, a damaged shoulder and other injuries. They were not properly treated earlier and eventually took their toll. At the time she died, I was hospitalized and was not permitted to attend the funeral. Her death dealt another blow, but I carry the image of her in my heart—with all the others who were so beloved.

Tsila married George Mangov and they are grandparents.

Kostaki, the prison baby, is also a grandfather. He is also a very successful businessman and owner of a large electric company in Toronto.

The Emblem

Prejudice is the child of ignorance.

WILLIAM HAZLITT, 1839

Before I became a *Begalets*, whenever I went to Lerin as I was growing up I always looked forward to getting there because of my Teta Traianka. She made my visits fun events because she was such a happy, positive person. We never pretended with one another. You could always expect Teta to be realistic and direct when discussing events or people. Never would she do or say anything that would be hurtful. She seemed to be goodness and kindness personified, always sharing with me as well as others, helping as much as and wherever she could. I can't remember her being worried, but she wouldn't pretend to be happy if she were not.

As a youngster, one year I spent an entire winter with her. We got to know each other well. I felt I learned so much from her perspective of people and events. I never had to pretend with her. I could be myself and that's why I loved her and appreciated her so much.

And now, after 4 years and a lifetime had passed, those of us who had survived were together again. Even those who had not, were with us. We were close to each other before the full horrors of two major wars tore our lives apart, but because of that separation and loss, we were now bound together even more closely.

What made our reunion even more enjoyable was that my cousins Goge and Kostaki liked soccer also. For whatever length of time I was to be in Lerin, I looked forward to the opportunity to teach them as much as I could about how to be more effective soccer players.

For the special occasion of my return home, Teta made a delicious *burek*, and did she know how to make it! Without any encouragement, I think I ate every piece that was available, and it was beyond delicious. Teta Traianka had outdone herself. Baba Vana, her mother-in-law, with whom Teta shared so much pain and sorrow, was there, also. I used to call her *Tsrvena* Baba Vana because of her very rosy complexion.

It was such a satisfying visit with loving, close relatives, with an outstanding feast, that no one was ready to stop talking or move. Finally, my young cousins decided that we ought to go to the center of town. That sounded interesting to me. So we did.

When we arrived in town Uncle Sotir's daughters, Vanglia and Tula, whom I hadn't seen since the winter of 1946, were there too, and so there were more rounds of surprised greetings, hugs and catching up. We met so many people, young ones who were friends of the cousins, as well as others, that I got a little confused with the names and relationships.

Ari, our neighbor's son, saw me and came over to welcome me home. What memories surfaced when I saw Ari, the friend of my pre-*Begaltsi* days! I recalled how my father had saved Ari's father's life from the clutches of the Germans and Bulgarians. Although Ari was born in Lerin, his dad was born somewhere in Asia Minor. His father came to Macedonia in 1922. I remember Ari saying, "I am going to become a Macedonian." Only he couldn't really speak Macedonian. In fact, we both laughed at his efforts, but he really tried to learn the language.

This was turning into the best day I had had since my return home, I felt, except for one thing. Too much Greek was being spoken, which I couldn't understand. What was puzzling me was that everyone we met knew that neither my sisters nor I spoke Greek, and I was beginning to get more than a little impatient with all that Greek chatter. In fact, it was getting on my last nerve, and I thought, I had better say something before I exploded.

"Listen, I don't have a clue as to what you are saying when you talk in Greek. And why are you doing that? From now on, speak to me in Macedonian!"

Well, they did from that day on, but they were very careful when and where they spoke in our mother tongue. The children were especially cautious. Ari and I moved aside and he asked me, "How about getting together tomorrow?"

I thought it was a good idea and nodded agreement.

Later, as the day slipped into evening, Mother and I had an opportunity to have a little private conversation, while Teta was putting the house in order. Mother wanted to discuss our sleeping arrangements, which apparently had been troubling her since we arrived home.

"Sote, our living and sleeping arrangements in the *kaliva* are too small now."

Where was she going with this? I asked myself.

"Oh, it's fine. We can make some changes, so don't worry about it."

Teta was listening to us, of course, and she came right to the point.

"Your mother is a little concerned about the sleeping, the water, and other things. You will come and stay with me in my house and I will not take no for an answer."

I guess that settled that. I was to be on the move again. I felt like excess baggage, but that had to be the arrangement until we moved into the house next to Uncle Sotir, which belonged to the *svatia,* the mother of his daughter-in-law, Mirianthy. Her mother and brother had left for Canada. Later, Mirianthy and Mite also left for Canada. Dedo, however, did not want to leave his *kaliva*, so some kind of accommodation had to be worked out to meet his and Baba's needs. Those needs were very simple. My sisters would bring their meals in daily and, since we all worked the fields together, it would only be at night that we would be separated. We made some repairs on the *kaliva* to make it more comfortable for Baba as well.

Sotir, the future star of the Partizan Soccer Club became a peasant and farmer all over again. Plowing and irrigating was no problem, but now I had to learn *kosenie,* cutting and bundling the hay, for our animals' winter feed. Gathering firewood was no problem, but the locations had changed. We needed the firewood not only for heating our house, but to sell to others in the *pazar* to supplement our income. Everybody needed wood, for it was the main resource for home heating. My partner in gathering wood was my best pal and favorite aunt, Teta Traianka. I looked forward to going up into any one of the mountains—Lokmata, Sokolets, or Luta—and working there all day. It truly was a full day's work, chopping, cutting, loading the horses and sending them to Lerin, where they were unloaded and sent back for more. The horses didn't have to be led. They knew their way back and forth. By the time the horses returned, we had more wood ready for loading.

I always felt so good whenever I was in our mountains. The air was fresh and invigorating. I enjoyed this chore because it also served as a workout for me, helping me build upper-body strength, for soccer was never far from my thoughts. Teta, noting how vigorously I took to the task of chopping, said to me, "I don't think I have ever seen anyone enjoy chopping wood as much as you."

"Teta, I am in training. I have to stay in good shape for football."

"Football?" She couldn't believe it. "Football? Are you out of your mind? You don't need football here. You need a plow, a *baltija, kopachki,* an axe, shovels. Sote, you have to get your priorities straight. You can't be doing silly things. You're home now, and your mother needs you to help her out. You're not here to run and play like some crazy kid!"

What could I say to that? If she couldn't understand, who was there who would? The answers to those questions were *nothing* and *nobody.* I kept my mouth closed. When I didn't respond, she looked at me for a few minutes and then spoke again.

"Listen, son, I hope you are not thinking of running off again and leaving us."

"Teto," I said, "I do have a plan, but I am not going to run off. I'm not going to leave now, but when I do, I'll let everybody know why I leave, especially you. I won't go without saying goodbye. How can I?"

"Be quiet, you pup," she said to me. She didn't know how to deal with what I said to her.

Teta decided to change the subject and began to talk about girls. In her mind, she had worked out a strategy to anchor me for good in Lerin, which was to marry and settle down. She had a very rich girl in mind.

"Teto, neither the girl nor I know each other. Don't you think that might be a problem? And besides, if she is beautiful, I'll marry her without taking her money. But if she is ugly, you marry her and keep her wealth. How does that suit you?"

She laughed. "You can say what you want, but if I were you, I would go after her and marry her without wasting any time."

"Fine with me. Let's go and we'll have the wedding this Sunday. How does that sound to you?"

Teta laughed again. "Go ahead, Sote, make fun of me. But wait till you see this girl. You will change your mind very fast."

"She is probably the ugliest, stupidest girl in town. If she is the way you described her, why isn't she already married? I think I will have to get you glasses so that you can see more clearly," I teased.

"*Abre, magare. Mulchi! Ochila mi trebalo!* Oh, you jackass. Shut up! I need glasses!" she retorted, highly insulted.

Even though both of us enjoyed this exchange, I decided it was time to change the subject and I started chopping again. By this time, others had joined us. I looked up and suggested there was better wood for chopping on the other side of the mountain from where we were. Simultaneously, I heard, "Oh, no. Not over there! There are lots of land mines over there. You can't go there!"

"Land mines? Who would mine that area? It's useless. Nobody goes there."

But both Pandel and Itso insisted, "It is full of mines."

I challenged them, "Let's check it out," and started walking in the direction leading to the other side of the mountain, but Teta stepped up and pulled me back.

"Have you lost your mind? Aren't there enough dead already, or do you want to kill us all? Nobody is going to go there!"

She was furious with me, and the message came through loud and clear. If Teta said that it was so, then it was so. I assured everyone that I was not really going to go there, and besides, it was time to return home.

By that evening, Teta had already told Mother about my near escapade in the woods. Before I even had a chance to wash up, Mother lambasted me. I don't ever recall seeing her this angry. She usually presented a calm, controlled manner, but not this evening. She was truly riled.

"I lost your father and your brother. I don't want to lose you. I can't lose you. After all we went through I didn't bring your home for. . . . "

"Listen, Mother. If you worry so much about me, if you are going to be this fearful, this protective of me, then I should go back to Yugoslavia. You can't worry about me every minute, every time I step outside. I am a big boy now. I understand the difference between right and wrong. I know what is dangerous, so don't worry about anything!"

She didn't know what to say. She just stroked my face with her palms to simmer me down and then, clearly upset, she left me.

I cleaned up and set out to meet Ari, whose full name was Aristides. We had made plans to go down to the *gipedo*, the stadium in Lerin. He was waiting for me on the steps of my uncle's house, talking to my cousin, Done. I wore my Partizan sweat suit. They both admired it and complimented me on it.

Lerin had two soccer teams, and I was filled with curiosity to see what kind of soccer they played. As we headed toward the stadium, I became aware of people staring at us. Every person eyeballed us. What are they looking at, I wondered. We were just three ordinary guys walking, talking, minding our own business.

I said to Ari, "I didn't know how popular you were. What did you do, kill or steal some chickens, or what?"

He shot back at me, "I think they are staring at you and your sweat suit."

"So what's wrong with it? Does it have any holes in it? It's brand new. Never washed. The Club gave it to me just before I left Belgrad."

"It's the emblem, or what is on the emblem, including the name Partizan. That's what they're staring at."

I still didn't get it.

We continued down past Platia Aron, the small sandy park with a bench on each corner. We were almost at the center of Lerin when two policemen and a civilian with a rifle on his shoulder came toward us. They carried themselves as if they owned a large part of the universe, and we should be properly impressed. Speaking with the tone of very important people who have been offended by us lesser beings and sounding quite harsh, they stopped us. Pointing at my sweat suit, in their arrogant and very rude manner, they began to harangue me. Although I didn't understand a word of what they were saying, I could guess what their problem was. My sweat suit seemed to be bothering them no end. Ari started to translate to me in broken Macedonian and that made me laugh. My laughter upset the three *very important people*. Their facial expressions spoke volumes of disapproval of my behavior.

I said to Ari, "I never thought that I would ever see the day when one *prosviga* would have to translate Greek into Macedonian!" I slapped Ari on his back and congratulated him, encouraging him to go on.

"You are doing a terrific job, Ari, very well done."

Apprehensively, Ari said to me, "It's not funny and it's hard. You know I don't speak Macedonian very well."

"You're doing fine as far as I'm concerned. Nobody is beating you up. We Macedonians speak Macedonian all the time, plus we get beat up for doing so! See what you're missing?"

"Listen, Sotiri, these idiots are serious," Ari pleaded with me.

When Ari said *idiots*, the civilian understood what he had said, because Ari had asked me how to say *idiots* in Macedonian. Ari explained to the two *horofilaka,* Greek policemen, what I told them. The civilian, whom I didn't know, was a *pushkar*, the word we use to describe a Grecophile or *grkoman,* took over the explanation. He knew Macedonian very well and told me that I was not allowed to wear this type of clothing here. And that was all I needed to hear!

I took a good measure of the situation and began, "Why not? Do you want me to go naked? What is wrong with my clothes?"

"You are wearing Communist clothes, with the red emblem. The name Partizan is on it, and that is not allowed here. That is a terrible name. Here in democratic *Elada*, Greece, Partizan is a bad, offensive name."

I told them to kiss my ass and started to walk away, leaving poor Ari to deal with them. One of the policemen grabbed my arm, warning me not to talk in such a vulgar way. I mumbled something that could pass for an apology. Then, almost in unison, the two policemen and the civilian told me to burn the sweat suit because it offended a lot of Greek citizens. Now this was really getting to be more than I was going to handle sweetly.

"Look, I just apologized for my crudeness, but you are forcing me to use vulgar language. Why don't you go to hell and leave me alone? Don't ever grab or touch me again or you will end up without any hands to hold your spoon!"

Poor Ari, still translating, told me that they were going to take me to the police station.

"Well, I'm sorry, but you are going to have to wait until I break one of your stupid laws!"

The civilian seemed more determined than the police to take me in. He kept on pointing and yakking about my suit, repeating that I should burn it, which only fed my fury.

"When you burn that garbage you are wearing, then maybe, just maybe, I will burn mine. So until then, see you around. Goodbye," and I, with Ari tagging along, took off.

They followed us to the stadium where we found even more police on the grounds. However, once we were in the stadium where one of the Lerin soccer teams was warming up, no policeman even seemed to care that we were there.

Soccer was the equalizer, I guessed.

One of the teams was named Elas, and Ari introduced me to a few of the players. I remember meeting Befa, Sote, Pandeli and Panagioti. Befa, who was from Armensko seemed to be the leader. He was living in Lerin and working in a bank. Pando was from Bapchor. Sote was from Nevoleni and Panagioti was a *prosviga*. All were Macedonians. Befa asked if I had played in *Servos*. Most of the people in Lerin referred to Yugoslavia as *Servos*, Greek for Serbia.

"No, I only played for Yugoslavia." I felt I needed to straighten out some things with Befa, whose name was Belcho.

"First of all, I am not Serbian and I didn't come from there. Secondly, I was born and raised in T'rsie and Lerin. Thirdly, I am a Macedonian just like you. And fourthly, I have played some soccer."

He and the others seemed surprised at what I said, but I only heard one comment, and that came from Pando. "Hey, you Macedonian from T'rsie!" I turned toward him.

With a smile on his face, he continued, "We are neighbors."

He was speaking in Macedonian, telling me that he liked my sweat suit very much. He began to ask me things about Yugoslavia and soccer. When I told them I knew Bobek, Chaikovski, Shostaric the goalie, Simanovski, Mitic Zebec and others on the team, and added that I played with the 18-year-olds and under, Pando and the Elas team were really impressed. As for me it felt so good to be able to talk about soccer again. Their expressions were something to see when I told them about the times when the first team let us play with them.

One of the boys asked me which team in *Veligradi*, Greek for Belgrad, I was with. When I pointed to the emblem on my chest and said, "This team, Partizan", their eyes nearly popped out of their heads. That was a great moment for me. I felt I was back among the living.

They asked if I would participate in their training session. Would I! I just needed a little time to warm up. I didn't have soccer shoes, so I had to use my tennis shoes, but I was ready. We waited around for about 15 minutes, but nothing was happening.

"When are they going to start?"

"Start what?" Pando asked.

"When are you going to start training?"

"We are, now!" was the answer.

Maikata! This was training? I thought to myself, are these people ever behind the times!

I started to shoot on goal. I had them in awe, so stunned that I could shoot like that. Then the requests started.

"Show us some of the different shooting techniques; curving the ball; chipping; dipping; low volley; high volley; skimmers on the ground . . . "

They weren't even aware that there are more than one or two ways of shooting and kicking the ball. After a few demonstrations, we called it quits. Befa asked me if I would join them at the next practice.

The other Sote said, "I would very much like to learn the shooting techniques."

To both of them I said, "No problem. I would like to join you."

Ari and I walked back together. As we were leaving, I felt pairs of eyes following us. However, no one stopped us and nothing further was said. I knew there was bound to be a follow-up to my encounter with the policemen.

A few days later Ari and I were both summoned to the police station by the same civilian, the one-eyed jack, and another policeman. No reason was given for the summons, but Ari urged me to clear up whatever the matter might be.

As we made our way to the police station, Aris was greeted by several people. Once we arrived inside the station, we were directed into a very plush office. In walked an obviously very important person. He was wearing a uniform, sporting a number of medals on his chest, some gold stars and ribbons. The gold-colored ropes that draped around his arms and over the shoulder were really something to see. For a moment I thought to myself, "Could this be the King of Greece?"

He greeted us with a cordial, "*Kalimera, pedia*, good morning, boys." With a sweep of his hand he motioned us to sit down. I was dressed again in the running suit, with the word Partizan across the emblem of the *Yugoslovensko Sportsko Druzhestvo*, flames sprouting up around a big red star. It still didn't penetrate my thick skull that I was wearing the most provocative symbol in the world to these people. I had my soccer shoes slung across my shoulder, not arrogantly, but just the way any guy would.

Although this man was obviously a ranking member of the police force, I had no idea what his rank was. He asked, "Do you know why you are here?"

Ari interpreted and I answered, "No, I don't"

"Well, look at you. Look at what you are wearing. People here resent it," he said, talking to Ari, but looking at me.

Here we go, I thought, another example of Greek *democratia,* democracy.

"I don't mean to be disrespectful, Sir, but I am getting sick of this harassment because of a sweat suit I am wearing. The only people who seem to be upset are you people and one *pushkar* in particular. No one else has objected."

A little more smoothly he replied, "Now, I have nothing against you, but you must understand our situation. We just finished a nasty war here. People do not want any reminder of that war. It is an insult to them."

"Hold on, Sir. It may be an insult to you and your like, but not to the people who were born, raised and died here. Isn't that what you are really trying to tell me?"

Even more smoothly, diplomatically, sympathetically, he continued, "You were kidnapped, *pedomazoma*. You didn't see the war. They took you and taught you the Communist system, so I know it's going to take some time before you adjust and realize you are free here."

I just laughed. He looked at me without anger, just puzzled.

Respectfully, without anger at him, I told him, "Sir, when I first saw you today, you appeared to be an intelligent man. But the more you talk, the more that initial intelligence that I thought I saw is beginning to evaporate. Neither I nor the 30,000 or more children were ever kidnapped. This is the first time I have heard that term used to describe us, the *Detsa Begaltsi*. The most important thing we were ever taught was that we must always remember our name, who we are, where we came from, and why we had to leave, which has saved us from death and destruction and the loss of our identity."

I went on, "We had our own Macedonian schools taught by Macedonian teachers in the Macedonian language. We were taught never to forget our birthplace, our country of origin. This is my country of origin. This is my birthplace, but since I have returned home, all I can see and everything I hear tells me that no one exists here except Greeks. You talk about being free here? About democracy here? I don't think so. You do not understand what freedom or democracy is."

Now I was beginning to get pissed off and getting a little heated. I could see that I was affecting him too.

He snapped at me, "Are you telling me that you were free under Communism?"

"Sir, the freedom that the Communists gave the people including the Macedonians in Yugoslavia is something you will never see here," I taunted him.

"I can see that you like the Communist system!"

"You know," I kept on, "I'll take any system that lets me be what I am; that doesn't attempt to change my name; that lets me speak my language and does not try to stop me from wearing what I want to wear. If that is your idea of a bad system, then you are mistaken."

His annoyance with me was showing now, and his facial expressions were changing, speaking volumes.

"We've been here at least a half hour," I said, taking charge, "I already told the soccer players that I would join them today."

He got up from his chair, walked around the room, thinking. I waited, silently. He came back to his desk again, and said, "I'll tell you what. You can keep your suit, but you can't wear it in public."

Determined to make my point, once again I said, "Sir, I will wear it whenever I wish and I will go wherever I wish to go. If you don't like it—or anybody else for that matter—too bad. If you think I broke any law, arrest me and lock me up right now. But before you do anything, I will have to notify the Red Cross in Geneva and Belgrad. I think I have had enough coercion and intimidation here to last me for a lifetime."

I felt that bold and that empowered because we kids were given telephone numbers to contact the Red Cross should we encounter any difficulty. I wanted to believe that the Red Cross might have some concern about the reality of how Greek democracy worked. As soon as I mentioned the Red Cross, he called someone from the other office and told him to get somebody on the phone. Turning to me, he switched subjects, asking where I came from; how we were treated in Yugoslavia, and did I like *podosvero*, meaning soccer.

He reflected, "There seems to be so much misunderstanding in the world today."

Did I say he was a smoothie? No, he certainly was not. He was a hypocrite, full of bullshit. I thought I should give him a little more to chew on.

"I shall be going back to Belgrad as soon as I can make arrangements."

I meant it. While sitting in his office, a loathing had begun to build in me for this man and everything he stood for. I knew that I would not be able to live like this, under unlawful, illegal, undemocratic restraints and threats. I was overflowing with regret that I had not stayed in Belgrad, giving up my dream of playing professional soccer. What was I thinking?

Defiantly, I continued, "Here, you are 50 years behind the times. I have been to Italy, Spain, Hungary, Germany, Romania, Bulgaria, Morocco, Sweden, Switzerland and France. I have never seen the kind of stupidity in the treatment of their own citizens in those countries as I have seen here. I could almost feel sorry for you Greeks, but I have no sympathy for you. My sorrow is for my Macedonian people."

I might have gone on, but we were interrupted by the telephone. He signaled to Ari and me to wait in the hall. While we were waiting, Ari's brother, Stefanos, and his uncle came in. I knew Stefanos but not his uncle, who happened to be a *horofilakos*. Ari explained the situation to them. They said that they would talk to the *Astonomos*, the police commissioner.

After a little time had passed, the commissioner called us back into the office. All four of us went in. Since the uncle happened to be a captain, he did the talking. After a little discussion, the commissioner turned to me and began in an expansive and conciliatory tone.

"There is no need to call anyone. You are as free as a *pulak*i, a bird. No one will bother you anymore. You will see, and we will prove to you young people that our system is better than any Communist system. You are free to go. *Adio*, goodbye."

I had to have the last word. "One thing, sir. You couldn't carry the *pintsi* of the Yugoslavs at any level. Goodbye."

We left.

What or who persuaded the commissioner to release me is a mystery to me to this day. Whether he had actually contacted the Red Cross or whether Ari's relatives persuaded him, I was never able to find out.

An hour and a half were lost, making me late for the practice at the stadium. I took out my frustration and anger on the soccer field. When I went home that evening, I could see worry written all over my mother's face. Word had gotten to her about my whereabouts. She began to voice her worry and to vent her anger with me, but I cut her off abruptly.

"Haven't I asked you not to worry about me? There is nothing to worry about. I am home after all, in one piece. So why waste your energy? It was just a simple misunderstanding."

"Please, Sote, get rid of your sweat suit. Burn it, before something terrible happens."

"No. That is something that will never happen. I will not throw this suit into the fire."

That was our first serious confrontation and disagreement since our reunion and return. Would it be our last?

I don't know when Mother succeeded in taking my mementos. Most of them disappeared, either burned or buried. Things like little club flags, small trophies, patches, shirts, jackets, everything from my soccer years that I had brought back with me was eventually gone. When I would ask her what happened to a particular item, she would always answer with the question, "Da ne gi ukradi nekoi? Maybe someone stole them?"

Only when I was able to bring her to America did she finally confess to me, even before I began to ask her again, "I buried them on the farm, down by the river."

I feel that she carried a sense of guilt about what she had done, especially after she saw that I had enclosed the Partizan emblem in glass and hung it on the wall of our home. It was the only remaining link to a brief, unbelievably happy chapter in my life as a Begalets in Yugoslavia.

A Palooka Gets his Due

The bigger a man's head, the worse his headache.

PERSIAN PROVERB

After my last visit to the police station, I didn't encounter any more serious problems with the police. I just thanked God that Lerin was the home city for two soccer teams. Beside the Elas team, there was another team called Megas Alexandros. These teams provided the only outlet for my frustrations in Lerin. A sense of camaraderie developed between the soccer players of both teams and me, due perhaps to the fact that word had spread that in Yugoslavia I was recognized as having some soccer talent. Was that what might have stopped the police and that *pushkar* from harassing me? Or was it my reference to the Red Cross when the police accused me of deliberately provoking the citizenry of Lerin by sporting my *subversive Communist* sweat suit around town? Who knows? I wore that Partizan sweat suit whenever I felt like it, without being bothered about it again by anyone in town, except for my mother and uncle.

The level of soccer in Lerin was far from the professional level to which I had been exposed in Belgrad. What a privilege that had been! However, in dry weather, as they say, even hail satisfies. Just being on a soccer field again was gratifying. A friendship developed among the soccer players based not only on our mutual love of the game, but also because we were young men with a Macedonian upbringing. Representatives from each team invited me to play for them. The choice was obviously mine, so I chose Elas because of my friendship with Pando, Sote, Befa, Panagioti, and Ilia.

Panagioti, a *prosviga* born in Lerin, carried himself as more Macedonian than some of the others. He was so proud to be one. He didn't seem to be intimidated. The other players were obviously fearful of the label "Macedonian" and didn't want any attention drawn to them.

The Megas team seemed to be the better team. The rivalry between them was great, especially since the Elas team had not been able to beat them in 2 years running! I love the nature of competition, so the juices in me began to surface, and I was looking forward to my first game of competitive play in Lerin. The game was scheduled on a Sunday at 4:00 p.m.

The soccer field itself was nothing but plain sand, no grass. My fellow soccer player, Pando, now a good friend, warned me to expect the unexpected. I smiled to myself. That's the story of my life, I thought, expect the unexpected. I felt the hostility between the teams hovering in the air around us. Pando again cautioned me, pointing toward their large defender whose name was Stafilidis, another *prosviga.*

I studied this palooka during the warm-ups. Yeah, he was large and he seemed strong, but his movements were clumsy. He used only his right foot to shoot, and that was it. He didn't display any accurate shots, even when he was clearing the ball defensively. My analysis was simply that the guy was unskilled, had little talent. Because of his size and his lack of skill as a player, other players were needlessly hurt. Knowing this, players stayed away from him.

I had a strategy that I thought would teach him a lesson or two. To the other Sote I explained, "For the first 25 minutes, we will go through the middle and bring the ball there. Then, we cross over from left to right, through the 18-yard line and watch for the ball. Every time we get the ball, we shoot on goal, *every time*!"

I instructed Panagioti, "Follow the middle zone about 10 yards back on both sides behind me." We made each player responsible for his position and when and where to deliver the ball.

"It's going to be hard for all of us at first, but we're going to make it harder for our opponents!"

During our practices, I had critiqued the players. Each one had been playing an "individual" type of soccer. I saw no teamwork, no leadership, no creativity, no set plays and worst of all no coordination. Without coordination, each player played as if he were a one-man team.

I had been told that Befa, the star of the team, was very shy and a little afraid to play. Now, how was I, the new man in town, supposed to tell the star that he can't start or play in any other position except center forward? After all, I wasn't the coach, and I didn't have the authority to name the line-up. When he had invited me to play with the team and asked me what position I played, I told him that in Yugoslavia we played all positions. It didn't matter to me. It really didn't.

When I gave the instructions on this Sunday, I told Sote where to look for the ball, figuring I would be playing center forward or striker. However, Befa put me in as a midfielder, and that was fine with me.

In the kick-off the Megas won the toss. A few minutes into the game only about three scrapes occurred. The game seemed so simple because each player was so predictable. There was precious little team coordination. Did I ever enjoy the game, succeeding with all my movements! It wasn't that I was a better man, but I was a skilled player because of the superior training I had been privileged to have in Yugoslavia. I was able to intercept the ball most of the time. For 30 minutes we played, neither side scoring.

Befa was useless against the palooka, Stafilidis, and I began to understand what the guys meant when they described Befa as "shy". He wasn't shy. He was just plain scared of the palooka. In any competitive arena, when one of our guys holds back and doesn't give his all, I get aggressive. You have to hustle in soccer and give as good as you get, if not better. So I took the bull by the horns and said to Befa, "Listen. You are scared of him, so there is no advantage for you to stay in this position. Let me play against him. I think I know how to handle him."

Befa didn't say anything, but we switched positions.

To Pando, I said, "As soon as we get possession of the ball, I want it."

Our team got possession of the ball and directed it to me. I began to dribble slowly toward the palooka. This was his moment to scare me as well. He started swearing at me, calling me names, and all kinds of Greek trash talk, trying his best to intimidate me with his facial expressions as well. Although I had learned only a few Greek words, I understood all that he was saying. But it didn't matter to me. I could give as good as I got. Vulgarity was no stranger to me. I was on the field to play soccer.

I made a move to the right. He followed. I turned sharply to the left, dragging the ball along with my right foot. He went to right field. I went toward the goal alone, one-on-one, faked out the goalie, and just pushed the ball into the net. It was 1 – 0 in our favor.

As I walked toward the center, palooka swung at me. I ducked, and one of the other players got clobbered, which started the melee. I watched until everything cleared and the game started again. Now Megas started to play a rougher game and, as a result, they played more stupidly, personifying the typical Greek ego, *pios ime ego!* Now the referee seemed lost. He had no idea what the rules of soccer were.

Mr. Palooka tried so hard to get me that he hurt his team more. He was way too slow and too dumb to catch me. I could anticipate his every move. We upped the score to 3-0 by the end of the first half.

During the break, I asked my team whether they would agree to my using some tactics to embarrass Mr. Palooka and teach him a lesson once and for all. When they gave me their blessing, I had already planned a strategy for this dummy. I promised myself I was going to make this son of a bitch remember this day forever and never forget who I was.

I asked the guys to tell me every vile word and name in Greek they could think of. They did, with pleasure. Then I asked, "Is he married? Does he have sisters?" I got my answers and my ammunition. I was ready for him.

The second half began. The first time he had possession of the ball near his goal, I made sure he knew I was close to him. In a voice that only he could hear, I said to him, "Boy, your sister—is real good."

What I said shocked him so, that he dropped the ball and started after me. I ducked, picked up the ball and scored. Now it was 4 – 0. The Megas team began to scream at each other. The referee waited for them to pull it together and come to the center to restart. As they moved toward the center still screaming at each other, I passed the palooka again.

"Hey, that wasn't your sister last night. That was your mother!"

He ran for me, chasing me around, but he couldn't catch me to save his life. He was much too slow.

The referee restarted the game. Once again we got possession of the ball because I timed my trash talk extremely well. At the point when one of their other players had the ball, palooka watched the play. When that happened, the nearest player on our team was to pick up the ball and make a long a pass to one of the wings. I timed my movements carefully, as I was near the palooka. His coach called to him, warning him not to fall for whatever the Servos—that was me—was saying. The agitation had aggravated the palooka so that his entire body was shaking with fury. Just before we made it 6–0, I taunted him, "Your wife told me last night that she needs a real man, not a boy!"

He couldn't take any more and went directly to the bench.

As I passed the bench playing the ball, I rubbed it in a little more deeply, saying to him with a jeer, "Your wife was right. You're not a man. You can't even finish a soccer game."

I kept on with the trash talk whenever I passed near him. He kept on calling me everything he could think of. He was good at dishing it out, but definitely could not take it.

The game finally ended. Elas was elated that we beat Megas to the ground. After 2 years of defeat, they were more than ready to celebrate. Later that evening, we met the palooka again. I asked Sote to introduce me formally. The guy was so surprised that I wanted to talk to him, that he didn't know what to say or how to handle the situation.

I said to him, "I want to apologize for saying all those nasty things to you, but, you know, you really have asked for it for a long, long time."

I wasn't sure what his reaction was going to be, but I was ready for anything, except for his response. "All I want to know is how a short kid like you can do all that you did today. I can't believe what I saw!"

I could see he was sincere, that he meant it, so I replied to him quite honestly, no boasting, "I had masters for teachers. They taught me everything they knew. When nastiness is called for, return it doubly, but always play the game. Both of our teams have a lot to learn about soccer. I don't mean it in a negative way, because Elas needs good coaching, too."

He was obviously listening, drinking in what I was saying to him. "You talk like an old man, but you sure don't play like one. Why don't you come and play for us? We are the better team."

I responded to him by saying, "If you guys were smart, you could form one hell of a team here and compete with Voden, Kostur, Kozhani, Negush and the rest of the teams in your league. There are teams in Solun, Yanina and Seres, you know."

There was agreement there on that point. There was consensus that it was a good idea and they ought to get together and discuss the possibility. But all the time I was in Lerin, they never got together. The two teams continued to compete separately against other teams. Elas played against Megas twice more. Although a truce existed between the palooka and me, we never could be friends. I really had no respect for him.

Mistiki Astonomia

In difficult situations when hope seems feeble, the boldest plans are the safest.

LIVY, 29 B.C.

My family was not at all pleased that I continued to indulge my passion for soccer. Among many households in Macedonia as well as among the Macedonian Diaspora, playing ball was nothing but a waste of a young man's time. Only bums drifted into football or soccer. A young man's time should be spent learning a trade, or studying for a profession, or working the fields, or marrying well—that is, into a family with money and property.

"*Abre* Sote, you will look like the biggest fool playing ball, and especially with the attitude you have, people won't want to have anything to do with you." Mother kept after me, speaking variations of those words—but it only built up my frustration and ardor for soccer.

Seeing that she was not even making a dent in my resolve to continue using my free time to play the game, in fear and desperation, she appealed to Uncle Sotir to see what he could do to make me understand what the family considered the error of my ways. They were so afraid of consequences, not for themselves necessarily, but for my sisters and me. That was the key concern for mother. I knew it then as well as I know it now.

Uncle Sotir was one of the most practical, pragmatic men. He kept his silence, except when he felt undercurrents of danger to any member of the family. When he did speak, the words came from the wisdom of experience, from his very soul. Knowing how much he had suffered during the war, we listened with respect. Uncle Sotir had been imprisoned, beaten, tortured, because of his nephew, Lazo, who was one of the first to join the Partizans. Lazo's father died during the Greco-Turkish War in 1922. Since then, Until Sotir had raised Lazo as his own.

One evening Uncle Sotir took me aside to speak to me privately. Out of earshot of the others, he began, "Listen to me, Sote. Listen carefully what I say to you. Don't think that because you came from Yugoslavia, you have some kind of protective shield around you. These Greek leeches will suck every ounce of your blood whenever they feel like it, and they don't even have to have a reason. Who will question these animals? Nobody in the world cares about us. They don't even know that we exist. But with your character and attitude, you are inviting disaster and destruction not only for yourself, but for your mother, your sisters, and your grandparents. Those Greeks will do things to you that will make your head, your total body shake and tremble like mine, *if* they let you live that long. They are masters of torture. The more they hear you scream, the greater the enjoyment for them."

He unnerved me with what he was saying. I stared ahead of me as he spoke, then turned to him and asked, "Why bring this up? It isn't as if I have broken a law or robbed someone. The truth is, I haven't done anything wrong."

"But that is not what I hear. People are talking about you, and when people talk the way they are now, it means trouble not only for you, but also for the rest of us. Whether what they are saying is true or not, those *gnusni,* stinking Greeks don't care. Don't think that you will have a trial, fair and square. Those words are not in their vocabulary.

"Sote, your mother lost her husband and her son. Think about that. Now do you want her to lose you, too? You are her only reason for living, her only hope for a future for your sisters. You must grow up quickly, Sote, and tend to your affairs. Don't talk back to those *kopili.* Keep your mouth shut because it will not only help you, but all of us as well. This family can't survive much longer if we lose one more of our own."

I still protested. His words were too painful to hear. "I have *not* done anything. I do mind my own business. There is no interference from me on anything, and I only speak when I am spoken to."

"I can say no more, Sote. All I say to you is be very, very careful what you say and what you do. Believe me, people who are on the "inside" are warning me, telling me that you talk too much. You challenge authorities and you taunt them! Can't you see the danger in that?"

Nothing I could say at this point would make any difference. He knew all too well the double standard the Greeks used against us. Things always meant one thing for the Greeks, but another for the Macedonians. To see my Uncle so defeated, so bitter, inundated with fear, was difficult to swallow. Who could blame him for his fear—this man who had been so tortured and beaten to a pulp that he was unable to keep his head from shaking? He had no nails left on his hands and feet. He showed me what they had done to him, "Do you want the same things done to you, Sote?"

He showed me the scars on his body, where he had been cut to the bone. It was an ugly picture he painted and I couldn't say anything that would erase the agonies he had lived through. Yet, how could I promise him that we could all still live here peacefully if I kept my mouth shut? What could I say to him that wouldn't be offensive or painful?

Nothing. There was nothing that could be said at the moment. Destiny had not shared her plans for us, and we had not been prepared to understand what had happened to our lives. Some were to die too early and sometimes anonymously, while others were to survive and live for another day, another time, and in a different place.

Uncle Sotir put his arm around my shoulders, each of us deep in our own thoughts, as we looked toward the sun setting over our familiar mountains.

The next day, I decided it was time to visit the police station. The station's official name was the *Mistiki Exotiriki Astonomia*, which was the investigative agency on external and internal matters. It was also the interrogation office. This fear that our family lived with because I mouthed back at the authorities and wore a particular sweat suit, or a shirt or a particular jacket were issues that had to be addressed. Previously, when I had been summoned to the police station, it was, more or less, an *orientation* to the protocol and the laws in Lerin. A kind of official *welcome home*—or sort of! At that time I was asked if I had any complaints, and whether I planned to file charges because I had been *kidnapped* by the Partisans.

This second visit reaffirmed that there were still people who were offended by the symbol on the sweat suit, and tried very hard to impress on me, subtly, possible consequences might develop if I didn't remove the symbol.

The police decided to give me a tour of the basement and the top floor. The guide assigned to me for this *tour* was a lawyer named Haralambos, who spoke fluent Macedonian. I hadn't asked for anyone, but according to Haralambos, it was the law. We walked up the stairs to the top floor. This had to be one of the grimmest places in all of Lerin. It really was a torture chamber. I wondered to myself how many of our Macedonians had been brought here and tortured.

Haralambos pointed toward some cupboards, or what looked like cupboards, measuring six by four feet. He explained, in a voice that showed no emotion, that a person could be locked in these cupboards for days.

The next points of interest were the electric prods, wires and clamps used on the head, ankles, and wrists of a prisoner, forcing him stand upright. Another object of interest to him was a long, grotesque, heavy table, with wide, black leather straps. On one side were some large kettles. It was very impressive, indeed. Teta's and Uncle Sotir's faces flashed through my mind, and I felt the flame of hatred sear my heart to think of human beings being treated worse than animals by other human beings.

Our tour came to an end, so I felt a question might be in order. I asked Haralambos, "Was this tour a scare tactic, to frighten me?"

Instead of responding to the question, he asked, "How were you treated in Yugoslavia? We have heard that it was very bad for you young people."

In a reasonable tone—as if he had asked me how I liked licorice ice cream—I responded, "No, you heard wrong. Things could not have been better."

"Even with constant guards?"

"There were no such things as guards. We were free, free as *sokols*. We could go anywhere. The food was very good and plentiful. We even had more clothes than we knew what to do with. They did not try to Serbianize us or make us into Communists. We were treated with dignity, as Macedonian children. They recognized the need for Macedonian schools, staffed with Macedonian teachers and books."

That aroused his curiosity. "Where did they get the teachers?'

"The teachers came from all over Macedonia, from Aegean Macedonia," I was happy to emphasize that point, "from Kostursko, Pipli, Voden, Engi-Vardar . . . ."

By this time, a number of staff people were listening, waiting for me to bad-mouth Yugoslavia. They didn't like what they heard. One of the men murmured, "*Bre tou kerata*!" whatever that meant!

I had made my point—and Haralambos and his superiors had made theirs with their lovely tour of the *Mistiki Exotiriki Astonomia*, thank you!

Tane Gets His Due

Many strokes overcome the tallest tree.

JOHN LYLY, 1579

A month later I had to appear at the *Ikastirio*, the Court, to get a permit to build onto our *kaliva*. We needed a length of wood that was 15 to 20 feet long and 3 to 4 inches thick. A permit was required to cut wood in the mountains, but we had the right to gather *prakie,* thick, long branches of trees

Dedo decided to come with me to show me which trees had the stronger branches, even though he couldn't see. I helped Dedo mount his horse, which he still could ride, and we trotted on horseback up toward the mountains. We reached an area that was further up the mountain, where I knew I could find good wood. Dedo insisted that he could show me which wood to cut. There were a few bushes and young trees nearby. He went over to them and ran his hands over the young trees. He grabbed the bottom of a young tree, indicating that this was a good choice.

"Chop this one."

"Dedo, it is too short and it won't do us any good."

"I have chopped so many just like this one. I've built houses and barns. Don't tell me what is good and what is not."

Although physically he had changed, his stubborn streak had not diminished. His way or no way, still! I was getting upset with him, but I chopped a few of those he pointed at. They weren't really very good pieces of wood. I went up further and selected the ones I wanted.

Having chopped what I needed, I went to get the horses. When I got there, the *dasolfilakas*, the forest ranger, was checking out what I had cut, talking to Dedo. When he saw me, he snapped at me immediately, "I should have known it was you. You don't have respect for anything. I am going to take you to court for this damage."

Dedo tried to reason with him, but to no avail. That was sad, because the man was a *T'rsianets*, living in the *T'rsianska mala*, a section of Lerin in which the people were primarily from T'rsie. His name was Tane, but everybody called him the *Arnautin*, the Albanian, which generally refers to an obstinate, stubborn or despotic person. I told him, "I'll chop wood wherever I please."

He tried to educate me, but when I refused to listen to him, he became quite angry. Apparently, certain areas had been designated for firewood chopping. That wasn't the reason for his animosity toward me; this *dasolfilakas* was a bully, Greek style. I'll tell you why I say this.

The *dasolfilakas'* name was Tane. He had wanted me to chop wood for him and I wouldn't, which really pissed him off. Tane had coerced other guys to chop for him, and then they had to load wood on his horse and mule and deliver it all the way to his home. Coercion was his trademark. He had coerced young villagers from T'rsie to do his chores and graze his cows and goats without paying them for their services, treating them as if they were his servants. He threatened most of those who were unwilling to do his bidding with a court suit. He actually fined some, pocketing the money.

Previously, this Tane, this *arnautin,* had confronted an older man, a Traian Mishovski, and some of the boys, Pandil, Itso, Mite and me on another part of the mountain. He insisted that I chop firewood for him and deliver it to his home. My response was typically Sotir Nitchov. "Why you must be running a fever. Not only that, but perhaps you are mentally ill, as well. Are you a cripple? That will be the day when I chop wood for you. But," I paused as if I were giving this some real thought, "I might consider it if you pay me for my service to you, and if the price is right."

His face turned red with anger, and he pulled out his gun.

"Nobody talks to me like this!"

"Well, then I'm the first one, right? So put that silly thing away before you hurt yourself."

Everyone moved, surprised and shocked. Everyone except Traian, who was sitting there, eating his lunch. Then he spoke quietly, "Why don't all of you go and sit down.

Finish your lunch. And you, Tane, go about your business, and put that away. Haven't we seen enough guns?"

Good advice, but the idiot was deaf to it. He kept tossing the gun from one hand to the other. He kept badgering me.

"You think you are in *Servos*. Maybe there you could insult people, but not here. You know that here we have the *Astonomia Dikastirio.*"

He named some other things that were supposed to frighten me, but it didn't matter to me. I had already seen some of their "toys".

"You talk like a *prazna vodenitsa,* a dry watermill. You are nothing but a pest, and it would be much better for you and the rest of us if you would shut up and leave us."

He started toward me angrier than before and swore at me. That did it. I jumped up. My built-up anger made me uncontrollable now. I grabbed him by the neck and gave him a hard punch to the stomach. He fell forward on the ground with his gun under him. He couldn't breathe because I had knocked the wind out of him. Pandil, Mite and Itso rushed toward us, and grabbed me so that I wouldn't hit him again. They got to him and helped him sit up. He reached for his gun again.

"If you try to shoot, I will put a hole in your arm," I warned him. I took his gun and threw it out as far away from us as I could, but fool that he was, he struggled to his feet, still threatening me.

Traian spoke up. "Aren't you ashamed? Leave him alone. You foolish kids, shame on you. You, boy," he was speaking to me, "leave him alone. Forget him."

To Tane, "Go on, Tane; get out of here and good riddance!"

Tane left, still muttering, but we would meet again

Soon after Tane left, the rest of us did also. Traian talked to me at length, counseling me not to lose my temper so easily.

"People like Tane should not be provoked, Sote. Yes, he is a stupid man, and since becoming a ranger, it has gone to his head. He is a bully, so avoid arguing with such a person. Tane and others like him think they have a lot of power over people. Just leave him alone, or he will cause you unnecessary trouble. You don't need that."

I thanked the old man for his sincere advice. Before we parted he warned the others, "I don't think it is necessary to talk about this to anyone. Agreed?"

Each one nodded yes, but as far as I was concerned, I didn't care who knew about it. My free time was spent at the stadium.

The affair, however, was not quite over. The following week I received a summons to appear in court on a designated date. There was no choice but to appear. The only two people there served as judge and jury. I was not given an opportunity to present a defense of any kind and was found guilty, with a fine of 5,000 *drachmas,* Greek dollars, for the damage I did when I chopped the wood. I honestly didn't think he would take me to court, which shows how naïve I still was.

Later that same week, I met Tane at the crossroads leading toward Luta and Lokmata near St. Bogoroditsa. In spite of all the advice that good old man Traian gave me, I felt I needed to confront Tane.

"Why did you take me to court?"

No response. It was if I was invisible to him. He couldn't see or hear me, so he felt he didn't have to respond to anything. But I knew something about him that no one else knew. I decided this was the moment to let him know that, and I did. He knew immediately what I was inferring because his look of sneering arrogance changed to that of a scared rabbit. In fact, I had scared the shit out of him. This is what I knew about him.

During the war, Tane served as a courier for the Partizans. I knew about each place that he received messages and where he had to deliver them, and my source was impeccable.

Tane froze. I thought he would drop dead right then and there. I didn't say another word to him, just walked away, as if talking to myself out loud, wondering, "Maybe I should go to the secret police and make a report. They would certainly fix his ass."

Hearing those words, Tane rushed toward me, trying to catch up. As he did, he spoke to me, whispering, "Sote . . . ." I brushed him off.

"Not now. We will talk on my terms, if and when I am ready to talk to you. Just remember, I know lots more." I rattled off some names that he knew and left him there. I just took a quick look at him and it was satisfying. The blood had drained from his face; his jaw had dropped. He looked as if had seen a terrifying apparition.

Tane learned a valuable lesson that day. The past eventually catches up with you in unexpected ways, especially if you try to keep the past buried and assume a phony past.

A few more days passed before my buddy, Lazo, from the village of Turie, and I finally met. Before we even mentioned the old days, the first thing he said to me after we greeted each other with handshakes, hugs, and back slaps was, "This place is not for you. I'll bet you're in trouble already."

"No way. You're wrong," I assured him.

"I don't believe you," and then Lazo proceeded to tell me about Tane who had also harassed many of the villagers from Turie. Chopping wood on the T'rsianska Mountain was prohibited by Tane.

I laughed. "They can chop all the wood they want to. I don't think he will bother them again."

This made Lazo wonder what I hold I had on Tane.

"I'll tell you about it another time. Right now, let's talk about our life here."

As we walked up into the mountains to a place we call Derveno, we talked and talked. Derveno was reached by the same road that the villagers from T'rsie used to and from Lerin. Before we met this day, when I first inquired about Lazo—remember he was one of the older *Begaltsi*—I was told that he had married and moved to Mala, a small village. We talked until sundown, about what it was like to come back and how different it was now. He and the older guys from Lagani and Kotori didn't like it here, either. The adjustment to the paranoia of the Greeks regarding our way of life, compared to the openness and freedom we experienced as *Begaltsi* in Yugoslavia, was depressingly difficult. We turned to the topic of Tane again, and made plans to scare him even further. It was going to be just a matter of time before we would apply the noose to his neck again, figuratively speaking. We both got a laugh out of that, and on that note, we parted.

From that time on, Tane began to see me almost daily, trying to be my friend. He even apologized to Dedo about the court summons and the fine. Tane even told me to forget that he had ever said that I would never leave here, and that if I should leave for either America or Australia, he would put a ring on his nose. In Macedonia we put a ring in the snout of a pig to keep it from digging. Very appropriate analogy.

But what he had said about America or Australia made me a little apprehensive. What had he heard that I hadn't? Nevertheless, there was no doubt that Tane had mellowed somewhat. Nobody had to cater to him anymore, because we had made a deal. He was to leave our villagers alone and not try to exert his authority over them. But I had to put one more scare into him, just so that he wouldn't be tempted to renege on his part of the deal.

On an afternoon when I had some free time, Itso Filipov and I went to Lokmata near the area Tane patrolled. We went to Lokmata because I wanted to get some target practice with my pistol. That was the pretext. Tane was walking along a narrow, secluded path below us, somewhat obscured by the thick branches of trees on either side. I began firing my pistol above his head and around his feet. He couldn't see who was shooting. "Don't shoot, don't shoot me!" he shouted, pleading, begging in the most piteous voice. He thought someone was really after him. So did Itso.

"Sote, Tane's not worth shooting."

I laughed at Itso. "I'm just putting a scare in him, Itso!"

I enjoyed this episode totally. It was the final and complete payback for me, to see and hear him pleading for his life. Itso saw the humor in it, but still was concerned. After we recalled a couple of episodes involving Tane and the villagers, we headed back, each to our own homes.

That evening when I returned home I arrived at the back of the house and walked around to the front. Four wide circular steps led to the porch. Overhead, the balcony covered the length of the porch. The door was open. As I was about to approach the porch, I overheard my mother and Uncle Sotir talking.

"The boy, Tsilo, is not for this place. He will not listen and he is totally without fear. He doesn't care what he says to anyone," Uncle Sotir was saying to Mother, "whether it is a magistrate or a policeman. He doesn't think of the consequences of what he says or does."

She replied helplessly, "What should I do? I don't know what to do. Who shall I write to, Kole in Australia or Vane in America? I don't even have an address for Vane!"

"*Barai chare*, find a solution, but Sote must not remain here. Whenever I go into the town, everyone warns me to teach Tsila's boy. . . . "

I couldn't believe what I was hearing. What was I doing that was so bad? Everyone, family, friends and enemies came to the conclusion that I was *bad*. If I had known this, that my own people would turn against me, I would never have come back. Why the hell did I? I interrupted both of them, by walking out again.

"Where are you going?"

"I'll be back later."

Almost in unison, both of them called out, "Don't get into any trouble!"

Why did they feel there was something wrong with me? I was still who I had always been, Sotir Nitchov. I was still the boy they raised, only a little older. Yes, I was independent. Yes, I felt I was free, free to express myself and that everyone had that right. I was born free! Rationally, I knew that they had been so beaten physically, emotionally and spiritually that the only strong feeling they had left in them was fear, and that I was feeding their fears. I didn't want to be the catalyst to drive them over the edge, so I made the decision I had been avoiding for some time now. I was going to go back to Belgrad. It was the only reasonable thing to do.

I decided at that moment to send a letter to the Partizan Soccer Club and not let anybody here know. When the right time came, I would tell the family. I had to be patient.

A week had passed since the night I had overheard Mother and Uncle Sotir discussing me. Mother and I found ourselves alone, so I asked her directly, "Why are you trying to get rid of me? If you didn't want me here, why did you send for me?"

I had created such a difficult situation for her and the family. She had always been a woman of great self-control. She knew instinctively what had to be done, how it had to be accomplished, and what had to be said. She always spoke directly to the point, but now, she didn't know how to answer me. It took her some moments, because she usually kept her emotions under wraps.

After a few minutes, having looked at her hands resting in her lap without seeing anything, she spoke. "I found out that they had taken you to the Mistiki Astonomia. Why didn't you tell me you were in trouble? We could have gotten a lawyer!"

I stopped her. "We didn't need a lawyer. I haven't done anything. Didn't I tell you not to be afraid and not to worry?"

Her eyes were red with concern.

"How did you find out?"

"Antigoni's fiancé, who is stationed there, saw you."

Antigoni, her first cousin's daughter, was engaged to a policeman, a higher level officer. He had access to information in the Astonomia, and he recognized me. I didn't know him at all. Usually I don't want to discuss in detail situations concerning me, especially if there are no consequences. Therefore, my assurances to Mother about the Astonomia did not make her any more comfortable.

"But what about Tane?" she asked. "Traian told me everything. Itso also told me. You know, we all know, what kind of person Tane is. We all know he is a *shpionin,* a spy, and they will believe whatever he tells the police. He works for them!"

Her fear was overwhelming her.

"Mother, stop. You are worrying for nothing. Tane will never bother anybody again. The Tane incident is over. But it is too bad that I didn't know about the *minise,* the fine, in advance. We never would have had to pay."

I don't know how much I convinced her during our talk. For an hour or two, Mother put every worry she had on the table. From that deep, open, heart-to-heart discussion, we came to a conclusion, which she accepted. As soon as possible, I would leave Macedonia. When I could work it out financially, I would send for her and my sisters without any delay. To our mutual relief, we had settled the problem. Each of us *thought* we had settled the problem. But Mother was thinking about America. I was thinking about Yugoslavia.

A Mother's Dilemma

Man is the only animal for whom his own existence is a problem which he has to solve.

ERICH FROMM, 1947

A week passed after Mother and I discussed the problems that existed between us. During that time I could see that we hadn't covered everything, because something was still troubling her deeply. She was lost in thought frequently, pausing in the middle of whatever task was before her, only to sigh deeply, and continue working. To see her like this, unable to unburden herself on me fully, made me understand how lonely and difficult it had to be for her without Father. He had been her life partner in everything. I was just a son, a generation removed. There had to be some issues that were difficult to discuss with me. I just hoped it wasn't something about me again.

I was hoeing in the vegetable patch, when I realized that Mother had come outdoors and had been watching me for a few minutes. I looked up.

"Mother, is something bothering you again? Don't keep it to yourself. Let's talk about it."

Her hesitation was so pronounced. She found it difficult to look at me, as she struggled for the right words. She looked away, and then down.

She began carefully, "Sote, a widower in Australia, a man from the village of Statitsa, has written to me. He wants me to come to Australia and marry him. He told me that I can bring my children with me!"

I felt shock cut through me like a saber, making me drop the hoe I held. Marriage? Marriage for my mother? Such an option was not even on my list of possibilities for the future! So engrossed was I in my own needs and wants, it had never occurred to me that my own mother had some needs and wants of her own—let alone, on a broader scope. For a solution to be right for her, it had to include the well-being of her children.

Marriage? It was the farthest thing from my mind. I didn't know what to say, how to respond. I could only move away from her. I walked a few yards and then turned around. She hadn't moved an inch. Her face was expressionless, but her eyes followed me intently. I went to her, took her by the hand, and led her toward the *livadia*, without ever uttering a word.

We stopped. There were so many thoughts swirling inside my head, so many emotions were gripping me. It was the thought of my father that kept me from speaking. For a brief moment I felt the way I did in Bela Crkva by the mulberry bush, after I had received word of my father's and brother's deaths.

Father. How could I call another man "Father"? I had one father, one brother. That was all that could be!

Flashing through my mind at the same time were conversations between my cousins Dina, Itso, Ilo and Krsto when they talked about how they were treated by their stepmother. No thank you! And that's when I spoke up.

"Look, Mother, if you want to go to Australia—go and marry—I will not go with you. I just can't see myself calling anybody else 'Father'. I have my own father and I can never forget him. I don't want to stop you. You must do what is best. I am old enough to take care of myself.

"However, about the girls, I don't know what to say. I don't know how they will feel. That's something you will have to find out for yourself. You will have to ask them. If they should decide they don't want to go, I promise you that I will look after them. I will take care of them, so don't worry about that part."

I meant what I said with all my heart. Mother just stood there, still as death. I had done all the talking. What I really wanted to say to her was, "Hell, no. You can't do this!" Because I loved her and respected her so much, because I was so overwhelmed with emotion that she felt she could confide in me and ask for my opinion, I had to be gentle and make it easier for her to make her decision. I truly did not want to stand in her way. I realized that she was sincerely thinking that a remarriage, far from the terrible memories she and the family had lived through, would make for an easier life and future for all of us, for me in particular. Everyone felt that I had to leave this damned Greece, including the Greeks who had their own twisted reasons. That was very clear.

I added, "If you decide to accept the offer from Australia, I want you to know you are and will still be *my* mother, no matter what happens, and no matter where you are. If you decide not to accept this offer, I give you my word, here and now, that I will do my best to take care of you forever. I promise you."

She squeezed my hand, let go, turned around and walked towards the *kaliva*. I could only stare at her back until she disappeared inside. I knew she was crying, because I was crying for her and with her. I stayed where I was for more than an hour, wondering about what I had said to her. Did I say the right thing? Did I do the right thing? How much of what I said hurt her? Who the hell was I to influence someone so strongly, even if it was my mother?

I just wasn't happy with myself, which made me so angry that I broke out into real sobs, like a little boy who had just lost his cndy. What was wrong with me? I should have asked her how she felt, what she would like to do. Damn it, why do I hurt her so much? She had said nothing in reply to me, but just walked away in that quiet, dignified way.

I didn't see Mother again until the next evening. There was no doubt in my mind that she had discussed the situation with my aunt and uncle. In fact, Teta confirmed that very fact to me, trying to intervene earlier in the day, saying in a casual conversational tone, "You know, your mother is still young . . . ."

I didn't give her a chance to finish. "Teto," I whipped around, "I don't want to hear or talk about my mother again, all right?"

It was never discussed again, not with anyone.

Mother had overheard us, and I think that was when she made her decision. It was *no!* When she rejected the offer, a heavy weight seemed to lift from my chest. I felt no guilt. Perhaps I was wrong, but I couldn't bring myself to accept a remarriage for my mother. I felt it would have been a rejection and betrayal of Father.

If only I had had the wisdom of more years.

Danti

Barbarism is the absence of standards
To which appeal can be made.

JOSE ORTEGA Y GASSET, 1930

The days dragged on. Life, such as it was, went on. Sometimes I felt I was 100 years old. In the evenings, when chores were done and with time permitting, some of us boys and girls would walk to the center of Lerin for an evening stroll. Sometimes we would rent bicycles, or just enjoy getting sodas. Sometimes we played cards in town. If there was what they called a *glendi*, a dance, once in a while we would go. That was the extent of the recreational outlets then.

One evening, some of the guys and I were walking toward the Platia Eron. In the back of the Platia, there was a little black shack. Some of the boys began to throw rocks at it—something which they had apparently been in the habit of doing.

"What's this all about?" I asked Pandel.

"Ah, there's an old demented guy that lives there. I think his name is Ilia Danti. Everybody says he's a little off," Pandel answered, twirling one of his hands around his head.

I told Pandil and Itsos to stop throwing the rocks. After all, the man wasn't bothering any of us.

The shack was a curious-looking structure, broken windows covered with cardboard and wooden planks. It intrigued me. I decided to go have a look at it. I walked up the road to where the shack stood on a steep hill, ignoring the guys who shouted to me that I was obviously nuts to go there. I reached the door and knocked. No response.

I knocked again. Still no response. As I was about to give up and walk away, I heard a voice.

"What do you want?"

I turned back. "I just want to apologize."

"You didn't throw any rocks, so why apologize?"

"Well, anyway . . . ," I paused. "you won't have any more trouble with my friends again."

"Are you sure they're your friends, letting you take the blame for their shenanigans?"

I didn't reply.

"Well, come up and come in if you would like to," he said, inviting me into his shack pointing to the door with his arm.

To my surprise as I walked in, it looked quite nice inside. Danti had a stove, chairs, a table, bed, cooking utensils, everything that a little house with one occupant needs. On top of that, it was very clean. Danti gestured toward a chair, and I sat down.

Looking at me, he asked me point-blank, "Aren't you afraid to come in here? Everybody in town thinks I am crazy."

"No, I'm not afraid. You don't talk or act like a crazy man. Why should anyone think that?"

Danti sat back. "Well, that's a very long story. Someday I'll tell you, when you have lots of time."

He got up as he spoke and, as is the custom of the Macedonian people, started to make Turkish coffee without asking me if I wanted any. Usually when the coffee is being prepared it means that the time for the visiting is almost at an end. I said to him, "You're going to make coffee? The old ones say that it means it's just about time for a person to leave."

He shook his head. "The old ones are very wise, but no, stay as long as you like. Where are you from?"

"I'm from T'rsie, but we have a house here in town as well."

"I didn't think I had seen you around before." He stirred the coffee a bit in the *zhezhveh*. "You don't sound like you're from here," Danti commented. "You speak excellent Macedonian. Very clean and clear." *Chisto Makedonski* was the way he put it.

"How do you know that? I haven't heard anybody say *'Chisto Makedonski'* since I left Yugoslavia. What are you, Greek, Macedonian or what?" I asked.

"Well, besides Greeks and Macedonians, who else live here?" he looked at me as he asked.

"Jews, Turks, Gypsies," was my easy answer.

"I am a *Vlach.* My parents were *Vlasi.* I learned Macedonian when they had schools here. They were Bulgarian schools. But, I also speak German, Albanian, Italian and Russian."

I was astonished. "And they call you crazy? Those who call you that are the crazy ones. You're amazing."

He reached under the bed and pointed, "Pull out that box and open it."

I did and received another pleasant surprise. He had all kinds of books in that box, the new Macedonian grammar book, and Russian, German, Italian and Turkish books. He even had a book about Lenin. Enjoying the look on my face, he said to me, "I have many more, hidden. I collect them. As you can guess, I have plenty of time to read."

I didn't see any book in Greek, except an old law book.

I wondered, aloud, "And nobody bothers you about these books? Has anyone seen them? Where did you get them?"

He chuckled. "Remember, I am crazy. No one bothers a crazy man. They stay away from that kind of fellow. I get the books from here and there. I was *Lohagos* in the Albanian War of 1939 until the German occupation."

I think he said he was the equivalent of a three-star general. After a pause he said, "There is no better fighter than the Macedonian."

He hit a nerve. "Then why did we lose the *Partizanski* war?"

In the most serious voice he had used so far, he replied, "The Macedonians didn't lose the war. The Greeks lost it for the Macedonians. They tricked the Macedonians. The problem for the Macedonians was that they put their trust in the Greek leadership. But Tito and Stalin had a lot to do with how the war ended. There were many complications."

This man, Danti, was full of surprises. As we were talking, some of the guys began to get impatient, and walked up to the windows.

"Sote, come on. Let's get going."

Danti asked, "Sote is your name? What is your surname?"

"Nitchov. My name is Sotir Nitchov."

"What is that old man up there, across from the church to you? Is he related to you?"

"He is my Dedo."

"Done was your father, then?"

"No. Mite was my father. Done is my uncle."

He looked closely at me. "The medic, Mitchko?"

"I don't know if he was called that. I do know that during the war he was known as *giatre*, the doctor. That is all I know."

Danti slapped his knee. "That is the one. I knew him very well, along with Traian and Krsto. They worked very hard for the Cause."

I couldn't believe this old man. Traian was Teta's husband. Krsto Stoikov was another T'rsianets who also was very involved in the uprising. He seemed like a living, talking encyclopedia to me. He knew more T'rsiani than I did. He began to tell me things about the past of which I wasn't even aware. To any question from me, he had an answer or explanation. Some of the events he was describing regarding Partisan activities I had seen for myself. The men he mentioned along with others were smuggling guns and other war materials, hand grenades and shells. Danti even knew where my father was killed. My jaw dropped as he spoke.

"The information about your father came to me by way of the military police. Your father was killed in Nausa, Negush."

I couldn't move or speak as he went on.

"If you want to see a picture of your father, go to the *Mistiki Astonomia*, and if they can be persuaded, they might, mind you, they might let you see his files. But don't count on it."

I finally found my tongue. "How do you know all of this? Everyone says you're out of your head. Were you working for the Greeks at one time or another? Are you working for them now? How did you get this information?"

He winked at me. "As a *crazy* man, I can do lots of things a sane man cannot. However, you better know here and now, that I have never, nor will I ever work for them, for those Greeks. I am too religious. I could not commit their atrocities."

I had to take him at his word, but he never did explain how he knew that there were files on the activities of my father and others kept in the *Mistiki Astonomia*. This information, nevertheless, made me determined to see for myself, somehow.

Danti could see that his words made quite an impact on me. He paused, and waited to see how I was going to handle this. So when I started to say that I had to rejoin my friends, he understood. I shook his hand, he nodded and I left.

As soon as I could find the time, without telling anyone in the family, I asked my friend Ari to go with me to the *Astonomia*. When the officer in charge asked my why I was there, I said, "I know that you have files on people, and one of them is my father. I would like to see his file."

I might as well have been talking in Chinese. The officers there tried to pretend they had no idea what I was talking about. Files? They were not going to admit knowing anything about files or about my father. I saw that I was not going to get anywhere and we left.

On the way out, we crossed paths with the Commissioner who had questioned me when I made my first appearance at the station. He stopped to ask me what I was doing there that day. Ari explained the purpose of my visit. His eyes, revealing nothing, took in my face and manner, inch by inch.

"I just want to see what my father looked like." I added. "I don't have a picture of either him or my brother. When your men burned down our house, everything we had, every memento burned also."

He had a response to that. "Are you sure it wasn't the *andartes* who burned your house?"

The Greeks referred to the Partizans as *andartes.*

In a firm tone I replied, "I am sure it was the *pushkari* and the *burandari*. We knew the Greek army police as *burandari*," I explained quite simply and without emotion. The *pushkar*i were Grecophiles who were given guns by the Greeks The Commissioner was all smiles and invited Ari and me back into his office. He called to one of his men and told him to bring the files of Mite Nitchov. In Greek he said, *"Ta hartia tou Dimitrios Nitsou."*

Within minutes he was handed an orange file filled with papers. The file name I could see began with Dimitrios to Vasilious Nitsou.

"O *paterasou itan nasokmois eh,*" he continued in Greek to me. I told him what I remembered, that my father was in the Greek army and then later with the Partizans.

He shot back at me, "I am sure, because it says so here along with everything else."

He looked through the papers and then handed me a single one.

"Here is a document with an old picture on it."

I grabbed it. This was the first picture I had seen of my father since the house had burned. The identification card, *taftotia,* had an old picture of him, ink stained and wrinkled. There was an illegible stamp on it.

"Could I have a copy of this?"

"Now you are asking too much. It cannot be taken out of here."

I persisted. "What if a photographer came here . . . ."

He cut me off, before I could finish the question, and stood.

"You do not appreciate what I have done for you. Now, I have work to do."

We were being dismissed. We got up to leave and as we reached the door, I turned, to appeal one more time.

"Sir, why do you need that picture of my father? He is dead, so it can be of no further use to you, but it would mean so much to the family and me. Why not let me have it?"

All I got was a dirty look as he spoke to Ari, "Get him out of here before he asks for my shoes." He obviously thought I did not appreciate the courtesy he had extended to me by showing me a dirty, wrinkled, stamped picture of Father.

In 1972 I made another try for the picture of my father, offering $500 American to anyone who could get me a copy of that picture. I approached lawyers and people we knew who might have access to the file, to no avail. The response to their inquiry was that no such file existed.

I wanted to see Danti again, this time without the company of my friends. I set out on my own one evening and walked into town, up the road leading to his little shack on top of the hill. I had scarcely finished knocking on his door, when it opened, Danti standing there with a welcoming smile on his face. We shook hands in greeting and he gestured toward the chair as before. As he had done previously he prepared Turkish coffee for us, talking to me about things in general.

We slurped our coffee in a companionable silence and, as I was finishing my cup, he told me to swirl the coffee cup several times and then turn it upside down on the saucer.

I did exactly as he instructed. He continued, "Cross the cup with the palm of your right hand."

I crossed the cup. Of course, he knew that I knew what he was going to do. Everyone gets their future foretold by the way the coffee grinds appear in the cup once the ritual is performed. I find the whole thing kind of silly, but I thought I would humor Danti to see where he was going to go. He picked up my cup and studied it for several minutes, looking at it this way, then turning the cup, looked at it that way, and then he spoke.

"You have an interesting cup that is telling me a lot."

Smart-ass that I am, I remarked, "It is more interesting when the cup is full. Besides, you don't know me well enough to predict my future!"

"Ah, but you see, you are mistaken on that point. The cup tells all. I just act as a translator. You are thinking of something very burdensome . . . but you are not going to accomplish this . . . . You will not go back to where you think you are going to go . . . . You are going over a large body of water . . . far away from here . . . . I see two relatives who are trying to bring you to them . . . but the one you don't know at all is the one you will join . . . . The other man is even farther away . . . . He will not succeed, even though he wants you very much . . . . He has tried before to bring you to him . . . . Let's see."

Danti kept studying the cup. "You are not aware of this now, but in about 3 months you will be traveling, I guarantee you. A little boy will be with you and this little boy will be a burden to you . . . . You will not like it where you are going . . . . It will be hard for you . . . but you will not leave. You will settle there . . . . You will marry . . . and you will establish your own home there."

I smiled at him tolerantly, enjoying his performance. "Ilia, you are good at this. You should open a shop and charge people. You'll make a lot of money!"

"I read cups only to certain people. They do give me a few drachmas."

"Do I have to pay?"

"No, you are a friend. You don't pay. Anyway, there is something else I want to ask you. Weren't you afraid to come in here? You know, to see a *ualf*, a fool, a *budala chovek*, stupid person?"

I replied to those questions in this way, "We are all crazy and stupid. I know I am often thought of as being that way, too. It's just that some of us are more stupid. I never think in terms of fear. That, in my opinion, is being stupid!"

"Now that you have seen me and talked to me, do *you* think I am crazy?"

I looked at him and answered, "To tell you the truth, there is something about you that I can't figure out. I can't put my finger on what it is."

"I'll tell you what it is. People talk about me, I know. You have heard something that doesn't quite fit. Let me tell you this. I am a very religious man. I believe in *Hristos* and I pray perhaps two, three times every day, but not in church!"

Not in church? I looked at him questioningly, "If not in church, then where do you go to pray?"

He pointed to the window and said to me, "Up there, at the big rock."

I looked.

"I guess you follow the primitive way. You don't kill any animal there, do you?"

"I see you are a non-believer," he commented. "Why is that?"

"I believe in my own way," I asserted. "I just don't want to fill up priests' pockets. They steal, lie and double-cross their own people . . . ."

He interrupted me. "You describe them very well. Anyway, come here any time you like. You've learned something about the outside world. You're a good young man and you're smart. You'll be fine. Don't forget to say goodbye before you leave for America."

"Oh, now, it's America, eh, Ilia?" I teased him.

But he was very serious. "I'll bet you anything you want to bet," he challenged.

I found that to be very funny and laughed. "I'll bet you and I will say goodbye when I leave for Belgrad, Ilia."

"You will not be going to Belgrad, I'm very sure of that," he answered firmly.

"Well, we'll see about that soon, won't we, Ilia?" I stood up. "I have to go. It has been a pleasure to talk with you. I'll visit you again. Why not come by us sometime and see my Dedo, since you know each other?"

He looked at me solemnly and said, "You are the first and only person to invite me anywhere, you know."

That seemed such a curious thing to me, this interesting man, to live so alone! We shook hands in parting. He watched me walk down the road. I turned to wave at him and he waved back.

I asked some friends about Ilia and was told that he did go to the rocks, where he stripped to the waist, wrapped a sheet around himself and just meditated. He read books there as well. One friend told me how he acted as his own lawyer defending himself when the city tried to evict him from his little house. I was told that he won every case he represented. He apparently received a military pension from the government and some monetary assistance from unnamed others.

And they called him crazy?

It was clear to me that Ilia Danti, too widely read, too wise, too experienced, had more intelligence than anyone Lerin.

After I had warned the guys from our T'rsianska Mala to leave him alone, eventually they began to speak to him nicely and refrained from throwing rocks at his home. I had to intervene just once more when Ari and I caught a couple of *prosvigi* kids still throwing rocks, while a few of the bigger boys harassed the man. I warned them that if they ever did that again, I would break their arms and bust their heads wide open.

Those darned kids called the police on us. When the police arrived, Ilia thanked Ari and me for intervening. Then he spoke to the police. Whatever it was that he said to them, the police looked apologetic and became a little tongue-tied. Each one responded to him with the phrase, *"Malista, Kirie Ilia."*

I laughed and laughed. Here was a man labeled "crazy", explaining the law to the people who were supposed to enforce the law, who didn't understand what their role in enforcing the law meant.

Ilia explained the situation like this: "The law itself is not clear. It was written by barbarians."

Ilia Danti, philosopher, religious mystic, warrior, lawyer, prophet, and among many other things, a little "crazy".

Danti! He was one of a kind.

I never saw him again.

A Friend in a High Place

If fate means you lose, give him a good fight anyhow.

WILLIAM MCAFEE, 1916

I always knew Father had a brother in America, although there was little communication between the two. The only thing I remember about Uncle Vane was that Father had received a package from him once. Uncle Vane had sent him a green coat and a pair of shoes that laced up to the ankle. It meant so much to Father to have been remembered by his brother. I don't know if they had been close as brothers or not. We didn't have an address for him. Imagine how I felt as Mother told me that Uncle had sent word that he was going to process the papers and documents to bring me to America!

"How did he know where we are now?" I asked her.

She told me she had written to someone else in Detroit who did know him. Whoever that "someone" was had contacted Uncle Vane, who responded to Mother's request immediately. I had no choice but to go with her to see Payo, an agent in Lerin. Payo seemed like a man who was actually a Macedonian, but to all intents and purposes you saw and heard only Greek. She told him the purpose of our visit and gave him the letters stating Uncle's willingness to sponsor me.

When we first met with Payo, he said, "I've known your family for a very long time. I know and hear things about you as well (meaning me). Now, don't get the wrong impression about me. I have to make a living. Do you understand? Do I have to tell you any more?"

I did understand what he meant, so I didn't question his role as an agent. As we exchanged a few pleasantries, he got down to the real reason we were there. I had some preliminary things to do, Payo told me, to start the process. There was no documentation about me, either in Lerin or T'rsie. The Greek authorities had erased my name and the name of my Cousin Ilo from the registry in the county. Ironically, my brother Stefo's records were intact. He was dead, but I—still alive—did not exist according to Greek records!

Payo gave us a list of what I had to have:

A birth certificate.
Names of witnesses who knew me and could verify my place of birth.
Parent's names.
Mother's maiden name.

Parents' place of birth.

Six passport pictures, not two or three, but six!

The information had to be notarized and sent to the police who had jurisdiction over T'rsie. Additionally, I had to get an affidavit from the police, verifying the information.

The Greek authorities did not accept my Yugoslav passport, as it was a Macedonian passport, stamped by Yugoslavia. I had never formally applied for either a Macedonian or Yugoslav passport. Whenever I traveled with the Partizan Club, I may have had some kind of official documentation, but I only remember signing something here and there.

Then Payo added, "It is going to be very difficult for you to get a passport, so don't get your hopes up too much. You may not be successful on a first try."

I didn't know whether that was the opening to offer a bribe or what. That was the pattern in Greece—if you needed something, you had to pay a price for it, one way or another. Money resolved many obstacles.

Difficult? It would be difficult did he say? Maybe I could add to that "difficulty." If I became meaner, nastier and more of a nuisance to the Greeks, then it might mean I would never get that passport to America, which would play right into *my* hands. Then maybe Belgrad would still be a possibility for me. I had nothing to lose, I felt.

Knowing exactly how the Greek authorities operated, almost from the time I was a toddler in T'rsie, I knew I could get my way by using reverse psychology on them. With these thoughts running through my mind, I could just visualize myself sneaking over the border, which was not very far from Lerin, and, *eto!* In just the twink of an eye I would be in Yugoslavia!

I smiled at him. The perfect plan! I could vent my spleen in Greece and get back to Belgrad. Things were going to work out, after all!

Having received the information we needed, Mother and I thanked Payo for his time and trouble and left. Mother seemed so dejected. *I*, however, felt so elated! I didn't show it outwardly, but on the inside, I was jumping with joy. I was going to get back to the PARTIZANS, to Belgrad at last.

My euphoria didn't last long. Within 6 weeks of our meeting with Payo, everything backfired. All the affidavits and documents had been prepared, approved and were ready for me. All that was missing was the ticket that Uncle Vane was to have sent for me. I had to take a trip to Solun to get my visa from the American Consulate there.

Payo was absolutely shocked. "I have been in this business for a long time. I have had all kinds of customers and clients. But *none*, none have ever received their documents as fast as you have."

I smiled at him. "You are not going to make much money on me. I did everything that was needed by myself. That's why everything came through so quickly."

But then Payo said something that rang so true, it should have been more obvious to me.

"They don't want you boys here. The Greeks accomplished their propaganda strategy, bringing some of you back from those other countries. They propagandized to the entire world that they had brought their 'kidnapped Greek' children back. Now, it seems that they can't wait to get rid of you. You are all potential political trouble for them."

His analysis was right on. I had seen many women going to Payo's office. Most if not all of the villagers had been clients of his at one time or another. There were many widows with and without children trying to get out of Greece.

I made my second trip to Solun by bus, which stopped at Gornichevo. Gornichevo was a police checkpoint. At first I thought it was just a rest stop. *Wrong*! Two policemen got on the bus, one stood by the driver, facing the passengers. The other said something to us, and then started to check for identification. When he came by, he said something to me, but I was far away, daydreaming, remembering and reliving some of the bus trips I had taken with the teams in Yugoslavia. I know I must have had a pleasant look on my face, until he nudged my shoulder.

"Are you deaf? I am talking to you. Your *taftolita,* identification card!" he demanded.

No one had mentioned that I had to have identification on me all the time. I didn't have it on my person.

He repeated his demand. I gestured again that I didn't have any identification on me. All kinds of words spilled out of his mouth, none of which I could understand, so I turned to some of the passengers who looked as if they had been frightened out of their wits. None of them dared to speak to me or for me.

Finally, a woman in black came over to me. I explained my situation to her. She then explained to the policeman that I told her that the war had been over for a few years, and that I didn't need one.

That was all he needed. He shouted, "*Exo*, out!" and out we went, headed for the office which was just a few yards from the bus. His superior officer, captain, or whatever, greeted us and motioned to me to sit down. As I looked at him, I thought . . . he reminds me of a Russian general with all of the medals and ribbons on his chest. There was hardly any fabric of the jacket he wore that you could see. Although he seemed to be polite, I detected a little note of sarcasm in his voice.

"I don't speak Greek," I told him. "I think you had better get someone who speaks Macedonian."

He shot back at me. "You mean *Vulgariki/giuftiki*, Bulgarian gypsy language?"

I, very politely, answered, "No, sir. I mean Macedonian."

He paused for a couple of seconds, and then, "What? Did your mother give birth to you yesterday? You seem to be a pretty big boy."

His implication was that I was so naïve as to claim to speak Macedonian, a language that didn't exist for him, I must have been born yesterday. So much for politeness.

So I said to him, still speaking Macedonian, "Those people are waiting in the bus.

If you stop your sarcastic remarks, we might be able to move on. I don't know what you want."

"Oh, I am so sorry," and he motioned to a policeman to the right who almost ran the 3 or 4 yards to reach his desk.

"Tell the boy that we have laws here which apply to all Greek citizens. They must have identification."

The policeman explained the law.

"I was made an official Greek citizen just 3 weeks ago," I replied. That's why I don't have any papers on me."

I surprised him.

"Explain."

"What is there to explain? Even though I was born in T'rsie near Lerin, the Greek law said that I had to apply to become an official Greek citizen. You know the law better than I."

We exchanged some comments, and then I added.

"I do have a passport, but if I were to show it to you, you might faint! It is a Yugoslavian passport, and it shows my nationality as Macedonian."

He finally caught on, or so I thought.

"Ah," he relaxed a bit. "*Pedomazoma*."

He used the term meaning "kidnapped children." That was the term the Greeks use when they referred to us. I interrupted him, "No *pedomazoma*! I left of my own free will."

He understood me very well, because things moved very quickly after that. He handed me a piece of paper indicating who I was so that at the next stop I would have some kind of identification paper on me.

As I boarded the bus, I told the policeman that if he had asked me in Macedonian, he would have had his response immediately. I had already guessed what this guy was, and couldn't resist the impulse to bait him further.

"You can't hide in that uniform. It is written all over your face, *bre bishe*, you pig!"

His face flushed. I had nailed him neatly. He was a Macedonian turncoat.

After the bus started to move, most of the women started to whisper to each other. Some even laughed! It was the first time I had seen anyone laugh, let alone talk, since we had left Lerin. I asked some of the women who sat near me, "What happened? Why are they laughing and whispering?"

An older woman, also in black, left her seat to sit next to me and asked, "Are you one of our children, *nashi detsa*, that left some years ago?"

I nodded my head. This opened the door for her to inquire about her children. She pulled out some pictures.

"This one is called Kole. They are in Polonia."

I had to disappoint her. She thought I might know something about them. She had thought Polonia and Yugoslavia were in the same country. Some of the other women from the villages of Vumbel, Breznitsa, and Rula summoned up their courage to ask me if I knew anything of their children. I did know some of the kids from their villages, but I couldn't help them. They were using the children's Greek names!

When we arrived in Solun, most of us went to the same hotel, the NIKI, which was owned by a man from Armensko village. We stayed there 3 days because of the unbelievable Greek bureaucracy. Still, very carefully, the women did relax a bit and discussed some of the problems they had encountered trying to get visas.

"This is my third attempt to get a visa for America."

"This is my sixth!"

Since there was nothing I could do for them for the time being, I went out to do some sightseeing.

We made several trips to the American Consulate, but were always told to come back the next day. This couldn't go on, I thought. I suggested to some of the women that we should try to get to the Consulate very early. We did that the next day, all arriving at the same time. I was sent into the Consul's office, where a Serbian translator was available to interpret for me.

She asked me in Serbian, "Do you speak English?"

I didn't.

"What did you study in school when you were in Bela Crkva? Why do you want to go to America?"

"I don't, really. The only place I want to go is Belgrad."

The Consul commented, "But they're Communists."

"I really don't care what they are. It doesn't interest me a bit. It's soccer that is the most important thing to me. I have a chance to play professionally in Yugoslavia. That is all I want to do." I spoke as honestly and as earnestly as I could.

"My mother and family feel it is not good for any of us if I remain in Greece."

I was speaking with this reasonable man candidly, and we talked for about half an hour.

"I can see why your mother wants you to leave. Here is a phone number and a name. Should you encounter any problems, call us."

And with that piece information and advice, I was granted a visa.

Little did he know that when I went downstairs to get the visa stamped, more delay was waiting, not only for me, but also for the other women as well. I lined up behind some of the ones who had been granted visas, and the others lined up behind me. When my turn came, I placed my visa on the desk of a thin, short, scarecrow of a woman, very heavily made up. She obviously needed some instruction on how to apply cosmetics and how much to apply.

Inside of my passport I had a document showing my uncle's name, address, and some other numbers. Uncle Vane spelled his name, John Nichoff, which was a different spelling from Nitchov, but phonetically pronounced the same.

Madam Scarecrow looked at the document and crackled, "Huh, you'll go to America and become Bulgarian."

At first I thought she was speaking to someone else. When no one else spoke, I realized she was speaking to me.

I told her, "It's none of your @%&!%* business what I become in America."

She threw my passport and visa into the corner of the room with as much effort and power she could muster. At the same time, with hatred in her voice and eyes, she was saying something. The women behind me began to whisper to me, "She won't give you the visa, and she will do the same thing to us again!"

I was stunned. Who did she think she was? Well, the Consul had told me that if I encountered any trouble at all to call. I didn't have to call. I just walked up the stairs and into his office. His secretary tried to stop me, but I went directly to his door, knocked, and walked in. He took one look at my face. Something had happened.

In Macedonian I tried to explain to him what the problem was. He was responding in English. The interpreter wasn't there. Neither of us understood the other. It was time for body language—I began to perform charades. I clutched my hands and then made a sound like *shusput,* as I used my arm to throw an invisible object toward the corner of the room. Then I grabbed his hand and led him down to the room where my passport still lay in the corner. I pointed toward it. He got the message.

The room was filled with people. He strode over to Madam Scarecrow, spoke to her very briefly and pointed to the corner. She got the message, picked up the passport and document and sat down at her desk. The Consul said something to me, which only he understood. I took his hand and shook it, gratefully, thanking him in Macedonian. I turned to the Scarecrow. The room was quite filled with people. She never took her eyes off me, as she held the documents. She was actually trembling, with anger, or was it with humiliation? I didn't care.

I gestured as I said, "Stamp! Now! Visa! Boom, boom! Passport!"

I was as sarcastic as I could be, even though she was a woman. It disgusted me that she was in a position of power, acting like a god, interfering and jeopardizing people's lives, willy-nilly. I couldn't wait to get out of there, and apparently she couldn't wait either. She hit a page with the stamp as hard as she could. I could see the indentation of the stamp on the next page, but I got my visa!

As I started toward the door, checking my papers, I overheard a couple of the women remarking, "*Ovaa kouchka pak neni dade visata*! This bitch again refused to give us our visa!" No visa again. The women who had been in line behind me said the same thing. That really pissed me off. I told the women to follow me, as I went back into the line. I asked the man who was next in line, if he would be good enough to let us step in ahead of him. He said words to the effect of, "Be my guest. She won't give me a visa anyway."

"We'll see about that!"

I took one of the women by the hand, held her passport up and placed it in the hand of the Scarecrow. I gestured and said, "Visa, Visa!" As if I were holding a stamp, I hit her desk hard. Why am I doing this act when there is a better way? I turned to the women and asked, "Who speaks good Greek?"

One of the women shoved a younger one toward me.

I said to her, "Tell this *kouchka* if she does not give all these people their visa, I will go back upstairs and bring the Consul back to talk to her. If she wants to keep her job, she had better start stamping right now."

Passport picture of a very unhappy young man.

As if by magic, Scarecrow opened to the right page of the passport and, boom! She began stamping passports and visas, so that within about 10 minutes the room had emptied. She hadn't even bothered to read anything in the passport or examine the documents as she had done so meticulously before. She just went into a stamping frenzy.

The three ladies who had been denied previously were outside waiting. I asked one of the other women to bring them back in. They, too, got their visas just like that!

As I left the Consulate, the women outside mobbed me. I was overwhelmed with hugs, kisses on the face, on the forehead, as I felt the tears on their wet faces. I tried to make light of the situation.

"Hey, what is this all about? Go and kiss that *kouchka.* She gave you the visa, not me. She had the stamp."

They began to tell me how some of them had been trying to get their visas since 1946 and 1947, but were always denied. Their family or someone in the family, either a husband, son, grandfather, uncle, someone was suspected of having been a Partisan, or had supported the Partisans, or were sympathetic to the Bulgarians. A name was always suspect if it ended in double "f"'. The women couldn't find words to thank me enough. It was interesting to me because they spoke in a variety of Macedonian dialects. Many of the women came from the Kostursko area. Finally, I had to tell them, "I'll see you at the hotel. The bus doesn't leave until 4:00 p.m."

And, with that, I went off to visit the *Edy Kula*, the White Tower in Solun. During the Ottoman period, it served as a Turkish prison. Before that, it was part of the walls and towers that surrounded the city.

The trip back to Lerin was a good one. We were relaxed and had a lot to talk about. We also laughed a lot. For half a day, I was treated with special respect and appreciation. That was a rare and terrific feeling.

My life seemed to cross many paths. It was ironic that one of the women who was with me that day and got her visa happened to be going to Detroit. Her son, Philip, and daughter, Tula, and I became good friends.

In fact, Fate had decided that we would travel to America together, sailing on the same ship.

Farewell, My Valiant Warrior

One may return to the place of his birth,
He cannot go back to his youth.

JOHN BURROUGHS, 1906

Until the time I left T'rsie to head for America, in truth, I don't think I had ever seen an ox as strong as Vesko. It wasn't that he was a huge animal. He really was just an average-size ox, with a very shiny, black-and-brown coat. That beautiful hide of his reflected the rays of the sun and even the glow of the moon.

Vesko, like my beloved Tome, was nurtured early on, by Baba. She had this maternal connection with all young living things. What a veterinarian she would have made! When Vesko had reached his maximum height and weight, my cousins and I took charge of him. That ox, as you may remember, was our ace in the competitions with other oxen from neighboring villages. He was quick and knew how to use his horns—which I kept needle-sharp.

When I returned from Yugoslavia, I learned that Dedo and Mother had to sell all our stock, all that survived the wars, including Vesko. They never told me how and to whom Vesko had been sold. The only animal we had left was a mean old mule.

Two years after I returned, two friends from T'rsianska Mala, Pandel and Itso, and I rode our bikes down toward the train station. As we were making our way there, we reached a wagon pulled by two oxen just in front of us. As we got closer, and closer, and as we talked to each other, one of the oxen started to get restless and began to grunt, turning his head toward us.

When I passed the man who was driving the wagon, he started whipping his oxen and cussing. They were getting more restless. We paused for a minute. The oxen looked so undernourished, gray, skinny and uncared for, and they were moaning. To me they sounded as if they were crying in protest. In Macedonian the word for the sound is *rika*.

The oxen were not cooperating with their driver. I got off my bike and walked the few steps to the wagon. Not understanding why this mean old man whipped the animals so hard, I walked up and stood very close to one of the oxen and placed my hand on his back. The ox looked at me so sadly, as if to say, "Why shouldn't I cry?" Those eyes, with their pitiful look, made me catch my breath for a moment. Could this be? Is it possible? Vesko?

I would never have recognized him. But it was Vesko. His owner was telling me that he had bought the ox 4 or 5 years ago from a widow who lives uptown, and that she lived with an old man.

That was it. There was no doubt, no doubt at all. Had Vesko not recognized my voice, I would not have known that it was our valiant warrior. I was just devastated. I couldn't believe it, I didn't want to believe that this undernourished, pathetic animal could be Vesko! Our Vesko was the strongest, shiniest, the most valiant ox in the district! I threw

Dedo.

my arms around Vesko, and wouldn't let go. I wanted him. I wanted to take him home where he belonged, where I would take care of him, just as I did before. I would bring the old Vesko back, back to the way he used to be. Itso came over to pull me away.

The old man wouldn't give me his name or tell me where he lived. With one more crack of his whip the oxen moved. I couldn't believe it. I felt I just couldn't part with another living thing from my past. Everything that had been good in my life was being taken from me. Everything I loved I could no longer reach out and touch!

I returned home in a murderous rage. Mother saw the signs.

"What's the matter? What happened? What's wrong? You look terrible."

I couldn't face her, and I couldn't answer her, so I mumbled, "Nothing."

My anger was so strong, I was afraid of what I might do or say—that I might regret my reaction if I stayed another minute. I had to go for a long walk to rid myself of the poison of this anger within me. I found myself walking toward the river. I walked for a long, long time. That solitary walk shed the present for me, enabling me to relive those few wonderful years with Vesko. Could I have been that happy then? Could that have been me? Whatever happened to that irresponsible, irrepressible, full-of-the-devil kid named Sote? Resentment, hatred, frustration at what had happened to us, to our lives and livelihood, to our beloved animals, was going to serve no good purpose. There was nothing that could be done now. The past was just that—past. Gone. Everything in that life that had given me such joy was no more.

By the time I returned home Pandel and Itso had told my mother that I had seen Vesko. She understood completely—hurt deeply for me, but could do nothing to console me.

Pain frequents us all at one time or another; sometimes physically often emotionally. The emotional pain I felt at losing the two most beloved of our animals, Tome and Vesko, may seem foolish and unmanly, but it is a pain that makes me cry without shame. A true bond and trust was built between Tome and Vesko and me. We were one spirit, unafraid, looking forward to challenges and meeting them with confidence and gusto.

Never again will I hear the beautiful sounds of those two wonderful creations of Nature, Tome, my joyful soul mate and Vesko, my shining, valiant warrior. Never will I see the likes of them again.

With their passing, my youth passed too. I was no longer Sote. Now my name was truly Sotir.

The Nitchov home as it looked in 1988.

Baba has passed away. Mother Tsila is standing to the right of Dedo Vasil, and Sotir is to his left, holding his cousin's hand.

Epilogue

Danti's reading of Sotir's coffee grinds was on target, for Sotir did cross a large body of water and came to a far-away land. But it was not the one he had thought it would be.

She was there on that August 17, 1952, waiting for him in the harbor. A faint outline at first; within moments larger than life. Holding her torch high toward the heavens, reflecting the golden promise of freedom, opportunity, and most importantly for Sotir, dignity, Lady Liberty welcomed him and his fellow passengers to America.

Sotir was about to begin another sojourn, this one with more freedom, responsibility, and opportunity than even he could ever have imagined.

Uncle Vane, whom he had only heard about back home in T'rsie, was there at the dock waiting for him. Neither knew what to expect.

As each individual in that large crowd scanned the passengers for a familiar face, and as Sotir's eyes roamed over that sea of faces, a pair of eyes locked firmly onto Sotir's. A man ran toward him shouting, "Sotir. Sotir," just as Sotir flew to him. They clasped each other tightly and held on, unable to speak. They cried together as only men do, for Sotir, at the age of 16, had become a man.

Sotir stayed with his Uncle Vane and the family for several years. Then, after about 5 years of working at many different kinds of jobs and gaining language skills, he earned enough money to bring his mother and sisters to America. Sofa came in 1957. Two years later he was financially able to bring his mother, Vasilka, and Mareto. However, because of the machinations of the incredible corrupt Greek bureaucracy, the two could not come together. Only his mother was allowed to come by herself. By 1960, they were all reunited, finally, in Detroit, Michigan.

Curiously, Danti's prediction of marriage and family for Sotir became a reality and unexpectedly. Soon after he arrived in Detroit, he met a beautiful blond, green-eyed Macedonian girl named Tina. Family and close friends affectionately call her Nouli. She and her family are also from Lerinsko.

Happily on July 10, 1960, Sotir and Tina were married in their Orthodox church. The priest performed the ages-old Macedonian wedding service in the Slavonic language. Their marriage was blessed with two children, a son, Stefo, named for his deceased uncle, and a daughter, Lena.

The constant changes of time and place, of personal difficulties and commitments, made it difficult and painful for Sotir to maintain any meaningful contact with the past. The exceptions were his family, friends, and especially that band of brothers and sisters, the *Detsa Begaltsi.* Sadly, Drago, *Gospozah* Iconia, Ivo, Kanachki, Marika, the outstanding soccer team that was the Yugoslav Partizan Soccer Club, Danti and Sotir would never see each other again.

Sotir never totally gave up on his dream to become a professional soccer athlete. His responsibilities, however, as a son, husband, and father, dimmed that vision over

Tina (Noulie) and Sotir at their engagement celebration.

Sotir and Tina with their children, Stefo, named after Sotir's brother, and Lena.

time. As he eventually realized that he would never fulfill his dream and ambition to play with the Yugoslav Partisan team, he channeled his old dream into a reality he never imagined . . . .

He used his energy and talent to guide younger generations of soccer enthusiasts. He offered his services to the local community college, passing on the skill and knowledge that he was privileged to have acquired under the tutelage of professionals in a previous lifetime. Over the years, his young, amateur teams have consistently placed near the top of their division, when not in first place. They have also earned trophies for multiple years. Their successes weres his successes as well.

The *Begaltsi* generation held a fiftieth year reunion in Skopje, Macedonia in 1988. Sotir and Tina attended. As they wound their way through the crowd, Sotir recalls how his face creased with smiles of recognition and how his heart tightened in his chest with pride.

They were not victims and they were more than survivors.

They were men and women who had made life better for themselves and for their families.

They were successful businessmen and women, entrepreneurs, and skilled tradesmen.

They were academic, medical and legal professionals.

Some had become engineers, chemists and pharmacists.

Others had entered artistic fields.

Within the Begaltsi generation a respected intelligentsia had emerged, and they were giving back to the communities that had given to them opportunity, security, and a new home.

Sotir coaching young American soccer enthusiasts.

Never have any of them forgotten who they are, where they were born, or their names. They have never forgotten the terrible history their parents, grandparents and great-grandparents lived. They have never forgiven those who wreaked such terrible havoc.

It makes one pause, doesn't it, to think how differently their history would have been written, if the world had heeded the plight of the Macedonian people during the last 150 years?

What worldly pleasure is untainted by grief?
What earthly glory remains unchanged?

All things are more feeble than shadows,
All things more deluding than dreams.
All human things are vanities.

Where is worldly charm?
Where the passing illusions?
Where the staff of servants and the noise

Then once more I looked into the graves
And saw the naked bones, and I said,
Now, who is the king and who the soldier?
Who the rich man and who the poor?
All are dust, all ashes, all shadows.

From the *Sticheras* by St. John of Damascus

Le symbole de l'esprit de ces splendides Macédoniens!
Coloriez-les INVINCIBLES!!

Symbolic depiction of the eternal Macedonian struggle for freedom.

Time Travel

Even though we have come to the end of Sotir's story, pause with me for just a moment and travel back in time about a hundred years or so. Come sit with me atop Mount Olympus as I share with you some of the observations of a respected American journalist, Albert Sonnichsen, from the book he published in 1906, **CONFESSIONS OF A MACEDONIAN BANDIT.**

Mr. Sonnichsen, who was born in San Francisco in 1878, traveled in Macedonia with the *voyvodas* and *chetas* in the late 1890's and early 1900's, at a time when the Macedonians were still under Ottoman rule.

The vignettes, which follow, are from his book reporting his first-hand experiences living among the Macedonian people. These excerpts underscore the reasons the Macedonians have fought for so long, so passionately for their dignity; for recognition as a people, for their freedom and independence.

One of the early organized efforts to achieve their goals was the formation of the organization IMRO (VMRO), the Internal Macedonian Revolutionary Organization. IMRO became an underground provisional system of government, established by the Macedonian peasantry, to replace Turkish anarchy.

Listen to Mr. Sonnischen's voice, as he begins on pages 93 and 94, describing the structure of the organization:

Vignettes

"The organization's system of administrative subdivisions coincided almost exactly with those of the Turkish government. Each caza or county was a rayon (region), governed by a rayon committee; represented in the field by the voyvoda (leader) and his armed escort, the cheta.

A number of cazas constituted the vilayet, or province, governed by a provincial committee, composed of one delegate from each of the rayons.

This superior committee was represented in the field by the revisor, who controlled the rayon voyvodas.

Above this came the famous Central Committee, composed of a delegate from each vilayet. Of all the vilayets, Monastir (Bitola) was considered the most important, for there the aggressive tyranny of the Greek church was most felt; there the most serious insurrections had occurred . . . "

CENTRAL COMMITTEE
1 Delegate from each vilayet

Revisor
Controlled rayonVoyvodas,
and was field representative
for Provincial Committee

Provincial Committee
Composed of one delegate
from each rayon

REGION COMMITTEE
One delegate from each rayon

VOYVODA
Field representative to the Rayon Committee

CHETA
Voyvodas' armed escort and fighting unit

VILAYET
Composed of several rayons

RAYON
A county or caza. . . . pp. 93–94

"A slip of paper, stamped with the seal of the Central Committee, passed us among the villagers. That slip of paper seemed a testimonial of our moral characters . . . Many voyvodas and chetniks had passed through . . . None had ever abused the naïve trust of these people."

Pp. 151–2

February 7, 1906

To my Brethren, the Villagers of Morenova, Kekovishitsa, and Yanchesta:

We learn that you are being persecuted by the Bulgar brigands, who are trying to force you to renounce your Greek nationality and faith. We learn they are forcing you to protest to the Europeans against the soldiers of the Faith, saying that we are persecuting you.

I beg you to open your eyes; make no more such protests in the future. I shall make it painful for those that do. Such we shall kill; their wives and children shall not be spared, for we shall cut their limbs asunder. We kill all who do not join us.

I hope you understand and will obey.
Your brother in the Faith,

Constantine Akritas

The missive had the imprint of Christ on the Cross.

Pp. 421

The Unholy Father Stavre

"There lived in the village of Pisoder, (Psoderi), a Greek priest who ranked next to the Bishop, but was even superior in planning mischief. This Father Stavre was the organizer of the system of espionage that supplied the church with such accurate information regarding the revolutionary agitators. He first distinguished himself in the insurrection (1903, Illinden) by the energetic help he gave the Turks in seeking out the members of the local committees. Twice he participated in a massacre. The peasants tell that once an old Turkish major refused the Father's company, publicly declaring before his soldiers that 'we can disgrace ourselves without the help of this savage'.

Then he (Father Stavre) endeared himself to the Church by having Lazar Poptrikov, one of the brainiest of the first organizers, betrayed and murdered. Father Stavre brought the head of Poptrikov to Kostur and had it photographed, distributing the prints among the peasants. But his masterwork was the massacre of Zagoritchani.

Now Father Stavre directed the operations of the terrorist bands. His location was exactly suited to this purpose, for Pisoder was a garrisoned village in the center of a district that was to be evangelized.

Curiously enough, this monster was a man of superior education and charming manners. He could hypnotize foreign journalists, and his power over women was tremendous. For this reason, the Church sent him abroad on diplomatic missions. He was head of the delegation 'from the Macedonian people', which was sent to meet the English King at the Olympics. During the previous summer he had made a tour of Europe, engaging the sympathies of diplomats and men of affairs for the cause of Greek expansion."

pp. 236–238

The Zagoritchani Massacre

"During the Macedonian Insurrection of 1903, Greek priests accompanied Turkish troops on punitive expeditions and pointed out the villages to be burned and the villagers to be executed. One of the most notorious incidents in Macedonian history occurred in this region, known even to Europeans: ***ZAGORITCHANI.***

The Greek priests bribed a Turkish officer to search the village of Zagoritchani repeatedly, thereby causing the villagers to hide their arms beyond immediate reach. Then a note was sent to the elders of the village, signed by a 'friend', warning them that another final search was to be made within a few days and which would be unusually thorough. Most of the villagers buried their guns.

On the date fixed, all the villagers were at church. When they heard a bugle call and saw a body of armed men approach, they thought this was the fulfillment of the warning that asker, Turkish soldiers, had come to search for arms.

Suddenly a volley had shattered the windows of the church, killing a dozen of the congregation. The worshippers rushed out in a panic and found themselves surrounded by a band of over a hundred soldiers at the church, some in Greek uniforms. Three of the leaders were in the uniforms of Greek officers.

In all, sixty villagers of Zagoritchani were massacred. Five of these were children under fifteen; seven were women, of whom two were in advanced pregnancy, and twenty-two were over sixty years of age. The Insurrection had left few houses standing, and of these, ten were burned along with twenty-eight temporary shelters. All this was done in broad daylight, near enough to a large garrison of troops for the rifle shots to be heard. All of this in the name of Christ, instigated by a church to whose head in Constantinople, representatives of European nations offer deference and consult when the 'will of the people' is to be sensed.

'I do not know how to indict a whole people,' said Burke, 'but when a whole people acclaim such a deed as this, through a unanimous press and pulpit, as patriotic and heroic, and glorify its perpetrators with public dinners, what is there left to say of such a people?'".

pp. 234–237

The Letter

One day a peasant woman found a letter on a mountain trail, evidently dropped by a passing courier. She carried it to the cheta. *Pando Klasheff opened it and recognized it as a letter in Greek cipher. In his boyhood he had been forced to learn Greek. He began carefully studying it. Appended was a list of several names which Klasheff recognized as those of Turkish gendarmerie officers. The names were in ordinary writing, but opposite each were words in cipher. Working on the rough guess that these might be the officer's stations, he began deciphering, and by this chance, discovered the key to the cipher.*

Though anonymous, the letter was evidently from the Greek bishop, and was addressed to Captain Vardas, commander-in-chief in the field. It unfolded a plan for the burning of Bouf, a large Bulgar village partly depopulated by emigration to America. The writer then directed Captain Vardas to send a certain Bellus to consult with Father Stavre, who would give the final instructions.

After consultation, Klasheff and Mitre called together all the cheta in the rayon (region) and went to the mountain overlooking Psoder. Among the minor chiefs was a graduate of the Greek gymnasium in Athens, who, of course was chosen as chief actor.

A few months before, the cheta had taken prisoner several members of a Greek band. They were disarmed and sent back to Greece in peasant clothes, their uniforms being kept as trophies. Kouze, the sub chief, and six of the chetniks dressed themselves in the Greek uniforms. Then a letter was written in the Greek cipher and sent down into Pisoder by a peasant. It requested an interview with Father Stavre on the "Bouf business" and was signed "Captain Bellus".

Several hours later the cheta, from its hiding place in the forest, saw two men from the village climbing the mountain. One was in a priest's cassock, and the other in the uniform of a Turkish gendarme. When these two arrived in a clearing half way up the mountain, they met a band of seven men in Greek uniform, one of whom stepped forward and introduced himself as Captain Bellus.

An hour later, when the garrison in Pisoder hurried up the mountain to investigate into the cause of a number of rifle shots, they found Father Stavre and his companion—both dead.

pp. 238–39

Pando Klasheff

"I have never met a voyvoda better equipped intellectually than Pando Klasheff. In appearance he was a clean-cut, aristocratic young fellow, his speech so pure that it approached Russian. He was dressed in a simple, close-fitting uniform; nothing except his canvass leggings, leather revolver holster and ammunition belt indicated his vocation. He had studied at the University of Sofia, and had, I believe, his degree of B.A. With him was his lieutenant, Kartchakoff, slightly younger, and also a college boy. No mere fighting men were they; they had definite theories of economic organization. They had established cooperative stores and flour mills. The karaool schools were of their making."

p. 236

The Karaool Schools

"Between Little Lake Prespa and Kostur rise the barren Korbus Mountains, presumably the Scarbul of antiquity. Crossing this range in late September, we came into a country differing much in character from any other part of Macedonia I had yet been in. It seemed almost as barren as the mountains we had crossed, rocky and bald of timber, but the floors of the small valleys were golden with grain and green with vineyards.

There was a village that was almost a town. Some of the houses were two storied stone structures with ornamental facades. The church had been bombarded and partly destroyed during the insurrection, but was again built with a tower almost like that of a western church. Here the fighting had been fiercest during 1903, yet recovery had been quickest. Most of the men were stonemasons who spent the winter months working at their trade in the bigger cities of the Balkan states. The effects of travel were visible in the active interest the villagers showed in political and general current events. One even produced a pamphlet sent him by a relative in America, in which I saw for the first time photographs of the ruins of San Francisco after the earthquake.

We entered the church. About a hundred children were gathered there, all seated on the floor, some reading, others writing, and one figuring out an arithmetical problem on a blackboard.

Two girls were presiding, both in peasant dress, but they addressed us in the Bulgarian of the Gymnasium.

'Why don't you have a schoohouse?' I asked, 'and why don't you have benches for the children?'

'Because this is a karaool school,' explained one of the teachers.

She took me to a window and pointed to a nearby hilltop. Two children sat there in the shade of a rock. I understood. They were the karaooli (Ottoman Turkish word for guardians). Should a file of asker (Turkish soldiers) appear along any of the approaching trails, their sharp eyes would perceive it in time. Before the soldiers could arrive in the village, there would be no traces of the school, and the two teachers would be churning butter or washing clothes.

Kostur is one of those districts whose secession from the Greek Church the government has not yet recognized, and therefore still under the temporal jurisdiction of a Greek bishop. Of course, he would forbid schools in which Bulgarian was spoken, and as the people are pure Bulgars speaking no Greek, it is natural that they would not tolerate teachers who could not even converse with them. The alternative was no schools at all.

Still they had them."

p. 233

Missions, Guerilla Bands and Political Organizations

ALO Allied Liaison Office unit of the AMM
AMM American Military Mission
ASNOM Anti-fascist Assembly for the National Liberation of Macedonia
BLO British Liaison Unit of the BMM
BMM British Military Mission
DAG Democratic Army of Greece
EAM Greek National Liberation Front
EDES National Republican Greek League
EKKA Greek National and Social Liberation Party, considered the political center, later incorporated by ELAS
ELAS Greek National Liberation Army
EOEOA National Bands of Greek Guerillas
IMRO Internal Macedonian Political Organization, one of the oldest Macedonian organizations
KKE Greek Communist Party
LNC Communist Party of Albania
NOF Macedonian Liberation Front in Yugoslavia
OC Opshestvena Cila, Bulgarian nationalist organization in Yugoslavia preparing ground for integration into Bulgaria, with political committees in Tetovo, Gostivar, Kichevo, and Debar
OHRANA The Bulgarian Guardians
OPLA Protection of the People's Struggle, units which provided the functions of a Gestapo and the and SS for the KKE
OSS Office of Strategic Services
PAO PAO evolved into the Pan-Hellenic Liberation Organization
PEEA Political Committee of National Liberation, the shadow government of EAM/ELAS in the mountains
SHTAB LNC General Staff
SNOF Macedonian National Liberation Front, equivalent of EAM among the Macedonians
SOE Special Operations Executive, reported directly to the British War Cabinet
X Pronounced khee in Greek. Direct action instrument of the Royalist right-wing
YVE Protectors of Northern Greece, which evolved into PAO

Bibliography

Eudes, Dominique. *The Kapetanios, Partisans and Civil War in Greece,* Monthly Press Review, New York and London, 1972.

Hamson, Denys. *We Fell Among the Greeks.* Oxford, Great Britain, 1947.

Kofos, Evangelos. *Nationalism and Communism in Macedonia.* Institute for Balkan Studies, Thessaloniki, 1964.

Myers, E. C. W. *Greek Entanglement.* Allan Sutton Publishing Limited, Gloucester, 1985.

O'Balance, Edgar. *The Greek Civil War.* Frederick A. Praeger, Publishers. NewYork, Washington.

Rossos, Andrew. Offprint from the *Slavonic Review,* Volume 69, Number 2, April, 1991, London.

Smiley, David. *Albanian Assignment.* Hogarth Press, London, 1948.

Sonniehsen, Albert. *Confessions of a Macedonian Bandit.* Duffield & Company, New York, 1909.

West, Rebecca. *Black Lamb and Grey Falcon.* Viking Press, U. S. A., 1941.

Woodhouse, C.M. *Apple of Discord,* Hutchinson & Co. London, LTD., 1948.